BIBLICAL AND RELATED STUDIES PRESENTED TO SAMUEL IWRY

BIBLICAL AND RELATED STUDIES PRESENTED TO SAMUEL IWRY

Edited by

Ann Kort and Scott Morschauser

Eisenbrauns
Winona Lake, Indiana
1985

Copyright © 1985 Eisenbrauns

Library of Congress Cataloging in Publication Data

Main entry under title:

Biblical and related studies presented to Samuel Iwry.

   Includes bibliographical references.
   1. Bible. O.T.—Criticism, interpretation, etc.—Addresses,
essays, lectures. 2. Near East—Civilization—To 622—
Addresses, essays, lectures. 3. Iwry, Samuel—Addresses,
essays, lectures. I. Iwry, Samuel. II. Kort, Ann.
III. Morschauser, Scott.
BS1192.B435   1985   221.6   85-16312
ISBN 0-931464-23-4

Samuel Iwry

CONTENTS

Preface and Acknowledgments   ix

Letters of Appreciation for Prof. Iwry   xi

List of Financial Contributors   xiii

Principal Abbreviations   xv

Did Alexander Yannai Negotiate an Alliance with the Parthians?   1
    MOSES ABERBACH

The First and Second Tithes in the *Temple Scroll*   5
    JOSEPH M. BAUMGARTEN

The Rhetoric of Psalm 145   17
    ADELE BERLIN

Levitical Cities: Archaeology and Texts   23
    ROBERT G. BOLING

Sargon and Joseph: Dreams Come True   33
    JERROLD S. COOPER

A Literate Soldier: Lachish Letter III   41
    FRANK MOORE CROSS

Prose Particles in the Poetry of the Primary History   49
    DAVID NOEL FREEDMAN

The Murder of the Merchants Near Akko   63
    BARRY M. GITTLEN

Adam's Rib   73
    HANS GOEDICKE

On Making Other Gods   77
    CYRUS H. GORDON

The Meaning of *Tkwnh*   81
    JONAS C. GREENFIELD

Cult and Prayer   87
    MENAHEM HARAN

Marginal Notes to the Biblical Lexicon   93
    MOSHE HELD†

A Difficult Curse in Aqht (19[1 Aqht] 3.152–154)   105
    DELBERT R. HILLERS

Cain, the Arrogant Sufferer 109
HERBERT B. HUFFMON

Originals and Imitations in Biblical Poetry: a Comparative Examination of 1 Sam 2:1–10 and Ps 113:5–9 115
AVI HURVITZ

Studies in Neo-Aramaic Lexicology 123
GEORG KROTKOFF

Philippi's Law Reconsidered 135
THOMAS O. LAMBDIN

The Worship of Baal and Asherah: a Study in the Social Bonding Functions of Religious Systems 147
GEORGE E. MENDENHALL

Hezekiah's Sacrifices at the Dedication Services of the Purified Temple (2 Chr 29:21–24) 159
JACOB MILGROM

Esther Revisited: an Examination of Esther Studies over the Past Decade 163
CAREY A. MOORE

Rib-Hadda: Job at Byblos? 173
WILLIAM L. MORAN

The New Jewish Version: Genesis of the Fourth Great Age of Bible Translation 183
HARRY M. ORLINSKY

Isaiah and His Children 193
J. J. M. ROBERTS

Isaiah 66:1–4: Judean Sects in the Persian Period as Viewed by Trito-Isaiah 205
ALEXANDER ROFÉ

Materials Toward a Biblical Grammar in the Bible Exegesis of the Tosefta 219
SAMUEL ROSENBLATT†

A Study of the Relationship of the Syriac Version to the Massoretic Hebrew, Targum Jonathan, and Septuagint Texts in Jeremiah 18 227
LEONA GLIDDEN RUNNING

Ernest Renan's Interpretation of Biblical History 237
LEIVY SMOLAR

New Gleanings on Resheph from Ugarit 259
YIGAEL YADIN†

PREFACE AND ACKNOWLEDGMENTS

Samuel Iwry has enjoyed a long and distinguished career as professor in the Department of Near Eastern Studies at the Johns Hopkins University, and professor and dean of the Baltimore Hebrew College. His remarkable knowledge, wit, humor and inspired teaching have touched the lives of generations of students. The fields of biblical and ancient Near Eastern studies owe the richness of much scholarship to the influence of this one teacher. It is an altogether fitting tribute to Prof. Iwry's achievements, as both scholar and teacher, that his many colleagues and friends have joined together to produce this festschrift in his honor.

The editors are greatly indebted to the faculty members of the Department of Near Eastern Studies at Johns Hopkins for their generous assistance during the preparation of this volume. Former chairman Prof. Hans Goedicke supported the project from its inception and kindly placed departmental facilities at the editors' disposal. The present chairman, Prof. Jerrold Cooper, generously extended his support, encouragement and assistance throughout all phases of the project. The editors also received many kind and helpful suggestions from Professors Delbert R. Hillers and Georg Krotkoff. Ms. Jane Dreyer, while performing her regular duties as department secretary, gave of her time and efforts, always with patience and good humor.

The editors are also grateful to Prof. Leivy Smolar, president of the Baltimore Hebrew College, and Professors Barry M. Gittlen, Moshe Aberbach and Joseph Baumgarten for their kind interest and support. Prof. Carey A. Moore of Gettysburg College also offered valuable advice and encouragement.

Mr. James Eisenbraun and his staff have provided indispensable expertise in the preparation of this volume. The editors are greatly indebted to Mr. Eisenbraun for his careful and skillful guidance and participation in the project.

From the beginning, the editors have been impressed by the enthusiasm, support and patience of all those who contributed articles to the volume. It should be noted that many papers were written in 1982 and 1983, and may therefore be somewhat different in content than if their authors had written them today.

Sadly, several contributors passed away before the volume could be completed. Prof. Mitchell Dahood, Sam Iwry's friend and fellow student from graduate school days, had intended to write a paper entitled "Ebla and the Psalms." He was unable to begin work before his death in March, 1982. Prof. Samuel Rosenblatt, a colleague at Johns Hopkins for many years and a personal friend, contributed his article early in the project. He passed away in January, 1983. Another fellow graduate student was Prof. Moshe Held, who hand-delivered his article and personally expressed his enthusiasm during a visit to Baltimore. Prof. Held died in June, 1984. Prof. Yigael Yadin, a close personal friend, agreed to contribute a paper while in Baltimore to deliver the 1983 William F. Albright Memorial Lecture. He passed away in June, 1984.

A project such as this festschrift cannot become reality without financial backing. The editors gratefully acknowledge and thank the many individuals and institutions whose kind and generous support made possible the realization of this tribute to Prof. Sam Iwry.

Ann Kort
Scott Morschauser

Baltimore
April, 1985

LETTERS OF APPRECIATION

I

Our friend, colleague, and teacher, Samuel Iwry, was born in Poland, where as a child and young man he acquired a European education, and especially a detailed and profound mastery of traditional Jewish learning. When the cruel twists and turns of fate through which World War II led him had finally abated, he was able to enter the Johns Hopkins University in Baltimore and there, under the guidance of Prof. William F. Albright, he proceeded to the doctorate through a broad program emphasizing archaeology and modern critical approaches to history, linguistics, and biblical literature. The outcome of this unusual mixture, displayed over a long and fruitful career, has been a scholar and teacher of extraordinary breadth, and a personality of the most engaging piquancy.

In biblical studies and in ancient epigraphy, it is evident that Samuel Iwry usually chose to write about the tough words and the difficult texts! It is remarkable, then, that his proposals, imaginative as they are, have consistently been models of good sense and persuasiveness, a result achieved no doubt by his ability to combine judiciously any number of scholarly approaches. The Dead Sea Scrolls have been a preoccupation of his since their discovery—one might almost say, since before their discovery—which found him already an expert on the Damascus Document. It must be gratifying for him to see that in recent times specialists such as Murphy-O'Connor have come to espouse views of Essene origins anticipated in Iwry's own early work.

Many readers of this volume and contributors to it will remember Samuel Iwry most appreciatively as a teacher. I would join that number, adding my impression that what makes this so is not only the vivacity of his classroom manner (which can only be experienced, not described), but his ability and inclination to *encourage* students. No austere figure barring the path forward, he is that rare teacher who invites young people to move ahead and is ready to praise extravagantly any sign of promise. I recall that Yigael Yadin cited this encouraging quality as characteristic of William F. Albright—quite correctly and perceptively, from my experience. Here there is a real resemblance between Iwry and his revered teacher.

All of Samuel Iwry's students and friends feel a great debt of gratitude to Ms. Ann Kort and Mr. Scott Morschauser for their devoted and skillful labors in bringing out this volume in honor of our beloved colleague and teacher. All of us hope he will accept it as a token of our

great respect and affection for him, and as an embodiment of best wishes
to him for many more happy and productive years.

DELBERT R. HILLERS
THE JOHNS HOPKINS UNIVERSITY

II

Nothing would have been more fitting than to pen in Hebrew these
words of tribute to Samuel Iwry, lovingly called Shemuel by his many
friends and colleagues in Israel. Deeply steeped in Hebrew learning and
the Jewish tradition, expertly trained in the broad field of ancient Near
Eastern cultures, Sam-Shemuel Iwry was eminently equipped to play an
important role in the furtherance of the study of these areas in a setting
in which they are taught in Hebrew. But fate decreed otherwise. The
vicissitudes of recent history and of his personal life caused Sam Iwry to
take root in the United States, his adoptive homeland.

As a result, we, his colleagues in Israel, could not maintain ongoing day to day contact with him. But his keen perception of issues—
whether in epigraphy, biblical literature or the Qumran texts—caught
our attention whenever his articles appeared in print. At congresses and
symposia we heard his presentations and discussed points of shared
interest into the small hours of the night. On these occasions we were
privileged to engage with him in the give and take which is the lifeblood
of scholarship.

Only once were Israelis given the opportunity to appreciate Sam
Iwry's outstanding abilities as teacher and mentor of budding scholars,
when he served as Fulbright Fellow in Biblical Studies at Haifa University in 1967/68. There was an instantaneous rapport with his students.
They flocked in large numbers to his courses in Bible studies, Hebrew
language, and Jewish history, appreciative of the remarkable combination of solid information and imaginative insight which was a hallmark
of his lectures.

The scholarly community in Israel is beholden to Samuel Iwry for
his contributions to shared pursuits and wishes him many more fruitful
years of teaching and research.

SHEMARYAHU TALMON
THE HEBREW UNIVERSITY

FINANCIAL CONTRIBUTORS

Meyerhoff Philanthropic Fund
Mr. Alvin H. Blum
Mr. Daniel Gordon
Mr. Jerold C. Hoffberger
Macht Philanthropic Fund
Mr. and Mrs. Gerald G. Eisenberg
Mr. Harvey M. Meyerhoff
Joseph Meyerhoff Fund
Dr. Liebe S. Diamond
Mr. Abraham M. Lilienfeld
Mr. Morton J. Macks
Mr. George Hugo Dalsheimer
Mr. and Mrs. Leonard Forman
Mr. Willard Hackerman
Mr. Bernard Manekin
Mr. and Mrs. Marvin Schapiro
Ms. Susan M. Mower

PRINCIPAL ABBREVIATIONS

AB	Anchor Bible
ADAJ	Annual of the Department of Antiquities of Jordan
AfO	*Archiv für Orientforschung*
AHW	W. von Soden, *Akkadisches Handwörterbuch*
AJA	*American Journal of Archaeology*
AJBA	*Australian Journal of Biblical Archaeology*
ANEP	J. B. Pritchard (ed.), *Ancient Near East in Pictures*
ANET	J. B. Pritchard (ed.), *Ancient Near Eastern Texts*
ASAE	*Annales du Service des Antiquities de l'Egypte*
AusBR	*Australian Biblical Review*
B.Bat	*Baba Batra*
Ber.	*Berakot*
BA	*Biblical Archaeologist*
BASOR	*Bulletin of the American Schools of Oriental Research*
BDB	F. Brown, S. R. Driver, and C. A. Briggs, *Hebrew and English Lexicon of the Old Testament*
Bib	*Biblica*
BibS(N)	Biblische Studien (Neukirchen)
BKAT	Biblischer Kommentar: Altes Testament
BMAP	E. G. Kraeling, *Brooklyn Museum Aramaic Papyri: New Documents of the Fifth Century* B.C. *from the Jewish Colony at Elephantine*, New Haven, 1953
BZAW	Beihefte zur *ZAW*
CAD	*The Assyrian Dictionary of the Oriental Institute of the University of Chicago*
CAH	*Cambridge Ancient History*
CAP	A. Cowley, *Aramaic Papyri of the Fifth Century* B.C., Oxford, 1923
CB	*Cultura Biblica*
CBQ	*Catholic Biblical Quarterly*
CBSC	Cambridge Bible for Schools and Colleges
CDC	Cairo Genizah Document of the Damascus Covenanters (The Zadokite Documents)
DISO	C.-F. Jean and J. Hoftijzer, *Dictionnaire des inscriptions sémitiques de l'ouest*
EA	*Die El-Amarna-Tafeln*, ed. J. A. Knudtzon
EncJud	*Encyclopaedia Judaica*
EI	*Eretz Israel*
GKC	*Gesenius' Hebrew Grammar*, ed. E. Kautzsch, tr. A. E. Cowley
HALAT	W. Baumgartner et al., *Hebräisches und aramäisches Lexikon zum Alten Testament*

HAT	Handbuch zum Alten Testament
HKAT	Handkommentar zum Alten Testament
HUCA	Hebrew Union College Annual
Ḥul.	Ḥullin
IEJ	Israel Exploration Journal
Int	Interpretation
Josephus, Ant.	Josephus' Jewish Antiquities
Josephus, J.W.	Josephus' Jewish Wars
JA	Journal Asiatique
JAOS	Journal of the American Oriental Society
JBL	Journal of Biblical Literature
JEA	Journal of Egyptian Archaeology
JEOL	Jaarbericht . . . ex oriente lux
JJS	Journal of Jewish Studies
JNES	Journal of Near Eastern Studies
JPS	Jewish Publication Society: The Holy Scriptures, 1917; new ed., The Torah, 1962
JQR	Jewish Quarterly Review
Jub.	Jubilees
KAI	H. Donner, and W. Röllig, Kanaanäische und aramäische Inschriften
Ketub.	Ketubot
KAT	E. Sellin (ed.), Kommentar zum A.T.
KB	L. Koehler and W. Baumgartner, Lexicon in Veteris Testamenti libros
LAS	S. Parpola, Letters to Assyrian Scholars
Lesh.	Loshenénu
LXX	The Septuagint
LXX^B	Codex Vaticanus
Maᶜas. Sh.	Maᶜaser Sheni
MAOG	Mitteilungen der altorientalischen Gesellschaft
Menaḥ.	Menaḥot
MSL	Materialen zum sumerischen Lexikon
MT	Masoretic Text
NAB	New American Bible
NEB	New English Bible
Ned.	Nedarim
NIV	New International Version
Or	Orientalia
OT	Old Testament
PEQ	Palestine Exploration Quarterly
Pesaḥ.	Pesaḥim
PRU	Le Palais royal d'Ugarit
Ps.-Jonathan	Targum Pseudo-Jonathan
I Q Isaᵃ	First copy of Isaiah from Qumran, Cave I
Q Temple	Megillat ha-Miqdash, Y. Yadin, 3 vols.
Rab.	Rabbah
RB	Revue Biblique
Rosh. Hash.	Rosh Haššana

RSV	Revised Standard Version
Sanh.	*Sanhedrin*
SBLDS	SBL Dissertation Series
SBLMS	SBL Monograph Series
SBLSCS	SBL Septuagint and Cognate Studies
Shab.	*Shabbat*
Ta'an.	*Ta'anit*
Tg.	*Targum*
USQR	*Union Seminary Quarterly Review*
UT	C. H. Gordon, *Ugaritic Textbook*
VT	*Vetus Testamentum*
VT Sup	Vetus Testamentum, Supplements
WO	*Die Welt des Oreints*
Yebam.	*Yebamot*
ZA	*Zeitschrift für Assyriologie*
ZAW	*Zeitschrift für die alttestamentliche Wissenschaft*
ZDMG	*Zeitschrift der deutschen morganländischen Gessellschaft*
ZDPV	*Zeitschrift des deutschen Palästina-Vereins*

DID ALEXANDER YANNAI NEGOTIATE AN ALLIANCE WITH THE PARTHIANS?

Moses Aberbach
Baltimore Hebrew College

I N the Talmud Yerushalmi *Ber.* VII, 2, 11a and *Nazir* V, 5, 54b—as well as *Genesis Rabba* 91, 3 and *Ecclesiastes Rabba* 7, 12—we are told an Aggadic story how Simeon ben Shetah, who was the brother-in-law of King Alexander Yannai (=Jannaeus), fled from the king and was ultimately permitted to return thanks to the intervention of "great men (or: dignitaries) from the kingdom of Persia" who happened to visit the king. While dining with Alexander Yannai, they noticed the absence of the sage "who used to say before us words of wisdom" (according to *Eccl. Rab.* and one *Genesis Rabba* version, "words of Torah," which is usually identified with wisdom both in Ben-Sira and in rabbinic literature[1]). At their request, the king summoned Simeon ben Shetah to return from exile, granting him safe conduct.[2]

---

[1] Cf. Sir 1:1–5, 26; 15:1; 24:1 ff.; 34:8; *t.b. Pesah* 87b; *Gen. Rab.* 1, 1 *et al.* Most rabbinic references mention Prov 8:22 ff., and in all cases pre-existent Wisdom is identified with Torah.

[2] Cf. *Y. Ber.* VII, 2, 11a; *Y. Nazir* V, 5, 54b: "Simeon ben Shetah was afraid and fled. Some time later, certain dignitaries from the kingdom of Persia came to King Yannai. While they were sitting and dining, they said to him: 'We remember that there used to be an old man here who spoke to us words of wisdom.' He told them what had happened (i.e., that Simeon had fled). They then said to him: 'Send for him and bring him here.' So he sent for him and gave him his word (*viz.*, that he would not harm him); whereupon he came . . .'' For parallel versions, cf. *Gen. Rab.* 91, 3 (Theodor-Albeck, pp. 1115f.) and *Eccl. Rab.* 7, 12. Cf. *t.y. Ber.* VII, 2, 11a; *t.y. Nazir* V,5,54b:

‎. . . דחל שמעון בן שטח וערק. (ל)בתר יומין סלקון בני נש רברבי(ן) מן מלכותא (נ"א: ‎ממלכותא) דפרס (גבי ינאי מלכא מן דיתבין אכלין), אמרין (נ"א: אמרו) ליה: נהירין אנן ‎(נ"א: הוינין) דהוה (אית הכא) חד גבר(א) סב והוה אמר קומין (נ"א: קומינון) מילין ‎דחכמה. תני לון עובדא. אמרין ליה: (נ"א: אמרון לון) שלח (ו)איתיתיה. שלח (ו)יהב ליה ‎מילא ואתא (נ"א: ואייתיתיה) . . ."

Cf. *Gen. Rab.* 91,3 (Theodor-Albeck, pp. 1115f.)

‎"שמעון בן שטח . . . ערק. בתר יומין אתון הלין פרסאי (נ"א: הוון בני אינשא רברבין מן ‎מלכותא דפרסאי) יתבין נגסין על פתורא דינאי מלכא. אמרון ליה: (נ"א: מרי מלכא) נהרין

Ever since the middle of the third century B.C.E., Persia had been under Parthian rule. Therefore the "great (or: important) men from the kingdom of Persia" who visited Alexander Yannai on at least two occasions (since they recalled Simeon ben Shetaḥ's "words of wisdom" during their previous visit) were most probably Parthian diplomats; for ordinary Persian or Parthian scholars or priests would hardly have bothered to travel to Jerusalem, of all places, nor is there any reason to think that ordinary idolators would have been welcome at the royal table. At any rate, the story as it stands would be inherently improbable, unless we assume that the "great men from the kingdom of Persia" were members of a diplomatic mission. In this connection, it should be pointed out that the Jews did not, as a rule, distinguish between Parthians and Persians;[3] and since talmudic and midrashic literature did not assume written form prior to the third century C.E.—by which time (about 227 C.E.) the Persians had successfully overthrown their Parthian overlords—it was natural for the distinction between Persians and Parthians to become blurred in the literature of the Jews.

What, then, would have been the purpose of a Parthian diplomatic mission at the court of the king of Judea? As pointed out by Yehoshua Ephron,[4] the Parthian victories against the Seleucid empire, and especially the decisive defeat inflicted by the Parthians on Antiochus VII Sidetes in 129 B.C.E., had enabled John Hyrcanus I, the father of Alexander Yannai, to gain total Jewish independence from the Seleucids. Moreover, the Parthian victory was an important factor in the progress of the Hasmonean state, which was henceforth in a position to expand the territories of Judea over the whole of Palestine. The Parthian empire, which reached up to the Euphrates, made its influence felt in Syria,

---

אנן דהוה הכא חד סב והוה אמר לן מילין דחכמה (נ״א: מילי דאורייתא). אמר לאחתיה: שלחי בתריה ואייתיתיה. אמרה ליה: הב ליה מילה (נ״א: מילא ושלח ליה עיזקתיה) ואתא".

Cf. *Eccl. Rab.* 7,12:

"שמע שמעון בן שטח וערק. בתר יומין הוו תמן בני נש רברבין מן מלכותא דפרס. הוון יתבין על פתוריה דינאי מלכא. מן דאכלין אמרין לינאי: מרי מלכא, נהירין אנן דהוה הכא חד סב והוה אמר לן מילי דאורייתא (נ״א: דאוריא). אמר לשלמצו אחתיה אינתתיה דינאי: שלחי יהב לה מילא ואתא . . . ". ואייתיה. אמרה ליה: הב לי מילא ושלח ליה עזקתך והוא אתי.

For a rather different version of the story, cf. *t.b. Ber.* 48a.

[3] Cf., e.g., *t.b. Sanh.* 98a–b, where we are told that R. Yose ben Kisma (second century C.E.) predicted that there would not be a palm tree in Babylonia to which a Persian (i.e., Parthian) horse would not be tethered—nor would there be a coffin in the Land of Israel out of which a Median horse would not eat straw. R. Yose ben Kisma was undoubtedly referring to a Parthian invasion which, he expected, would drive out the Romans from the Near East—a scenario that had actually come to pass in 40 B.C.E.

[4] Cf. *Essays in Jewish History and Philology—In Memory of Gedalyahu Alon* (Hebrew), Tel Aviv, 1970, 71.

where the Parthians frequently intervened in the internal affairs of what remained of the Seleucid empire.[5] It was natural and logical for the Hasmoneans to establish contacts with the Parthians, since their interests coincided. Both wanted to weaken and, if possible, destroy their common enemy, the Seleucids. Thus, Demetrius III Akairos, a Seleucid king who defeated Alexander Yannai in battle,[6] was himself defeated and captured by the Parthians.[7] Ephron also points to a potential "spiritual" contact between the Parthians and the Jews, since the latter held scholars in great honor (hence the presence of Simeon ben Sheṭaḥ at the court of King Alexander Yannai), while the former had a "Synedrion of sages and magi"[8] occupying a similar place of honor among the supreme institutions of the empire.[9]

While the basic validity of these arguments is undeniable with regard to the earlier stages of the relations between Judea and Parthia, the need for a Parthian diplomatic mission during the reign of Alexander Yannai for the sole purpose of establishing a common front against the dying Seleucid empire seems questionable, to say the least. The gravely weakened Seleucid rulers no longer posed the slightest threat to the expanding powerful Parthian empire. The fact that King Mithridates II of Parthia (reigned ca. 123 to 88/87 B.C.E.) treated the captive Seleucid king, Demetrius III, with "the greatest honor"[10] indicates that the hostility between the two empires had run its course. From the Parthian point of view, there was no need for an anti-Seleucid alliance.

What, then, was the purpose of this diplomatic activity? An examination of the contemporary history of the Near East leaves no doubt that both Parthia and Judea were facing a new unexpected common threat from the growing power of King Tigranes of Armenia. As a matter of fact, during the reign of Alexander Yannai as well as that of his widow, Alexandra Salome, Tigranes was by far the most powerful Near Eastern ruler who conquered much of Asia Minor and most of Syria and Phoenicia. Eventually, he even besieged Acco (=Acre)—at the time a Phoenician city—and threatened Judea, forcing Queen Alexandra Salome to buy him off by means of valuable gifts.[11] Earlier in his reign, he had also fought the Parthians and had succeeded in reconquering areas which he had previously ceded to them. The Parthians, who were going through a period of internal disunity and weakness, tried to forge an alliance with

---

[5] *Ibid*, p. 72.
[6] Cf. Josephus, *Ant.* 13.14.1 § 378; *J.W.* 1.4 § 95.
[7] *Ant.* 13.14.3 § 385.
[8] Strabo, *Geographia*, 11.9.3 (515).
[9] Ephron, *Essays in Jewish History and Philology*, 72.
[10] *Ant.* 13.14.3 § 386.
[11] Cf. Josephus, *J.W.* 1.5.3 § 116; *Ant.* 13.16.4 § 419.

the Romans.[12] Since there was an alliance of sorts between the Romans and most of the Hasmonean rulers, it would have been a logical corollary for the Parthians to attempt to establish a common front with Judea and its successful, warlike ruler against a potential common enemy, namely Tigranes. As the sequel showed, Tigranes' growing power alarmed Queen Alexandra Salome, and may, conceivably, have been seen as a future threat by her husband. Since Alexander Yannai spent most of his life in more or less successful military expeditions, he could not have been indifferent to the potential threat from the north.

Whether an alliance between Parthia and Judea was indeed concluded as early as the reign of Alexander Yannai is uncertain, and there is no direct evidence that it was. In favor of such an assumption is the fact that Alexander Yannai's grandson, Antigonus, the last of the Hasmonean kings, did conclude an alliance with the Parthians against Herod and his Roman supporters in 40 B.C.E.[13] This alliance would have been greatly facilitated by an earlier understanding between Parthia and Judea.

Viewed from a wider historical context, it is certainly significant that throughout antiquity a limited but important identity of interests between Iran and Judea, necessitated primarily by the need to resist common enemies (Babylonian, Hellenistic-Seleucid, Roman and Byzantine), tended to make the overlords of Iran—Persians and Parthians alike—unequal and often uneasy allies in war and peace alike. If our assumption is correct, Tigranes and his Armenian empire must be added to the list of common enemies who helped to form an Iranian-Judean alliance during the first quarter of the first century B.C.E.

[12] Cf. Pauly-Wissowa, *Realencyclopädie der Classischen Altertumswissenschaft*, Vol. 18, Part 2 (Stuttgart 1949), col. 1990; ibid. *Zweite Reihe* (Second Series), Vol. 6 (Stuttgart 1937), cols. 970–71, where the sources are cited in full.

[13] Josephus, *J.W.* 1.13.1ff. §§ 248–69; *Ant.* 14.13.3ff. §§ 330–84.

THE FIRST AND SECOND TITHES IN THE *TEMPLE SCROLL*

Joseph M. Baumgarten
Baltimore Hebrew College

A MONG the religious criteria which served, according to rabbinic sources, to distinguish the Ḥaber from the ʿAm-ha-Aretz there were two of primary importance: (1) the observance of ritual purity and (2) the scrupulous separation of the tithes.[1] With regard to the pre-rabbinic Essene-Qumran community, we have a fair picture of the role of purity in their daily regimen from Josephus' description as well as the pertinent Qumran texts.[2] However, the hitherto available sources do not give us any information about the manner in which the laws of *maʿasrot* were interpreted and observed outside the sphere of Pharisaic tradition. The lack is now to some extent filled by the recently published *Temple Scroll* (*11QTemple*).[3] This supplement to the Torah, presented as the direct word of God, contains rules about the various perquisites of the priests and the Levites, such as their portions from the booty and the hunt, as well as a "tithe" of two percent from wild honey.[4] In this paper we shall be primarily concerned with the Scroll's elaboration of the two major tithes found in the Pentateuch, the levitical tithe in Numbers 18 and the so-called "deuteronomic tithe" of Deuteronomy 14.

We should note at the outset that contrary to modern exegetes who view the tithes in the priestly legislation and that of Deuteronomy as alternative interpretations or revisions of a single tithe, the sources available from the Second Temple period are in agreement with rabbinic halakha in requiring the separation of two distinct tithes. This is already evident from the *Book of Jubilees* which refers to the "second tithe" to

מוקדש בהוקרה לידידי שמואל שכל שבילי הספרות נהירין ליה

[1] *b. Ber. 47b* and parallels. For a recent study of the sources see A. Oppenheimer, *The ʿAm Ha-aretz* (Leiden, 1977).

[2] For a preliminary evaluation of the bearing of the Temple Scroll on this subject, see the writer's article, "The Pharisaic-Sadducean Controversies about Purity and the Qumran Texts," *JJS* 31 (1980) 157–70.

[3] Y. Yadin, *Megillat ha-Miqdash*, 3 vols. (Jerusalem, 1977).

[4] This is discussed in the writer's forthcoming paper, "On the Non-literal Use of *Maʿaser/Dekatē*," (*JBL* 103 [1984] 245–51).

be "fulfilled from year to year" by eating it before the Lord (32:11). *11QTemple*, likewise, has two distinct pericopes dealing with the levitical tithe (60:6–7) and the deuteronomic one (43:2–17) respectively.

Moreover, as we shall see, *11QTemple* throws valuable light on a related exegetical problem which has exercised commentators both ancient and modern, the nature of the enigmatic tithe of Lev 27:30–31:

> All tithes from the land, whether seed from the ground or fruit from the tree, are the Lord's; they are holy to the Lord. If a man wishes to redeem any of his tithes, he must add one fifth to them.

Rabbinic tradition identified the tithe in this passage with the 'second tithe' of Deuteronomy,[5] while modern scholars tend to connect it with the levitical tithe. Since the tithe here is spoken of as belonging to the Lord, which is presumed to mean to the priests of the sanctuary rather than the Levites as in Numbers 18, Kaufmann and Weinfeld point to a bifurcation of views concerning the tithe within the Priestly literature: "According to the stratum embodied in Leviticus 27 the tithe is considered the property of the Sanctuary and the priesthood. According to the later stratum (Num 18:21ff.) the tithe is given to the Levites who were the non-officiating class of the Temple personnel."[6] The idea of pentateuchal strata was, of course, alien to the conceptual framework of the author of *11QTemple*. Yet, it is interesting to observe that he, too, was impelled by the aforementioned exegetical problem to the assumption that there were "stages" in the history of the allocation of the tithe. This emerges from the brief, but significant pericope concerning the levitical tithe in *11QTemple* 60:6–7.

A. THE LEVITICAL TITHE

> And to the Levites belongs the tithe of grain, wine, and oil which they formerly consecrated unto me.

Yadin has properly pointed out that the phrase הקדישו לי must be derived from Lev 27:30 where the tithes are termed קדש לה'.[7] The transposition to the first person is in accord with the general format of the Scroll as the direct word of God. Less convincing is his suggestion

---

[5] See *Siphra* ad locum (ed. Weiss 115a), and D. Hoffman, *Das Buch Deuteronomium* (Berlin, 1913) 144.

[6] M. Weinfeld, art. "Tithe," *EncJud* 15 (1971) 1156–62; cf. Y. Kaufmann, *Toledot ha-ʾEmunah ha-Yisraʾelit* 1 (Tel Aviv, 1960) 148–54, and M. Haran, art. "Maʿaser," *Encyclopaedia Miqraʾit* 5 (1968) 204–12.

[7] *Megillat ha-Miqdash* 1, 126; cf. J. Milgrom, "Studies in the Temple Scroll," *JBL* 97 (1958) 519.

that the word לראישונה echoes the term מעשר ראשון, used as a designation for the levitical tithe in rabbinic literature. לראישונה occurs elsewhere in *11QTemple* in the sequential sense of something done before
something else. Here its most plausible connotation is that of something
done in former times, but now modified as in Gen 28:19 and Judg 18:29.[8]
Formerly, the tithes were consecrated to the Lord (Lev 27:30), but henceforth they are to belong to the Levites. Since the Levites in the author's
view were chosen "to stand in my presence and to minister" (60:11), they
were entitled to the emoluments properly belonging to the Sanctuary.
We may further surmise that this was the author's understanding of
Num 18:21: "And to the Levites I hereby give all the tithes in Israel as
their share in return for the services that they perform." The original
priestly claim to the tithes is nevertheless recognized in the 'tithe of the
tithe' which the Levites are required to set aside "as a gift to the Lord"
(Num 18:25).

The former practice of dedicating tithes to God or to the priesthood
is further illustrated in the narratives of Genesis. Thus, Abraham gave
"a tithe of everything" to Melchizedek, the priest of the Most High God
(Gen 14:20). In *Jub.* 13:25 this incident serves as a precedent for the ordinance to give the title "to the priests who served before Him." Some
have taken this to mean that according to *Jubilees* the tithe is still to be
given to the priests, rather than the Levites as prescribed in Numbers 18.[9]
Yet, in *Jub.* 32:2–9, Jacob is described as giving the tithe which he had
vowed to Levi. Although Levi was a "priest" there (32:9), he was recognized as the ancestor of both priests and Levites, who together minister
before the Lord (30:18). The ambiguity is most likely to be resolved in
the manner indicated in *11QTemple*. The tithes were originally consecrated to the Lord and were therefore assigned to the priesthood. When
the Levites were chosen to minister in God's presence, they became the
exclusive recipients of the levitical tithe.

The "historical" theory adumbrated in *11QTemple* is in striking
contrast with what is generally supposed to have been the history of the
disposition of the levitical tithe in the Second Temple period. Despite
the provisions in Numbers 18 assigning the tithe to the Levites, scholars
have noted apparent indications of the diversion of the tithe to the
priests according to the prevailing practice.[10] J. Milgrom, who has effectively demonstrated the higher status of the Levites in the ritual law of
11QTemple, suggests that the emphatic assignment of the tithe to the

[8] Cf. בראשונה in Mishnaic Hebrew, e.g. *Ned.* 11:12, *Roš.Haš.* 2:2, 5.
[9] See Y. M. Grintz, *Sefer Yehudith* (Jerusalem, 1957) 191; cf. the more judicious evaluation of Oppenheimer, *The ᶜAm Ha-aretz* 39–40.
[10] Cf. J. Jeremias, *Jerusalem in the Time of Jesus* (Philadelphia, 1969)
106–8.

Levites is in reaction to its usurpation by the contemporary priests.[11] But when did this usurpation occur? We have recently had occasion to review the evidence and it does not appear to be as early nor as unequivocal as some have supposed.

In the Book of Nehemiah the Levites, rather than the priests are regarded as the legitimate recipients of the tithe, whose collection had fallen into neglect.[12] There is a talmudic tradition which attributes the diversion of the levitic tithe to the priests to Ezra, who is said to have penalized the Levites for their failure to take part in the migration to Jerusalem.[13] However, the books of Ezra, Nehemiah, as well as Chronicles show no trace of a punitive attitude toward the Levites; on the contrary, they underline their ritual function in the Temple, and their role as teachers.[14] The implication of Ezra 8:15 that the Levites were conspicuous by their absence from Ezra's caravan is largely neutralized by 1 Esdr 8:42, where both priests and Levites are said to have been lacking.

Jdt 11:13 describes the besieged Jews as consuming the firstfruits "and the tithes of the wine and oil, which they had consecrated and set aside for the priests, who minister in the presence of our God." The prevalent explanation of the author's assignment of the tithes to the priests, rather than the Levites, is either that he was not concerned with the distinction, or that the practice in his day already allowed the levitic tithe to be given to the priests. However, in a recent paper we pointed out that the word $ma^c aser$ was frequently used in the generalized sense of any priestly gift, including the Terumah.[15] This would explain the statement in Jdt 11:13 that "it is not lawful for any of the people so much as to touch these things with their hands." In normative rabbinic halakha, no such restriction was applied to the levitic tithe.[16] The possibility, nevertheless, must be kept in mind that pre-rabbinic sources, including, as we shall see, *11QTemple*, may have held stricter views on this matter.

The use of *dekatē*, not only for the tithe, but as a general term for the priestly portions from the harvest may likewise serve to explain the ambiguity found in the Book of Tobit. Tobit went to Jerusalem "with the firstfruits and the tithes (*tas dekatas*) of the increase and the first shearings of the sheep," which he gave to the priests, the sons of Aaron (1:6-7, BA rescensions). Yet, immediately afterward he is said to have given the tithe (*tēn dekatēn*) to the sons of Levi, who ministered in Jerusalem (1:7). The premise put forth by some scholars that this contra-

---

[11] J. Milgrom, "Studies in the Temple Scroll," 503.
[12] Neh 10:38, 13:10.
[13] *b. Yebam.* 86b, *b. Bat.* 81b, *Ketub.* 26a, *Ḥul.* 131b.
[14] Ezra 3:8, 10; 6:20; 8:30, Neh 8:7-11.
[15] See above, n. 4.
[16] cf. *m.T.Yom* 4:1.

diction reflects the tension between the law in Numbers and the contemporary encroachment of the priests on the levitic tithe does not seem convincing. We have no substantial evidence for such encroachment from the early Second Temple period.

More plausible is the possible connection between the assertion of priestly claims to the tithe and Hasmonean innovations. A. Schalit[17] has described the policy of the Hasmonean kings to take control of the tithes and to use them for their own purposes. A. Oppenheimer more recently has surveyed the relevant rabbinic sources.[18] Of specific interest is the ordinance attributed by tannaitic tradition to John Hyrcanus I: "Johanan the high priest abolished the confession that the tithe had been given . . . and in his days one had no need to inquire concerning *demai*" (*m.Soṭa* 9:10). The abolition of the confession was apparently connected with the diversion of the tithe to the priests: "Because people were not presenting it as prescribed. For the divine law states that it is to be given to the Levites, whereas we give it to the priests." (*b.Soṭa* 47b) However, if Johanan were concerned with preserving the rights of the Levites, why did he abolish the confession rather than reform the prevailing practice? The confession, it has been inferred, became obsolete as a result of the new and more stringent methods of collecting the tithe instituted in the days of John Hyrcanus, which also removed any doubts about whether the obligatory separation had been performed.[19] "Pairs" were appointed to supervise the collection of the tithe and presumably priests were now recognized as legitimate recipients under the aegis of the "treasury."[20]

11QTemple, as we have noted, assigns the tithe exclusively to the Levites. It is possible to see this as a reaction to the preemption of the tithe by the priests. Since no conclusive evidence for such preemption is available before the Hasmonean period, one might be inclined to view this as corroborating the hypothesis of a Hasmonean date for the Scroll.[21] However, it is equally possible to relate the pro-Levitic posture of the Scroll to the similar tendency found in Chronicles and other sources from the early Second Temple period.

Before leaving the provisions in *11QTemple* concerning the levitical tithe, we must consider a halakhic question which arises from the wording of the text. The tithe is described as that "which they formerly *consecrated* unto me." We have noted that the phraseology derives from Lev 27:30 where the tithes are termed "holy to the Lord," requiring a surcharge of one fifth for redemption as for other sacred dedications.

[17] A. Schalit, *König Herodes* (Berlin, 1969) 262–71.

[18] Oppenheimer, *The ʿAm-Ha-aretz*, 29–42.

[19] Ibid., 34.

[20] *y. Maʿaś. Š.* 56d and *y. Soṭa* 24a.

[21] Yadin, *Megillat ha-Miqdash* 1, 298; cf. J. Milgrom, "The Temple Scroll," *BA* 41 (1978) 119.

Does this mean that the tithe was considered as sacred and forbidden for consumption by non-Levites? Rabbinic tradition, as was mentioned, did not apply Leviticus 27 to the "first tithe." Moreover, the halakha ultimately accepted as normative specifically denies any sacred character of the levitic tithe and regards its consumption by Israelites as merely a matter of misappropriation.[22] Yet, there were opinions which forbade the tithe to any but Levites.[23] *11QTemple*, which describes the tithe as "consecrated," is most probably to be understood in this sense, though the word is used in the context of what was done "formerly." The implied change is most likely to be taken as affecting the recipients of the tithe, i.e., Levites rather than priests, but not its sacred status.[24] The tithe would thus be consecrated exclusively to the Levites in the same manner that the Terumah was restricted to the priesthood.

Finally, we may infer that the collection of the tithe was to be centralized at the Sanctuary. This is indicated by the juxtaposition of the tithe with the shoulder portion of the sacrifices, which is likewise assigned to the Levites, in recognition of their ministering at the Temple. According to rabbinic halakha it was permissible to give the tithe to any Levite wheresoever one wished. However, it has already been pointed out by several scholars, that during most of the Second Temple period the practice was to bring the tithe to Jerusalem for central distribution.[25]

B. THE SECOND TITHE

Although the term "second tithe" is not found in the extant portions of *11QTemple*, comparison with *Jub.* 32:9–10 indicates that it is this tithe which is the subject of the rules elaborated in *11QTemple* 43:2–17:

2   ]on the Sabbath days and the days[

3   ]and on the days of first fruits for grain, for w[ine and for oil]

4   [and on the appointed day for the w]ood offering; On these days shall it be eaten. And they shall not allow it to re[main]

5   [from one] year to another. For thus shall they eat it:

---

[22] *b. Yebam.* 85b–86a; cf. the formulation of Maimonides, *Yad, Laws of Ma^{c}aser* 1,2: "The first tithe may be eaten by Israelites and in a state of impurity, for it has no sanctity whatsoever."

[23] According to R. Meir, the levitic tithe was prohibited to non-Levites (*b. Yebam,* 86a); cf. Z. Karl, "The Tithe and the Terumah" (Hebrew), *Tarbiz* 16 (1944) 11–17.

[24] J. Milgrom, "Studies," 519 suggests that the author of the Temple Scroll might also have derived the sanctity of the first tithe from Deut 26:13, where the tithes which accumulated in the third year of the cycle are called "holy."

[25] See Oppenheimer, *^{c}Am ha-Aretz*, 30–38.

6   From the first fruit festival for wheat grain let them eat the grain

7   until the following year, until the day of the first fruit festival; as for wine, from the day

8   appointed for wine until the following year, up to the appointed day

9   for wine; as for oil, from its appointed day until the following year

10 up to the appointed day for the offering of new oil on the altar. And whatever

11 remains from their appointed times shall be sacred; it must be burned in fire, and may no longer be eaten

12 for it has become sacred. And those who dwell at a distance from the sanctuary of three

13 days journey, whatever they are able to bring, let them bring; if they are not able

14 to carry it, let them sell it for money. They shall bring the money and buy with it corn

15 wine, oil, cattle, and sheep. And they shall eat it on the appointed days, and not

16 eat of it on workdays in their uncleanliness, for it is holy.

17 On the holy days let it be eaten, it may not be eaten on workdays.

This expansion of Deut 14:22–26 is found in the Scroll after the description of the booths constructed in the outer court of the Temple for the celebration of Sukkot. Similarly, *Jub.* 32:10–11 elaborates on the second tithe in the context of the account of Jacob's celebration of Sukkot. Since Sukkot was the festival of ingathering and concluded the harvest season, it served as a terminal point for the separation of the tithe. The one-year time limits on the consumption of the tithe from each category of harvest unparalleled in rabbinic halakha, is likewise found in *Jubilees*.[26] However, the requirement to eat the tithe only on holy days is not found elsewhere.

The exclusion of workdays derives from considerations of purity as indicated by the term לאונמה. The word און, originally referring to mourning for the dead, appears in Deut 26:14 in parallel with טמא as a typical example of ritual defilement which renders one ineligible to eat the sacred tithes.[27] Our text implies that ritual uncleanliness was associated with all workdays. What is the nature of this uncleanliness? A clue may perhaps be found in Josephus' description of the daily routines of the Essenes (*J.W.* 2.128–30).

---

[26] Yadin, *Megillat ha-Miqdash* 1, 81–98; cf. this writer's paper, "4QHalakah[a] 5, the Law of Ḥadash, and the Pentecontad Calendar," *JJS* 27 (1976) 36–46.

[27] Cf. Hos 9:4 where לחם אונים (*Tg.* לחם מרחק, "defiled bread") makes unclean those who eat it.

Before their morning prayers, we are told, the Essenes utter no word on mundane matters (*tōn bebēlōn*). They then go off to their various occupations until the fifth hour. The communal meal in the refectory must be preceded by a bath for purification. Such purification, it appears, was not for the purpose of removing uncleanliness stemming from corpses, carrion, creeping animals, or other biblical categories of defilement. If that were the case, a minimal waiting period after the bath until sundown would have been required.[28] Rather the uncleanliness stems from the secular activities, themselves. Just as the priests in the Temple, even when clean, were required to undergo immersion before performing their rites, so the Essenes' ablution served as a ritual demarcation between their secular occupations and the sacred meals. It is this concept of workdays as inherently "defiling" because of their mundane nature[29] which may serve to explain the rule in *11QTemple* excluding the consumption of the tithe on such days.

The other time restriction which *11QTemple* applies to the second tithe, the one-year limit for each category of harvest, likewise derives from its holy status. Just as sacrificial food has a prescribed period for its consumption after which it becomes unfit (Exod 29:34; Lev 7:17, 8:32, 19:6), so does the tithe "become sacred" after the following harvest festival. Although rabbinic halakha considered the second tithe as "holy to the Lord" (Lev 27:30), it rejected the imposition of such restrictions.[30]

C. THE REDEMPTION OF THE SECOND TITHE

Let us now turn to the provision for the redemption of the tithe. Comparison of the phraseology in *11QTemple* with its source, Deut 14:25–26, reveals some interesting changes:

---

[28] *11QTemple* 51:4–5; cf. 49:19–21 and my paper, "The Pharisaic-Sadducean Controversies," 158–59.

[29] The idea of ritual impurity associated with the workdays may perhaps serve to explain the practice of bathing on the eve of the Sabbath, of which mention is made in various sources. 2 Macc 12:38 says of Judah and his men: "And as the following day was the seventh, they purified themselves according to custom (*kata ton ethismon*) and celebrated the Sabbath there." It does not appear that this was done only because of the preceding battle. In CDC 10:10 the laws of purification, under the rubric על הטהר במים are placed immediately before those of the Sabbath. Among the latter we find a rule forbidding the wearing of unwashed garments (CDC 11:3–4). G. Allon (*Meḥqarim* 1, 306) pointed out the interesting reference in *Barn.* 15:1 to sanctifying the Sabbath "with pure hands and a pure heart." A vestigial remnant of this practice may be found in the hot baths which R. Judah used to take on the eve of the Sabbaths (*b. Šab.* 25b). Cf. the recent discussion in L. Schiffman, *The Halakhah at Qumran* (Leiden, 1975) 107.

[30] See *b. Tem.* 21b where the rule that "(second) tithe is not disqualified from one year to the next" is taken for granted.

Deuteronomy 14	*11QTemple*
ונתת בכסף	ימכרהו בכסף
ונתת הכסף	ולקחו בו

We note that *11QTemple* has replaced the rather vague wording ונתת
בכסף "and you may convert (the tithe) into money," with the more precise
directive "let him sell it for money." This contrasts sharply with the
mishnaic ruling found at the beginning of the tractate *Maᶜaśer Šeni*: אין
מוכרין מעשר שני "The second tithe may not be sold." The type of sale in
question is illustrated in *t.Maᶜaś. Šeni* 1:1: He may not say to him (the
buyer), "Take two-hundred (zuzim) and give me one hundred." Since
the tithe is subject to the restriction of being consumed only in Jerusalem,
it is assumed that no one would be willing to buy it at par value. The
ruling, however, excludes any sale because it constitutes a disgrace of a
sacred commodity.[31] The only conversion sanctioned would be redemption of the tithe, in accordance with Lev 27:31. This is likewise indicated
by the rendering of Deut 14:25 in the Targumim, *Ps.-Jonathan* (ותחלל)
and *Neofiti* (ותפרקון). *11QTemple*, which prescribes selling rather than
redeeming the tithe, thus presents us with an interesting polarization of
exegesis.

We note that both methods of converting consecrated objects are
mentioned in Leviticus 27. Thus, non-offerable animals which were devoted to the sanctuary were either assessed for their salable value by the
priest (v 12) or redeemed with a one fifth surcharge by the donor (v 13);
similarly, for real property (vv 14–20). Offerable animals and anything
devoted as *ḥerem* could "neither be sold nor redeemed" (v 28). To an
intermediate status belongs the "tithe of the land" for which redemption
is possible (v 31), while disposal by sale is not indicated. The identification of this tithe, described as "holy to God," as we have noted, has been
an ancient *crux interpretorum*.

Rabbinic exegesis, proceeding from the premise that the levitic tithe,
once the priestly Terumah has been deducted from it, could not be
termed "holy," arrived at the conclusion that the tithe of Lev 27:30–31
was the "second tithe."[32] They therefore identified the conversion procedure of Deut 14:25 (ונתת בכסף) with redemption. Ordinary sale was
deemed inappropriate for the second tithe.

At the same time, tannaitic halakha extended the procedure for redemption from the owner of the tithe, who was subject to the one-fifth
surcharge (Lev 27:31), to others who were exempt.[33] This opened the door
to certain evasions with considerable economic consequences. In a marginal economy burdened with taxation and already subject to the levitic
tithe, the additional imposition of a second tithe whose consumption

---

[31] Cf. S. Lieberman, *Tosefta Ki-fshutah, Zeraᶜim* II, 712.
[32] See *Siphra* (ed. Weiss 115a).
[33] *m. Maᶜaś. Š.* 4:3.

was restricted to Jerusalem no doubt constituted a serious problem. It is therefore interesting to read in the Mishnah:

> If someone had (second-tithe) money in Jerusalem and he had need for it (for other than food) and his fellow had produce, he may say to his fellow, "Let this money be rendered free for common use by (exchange with) your produce." The result will be that this one will eat his produce in cleanliness (as second tithe) and the other may do what he will with his money. (m. Maᶜaś.Š. 3:3)

Here the tithe money is ostensibly exchanged for unconsecrated produce which now becomes subject to the restrictions applicable to the second tithe. However, neither the produce nor the money really change hands. They are regarded as gifts from the seller to the buyer and vice versa. The original owner of the produce must now eat it with proper regard for ritual purity, a burden which he was willing to assume, perhaps in return for a service fee. Moreover, an analogous procedure was extended to the situation where the money was in the province while the fruit was in Jerusalem (m. Maᶜaś.Š. 3:4), thus sparing the owner of the second tithe the trouble of making the pilgrimage altogether. In effect, such a procedure would allow residents of Jerusalem to become surrogates for their brethren in the provinces in the consumption of the second tithe. Our sources do not indicate how widely this particular evasion was used, but when one considers that Jerusalem had approximately one-tenth of the population of Judea (Nah 11:1), the economic practicality of such an arrangement for disposing of the tithe becomes apparent. Its legality, however, depends ultimately on the identification of the redeemable "tithe of the land" in Lev 27:30–31 with the second tithe.

11QTemple, however, indicates its sharp dissent with such exegesis. The second tithe may be converted to money, but only through a bona fide sale, not by redemption. Redemption with the one-fifth surcharge, the author may have reasoned, was appropriate only where the sanctified object was to be conveyed to a recipient other than the original owner, as in the case of dedications of property (Leviticus 27) or the inadvertent consumption of Terumah by a non-priest (Lev 22:14). The deuteronomic tithe, however, was to be consumed by the owner, himself; hence, no redemption was indicated. The "tithe of the land" which according to Lev 27:31 was redeemable could thus only be the levitic tithe. This tithe was to be delivered to the Levites, and unlike the rabbis, Qumran exegesis held it to be sacred.

The aforementioned evasions of the second tithe are further eliminated by the manner in which the bringing of this tithe is elaborated in 11QTemple. First, the duty of bringing either the fruit or the proceeds from its sale to the sanctuary is taken quite literally. Second, by restricting its consumption to holidays and imposing a one-year limit for each species of crop, the quantity of tithe which could be consumed in Jerusalem was sharply reduced. The economic consequences of such restrictions were probably of little concern to the authors of the *Temple Scroll* and the *Book of Jubilees*. What mattered was that the rules were believed to be in accord with what was inscribed on the Tablets of Heaven.

THE RHETORIC OF PSALM 145

Adele Berlin
University of Maryland

IT is never easy to understand a poem. It is not enough to know the meaning of the words or to be able to analyze the syntax. One must make a leap from the linguistic level of the poem (words, grammar, etc.) to the poetic level—the level at which one grasps the essence of the poem, its message, its *raison d'être*. For biblical poetry the task is even more formidable, for words and grammar often remain obscure, and problems of textual accuracy always lurk beneath the surface. Nevertheless, if we stop when we have established correct readings, philological and grammatical analyses, and even historical or social reconstruction, we may still fall short of understanding what a particular poem is all about. This study is an attempt to get at the meaning of Psalm 145—to use the linguistic and structural clues of the psalm in order to elucidate its purpose and to show how it achieved this purpose.[1]

The study will be, of necessity, brief and superficial. There will be no effort to explicate individual verses or even all of the subdivisions of the psalm. Rather we will take an overview of the psalm as a whole, commenting only on its most outstanding features. The methodology employed is that currently subsumed under the label "rhetorical criticism," although actually some scholars were using it long before James Muilenburg coined the term. It consists of looking for repetitions and patterns in the use of words and phrases, for the particular structuring of words and ideas, and for various other rhetorical or poetic devices, such as chiasm and inclusio. The potential success of rhetorical criticism lies in the fact that the devices and symmetries that are present in a poem are not merely decorations—esthetically pleasing ornaments surrounding the meaning—but are pointers or signs which indicate what the meaning is.

---

[1] The studies of Psalm 145 cited in this article are Z. Adar, ספר תהלים (Tel Aviv, 1976) 178–80; M. Dahood, *Psalms III* (AB 17A; Garden City, 1970), 334–39; J. Liebreich, "Psalms 34 and 145 in the Light of Their Key Words," *HUCA* 27 (1956) 181–92; W. G. E. Watson, "Reversed Rootplay in Ps 145," *Biblica* 62 (1981) 101–2; A. Weiser, *The Psalms* (Philadelphia, 1962) 825–28; M. Weiss, "תהלה לדוד (תהלים קמה)," *Yuval Shay; a jubilee volume dedicated to S. Y. Agnon on the occasion of his seventieth birthday* (Ramat Gan, 1958) 185–209.

17

To understand how a poem is constructed is to begin to understand what it expresses.

1. THE ACROSTIC

The psalm is in the form of an alphabetic acrostic (slightly defective, the *nun* line is missing in the MT[2]). Acrostics are often viewed as a mnemonic or didactic device. Some scholars feel that the use of an acrostic diminishes the artistic merit of the poem, while others feel that it need not do so. Although the acrostic form does limit to some extent the alternatives for opening each verse, and in some cases a particular word choice may have been due to the acrostic, the poem still has to make sense. A good biblical poet could not let the structural demands of his work undermine his poetic creation any more than the composer of sonnets or haiku could. Moreover, since biblical poetry does not require acrostics, we must ask why the poet chose this form. Although the psalm has a didactic element (to be elaborated below), it is not generally considered to be a wisdom psalm,[3] and so the acrostic form was probably not used for scholastic reasons. Rather it may have been used because it expresses a totality. The poet praises God with everything from A to Z; his praise is all-inclusive. More than that, the entire alphabet, the source of all words, is marshalled in praise of God. One cannot actually use all of the words in a language, but by using the alphabet one uses all potential words. So the form is made to serve the message.

2. THE INCLUSIO

The occurrence of תהלה and תהלת in the first and last verses has been noted by Liebreich (cf. also Dahood), and the larger inclusio containing ברך ,שם and לעולם ועד has been discussed by Weiss (207–8). It seems clear, and is borne out by the analysis of the rest of the psalm, that the inclusio contains the most important idea in the psalm: praising the name (of God) forever.

3. KEY WORDS

Searching for key words (*leitwörter*) has yielded results even before it was made popular by rhetorical criticism. Liebreich's was the first and most thorough study of key words in Psalm 145. It noted, in addition to the inclusio, word repetitions that served as the basis for subdividing the

---

[2] Cf. *b. Ber* 4b and Dahood, 335.

[3] As far as I know, the only one who considers Psalm 145 to be a wisdom psalm is S. Holm-Nielsen, "The Importance of Late Jewish Psalmody for the Understanding of Old Testament Psalmodic Tradition," *ST* 14 (1960) 1–53.

poem into sections. For example, in vv 3–9 the words "greatness" and "goodness" predominate, in vv 11–13 the main word is "kingdom." More recently Watson has found the letters, *mem, lamed, kaph*, that make up the root for "king, kingdom" repeated in various places throughout the psalm. He concluded that the basic theme of the poem is God's eternal and universal kingship. Weiser (827) and Weiss have also emphasized the significance of the psalmist's view of God as king. But the word that occurs more often than any other is כל (17 times; Liebreich noted the frequency of this, too). This stresses the idea of "everyone" and "always." In the majority of cases it is used in association with those who benefit from God, e.g., "The Lord is good to all" (v 9), but it also appears in connection with when to praise ("every day"; v 2) and who will praise ("all flesh"; v 21). So there is created a relationship between God's universal beneficence and the universal praise of him. God is doing good to *all*, and *all* should *always* praise him.

In addition to repeated words there may be main ideas repeated through synonyms. In Psalm 145 there are two oft-repeated ideas, phrased differently, which are grouped into the two halves of the psalm. In the first half verbs of speaking or uttering praise predominate: אברכה, אברכך, אהללה, ישבח, יגידו, אשיחה, יאמרו, אספרנה, יביעו, ירננו, יודוך, יברכוכה, יאמרו, ידברו. It is not only God's praiseworthiness that is emphasized, but, even more, the many ways in which praise for him can be expressed. In the second half of the psalm the main idea is the actions of God towards his creatures; he supports them, gives them food, hears their cries, etc.

4. MAJOR SUBDIVISIONS

On the basis of recurring words and general contents the psalm can be subdivided into two, approximately equal, halves. Liebreich made v 10 the dividing point and saw the structuring word ברך as marking the beginning (vv 1, 2), middle (v 10), and end (v 21) of the psalm. Watson found a reverse acrostic of the letters *kaph, lamed, mem* ("king") in vv 11–13. This would place the central word/idea at the center of the poem.[4] Vv 11–13 also contain other features that mark them as the pivotal point in the psalm. There is a chiasm in vv 11–12

כבוד מלכותך . . . וגבורתך

. . . גבורתיו וכבוד הדר מלכותו

---

[4] The placement and arrangement of these letters would seem to be more a factor of the alphabetic acrostic rather than a desire for a reverse acrostic of *mlk*. More persuasive of the importance of the kingship theme is the use of *mlkwt* in vv 11, 12.

And one can also find in the word עולם the same kind of structural marker that Leibreich saw in ברך.

v 1	לעולם ועד
v 2	לעולם ועד
v 13	עלמים
v 21	לעולם ועד

Thus in vv 10-13, the heart of the psalm, there is a dense accumulation of the main words and themes: blessing, kingship, and forever (the same is true of v 1). The exact midpoint of the psalm remains somewhat ambiguous, but on the basis of content, supported by the structuring terms, I would place it at v 12 or v 13. As I noted in the previous section, the main thrust of the psalm from vv 1–12 is on speaking, telling, etc. This is not actually a praise of God; it is potential praise. The psalmist talks about praising, and does so at length, by heaping up verbs of saying, informing, speaking, etc. The impact is to illustrate a variety of ways of uttering or expressing praise. The first part of the psalm shows how to speak God's praise.

In the second half of the psalm the emphasis is on God's omnipresence and his actions in relation to the inhabitants of the world. God's beneficence is described in a general, universal way. The psalmist never says whether he himself has witnessed or experienced this beneficence; this is not a personal testimony. Rather it is like a catalogue of attributes that may, indeed, have been well known by the poet's audience.[5] This listing of God's deeds, many of which resemble phrases in the Book of Psalms and elsewhere, provides reasons for praising him and is a form of praise in itself. He is praised because he is praiseworthy;[6] and declaring him praiseworthy adds to his praise.

Thus, taken together, the two halves of the psalm constitute a poetic lesson in how to speak about God and what to say. In the next section we will see how the movement within the first half, and from one half to the other, reinforces the psalm's meaning and intent.

5. MOVEMENT AND CHANGE

We are usually so delighted to find key words and/or symmetrical structures that we rarely notice that often they are accompanied by a

---

[5] I am not suggesting that it is a formal catalogue of rubrics, though this remains a possibility. Compare the suggestion that Psalm 68 is a catalogue of incipits: W. F. Albright, "A Catalogue of Early Hebrew Lyric Poems (Psalm LXVIII)," *HUCA* 23 (1950–51) 1–39; S. Iwry, "Notes on Psalm 68," *JBL* 71 (1952) 161–65.

[6] This corresponds to the idea behind אהללה and מהלל in vv 2–3; cf. Weiss, 195.

change of some sort; and that change may be as significant as the repetition. (It is the repeated information that allows the change to stand out by contrast.)

The first and most noticeable shift is from the first person to the third person in the verbs of the first half. The psalm begins with first person (4 verbs), then fluctuates between first and third (5 verbs), and then remains with third person (6 verbs) (cf. Weiss, 192ff.). This is not a random pattern, but one that emphasizes the major purpose of the psalm: through the psalmist's praise everyone will come to praise God. This is expressed more directly in the last verse which sums up the point: "My mouth speaks the Lord's praise so that all flesh will bless his holy name forever." There is a sense of cause and effect here.[7] It should be recalled that this verse forms an inclusio with v 1, and here again the differences are as important as the similarities. For one thing, the same movement from first to third person is evident: from אברכה to יברך. Second, as Weiss has noted (208), שמך becomes שם קדשו. By the end of the psalm something more of the specialness of God's essence has been articulated. Finally, what began as a direct address to God, using the second person, "*your* name," ends as an indirect statement about God, "all flesh will bless *his* holy name." This kind of shift is not uncommon in the Bible, and it occurs several times within this psalm. But here it serves to emphasize the psalm's dual purpose: to praise God directly and to cause others to praise him. The psalm, then, is a lesson in how to praise God—ways to enunciate and what to say; and at the same time it is a good example of the very kind of thing that it is advocating. It succeeds in proclaiming praise to God.

In this brief study I have tried to show how attention to linguistic details—words, grammar, rhetorical structures and devices—can be useful in textual interpretation. These details are not ends in themselves, but signs pointing to a meaningful whole. This can be seen even from a superficial survey, as we have done, before moving to the analysis of individual verses. I have used the term "rhetorical criticism" and the methodology associated with it, but as it turns out, Psalm 145 is rhetorical not only in that it employs poetic devices, but in the classical sense as well. It is a poetic "argument" aimed at persuading the hearer to do what the psalmist has done, namely, praise the Lord always. How well the psalm succeeded is the subject of the postscript.

POSTSCRIPT

Psalm 145 occupies a prominent place in the Jewish liturgy; it is recited thrice daily (cf. Weiss, 185–86 for details). At its beginning were

---

[7] For the syntax of cause and effect sentences cf. P. Jouön, *Grammaire de l'hébreu biblique* (Rome, 1923) §§ 115c, 170a and F. I. Andersen, *The Sentence in Biblical Hebrew* (The Hague/Paris, 1974) § 8.3.

affixed two verses: Ps 84:5 אשרי יושבי ביתך עוד יהללוך סלה and Ps 144:15
אשרי העם שככה לו אשרי העם שה' אלהיו. And at its end was added Ps 115:18
ואנחנו נברך יה מעתה ועד עולם הללויה. Z. Adar (179) has suggested that
these additions add a nationalistic tone to a psalm which was originally
universal (God helps all who call upon him, satisfies all the living, etc.).
This is probably true, especially as regards Ps 144:15, but Ps 84:5 and
115:18 serve a more interesting function. They form an inclusio which
parallels the original inclusio. They echo the תהלה with יהללוך and
הללויה, and, more to the point, they hint at the essence of the meaning of
the psalm that I have tried to explicate. "They will ever (עוד) praise you"
becomes "we will praise the Lord from now till forever." All of the
elements of the first inclusio are present here: "praise," "the Lord," "forever"; the direct address to God and the indirect statement about him;
and the movement from third to first person. This last is a significant
reversal from the original inclusio. Whereas Psalm 145 moves from first
to third person, the addition moves in the opposite direction. What does
it signify? That the psalmist has been successful. Through his praise
others have come to do likewise. There will always be those who praise
God; they will keep on praising him indefinitely (עוד יהללוך). And the
circle is completed when the "they" becomes "we." The "we," i.e., the
present worshippers, join themselves to the never-ending chain of praise.
Ps 115:18 in this context[8] becomes a response to the author of Psalm 145:
"Here we are, psalmist, fulfilling your purpose by reciting praise to the
Lord." It would appear that those who made these additions understood
the poetic message of Psalm 145.

---

[8] In its original context in Psalm 115 the verse contrasts "we," i.e., the living,
who can praise God with "they, the dead" who cannot.

LEVITICAL CITIES: ARCHAEOLOGY AND TEXTS

Robert G. Boling
McCormick Theological Seminary

I T is a curious fact that the Book of Joshua, after devoting twelve chapters to stories of a prolonged mobilization and a hyperbolic warfare sequence, followed by another seven chapters describing the impartial delineation of tribal allotments by divine determination, should at last single out two social institutions for special attention before presenting Joshua's farewell address and a concluding account of the Shechem covenant. The two chapters on the Cities of Refuge (Joshua 20) and towns designated to guarantee residence and pasture rights for dispersed levites (Joshua 21) thus occupy a position of penultimate structural significance in the Book of Joshua.

The first of these institutions, three Cities of Refuge on each side of the Jordan River dedicated to curbing the blood feud, is at least broadly comprehensible as compensatory action in early Israel's opposition to urban Canaanite culture and Israel's dismantling of the older city-state governments. But the origin and purpose of the system of levitical towns is not so clear. Four kinds of questions confront the critical reader of Joshua 21. First is the question of content and organization of the list, with its doublet in 1 Chronicles 6. Second is the question of the origin and purpose of the *system* in which certain towns have obligation to provide the levite with residential and pasture rights. Third is the question of historical geography and the date of the surviving list(s). And fourth is the structural effect in context of the list's redactional use in the Book of Joshua.

1. CONTENT AND ORGANIZATION

Reconstruction of the list is greatly facilitated by the parallel 1 Chr 6:39–66 (54–81E). That these are two scribal recensions of a single list, rather than separate and distinct traditions, was shown by W. F. Albright.[1] In the following summary chart of names correlated with site

---

[1] W. F. Albright, "The List of Levitic Cities," *Louis Ginzberg Jubilee Volume* (New York: American Academy for Jewish Research, 1945) 49–73.

23

proposals and archaeological evidence, seven names require special comment. The bulk of the text is covered by our Textual Notes in the Anchor Bible on *Joshua*, from which the chart is also adapted.[2]

The name *Ashan* in v 16 (Judah/Simeon) follows 1 Chr 6:44 (59E). The common place name *Ain* in Josh 21:16 may refer to the same place.

The name *Joqmeam* in v 22 (Ephraim) follows 1 Chr 6:53, and was perhaps lost by haplography in MT. LXX[B] dropped *Qibzaim*. Conceivable but less likely is either alternative explanation: that one name is a corruption of the other, or that one represents an actual change of a town's name.

The name *Ibleam* in v 25 (Manasseh) follows 1 Chr 6:55 (70E). MT repeats *Gath-rimmon* from the Dan section (v 23).

The name *Qishion* in v 28 (Issachar) has a variant *Qedesh* in 1 Chr 6:56 (72E), but the relationship is obscure. Similarly *Helqath* in v 31 (Asher) alternates with *Huqoq* in 1 Chr 6:60 (75E); but the latter is a Naphtalite place in Josh 19:34.

The name *Qartah* in v 34 (Zebulun) is a *hapax*, with no parallel in 1 Chronicles 6. It is possibly a partial dittography of Naphtali's *Qartan* (v 32), displacing reference to *Tabor* in 1 Chr 6:62 (77E). Mount Tabor is clearly within Zebulun, as the border is drawn in 19:12. But the town *Chisloth-tabor* is just as clearly within Issachar. The problem is compounded by the fact that Qartah/Tabor is the only entry in the entire configuration for which we do not have at least one plausible site.

The name Rimmon restored in v 35 (Zebulun) agrees with 19:13 and 1 Chr 6:62 (77E) where it has a suffix. MT *dmnh* shows scribal confusion of *d* and *r*; LXX omits.

The summary figure of "48" cities in Josh 21:41 seems to imply four per territory. Such symmetry does not show in the reconstructed list. In order to achieve the symmetry we might subtract Hebron and Shechem as secondary additions (perhaps under the influence of the preceding Cities of Refuge list) and read *Hammoth-Dor* in Naphtali as two names. There can be no doubt, however, that both Shechem and Hebron had at one time or another very influential levitical-priestly personnel. It is better to assume that unless there is in the text the mechanism for some common scribal lapse, then there is high probability that the places named together comprised at one time or another a system that was ideally conceived (and perhaps originally established) to have the symmetry of four such towns per territory.

The list is organized according to a standard segmented genealogy of Levi, in three *mišpāḥôt*. First in our chapter come the Bene Qohath, among whom are to be found the higher clergy, the Bene Aaron, mentioned at the very outset. The Bene Aaron are concentrated in Hebron

---

[2] Robert G. Boling and G. Ernest Wright, *Joshua* (AB 6; Garden City, NY: Doubleday, 1982) 481–84.

Group	City	Identification	TENTH	NINTH	EIGHTH
	JUDAH/SIMEON				
	v 11 Hebron	(Jebel er-Rumeida)			x
	v 13 Libnah	(Tell Bornat)		x	x
	v 14 Jattir	(Khirbet Attir)			x
	Eshtemoa	(es-Semuᶜ)		?	?
	v 15 Holon	(Khirbet Alin)	?	?	?
	Debir	(Tell Rabud)	x	x	x
Bene Aaron	v 16 Ashan	(Khirbet Asan)	inaccessible		
(of the	Juttah	(Yatta)	unclarified see 15:55		
Bene Qohath)					
	Beth-shemesh	(ʾAin Shems)	x	x	x
	BENJAMIN				
	v 17 Gibeon	(el-Jib)		x	x
	Geba	(Jeba)			x
	v 18 Anathoth	(Ras el-Kharrubeh)		x	x
	Almon	(Tell Almit)		x	x
	EPHRAIM				
	v 21 Shechem	(Tell Balatah)	x	x	x
	Gezer	(Tell Jezer)	x	x	x
	v 22 Qibzaim	(Tell el-Mazar)		x	x
	Joqmeam	(Tell esh-Sheikh Dhiab)	x	x	x
	Beth-horon	(Beit ᶜUr)			
Other Bene Qohath	Upper	(el-Foqa)	x	x	x
	Lower	(el-Taḥta)	x	x	x
	DAN				
	v 23 Elteqe	(Khirbet el-Muqennaᶜ)		x	x
	Gibbethon	(Tell Malat)		x	x
	v 24 Aijalon*	(Tell Qoqa + Yalo)	x	x	x
	Gath-rimmon				
		(Tell Abu Zeitun)	x	x	x
		(Tell Jerishe)		x	x
	MANASSEH (WEST)				
	v 25 Taanach	(Tell Taᶜannak)	x	x	x
	Iblcam	(Tell Belᶜameh)	x	x	x
	MANASSEH (EAST)				
	v 27 Golan	(Sahem el-Jolan)	inaccessible		
	Ashtaroth	(Tell Ashtarah)	x	x	x
	ISSACHAR				
	v 28 Qishion	(Tell el-Muqarqash)		x	
	Daherah	(Deburiyeh)	Iron Age: unclarified		
Bene Gershon	v 29 Jarmuth	(Kokab el-Hawaʾ)		x	x
	En-gannim	(Khirbet Beit Jann)	x	x	x
	ASHER				
	v 30 Mishal	(Tell Kisan)		x	x
	Abdon	(Tell Abdon)		x	x
	v 31 Helqath	(Tell el-Qassis)	x	x	x
	Rehob	(Tell el-Gharbi)	x	x	x
	NAPHTALI				
	v 32 Qedesh	(Tell Qades)			x
	Hammoth-dor	(Tell Raqqat)			x
	Qartan	(Khirbet el-Qureiyeh)	unclarified		
	ZEBULUN				
	v 34 Joqneam	(Tell Qeimun)		x	x
	Qartah/Tabor	(?)			
	v 35 Rimmon	(Rummaneh)	?	?	x
	Nahalal	(Tell en-Nahl)	x	x	x
	REUBEN				
	v 36 Bezer	(Umm el-Amad)	x	x	x
Bene Merari	Jahaz	(Khirbet el-Medeiyineh al-Themed)	LB-Iron I: unclarified		
	v 37 Qedemoth	(es-Saliyeh)	Iron Age: unclarified		
	Mephaath	(Tell ej-Jawah)	x	x	x
	GAD				
	v 38 Ramoth-in-Gilead	(Tell er-Rumeit)	x	x	x
	Mahanaim	(Tell edh-Dhahab el-Gharbiyeh)	Iron Age: unclarified		
	v 39 Heshbon	(Tell Hesban)	x	x	x
	Jazer	(Khirbet Jazzir)	Iron Age: unclarified		

and the hills south of it, in the Judean Shephelah, and in Benjamin. Others, apparently lower ranking Qohathites, are mostly dispersed at the fringes of the north-central hill country (Ephraim, Dan, W. Manasseh). Shechem is the major exception to the pattern here.

For the two remaining *mišpāḥôt* (Gershon and Merari) towns are designated in the far north and in Transjordan.

The pride of place here granted to the Bene Qohath and to the Aaronite priests among them is also reflected in the description of tabernacle responsibilities (Num 3:23–26; 4:24–27; cf. 10:17). At one time or in other circles, however, Gershom/n was the dominant levitical family, to judge from its frequent appearance in first position, where the three families are listed in other texts (Gen 46:11; Exod 6:16; Num 3:17; 26:57; 1 Chr 6:1, 16; 23:6). One explicit reference to such a priesthood, headed by "Jonathan, son of Gershom, son of Moses" locates it precisely in the far north at the town of Dan (Judg 18:30). If the patronymic of Gershom is to be understood as a clan name, then it may be plausibly related to the family of the Mushites in the fragment of an alternative genealogy of Levi in Num 26:58a. It is therefore possible, as Frank M. Cross began to do,[3] to trace the influence of an ancient polarity of priestly houses claiming legitimacy through direct descent from either Moses or Aaron.[4] The organization of our list reflects the victory of the Aaronites, to be observed as early as the Solomonic establishment, in the elevation of Zadoq and the suppression of the Shilonite house of Abiathar.

2. ORIGIN AND PURPOSE OF THE SYSTEM

It is a reasonable working hypothesis that our tradition is ultimately rooted in the religious conversion of "levitical" families left more or less isolated in Egypt after events that are reflected, however dimly, in stories such as the rape of Dinah (Genesis 34) and in archaic poetry such as the Testament of Jacob (Genesis 49). The latter is an eleventh-century poem which recalls an earlier time when Levi and Simeon were banished from the league, on a single charge:

Cursed be their wrath—how fierce it was!
And their rage—how cruel it was!

[3] Frank M. Cross, *Canaanite Myth and Hebrew Epic* (Cambridge: Harvard University, 1973) 195–215.

[4] Robert G. Boling, "Levitical History and the Role of Joshua," in *The Word of the Lord Shall Go Forth*, eds. Carol Meyers and M. O'Connor (Winona Lake, IN: Eisenbrauns, 1983) 241–61.

I will divide them from Jacob,
And I will banish them from Israel.[5]

The Jacob/Israel organization from which Levi and Simeon were expelled must have been a pre-Mosaic league centering on the cult of the patriarchal god El.

The Testament of Moses, on the other hand, with its emphasis on Levi's responsibility for handling the priestly lot, guarding the oracle, protecting the *berît*, teaching *tōrâ* and *mišpāṭ* (Deut 33:8-10), seems to voice a hope based on *late* eleventh century reality.[6] In other words, the suggestion is that a significant portion of the patriarchal (pre-Yahwist) tribe of Levi found its way, after expulsion from a league in Canaan, to Egypt where it later experienced religious conversion and was revitalized as the core of the Yahwist movement. The discovery of a Hittite parallel for shared guardianship of the sanctuary[7] suggests an example of what Max Weber called "hereditary" or "office" *charisma*[8] which would have left pre-Mosaic Levi predisposed toward the role of palace guard in Mosaic Israel, the latter understood as Kingdom of Yahweh in fact. In sociological terms, the Levites in post-Mosaic Israel may be understood as "a quasi-guild structure or caste into which one might gain entrance by choice and appointment *or* by heredity."[9]

Dispersal of the levitical carriers of militant Yahwism throughout the territory of Israel was thus institutionalized in the appointment of levitical towns. Josh 21:2 asserts Mosaic authority for the institution; Yahweh had anticipated a time when levites would no longer be serving only the function for which they are especially noted in the epic sources—guarding the portable palace and throne of the divine king, as at the Jordan crossing (Joshua 3-4) and at the Shechem Valley ceremony (Josh 8:30-35). In the new circumstances the militant levites were to be dispersed for the purpose of teaching the old Yahwist duties. There is nothing implausible about the specific concern of this institution. City

---

[5] Gen 49:7, tr. David Noel Freedman, "Early Israelite History in the Light of Early Israelite Poetry," in *Unity and Diversity: Essays in the History, Literature and Religion of the Ancient Near East*, eds. H. Goedicke and J. J. M. Roberts (Baltimore: Johns Hopkins University, 1975) 17.

[6] David Noel Freedman, "Divine Names and Titles in Early Hebrew Poetry," *Magnalia Dei: The Mighty Acts of God*, eds. Frank Moore Cross, Werner Lemke, and Patrick D. Miller, Jr. (Garden City, NY: Doubleday, 1976) 55-102.

[7] Jacob Milgrom, "The Shared Custody of the Tabernacle and a Hittite Analogy," JAOS 90 (1970) 204-9.

[8] Max Weber, *Ancient Judaism*, tr. Hans H. Gerth and Don Martindale, (New York: The Free Press, 1952) esp. 1-27.

[9] Timothy Polk, "The Levites in the Davidic-Solomonic Empire," *Studia Biblica et Theologica* 9 (1979) 3-22.

houses in themselves had no economic function in the society; there could be no well-being without access to land outside the town.[10]

Historical precedent for this system in early Israel has been recognized in Egypt's Late Bronze Age administration, where "certain cities had been confiscated . . . turned into royal estates and dedicated by Pharaoh to the great gods of the Egyptians."[11] While Mazar sought to correlate the distribution of levitical towns with Solomonic administration of neighborhoods at last conquered by David, it was never explained how the supposedly Solomonic creation came to enjoy explicit Mosaic authority in the Deuteronomic corpus of material. It is, however, advisable to distinguish between the origin of the system as sacred institution and the actual roster of names which survives. It seems clear enough that places such as the outlying towns in Dan and perhaps Gezer could not have been part of the system any earlier than the tenth century. For the creation of the system on a modified Egyptian model, we should have to recognize that it was Yahweh as king of pre-monarchic Israel who instituted the system in imitation of Pharaoh his royal counterpart. On this view it was such developments as Solomon's manipulation of an already existing system (e.g., the sale of the Cabul district to Hiram of Tyre in 1 Kgs 9:13), followed by the alienation of Shechem when the northern capital was moved to Tirzah, and the continuing impoverishment of northern levites by the priestly appointments of Jeroboam I, that nourished levitical discontent and generated a reform movement which we know from later centuries as Deuteronomism.[12]

In the Book of Deuteronomy it is the deeply rooted teaching function of the levites that calls for recognition.[13] In contrast presumably to those prestigious clergy whom Deuteronomy styles "the priests the levites"[14] (like the bearers of the ark in epic sources), the mass of levites in Deuteronomy are impoverished and especially in need of the community's benevolence and protection, along with the widow, the orphan, and the resident alien.[15]

---

[10] Menaḥem Haran, "Studies in the Account of the Levitical Cities," *JBL* 80 (1961) 45–54, 156–65. Haran concludes that a historical situation lies at the basis of what he regards as essentially a utopian creation in this list.

[11] Benjamin Mazar, "The Cities of the Priests and the Levites," *VT* Sup 7 (1960) 193–205.

[12] See the studies of Baruch Halpern, "Sectionalism and the Schism," *JBL* 93 (1974) 519–532; "Gibeon: Israelite Diplomacy in the Conquest Era," *CBQ* 37 (1975) 303–16; "Levitic Participation in the Cult of Jeroboam I," *JBL* 95 (1976) 31–42.

[13] G. Ernest Wright, "The Levites in Deuteronomy," *VT* (1954) 325–30. In response see J. A. Emerton, "Priests and Levites in Deuteronomy. An Examination of Dr. G. E. Wright's Theory," *VT* 12 (1962) 129–38.

[14] Deut 17:9, 18; 18:1; 24:8.

[15] "The levite" or "all the tribe of Levi," in 12:12, 18; 16:11, 14; 26:11, 13. Also in 18:1 "the priests the levites" is immediately explained appositionally as "all

If Deuteronomy is originally most deeply rooted in the north, the Arad ostraca on the other hand provide additional evidence for levitical activity in the south, where persons with levitical names are involved in fiscal administration and accounting for stores of wine, flour, and oil on behalf of the "House of Yahweh" (whether at Arad or elsewhere is a moot question). Here there is considerable data that lends credibility to the Chronicler's report of King Jehoshaphat's reforms in ninth-century Judah (ca. 873–849). A team of eight levites and two priests was dispatched to "all the cities of Judah" with the purpose of teaching the people from the Book of Yahweh's Torah (2 Chr 17:7–9), while in Jerusalem there were levites and priests announcing the decisions of Yahweh and adjudicating cases.

Many of Jehoshaphat's teaching levites were no doubt related to folk who had fled from the north half a century earlier, expelled from office by Jeroboam I but welcomed by the son of Solomon because, as the Chronicler was pleased to say, "they walked in the ways of David and Solomon," i.e., they regarded the Jerusalem throne as the legitimate one (2 Chr 11:13–17). In other words, there were in both of the divided kingdoms elements of two major levitical factions, divided primarily over the legitimacy of the Jerusalem establishment.

3. HISTORICAL GEOGRAPHY AND THE DATE OF THE LIST

If we look for a period when all the towns in the list were most likely to have been occupied concurrently, the trail leads rather directly to the eighth century. The pattern of occupation described on the chart draws heavily upon the unpublished dissertation by John L. Peterson; the bulk of Peterson's work supplements the excavation reports with topographical surface survey, covering some 74 sites that have been associated with the roster of levitical towns.[16]

Question marks in the chart indicate lack of success by Peterson's team in finding confirmatory evidence for a previous dating. In some

---

the tribe of Levi." The latter may well be a gloss claiming for all levitical persons the prerogatives of "the priests the levites." Emerton's objection to Wright's theory cannot stand if the apposition is read dialectically. Cf. Boling, "Levitical History and the Role of Joshua."

[16] John L. Peterson, "A Topographical Surface Survey of the Levitical 'Cities' of Joshua 21 and 1 Chronicles 6: Studies on the Levites in Israelite Life and Religion," unpublished Th.D. dissertation, Chicago Institute for Advanced Theological Studies: Seabury-Western Theological Seminary, 1977. My few disagreements with Peterson have to do with the textual integrity of Qartah in Zebulun (v 34) and the locations of Helqath in Asher (v 34) which Peterson finds at T. Regev, and Mahanaim in Gad (v 38) where Peterson settles for T. Hejjaj.

cases a large modern village (Juttah, Daberath) or modern urban expansion (Ashan, Hebron), or a nearby international border (Golan, Ashtaroth, Qartan) have either reduced the value of surface sherding or made it impossible.

The location of Elteqeh in Dan (v 23) is uncertain, but the site of T. Miqne (khirbet el Muqennaᶜ) remains the best candidate. Elteqeh is left in limbo if Miqne is Eqron, as recently proposed.[17] Despite the impressive evidence of Philistine presence at Miqne, we will await further excavation and surveying, since it seems likely that our list refers to an eighth-century town. If T. Miqne is Eqron, then we must look for Elteqeh somewhere north to northeast of Miqne. This rules out Tel esh-Shalaf (an archaeological blank anyway) and raises a question about Tel Melat (which is already better identified as Gibbethon).

The route taken by the cows from Eqron in returning the ark according to the story in 1 Samuel 6 is not admissable as evidence here, since it was not a matter of cows at a crossroads deciding which road to take and choosing the most direct one,[18] but a question of whether or not the cows would immediately forsake their calves, because, it is implied, they were driven to do so by Yahweh.

There is also a plausible reading of the account of Sennacherib's campaign which does not pose a problem. Sennacherib's itinerary is clearly explained as due to the arrival of the Egyptian army "in the plain of Eltekeh,"[19] which would interrupt the Assyrian's unhindered suppression of various towns. The implication is that Eqron was bypassed of necessity, in order to deal first with the main Egyptian force. The victory led to the rapid reduction of nearby Elteqeh and Timna before turning back to take Eqron. These conditions all are met with Eqron at Qatra and Elteqeh at Muqennaᶜ (the latter ought also to be producing some Hellenistic evidence if it is the site of Eqron). The argument that Elteqeh was too insignificant for the large site of Muqennaᶜ is not totally convincing. Elteqeh was certainly prominent enough for Sennacherib's scribe to use it as a major point of reference.

Allowing a wide margin for the inadequacies of surface surveying without stratigraphic excavation, which would surely modify the picture in considerable detail, a reliable general view of the occupational history of these towns in the tenth to eighth centuries is clear, with only one exception in the eighth-century column (Tell el-Muqarqash, possibly Qishion in Issachar). Developments in the eighth century make it precisely the sort of period in which such a system might flourish—the era of the long and brilliant reigns of Jeroboam II in the north (ca. 786–746) and Uzziah in the south (ca. 783–742), rapidly eclipsed by the swift

---

[17] J. Naveh, "Khirbat al-Muqannaᶜ-Ekron: An Archaeological Survey" *IEJ* 8 (1958) 87–100 (Part I); 165–70 (Part II).

[18] Naveh, "Khirbat al-Muqannaᶜ-Ekron," 168–69.

[19] *ANET²* 287–88.

decline and fall of the northern kingdom and severe vassalage imposed upon the south. The great eighth-century prophets are increasingly recognized as having close connection to the same levitical circles which produced the core of Deuteronomy. The latter seems clearly enough to reflect a vigorously transmonarchical (not necessarily "antimonarchical") reform movement. There is much new archaeological evidence to suggest that in matters military, as well as civil and administrative, the power of Hezekiah, with whose reforms the nucleus of Deuteronomy is generally associated, was actually superior to that of Josiah a century later.[20] A support-system for the network of levitical torah-teachers which embraced north and south and extended to both sides of the Jordan is one which apparently had not acknowledged the permanence of political divisions and had not made peace with the redefinition of Israel in terms of the monarchic nation-states. There is nothing to gainsay a claim that the rationale is Mosaic in origin.

Peterson proposes that the levitical towns were teaching centers of the Yahwist covenant, where the levites taught what was involved in covenantal living. On this view it was the word of Yahweh that created the system early in Israel and later revived it.

Such a roster of towns would surely tend to fluctuate. If our list represents a distribution of major levitical centers roughly a century after the reforms of Jehoshaphat, assignments made for the Bene Aaron are very interesting. Although the list reflects the priority and predominance of the Bene Aaron, no special importance is attached to them. They appear to have no special relation to Jerusalem; and they have no support towns at all in the heartland north of Hebron. These observations bring into sharper focus the final question of this paper.

4. REDACTIONAL EFFECT

This is not the place to recapitulate the variety of indicators which suggest that the position of the list in Joshua 21 is a contribution of the latest (that is, post-Josianic) redaction.[21] The redactor, we have argued elsewhere, was an intellectual heir if not a genealogical descendent of a northern levitical family that fled south, perhaps after 721, later to have the last word in forming the Dtr-corpus.[22] By that time (late seventh to early sixth centuries) the list of levitical towns was more than a century old. The redactor understood it, however, as preserving the actual assignments made by Eleazar, Joshua, and the Bene Israel. It was at last included in the Dtr-History, not because it was a living institution, nor a utopian one, but for its high symbolic value conveying the lessons of

---

[20] See J. Rosenbaum, "Hezekiah's Reform and the Deuteronomistic Tradition," *HTR* 72 (1979) 23–43.

[21] Symbol Dtr 2. Boling and Wright, *Joshua*, 132–35, and 478–97.

[22] Boling, "Levitical History and the Role of Joshua."

history. As the very next chapter of Joshua makes clear, in the account of narrowly avoided civil war at the end of the Joshua era, the point of view represented by the redactor's use of the levitical cities list is anything but utopian.

Now that the land has been fairly allotted, with institutions in place for combatting private vengeance and for the promulgation of Yahwist ethic, how will the Bene Israel conduct themselves as citizens of the Yahweh-kingdom? With the record filled out to the satisfaction of the final redactor, transition to the following era is effected in a characteristic way, by adding the tragicomic story in chap. 22. At the end of the succeeding book there are two such chapters (Judges 19–20 and 21).[23] But first comes a summary at the end of Joshua 21 emphasizing the quality of Yahweh's faithfulness to his promise and oath: "Not a word of all the Good Word which Yahweh had spoken to the house of Israel proved untrue. It all happened" (Josh 21:45).

[23] Robert G. Boling, *Judges* (AB 6A; Garden City, NY: Doubleday, 1975) 271–88 and 289–94.

SARGON AND JOSEPH: DREAMS COME TRUE[1]

Jerrold S. Cooper
Dept. of Near Eastern Studies
The Johns Hopkins University

T HE recently published Sumerian account of Sargon of Akkad's rise to power[2] tells us that his ascendancy was foretold to him in a dream. At the time, Sargon was serving as cupbearer to king Urzababa of Kish,[3] and the latter, not unsurprisingly, was extremely displeased to learn of Sargon's dream, and went to great lengths to avoid the consequences that it prophesied. But even before Sargon had his dream, Urzababa himself had nocturnal premonitions of his downfall, to which he reacted in the same way that Naramsin reacted to a dream foretelling his own doom in *The Curse of Agade*:[4] "He understood, but would not articulate it, nor speak about it with anyone" (line 4). If Urzababa's uneasiness at this point cannot simply be ascribed to a bad manuscript tradition (there is only one manuscript preserved, and the line occurs again later in the composition at a more appropriate place), then we ought to assume either an earlier prophetic dream of Sargon or some other ominous event in the lost part of the composition that preceded the beginning of the new text. In any case, a week or so after these first premonitions, Urzababa had a genuine conniption ("Like a lion, he was dribbling urine, filled with blood and pus, down his legs, / He struggled like a floundering salt-water fish, he was terrified there"; lines 10f.), and only then did Sargon "lay down not to sleep, but lay down to dream" (line 13).

The dream itself is first presented in the narrative in a brief and intentionally ambiguous form: "Holy Inana, in the dream, was drowning him (Urzababa) in a river of blood" (line 14). That Urzababa (and

---

[1] I would like to thank A. Kort for her assistance with the research for this paper.

[2] J. Cooper and W. Heimpel, *JAOS* 103 (1983) 67ff.

[3] For the literary traditions surrounding Sargon's career, see B. Lewis, *The Sargon Legend*, ASOR Dissertation Series, (Cambridge: ASOR, 1980).

[4] See J. Cooper, *The Curse of Agade* (Baltimore: Johns Hopkins University, 1983), lines 87 and 93a.

not Sargon) is the antecedent of "him" is clear from what follows, and certainly must have been clear to Sargon himself; only the reader/auditor is temporarily left in suspense. The reader is even led toward concluding, incorrectly, that Sargon is the antecedent by the reaction of Sargon in the next line: "Sargon, screaming, gnawed the ground." The true interpretation is revealed when Urzababa, having heard Sargon's screams, summoned Sargon and asked him to recount his dream. Sargon's reply consists of a more elaborate and more specific account of the dream:

> "Oh my king, this is my dream which I will have told you about:
> "There was a single young woman, she was high as the heavens, she was
>   broad as the earth,
> "She was firmly set as the base of a wall.
> "For me, she drowned you in a great [river], a river of blood." (lines 21–24)

Here there is no ambiguity, nor is there any possibility that Sargon's perception is incorrect: Urzababa's earlier premonitions and the course of action he is about to take, the role of Inana in Sargon's career, and that career itself, as known from both historical and literary-historical sources, leave no doubt that according to the dream it is Urzababa, not Sargon, who will perish. Sargon's screams could not have been caused by the ultimate outcome foretold by the dream, which was in his favor. Rather, it was the prospect of supplanting a master whom he perhaps loved, and the possible consequences when Urzababa would learn of his coming demise, that so unnerved Sargon.

Sargon had reason to worry. Urzababa reacted to Sargon's dream with apprehension (line 25), but then turned to his chancellor and provided the dream with a new interpretation:

> "[ ] my royal sister, holy Inana,
> "[ ] is going to put my finger into a . . . of blood,
> "[The]n she will drown Sargon, the cupbearer(?), in a great river."
> (lines 27–29)

Knowing in his heart that Sargon had correctly reported and understood the dream, Urzababa publicly proclaimed his own bravado interpretation, which predicted the demise of Sargon instead of himself. And he set in motion a vain plot to turn his new interpretation into reality. The details of this plot form the least intelligible part of a generally difficult text, but Inana protects Sargon and he returns unscathed to Urzababa's palace, much to the latter's horror.

Sargon's dream of replacing his master and ruler is reminiscent of the dreams of Joseph in Genesis 37. Before the dreams are recounted, we are told that as his father's favorite, Joseph was unpopular with his elder brothers, information that foreshadows both the mistreatment of Joseph by his brothers, and his eventual ascendance over them. The slightly sinister mood this casts at the tale's beginning can be compared with the atmosphere of foreboding created by Urzababa's apprehension and fit *before* Sargon even has his prophetic dream. Unlike Sargon, Joseph was not at all disturbed by the prospect of dominating his brothers and parents. Whether due to youthful arrogance or confidence in the destiny god has assigned to him, his matter-of-factness here makes him a not entirely sympathetic figure.

Like Sargon's dream, the dreams of Joseph belong to Oppenheim's category of the symbolic dream:

> a series of more-or-less rational activites, actions, and gestures are performed for the benefit of the dreamer, as a rule silently and with gods, stars, animals, and objects of every description as actors.[5]

As we know from Joseph's later career in Egypt, such dreams usually require interpretation. Even the very obvious dream of Gudea, ordering him to build the temple of Ningirsu,[6] required an elaborate interpretation. But, continues Oppenheim,

> There are, however, a few instances of "symbolic" dreams in which interpretations can be dispensed with. Such are the self-explanatory dreams of Joseph foretelling his future supremacy over his family.

Such, too, is the dream of Sargon. The action of the goddess and what it prophesies is clear both to Sargon and Urzababa, despite the latter's desperate and insincere attempt at reinterpretation. Had there been any real doubt, Urzababa could have turned to a professional interpreter, or to the goddess herself.[7]

The appearance of the goddess Inana in Sargon's dream guaranteed its authenticity. Joseph's dreams contained no such theophany, and the questioning of both his brothers and father suggest that neither entirely believed that the message was authentic. As Von Rad has noted,[8] this lack of divine presence makes Joseph's dreams ambiguous: do they represent the hubris of a brash young man, or genuine prophecies of future greatness? Whichever, the increased hatred of his brothers, and his father's thoughtfulness, are appropriate responses. One might compare Jacob's

---

[5] Oppenheim, *The Interpretation of Dreams in the Ancient Near East*, Transactions of the American Philosophical Society, N.S. 46/3 (Philadelphia: American Philosophical Society, 1956) 206.

[6] Oppenheim, *Dreams*, 211f. Gudea's dream begins very much like Sargon's; see *JAOS* 103 (1983) 80.

[7] Cf. Oppenheim, *Dreams*, 221.

[8] *Genesis: A Commentary* (OTL; Philadelphia: Westminster, 1961), 346.

believable mixture of annoyance and thoughtfulness to Urzababa's desperate distortion of the dream's message. The former then unwittingly sent Joseph into his brothers' trap, whereas Urzababa deliberately sent Sargon into an unsuccessful trap. Inana protected Sargon from Urzababa, but Joseph's salvation was more circuitous: he succumbed to his brothers, but his sale into Egyptian bondage turned out to be a part of a divine scheme that ultimately saved his father and the very brothers who tried to do him in.

The folkloric character of the Joseph story has long been recognized.[9] Stith Thompson's *Motif-Index of Folk-Literature*[10] lists the following relevant motifs: Dream of future greatness for youth (M312.0.1), dream (prophecy) of future greatness causes punishment (imprisonment) (L425), and vain attempts to escape fulfillment of prophecy, of which there are many subtypes (expulsion, confinement, killing; M370ff.). In Aarne-Thompson, *The Types of the Folktale*,[11] two types bear resemblance to the Joseph story. In No. 517, a boy understands the language of the birds, who prophesy that his parents will humble themselves before him. The parents drive him away in anger, and the boy becomes a great man, returns unknown to his parents, and the prophecy is fulfilled. In No. 725, a boy dreams that his parents and the king shall serve him. He is driven away, but after many adventures, his dream comes true. These tale-types and motifs[12] are found world-wide; one of the most striking parallels is from pre-Columbian Peru:[13]

Two brothers, jealous of a third brother's superhuman powers, lured him into a cave where they sealed him up. After some time, when the brothers were certain that the third brother was dead, he appeared to them "flying through the air on great wings of colored feathers, and with the fear the sight of him aroused in them, they tried to run away. But he quickly dispelled that fear, saying: 'Do not be afraid or troubled; I come only that the empire of the Incas shall begin to be known. Therefore leave, leave this settlement which you have built, and go farther down until you come to a valley where you will then found Cuzco.' "

[9] See especially Gaster(-Frazer), *Myth, Legend and Custom in the Old Testament* (New York: Harper and Row, 1975 [1969]), 216f., and Redford, *A Study of the Biblical Story of Joseph*, VT Sup 20 (1970), chaps. 4 and 7.

[10] Bloomington: Indiana University, 1955–58.

[11] Folklore Fellows Communications, No. 184 (1964).

[12] For a critical discussion of the tale-type and motif as analytical units, see Dundes, *Analytic Essays in Folklore*, Studies in Folklore, No. 2 (The Hague: Mouton, 1975) 62ff.

[13] Pedro de Cieza de Leon, *The Incas* (Norman: University of Oklahoma, 1959) 32ff.; cited by Gaster, *Myth*, 216f.

Neither the Joseph story nor the story of Sargon's rise to power are folktales. The Joseph story is the culmination of the patriarchal narrative that brings the family of Jacob into Egypt, setting the stage for the charter myth of the nation of Israel as recounted in Exodus. The Sargon text, whose introduction depicts a prosperous Kish ruled by Urzababa, is part of a group of Sumerian "historical-literary" compositions that relate the rise and fall of every major Mesopotamian hegemony prior to the Old Babylonian period.[14] In both texts, "motifs from folk literature" are being used as "building stones" in literary compositions.[15] Nevertheless, the motifs and tale-types mentioned above bear a much closer resemblance to Joseph than to Sargon. The transformations involved are obvious: son/junior sibling (subordinate to parents and brothers) > courtier (subordinate to king); dream that superiors (parents and brothers) will serve him > dream that superior (king) will be killed and he will replace him. The functions remain essentially identical, yet it is the Joseph story which finds so many parallels in its specifics. I have not found any precise parallel to the Sargon story, in which a courtier dreams of replacing the king.[16]

The reason for this is to be sought in the natures of Mesopotamian and Israelite literature. In an article entitled "How Old are Folktales?",[17] Jason and Kempinski note that since

> no people on Earth has been found to lack oral tradition, the assumption is that oral tradition did exist in the same measure among all the ancient people too. From this oral tradition the folk literature was committed to writing according to the scribal tradition specific to each culture.

Nevertheless, the folk materials preserved in Mesopotamian literature are "very few," but "much richer" in the OT. This is because Mesopotamia had a millennia-long tradition of scribal literacy, for which "the popular story in the vernacular was something so entirely different that only rarely did it attract the attention of the scribe-literatus," whereas

> Israelite scribal tradition was young at the time when it produced its great works. . . . As the Israelite scribes had no impressive written tradition to build upon, they turned to folk tradition.

This, then, accounts for the closer resemblance between the Joseph story and the materials in the corpora represented in the motif and tale-type indices.

[14] Cooper and Heimpel, *JAOS* 103 (1983) 73f.

[15] Jason, *Folklore and Oral Communication* 1980, 170.

[16] But cf. the King of Heaven replaced by his butler/cupbearer in the Hittite Kumarbi myth (*ANET*, 120).

[17] *Fabula* 22 (1981) 1ff.

Sargon and Joseph both dreamed of surpassing their superiors, and both survived attempts to prevent their prophetic dreams from becoming reality. Can we postulate some sort of genetic relationship between the two stories? It is not my intention to add to the long list of alleged Mesopotamian materials in Genesis. Not only are the actors in the two stories different, but the stories have no specific details in common. Thus, there can be no question of Babylonian influence here, as there most certainly is in the Noah story (this may well be the only certain instance of the influence of a Mesopotamian literary work on the OT).[18] Perhaps the stories have some remote common ancestor, but the universality of the motifs they have in common suggests that this need not be so. No one would suggest that there is any genetic relationship between the Joseph story and the Incan legend of the founding of Cuzco cited above. In his *Morphology of the Folktale* Propp asks: "How is one to explain the similarity of the tale . . . when the contact of peoples cannot be proven historically?"[19] A simple yet adequate answer, consonant with the mentalist premises of recent linguistics, was provided by Stith Thompson: "The very nature of human thought has undoubtedly produced many natural parallels."[20] He goes on to add that "there has also been a great deal of diffusion." And here is the difficulty in attempting to understand the relationship between the Sargon and Joseph stories. When the materials are not so close that a genetic relationship is obvious, yet the cultures are not so distant that some kind of genetic relationship can be categorically denied, it is often impossible reach any conclusion at all.[21]

Then why bother to write about such resemblances? I believe it is important to recognize the folkloric "building stones" in ancient Near Eastern literature in order to comprehend the architecture that employed them and reconstruct and appreciate the edifices of which they are a part. Jason is correct when she writes that "a thorough examination [of a text] with the aid of ethnopoetic tools . . . can help solve philological text-critical problems otherwise unsolvable."[22] The story of Sargon's rise to power is a very difficult text, and it was the recognition of the folkloric motifs in it that provided one of the bases of a confident interpretation, even though many of the details remain murky. The recognition of these motifs and tale-types in Mesopotamian "historical-literary" compo-

---

[18] But note the reservations of Irvin, *Mytharion*, (AOAT 32; Kevelaer: Butzon und Bercker, 1978), 113.

[19] P. 16 of the second English edition (Austin: University of Texas, 1968).

[20] *Narrative Motif-Analysis as a Folklore Method*, Folklore Fellows Communications, No. 161 (1955) 4.

[21] Cf. the discussion of Irvin, *Mytharion*, 114.

[22] *Folklore and Oral Communication* 1981, 173.

sitions[23]—and in the Bible—provides yet one more argument for studying these documents primarily as works of literature, and not as records of past events that can be sieved for historical kernels.

[23] Cf. Cooper, *The Curse of Agade*, chap. 2.

A LITERATE SOLDIER: LACHISH LETTER III*

Frank Moore Cross
Harvard University

1.0 Ostracon III from Lachish, a letter from a junior officer, Hoshaiah, to his commander at Lachish, Ya²osh, is perhaps the most fascinating of the Lachish corpus. It speaks tersely and tantalizingly of troop movements between Judah and Egypt in the last days of Judah, of a letter containing, apparently, the warning of a prophet, and, in the midst of allusions to great events, expresses the hurt and injured pride of a man accused by his superior of not being able to read and understand a letter, in effect of being illiterate. It is the last-mentioned section of the letter that particularly interests us here. In the forty-five years which have passed since the *editio princeps* of the ostracon, most of its material readings have been solved;[1] ironically we still have difficulties in understanding—reading—the author's argument defending his ability to read a letter.

1.1 TRANSCRIPTION

Recto
1. ᶜbdk.hwšᶜyhw. šlḥ. l
2. hgd l²dny y²wš yšmᶜ.

---

* Note the following special abbreviations:

Albright: W. F. Albright in *Ancient Near Eastern Texts Relating to the Old Testament*, ed. J. B. Pritchard (Princeton: Princeton University, 1950), p. 322.

EHO: F. M. Cross and D. N. Freedman, *Early Hebrew Orthography*. AOS 36 (New Haven: American Oriental Society, 1952).

LeMaire: A. LeMaire, *Inscriptions hébraïques. Tome I: Les ostraca* (Paris: Les éditions du Cerf, 1977).

Michaud: H. Michaud, *Sur la pierre et l²argile*. (Neuchâtel: Delachaux et Niestlé, 1958).

Pardee: Dennis Pardee *et al.*, *Handbook of Ancient Hebrew Letters*. SBL Sources for Biblical Study 15 (Chico, California: Scholars Press, 1982).

[1] For bibliography, see *Pardee*, 81–83.

3. yhwḣ ᵒẗ ᵓdny. šmᶜt.šlm
4. wšmᶜt. ṭb[.] wᶜt.hpqḥ
5. ṅᵓ[.]ᵓṭ ᵓzn[.]ᶜbdk.lspr.ᵓšr.
6. šlḥth[.]ᵓl ᶜbdk.ᵓmš.ky.lb
7. ᶜbdk dẇh. mᵓz. šlḥk. ᵓl. ᶜbd
8. k[.]ẇky[.]ᵓmṙ. ᵓdny.lᵓ .ydᶜth.
9. qrᵓ spr ḥyhwh.ᵓm.nsh.ᵓ
10. yš lqrᵓ ly.spr lnṣḥ.wgm.
11. kl spr[.] ᵓšr ybᵓ. ᵓly[.]ᵓm.
12. qrᵓty. ᵓth wᶜẇd. ᵓtnnhw
13. ᵓl.mᵓwmh wlᶜbdk. hgd.
14. lᵓmr. yrd šr. hṣbᵓ
15. knyhw bn ᵓlntn lbᵓ.
16. mṣrymh. wᵓt

Verso
17. hwdwyhw bn ᵓḥyhw w
18. ᵓnšw šlḥ. lqḥt.mzh.
19. wspr.ṭbyhw ᶜbd.hmlk.hbᵓ
20. ᵓl. šlm. bn ydᶜ.mᵓt.hnbᵓ.lᵓm
21. r. hšmr. šlḥh. ᶜb<d>k. ᵓl. ᵓdny.

1.2 PROVISIONAL VOCALIZATION

1. ᶜabdak. hawši-yahū.šalaḥ.la-
2. haggīd laᵓadōnî yaᵓuš yašmiᶜ.
3. yahweh ᵓet ᵓadōnî. šamūᶜōt. šalōm
4. wa-šamūᶜot. ṭōb. wa-ᶜit hippaqiḥ
5. naᵓ. ᵓet ᵓuzn. ᶜabdak. las-sipr. ᵓašar.
6. šalaḥtōh. ᵓel. ᶜabdak. ᵓamš.kī. lib
7. ᶜabdak. dawēh. mi-ᵓaz. šulḥak. ᵓel. ᶜabd-
8. -ak. wa-kī. ᵓamar ᵓadōnî. lōᵓ. yadaᶜtōh.
9. qaraᵓ sōpir ḥay-yahwēh. ᵓim. nissāh ᵓ-
10. -īš la-qruᵓ lî. sipr la-niṣh. wa-gam
11. kul sōpir. ᵓašar yabōᵓ. ᵓilay. ᵓim.
12. qaraᵓtî. ᵓōtōh wa-ᶜawd. ᵓettininhū
13. ᵓal. maᵓūmāh. wa-la-ᶜabdak huggad
14. lēᵓmur. yarad śar. haṣ-ṣabāᵓ.
15. kun-yahū bin ᵓilnatan la-bōᵓ.
16. miṣraymāh. wa-ᵓet
17. hawdaw-yahū bin ᵓaḥī-yahū wa-
18. -ᵓanašaw šalaḥ. la-qaḥt. miz-zēh
19. wa-sipr. ṭōbî-yahu ᶜabd.ham-malk.hab-bāᵓ
20. ᵓel. šallūm.bin yaddūᶜ. mi-ᵓit.han-nabīᵓ. lēᵓmu-
21. -r. hiššamir. šalaḥōh. ᶜab<d>ak. ᵓel. ᵓadōnî.

1.3 TRANSLATION

1. Your servant Hoshaiah: he has sent to
2. report to my lord Ya²osh. May
3. Yahweh let my lord hear tidings of peace
4. and tidings of good. And now: let be opened,
5. pray, the ear of your servant concerning the letter which
6. you sent to your servant yesterday evening; for the heart
7. of your servant has been despondent since you sent (it) to your servant,
8. and that my lord said, "you did not understand it.
9. Call a scribe!" As Yahweh lives, no one has tried
10. to read a letter to me ever, and furthermore,
11. any scribe who might have come to me, I did not
12. summon him and, further, I would pay him
13. nothing! Now it has been reported to your servant,
14. saying: "The commander of the army has gone down—
15. Coniah son of Elnathan—to go into
16. Egypt and
17. Hodaviah son of Ahiah and
18. his men he has sent for, taking them away from here."
19. As for the letter at Tobiah the servant of the king which came
20. to Shallum son of Jaddua at the instance of the prophet, saying:
21. "Beware!" thy servant has forwarded it to my lord.

2.0   The transcription above (based on Figure 1) reflects the writer's study of the original ostracon, new photographs, which, alas, reveal fading of the ink which new photographic procedures have not overcome, and study of old photographs, especially a postcard published many years ago by the (then) Palestine Archaeological Museum. The vocalization of the text presumes the development of pre-Exilic Hebrew reflected in inscriptions and transcriptions in vocalized languages notably in Akkadian and Greek. At many points it is theoretically based with little or no direct evidence. For example, we do not know when certain types of tone-lengthening took place; in such cases we reconstruct forms with the earlier (short) vowels. We offer it, not as an exercise in historical Hebrew, but as a laying bare of our grammatical analysis, so often obscured in ambiguity when translations alone are given.

2.1 COMMENTARY ON MATERIAL READINGS

The beginning of line 4 has been long misread. *Michaud* and *LeMaire* have correctly reconstructed wšm ʿt.ṭb. The š is partly preserved; traces remain of the top of the *m* as well as the cross-bar of *taw*. The *ṭet* I regard as certain, and a trace conforming to the bottom of *bet* exists.

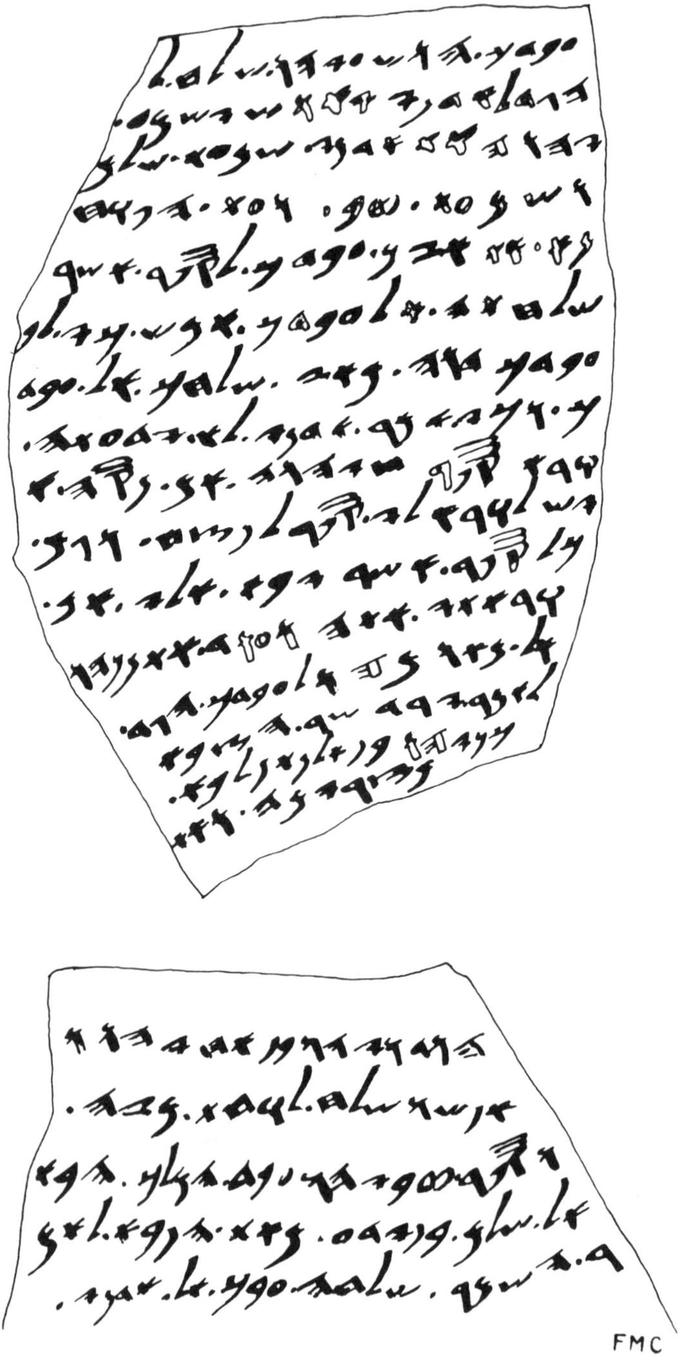

Figure 1. A Tracing of Lachish Ostracon III

There is a space before the *waw* of *w ʿt*, and a blob of ink. It is possible to read *wšm ʿt.ṭbt*.

In line 5 the reading *ʾzn* is certain; it is mystifying that this rendering emerged so late in the study of the ostracon, and is still unrecognized by some.

The beginning of line 6 must be read *šlḥth.ʾl.ʿbdk*. Only the *ʾalep* is in doubt. The cross-stroke of the *taw* and its lower shaded stroke are preserved, and *he* is very clear.

The end of line 12, *ʾtnnhw*, and the beginning of line 13, *ʾl.m ʾwmh̊*, despite the difficulty the reading occasions, are, I believe, beyond questioning.

The reading remains a crux.

2.2 COMMENTARY ON THE TEXT AND TRANSLATION

The introduction in lines 1-2 is unusual. Syntactically it can be understood most easily as a *casus pendens*, "Your servant Hoshaiah," followed by the perfect (or suffixal) tense. The body of the letter, introduced as usual by *w ʿt*, begins with a request for an explanation of a reprimand received in a previous letter from Yaʾosh. The phrase *hpqh ʾt ʾzn* is to be taken as the *nipʿal* imperative with the object of the active construction still subordinated in the accusative with *ʾt*.[2] There is no reason to propose an unattested *hipʿil* (*pace* Pardee). *šlḥth* in line 6 must be taken as the perfect, 2.m.s. with the retrospective pronoun. Regularly in pre-Exilic Hebrew prose the 2.m.s. form without the suffix is written without *he*, the 2.m.s. form with the 3.m.s. suffix with *he*: *qatalt* (the short form) and *qataltōh*.[3]

In line 8/9 a crucial reading is *lʾ.yd ʿth.qr ʾ spr*. *yd ʿth* should be taken as the 2.m.s. perfect with the 3.m.s. suffix, "you did not understand it" or "you have no knowledge of it," referring no doubt to a previous letter. *qr ʾ spr* has been taken to mean "call a scribe" (Albright), or "to read a letter." The latter reading is difficult. We should have expected *l ʾ yd ʿt lqr ʾ ʾt hspr*, "you do not know (how) to read the letter" or, much more harshly, *l ʾ yd ʿt qr ʾ spr*, "you do not know (how) to read a

---

[2] *GKC* § 121 ab.

[3] See *EHO*, 65-68. In the Arad Letters, e.g., compare *wntt* (2.7-8); *wṣrrt* (3.5); *wiqht* (3.8; 17.3-4) over against *ktbth* (7.5/6), and in the Lachish ostraca, *šlḥt* (5.4; 9.3[?]) vs. *šlḥth* (3.6); *yd ʿth* (2.6; 3.8). It should be noted that the 3.m.s. suffix here and with the singular noun is not derived from **-ahu > *aw > *ô*; diphthongs had not yet contracted; the development of the nominal suffix was **-uhu *>uh >ō*. This is the reason for the use of *he* as a *mater lectionis* regularly for this form of the suffix in pre-Exilic Hebrew. The verbal suffix is surprising; we should have expected **qataltaw* (*<*qataltahu*) or **qataltah* (*<qataltahu*). It may be the verbal suffix has been secondarily replaced by the nominal form in massoretic Hebrew.

letter." Conceivably the pronoun could be prospective: "you do not know it (namely) to read a letter." But this is awkward and most improbable.[4] The simplest reading, therefore is, "you did not understand it. Call a scribe!" The discussion of a scribe reading to Hoshaiah in lines 10–13 then follows naturally from Ya'osh's directive, "call a scribe!"

The oath formula *ḥyhwh . . . 'm* is continued by *'m* in line 11. The attempt to take the second *'m* as "if" is a *pis aller*, forced by a misunderstanding of *'tnnhw 'l m'whn* line 12/13. We should read, I am convinced, "as Yahweh lives, no one has tried to read a letter to me ever, and furthermore any scribe who might have come to me, I did not summon him . . ."

'tnnhw 'l m'wmh as we have noted is a certain reading. How is it to be understood? The context reminds one of 2 Sam 3:35: *kh y'śh ly 'lhym wkh ysyp ky 'm . . . 't'm lḥm m'wmh*, an oath formula affirming determination to taste no bread nor anything else. *'l m'wmh* is to be vocalized *'al ma'ūmāh* "not anything," "nothing." *'al* construed with substantives is not rare, appearing without verbs or with the verb at a remove.[5] *'tnnhw* has been taken to be an imperfect of *ntn*: *'ettininhū* or better *'ettininnahū*,[6] "I would give (i.e. pay) to him." Alternately it could be analyzed—without the unexpected energic (or emphatic) -*n*-unassimilated or the archaic -*nn*- energic—as deriving from the root *tnn*. Biblical *'etnan* and Ugaritic *'itnanu*[7] "fee" suggest that a denominative, "to pay a professional fee" may have existed. To be sure, the biblical usage is, for the most part, restricted to the harlot's price, a "professional fee" in a narrowed sense, but the meaning may have been more general. In this case, we could vocalize *'etōninihū*, "I would pay him (no) fee, nothing!"

[4] Generally those who have elected to interpret the phrase as meaning "you do not know to read a letter" take *yd'th* as a long (formal) *qataltāh* without suffix. Methodologically I believe this is unsound—until it can be shown that the two forms were used interchangeably in pre-Exilic prose. This is not this case; elsewhere the distribution appears to be systematic. Later, of course, different scribal schools tended to level one or the other forms through the biblical text with the resultant mixed orthography of the Qumrân texts, the second column of the Hexapla, and the Massoretic Text. See *EHO*, 65–70, and F. M. Cross, "The Contribution of the Qumrân Discoveries to the Study of the Biblical Text," in Cross and S. Talmon, *Qumrân and the History of the Biblical Text* (Cambridge: Harvard University, 1975) 286f.

[5] Cf. *'l ṭl w'l mṭr* 2 Sam 1:21); *w'l r'* (Amos 5:14); *w'l ksp* (Prov 8:10); *'l mwt* (Prov 12:28); *'l ngh* (Deir 'Allā I, 6); cf. l'l "to nought" (Job 24:25).

[6] Compare such forms as *'rmmnhw* (Exod 15:12), probably to be vocalized *'ărōmĕmennahū*.

[7] Ugaritic V.6.75: *ytt.nḥšm. mhrk*
 bn btn. 'itnnk
"I have given serpents as your bridal price
Dragon's sons as your (conjugal) fee."

It should be noted that the negative force of *ʾm* carries through to the end (lines 12–13) so that literally we should render with a double negative, "I would *not* pay him—nothing!"

The vocalization *kun-yahū* (line 15) is a haplological reduction of *yakun-yahū*, bibl. *yĕkōnyahū*. *m*ʾ*t* (line 20) has been understood as meaning "by the instrumentality" of the prophet, comparing 2 Kgs 3:11. However, more natural is the meaning, "at the instance of," suggesting that the warning originates from the prophet.

3.0   The aggrieved soldier, it must be said, spends a disproportionate space in his letter, to judge from other events to which he alludes, defending his skills in reading. The suggestion of his commander that he needs a scribe to assist him in reading letters prompts a vigorous and passionate response. Hoshaiah's expressions of hurt and pride lend a pathos to the letter as we read it, aware as we are of the fate which shortly descended on Hoshaiah and his fellow soldiers manning the outposts of Judah. At the same time the letter yields some data by which we can estimate the extent of literacy in Judah in the early sixth century B.C.E. A minor army officer is "sick at heart" if his ability to read accurately and easily is questioned. At the same time the importance of the scribe in the life of Judah is underlined by the assumption of all parties that a scribe is near at hand. It should be added that there is every reason to believe that the skilled and elegant hand of the letter which appears on Ostracon III is not the hand of Hoshaiah, but the hand of an army scribe. Literacy was wide spread in Judah, but the writing of documents was primarily the task of a scribal elite.

It is with great pleasure that I dedicate this brief paper to Professor Iwry, a school mate from olden days at Johns Hopkins, and through the years, a cherished friend and respected colleague.

January 3, 1983

PROSE PARTICLES IN THE POETRY OF THE PRIMARY HISTORY*

David Noel Freedman
Program on Studies in Religion
The University of Michigan

A long-recognized distinctive feature of biblical poetry is the striking rarity of certain familiar particles found regularly and frequently in biblical prose, specifically, ʾăšer (the relative pronoun), ʾēt (the sign of the definite direct object), and h (the definite article). Although it is generally agreed that prose and poetry differ sharply in their use of these particles, and although their use as a reliable criterion in distinguishing prose from poetry has long been asserted and relied upon, the statistical data for a given set of poems and a comparable prose corpus have never been developed and published; the empirical base for this important and useful distinction has not been established. Similarly, the implications of the particles' occurrence for genre-classification, both within the two categories and between them, and possible patterns of evolution in their use have not been seriously examined. The present study of the three "prose particles" is intended as a model for the analysis of material comprising both prose and poetry. Its findings and inferences are available for application on a broad scale to the rest of the literature of the Hebrew Bible.

Eleven substantial poems of varying length have been incorporated into the Primary History of the Hebrew Bible, that is, the Torah and the Former Prophets, the prose narrative that runs consecutively from Genesis through Kings. These easily identified poems constitute an interesting group for various kinds of research. Not only do most of them derive from the earliest period of Israel's history, but they share a similar if not common transmissional history as part of the canonical core of the Hebrew Bible, the oldest part to be standardized and fixed textually. Four of them have been transmitted in metrical form as far back as scholars can

---

*After this article was submitted for publication, all the data about the prose particles appeared in print in the article by Andersen-Forbes listed in the Bibliography. This present paper, however, was written and submitted in final form before the Andersen-Forbes article appeared.

trace them through the manuscript tradition: (1) the Song of the Sea, Exodus 15 (not preserved in the Aleppo Codex, but confirmed by other medieval manuscripts in a stichometric arrangement); (2) the Song of Moses, Deuteronomy 32 (not only in the Aleppo Codex, but also in metrically arranged fragments from the Dead Sea Scrolls, about a thousand years earlier); (3) the Song of Deborah, Judges 5 (metrically arranged in the Aleppo Codex, although in a pattern different from that in the Pentateuch), and (4) the Psalm of David, 2 Samuel 22 (equivalent to Psalm 18). The seven other poems, while not metrically specified in the manuscripts, have been identified through recent scholarly research; there exists broad agreement as to their existence and boundaries: (1) the Blessing of Jacob, Genesis 49; (2) the Oracles of Balaam, Numbers 23–24; (3) the Blessing of Moses, Deuteronomy 33; (4) the Song of Hannah, 1 Sam 2:1–10; (5) the Lament of David over Saul and Jonathan, 2 Sam 1:19–27; (6) the Testament of David, 2 Sam 23:1–7, and (7) the Prayer of Hezekiah, 2 Kgs 19:21–28 = Isa 37:22–29.

Recent critical editions of the Hebrew text reflect the scholarly consensus regarding these poems; this paper follows the delimitation and demarcation of the poems in the recent Stuttgart edition of the *Biblia Hebraica*. Ten of the eleven relate and reflect events and circumstances of the early history of Israel, from the 13th to the 10th centuries B.C.E., and are the products of roughly the same period, perhaps the 12th to 9th centuries B.C.E. These ten will be treated together. The eleventh, the Prayer of Hezekiah, clearly belongs to a much later period; it will be dealt with separately, for purposes of control and comparison.

A principal value of these poems, separately and together, is that they originated apart from the prose narrative in which they are embedded. At the same time they share the transmissional history of those books which constitute the Primary History from the time that it was formally promulgated as the canonical core of the Hebrew Bible, probably by the middle of the 6th century B.C.E. Preserved differences in the treatment of poetry and prose in this corpus probably reflect the standard but separate forms of the two literary types at the time of incorporation rather than later developments in the principles or techniques of scribal copying.

As this study aims centrally to confirm the hypothesis that the three particles ᵓăšer, ᵓēt, and h occur significantly more often in prose than in poetry, each poem is examined in company with a corresponding prose passage. Tables below list the occurrence of particles in each poem and in its corresponding prose passage. This approach allows comparison of materials similar in content and textual history so as to emphasize the essential distinction between poetry and prose while eliminating all incidental or accidental factors. As the ordinary use of the particles in prose varies considerably from literary type to literary type, and even from sentence to sentence within a single genre, it is important to examine a large sample, one drawn from radically different segments of the narrative.

The data in this study have been derived from a standard text of the Hebrew Bible, the Stuttgart edition, and the same method of analysis has been followed in all passages, prose or poetry. Words are defined as single contiguous groups of letters separated by spaces (ignoring the *maqqēp*) and counted accordingly. The particles are identified in accordance with the Massoretic writing and scholarly traditions.

Despite every effort at scientific objectivity, certain ambiguities inherent in the text remain. For example, the particle *ʾēt* has a homograph in the preposition meaning "with"; while most cases are easily differentiated, some are disputed. The same is true of the definite article, which is identical in form to the vocative particle; it is possible that the prevailing usage varied. So as not to slant the results, ambiguous terms are in almost all cases included in the totals.

The article, however, is not so included when the only sign of its presence is the *dagesh forte* in the next consonant. (It is clear that the Massoretes recognized no distinction between prose and poetry in this respect; they inserted the *dagesh* whenever they believed it belonged according to their grammatical rules. In fact, one should count the cases in which the dagesh occurs in prose and discount those in poetry, but that would be begging the question.)* Once the particle counts have been established, individual cases will be examined, the data will be analyzed, and interpretations will be suggested.

With respect to the Song of the Sea (Exodus 15) and the Song of Deborah (Judges 5), prose narratives dealing with the same events appear in contiguous chapters of the Hebrew Bible: Exod 14:1-31 and 15:19-21a and Judg 4:1-24. The poetic and prose accounts will be directly compared in each case with their corresponding particle counts; the actual number of occurrences for each particle and the frequency percentages will be given in order to establish a valid comparison, as the poems and the prose passages are not of equal length.

The four poems of the Oracles of Balaam are embedded in a larger prose narrative extending through Numbers 22-24. Here the prose materials provide a framework for the poems rather than running parallel to them. The proximity of the materials and the fact that prose and poetry here deal with the same persons and form a single story make the comparison valid and useful.

Similar comparisons for the other poems must come from contiguous passages before and after the poems; we must rely on the editors and scribes who combined the materials and transmitted the text to have kept it essentially intact once fixed. Deuteronomy 31 and the prose materials in Deuteronomy 33 (vv 44-52) and 34 establish the prose context and comparison for the Song and Testament of Moses (Deuteronomy 32-33). Gen 48:1-22 and Gen 49:28-33 provide the prose passages to compare with the Blessing of Jacob (Genesis 49). In the case of the poems in Samuel, contiguous prose passages are also used: for the Song of Hannah, 1 Sam 1 and 2:11-36, and for the Lament of David, 1 Samuel 31 and

2 Sam 1:1–18. For the Psalm of David (2 Samuel 22) and the Testament of David (2 Samuel 23), I have used 2 Samuel 21 and the remainder of chapter 23. Because chapter 23 has peculiar features, I have also examined chapter 24 and have given those figures; the results are much the same. The remainder of 2 Kings 19 is used for comparison with the Prayer of Hezekiah.

The following tables contain the summarized results of these comparisons:

	POETRY		PROSE	
	Genesis 49		*Genesis 48–49*	
Words	259		445	
		%		%
$^{\circ}\check{s}r$	0	0.00	11	2.47
$^{\circ}t$	1	0.39	34	7.42
h	4	1.54	30	6.74
Total	5	1.93	75	16.82
	Exodus 15		*Exodus 14, 15:19–21a*	
Words	177		510	
		%		%
$^{\circ}\check{s}r$	0	0.00	4	0.78
$^{\circ}t$	0	0.00	31	6.08
h	0	0.00	51	10.00
Total	0	0.00	86	16.86
	Numbers 23–24		*Numbers 22–24*	
Words	253		1049	
		%		%
$^{\circ}\check{s}r$	1	0.40	22	2.10
$^{\circ}t$	1	0.40	44	4.19
h	4	1.58	54	5.15
Total	6	2.37	120	11.44

	Deuteronomy 32		Deuteronomy 31	
Words	462		553	
		%		%
ᵓšr	1	0.22	18	3.25
ᵓt	0	0.00	42	7.59
h	3	0.65	71	12.84
Total	4	0.87	131	23.69

	Deuteronomy 33		Deuteronomy 32–34	
Words	304		329	
		%		%
ᵓšr	2	0.66	17	5.17
ᵓt	2	0.66	20	6.08
h	3	0.99	36	10.94
Total	7	2.30	73	22.19

	Pentateuch				
Words	1455		2886		
		%		%	Ratio
ᵓšr	4	0.27	72	2.49	× 9.22
ᵓt	4	0.27	171	5.93	× 21.96
h	14	0.96	242	8.39	× 8.74
Total	22	1.51	485	16.81	× 11.13

	Judges 5		Judges 4	
Words	352		422	
		%		%
ᵓšr	1	0.28	7	1.66
ᵓt	0	0.00	22	5.21
h	8	2.27	26	6.16
Total	9	2.56	55	13.03

	1 Samuel 2		1 Samuel 1	
Words	113		415	
		%		%
ˀšr	0	0.00	4	0.96
ˀt	0	0.00	19	4.58
h	0	0.00	23	5.54
Total	0	0.00	46	11.08

	2 Samuel 1		1 Samuel 31–2 Samuel 1	
Words	110		459	
		%		%
ˀšr	0	0.00	7	1.53
ˀt	0	0.00	24	5.23
h	7	6.36	40	8.71
Total	7	6.36	71	15.47

	2 Samuel 22		2 Samuel 21	
Words	365		419	
		%		%
ˀšr	0	0.00	12	2.86
ˀt	2	0.55	25	5.97
h	7	1.92	32	7.64
Total	9	2.47	69	16.47

	2 Samuel 23		2 Samuel 23	
Words	86		354	
		%		%
ˀšr	0	0.00	4	1.13
ˀt	0	0.00	7	1.98
h	1	1.16	50	14.12
Total	1	1.16	61	17.23

Former Prophets (Judges–2 Samuel)

Words	1026	%	2069	%	Ratio
ʾšr	1	0.10	34	1.64	× 16.4
ʾt	2	0.19	97	4.69	× 24.68
h	23	2.24	171	8.26	× 3.69
Total	26	2.53	302	14.60	× 5.77

Totals

Words	2481	%	4955	%	Ratio	
ʾšr	5	0.20	106	2.14	× 10.70	(11)
ʾt	6	0.24	268	5.41	× 22.54	(23)
h	37	1.49	413	8.34	× 5.60	(6)
Total	48	1.93	787	15.88	× 8.23	(8)

2 Kings 19   2 Kings 19

Words	114	%	455	%
ʾšr	1	0.88	13	2.86
ʾt	3	2.63	17	3.74
h	0	0.00	35	7.70
Total	4	3.51	65	14.29

Former Prophets (Judges–2 Kings)

Words	1140	%	2524	%	Ratio
ʾšr	2	0.18	47	1.86	× 10.33
ʾt	5	0.44	114	4.52	× 10.27
h	23	2.02	206	8.16	× 4.04
Total	30	2.63	367	14.54	× 5.53

SUMMARY

	POETRY		PROSE		RATIO	
Words	2595		5410			
		%		%		
ᵓšr	6	0.23	119	2.20	× 9.57	(10)
ᵓt	9	0.35	285	5.27	× 15.06	(15)
h	37	1.43	448	8.28	× 5.79	(6)
Total	52	2.00	852	15.75	× 7.88	(8)

On the basis of the samples given, the ratio of particle frequency between prose and poetry in the Primary History is 8 to 1. That is, the particles occur eight times as often in prose as in poetry. When the particles are considered separately, the ratio is 10:1 for ᵓšr, 15 : 1 for ᵓt, and 6 : 1 for h. Without 2 Kings 19, the figures vary as follows: ᵓšr 11 : 1, ᵓt 23 : 1, h 6 : 1. There is a wide variation in specific matchups, but probably this in only a random effect, as individual samples are small.

Except in the rarest circumstances the range for occurrence of particles in poetry and prose in given categories does not overlap; 2 Kings 19 is a special case, but this poem belongs to a later age and may reflect a gradual blurring of the distinction between poetry and prose in the use of the particles. Overall there is a marked gap: the range for poetry is 0.00 to 6.36, while for prose it is 11.08 to 23.69. Only two poems have a ratio exceeding 2.56—2 Kings 19 at 3.51 and the Lament of David at 6.36. The high count of the latter results entirely from cases of the definite article. In its total lack of ᵓšr and ᵓt the poem conforms to the general poetic pattern and specifically matches three other poems, including two from the same early period of the monarchy (2 Samuel 1 and 2 Samuel 23); Exodus 15 is the other poem in which ᵓšr and ᵓt do not occur. Genesis 49, Deuteronomy 32, and Judges 5 have only a single instance of either ᵓšr or ᵓt, while 2 Samuel 22 and Numbers 23–24 have two.

Excluding the poem in 2 Kings from the examination of a fairly homogeneous corpus of poems from the early period of Israel (12th to 10th or 9th century), we note the extreme paucity of occurrences of ᵓšr and ᵓt. Separation of the five poems in the Pentateuch from the five in the Former Prophets yields the following figures:

	Words	ʾšr		ʾt	
			%		%
Pentateuch	1455	4	0.27	4	0.27
Former Prophets	1026	1	0.10	2	0.19

As this chart shows, these particles occur even more rarely in the Former Prophets than in the Pentateuch; examination of the individual examples should produce additional important information.

In the five poems of the Former Prophets the single example of ʾšr occurs in the Song of Deborah (Judg 5:27), one of the oldest poems in the Bible. The circumstances of and comparative data from this poem immediately cast doubt upon the authenticity of the occurrence of ʾšr. The most important consideration is the use of a different relative pronoun in the poem, ʾša twice in v 7. Apparently ʾšr is a secondary insertion here. If it is original, however, it should be interpreted not as the relative pronoun, but as the underlying noun, meaning "place." Hence the rendering: "in the place where he fell. . . ." In either case ʾšr may be dropped as an instance of the relative pronoun in any of the five poems in the Former Prophets.

The two cases of ʾt may be considered next. Both occur in 2 Samuel 22 (vv 20, 28), there being none in any of the other four poems. Comparing this poem with Psalm 18 (the parallel and equivalent poem) shows up the dubious nature of both examples. First, Psalm 18 does not contain ʾt at all. The verse containing the first instance, 2 Sam 22:20, parallels Ps 18:20. Both verses contain a verb with suffix, but Psalm 18 attaches the pronominal suffix directly to the verb (wayyôṣîʾēnî), while 2 Sam 22:20 uses the particle ʾt (wayyōṣēʾ . . . ʾōtî). Although both uses are well attested, the weight of the evidence from the five poems of the Former Prophets and the particular example of Psalm 18 show that ʾty is secondary in 2 Samuel. In the second instance (2 Sam 2:25 = Ps 18:28), the word ʾt in 2 Samuel is written ʾattâ in Psalm 18 and vocalized as the second masculine singular pronoun, undoubtedly the correct original reading. The word is the same in 2 Samuel but, having been written defectively, was misunderstood by the Massoretes.

The five poems in the Former Prophets, then, contain not one well-attested and confirmed example of either particle, ʾšr or ʾt. These particles were not used at all in such poetry. If that seems to be a radical or extreme judgment, it is only necessary to examine the data. From a statistical point of view it is of no consequence whether we retain or remove these few examples; the evidence is overwhelming. Three of the five poems make no use of either particle, and four of the five use only one or the other. The conclusion is inescapable: in this group of poems the use of the two particles is practically zero, and the few exceptions can and should be explained as intrusions.

The poems in the Pentateuch present much the same picture, despite a few more instances of each particle: the texts as preserved contain four examples of each, twice as many as in the Former Prophets. However, the percentage is still very low, 0.56%, or about 1/2 of 1%. Examination of the specific instances indicates that either the reliability of the text or the originality of the reading may be questioned. One poem, Exodus 15, has neither particle; a second poem, Genesis 49, has no instance of ʾšr, and Deut 32 makes no use of ʾt. The four instances of ʾšr are distributed among Numbers 23–24 (1), Deuteronomy 32 (1), and Deuteronomy 33 (2). The ʾšr in Num 24:4 is clearly secondary: comparison with 24:16 (where ʾšr does not occur, although the texts are virtually identical) makes it clear that a colon has fallen out in 24:4 (wydᶜ dᶜt ᶜlywn), and in its place this dubious relative pronoun has surfaced. The occurrence in Deut 32:38 poses no particular textual or grammatical problem. It might, however, be questioned on metrical grounds, since it unbalances the bicolon in v 38a.

The two occurrences in Deut 33:8 and 29 are more difficult. Questions about the originality of vv 8b–9a have arisen for a variety of reasons, reinforced by the occurrence of ʾšr once and ʾt twice in these three bicola, the highest concentration of these particles in the whole corpus under consideration. In the immediately surrounding materials (vv 8a and 9b–10a) ʾt is not used, although there would be reason to use it as many as six times with definite direct objects (tmyk, w ʾwryk after hābû lēlēwî, which must be supplied to MT on the basis of Q and LXX, ʾmrtk wbrytk, mšptyk, wtwrtk). Vv 8b–9a seem to be a secondary insertion betraying signs of later composition.

The occurrence of ʾšr in v 29 is also anomalous. It is the only instance of ʾšr (or ʾt) in the Prologue and Epilogue or in the body of the Blessing apart from vv 8b–9a, and it disturbs the symmetry of the passage. While it is grammatically appropriate in the passage, it should be matched by ʾšr before mgn ᶜzrk // ḥrb gʾwtk. Its absence in the first phrase suggests that it was originally also absent in the second phrase.

In the Pentateuch poems ʾt does not occur at all in Exodus 15 or Deuteronomy 32. It occurs twice in Deuteronomy 33, both times in v 9, but both cases raise questions. The other examples of ʾt in these poems are in Gen 49:15 (ʾet-hāʾāreṣ, a common and unexceptionable but clearly prosaic expression) and Num 23:10 (ʾet-rōbaᶜ yiśrāʾēl, a problem, but not for grammatical or syntactic reasons).

Of the eleven examples of ʾšr (5) and ʾt (6) preserved in the ten poems under consideration, the following cases are doubtful:

ʾšr: two in Num 24:4 (on the basis of parallel usage) and Judg 5:27 (on the basis of internal evidence). The three remaining cases, in Deut

32:38 and Deut 33:8 and 29, can only be challenged on metrical and symmetrical grounds, and while there may be a case, the point need not be pressed here.

ʾt: of the six occurrences, the two instances in 2 Sam 22:20 and 28 may be challenged on the basis of the parallel passages in Psalm 18. As for the others, there is no compelling reason to doubt the readings in Gen 49:15 and Num 23:19. In Deut 33:9 there appears to be a problem with the whole passage vv 8b-9a, but not with the two occurrences of ʾt. Of the five occurrences of ʾšr, then, two may be effectively eliminated; of the six occurrences of ʾt two may be dropped.

The percentages of the eleven examples of ʾšr and ʾt in the poems from the Pentateuch are shown below:

Total Words		2481		2481
		%		%
ʾšr	5	0.20	3	0.12
ʾt	6	0.24	4	0.16
Total	11	0.44	7	0.28

The difference is substantial, although the conclusion is the same and inescapable. For all practical purposes, neither ʾšr nor ʾt was used in early Hebrew poetry, certainly not in the poems preserved in the Primary History. The few surviving examples resulted either from error or false correction (two of each); all others slipped in through scribal inadvertence in the long process of transmission.

The very rarity of these accidents is surprising; the scribes' faithful preservation of this peculiarity of Hebrew poetry is quite remarkable. One or two instances of ʾšr and ʾt may be part of the original composition, as was doubtless the case in the composition of some later Hebrew poetry, e.g. 2 Kings 19, but originality would be difficult to demonstrate in any particular instance.

The thirty-seven examples of the use of he as the definite article remain. While a few of these may be questioned, such as the misdivision in Num 24:3, 15, which produced an article not original to the text (read šětummâ ʿāyin for MT šětūm hāʿāyin) and may on reasonable grounds be excluded, a sufficient number remain to require recognition as part of the armory of the poet and intrinsic to poetry even of the earliest Israelite period.

Among the rest, at least two categories of usage should be noted, as they imply a use of the article apparently antedating the general use of the definite article he and relatively independent of it:

1) Its use with participles to form the equivalent of a relative clause, as "the one who clothed you" (2 Sam 1:24). Examples of this usage appear in several poems, in David's Lament (4: vv 23-24), Deborah (1: v 9), Genesis 49 (2: vv 17, 21), 2 Samuel 22 (David's Hymn 2: vv 31, 33), nine occurrences in all.

2) Its use as an attenuated demonstrative, especially in stereotyped phrases, e.g., *nĕʾūm haggeber* = "oracle of *that* man" (Num 24:3, 15; 2 Sam 23:1). This expression occurs three times in the corpus, always with the article (especially striking in 2 Sam 23:1, where otherwise not a single instance of any of the particles here discussed appears). The expression *byn hmšptym* occurs twice, both times with the article (Gen 49:14, Judg 5:16). The article appears repeatedly with El in Deuteronomy 32 and 2 Samuel 22 = Psalm 18.

3) Finally, two instances occur in which the prefixed *he* may be the vocative particle rather than the definite article: Deut 32:1 and perhaps 2 Sam 1:19.

Those remaining may be regarded as belonging to the original poems. As the ratio of prose particles in the text preserved by the Massoretes may be set at slightly less than 2%, the case is already firm, especially when the ratio is compared with that in standard prose, where it is about 15%. With the removal of the most glaring examples of forced entry, the percentage total may be reduced to somewhere between 1 and 1.5%. The evidence could hardly be more clear.

The earliest biblical poetry characteristically does not include these particles. To be more precise, the particles *ʾšr* and *ʾt* are so uncommon in this material (eleven occurrences in 2470 words) that all surviving examples may be regarded as secondary. As for the more numerous instances of the definite article, some appear to be secondary, while others have specialized functions or meanings (as relative pronouns, attenuated demonstratives, or vocatives); only a handful can be seen as simple definite articles. Early poets seem by and large to have shunned these particles, making use only of the preformative *he* to any extent.

As the present text of the poems in the Primary History has an overall percentage of less than 2% use of these particles, the original poetry can be assumed to have shown an even lower figure, perhaps 1.0 to 1.5%. Several poems fall within a narrow range, from just under 1% to just over 2.5%. Two poems have no prose particles at all (Exodus 15 and 1 Samuel 2), while one is remarkable for the large number of such particles included (David's Lament in 2 Sam 1:19-27). The anomaly of this poem is difficult to explain, for the text is generally in good order and the early date of the poem (ca. 1000 B.C.E.) is assured. It may clarify the puzzle to note that neither *ʾšr* nor *ʾt* occurs in the poem, in accord with the best classical usage, while the definite article occurs in 7 of 110 words. Of these, 4 are attached to participles (vv 23-24), seeming to reflect a specialized function requiring their use in poetry as well as in prose. A fifth instance is attached to the first word, $h\d{s}by$, and this may be an example of the vocative *he* rather than the article: "O Gazelle of Israel!" rather than "The Gazelle, O Israel, is slain. . . ." That reading would leave two fairly normal occurrences of the article in the poem (vv 20, 25); the total particle count, noting the absence of $^{\circ}\check{s}r$ and $^{\circ}t$, would then be less than 2% of the total number of words, in conformity with the other poems.

The conclusion of the matter is that classic Hebrew poetry is easily distinguished from Hebrew prose by the criterion proposed, namely, the relative frequency with which the three common particles—$^{\circ}\check{s}r$, $^{\circ}t$, and h—occur in the two forms of discourse. The virtual absence of the first two even in the current Massoretic text confirms that they were simply not used by ancient Hebrew poets. The case with the definite article is somewhat different. The occasional occurrence of this particle in the surviving text indicates that some limited use of it was permitted and practiced by classic Hebrew poets. In spite of this qualification, h is still used markedly less frequently than in prose. Overall, the contrast between the frequencies in prose and poetry is so great (eight times on the average) that we may regard the criterion as firmly validated by the evidence.

*The following table shows the frequency with which the definite article is indicated by the *dagesh* alone in the poetry and prose samples, e.g., *baggôyīm* (Num 23:9):

POEM	words	dagesh %	PROSE	words	dagesh %
1) Gen 49	259	6	1) Gen 48	445	3
2) Exod 15	177	9	2) Exod 14–15	510	11
3) Num 23–24	253	2	3) Num 22–24	1049	16
4) Deut 32	462	3	4) Deut 31	553	6
5) Deut 33	304	1	5) Deut 32, 34	329	3
6) Judg 5	352	7	6) Judg 4	422	5
7) 1 Sam 2	113	3	7) 1 Sam 1	415	1
8) 2 Sam 1	110	2	8) 1 Sam 31– 2 Sam 1	459	4
9) 2 Sam 22	365	5	9) 2 Sam 21	419	7
10) 2 Sam 23	86	3	10) 2 Sam 23	354	11
Total	2481	41 (1.7%)	*Total*	4955	67 (1.4%)
11) 2 Kgs 19	114	1	11) 2 Kgs 19	455	11
Total	2595	42 (1.6%)	*Total*	5410	78 (1.4%)

It is evident that there is no significant difference between the two columns insofar as the frequency of this form of the definite article is concerned. What it shows is that the Massoretes made no distinction between poetry and prose when it came to marking the presence of the definite article by the appropriate punctuation. The difference between this set of statistics and the data for the use of the article as indicated by the prefixed letter *h* is so striking as to constitute a *prima facie* case for the actual difference in biblical prose and poetic usage, or for the indifference of the Massoretes to this phenomenon.

BIBLIOGRAPHY

Andersen, F. I., and Forbes, A. D.
  1983   " 'Prose Particle' Counts of the Hebrew Bible," in *The Word of the Lord Shall Go Forth: Essays in Honor of David Noel Freedman in Celebration of His Sixtieth Birthday*. Ed. Carol L. Meyers and M. O'Connor. Winona Lake, IN: Eisenbrauns/American Schools of Oriental Research.
Andersen, F. I., and Freedman, D. N.
  1980   *Hosea*. Anchor Bible, vol. 24. Garden City, NY: Doubleday.
Freedman, D. N.
  1977   "Pottery, Poetry, and Prophecy: An Essay in Biblical Poetry," *Journal of Biblical Literature* 96: 5–26. Reprinted in Freedman, D. N., *Pottery, Poetry, and Prophecy*, Winona Lake, IN: Eisenbrauns, 1980, pp. 1–22.
  1976   "Divine Names and Titles in Early Hebrew Poetry," in *Magnalia Dei: The Mighty Acts of God*, ed. F. M. Cross, *et al.*, pp. 55–107. Garden City, NY: Doubleday & Co. Reprinted in Freedman, D. N., *Pottery, Poetry, and Prophecy*, Winona Lake, IN: Eisenbrauns, 1980, pp. 77–129.

THE MURDER OF THE MERCHANTS NEAR AKKO

Barry M. Gittlen
Baltimore Hebrew College

Serendipity. How often do chance and circumstance combine in a fleeting moment to generate a new approach or solution to a problem? One such moment, occurring during a felicitous meeting in Jerusalem in August 1981, was the genesis of the following contribution. Sam Iwry had urged me to deliver a message in person to Abraham Malamat while I was in Jerusalem. Always the gracious host, Malamat found time in an unusually hectic schedule to meet with me late on the night of August 11. During the wide-ranging conversation that ensued I mentioned my interest in the Late Bronze Age cemetery discovered ten years earlier near the Persian Garden, just north of Akko's ancient tell. Malamat, having had a similar interest, immediately suggested that I look at Amarna Letter 8 and pulled a well-used copy of Mercer from his shelf. As we discussed the incident described in EA 8, I impetuously sought to link the letter's events with the cemetery but Malamat urged caution, saying that the cemetery might "reflect" the kind of conditions described in EA 8. It is therefore fitting to dedicate this presentation to Sam, who urged me to see Malamat, and to Malamat who originated the idea of linking the cemetery with EA 8.

A rchaeologically, the good that men do as well as the evil all too often lies buried with their bones. So it is with the occupants of the five graves excavated by Sarah Ben-Arieh and Gershon Edelstein near the Persian Garden, 2.5 km north of Tell Akko in Israel's coastal plain.[1] The skeletal remains of the nine individuals recovered from the cemetery in 1971 were in such poor condition that it was impossible to determine familial ties or causes of death.[2] Nevertheless, something of the history

---

[1] Sarah Ben-Arieh and Gershon Edelstein, *Akko: Tombs Near the Persian Garden* (Jerusalem: Israel Department of Antiquities, 1977; Atiqot, English Series, 12), hereafter referred to as *AKKO*. The writer has reviewed this excellent publication in *BASOR* 248 (1982) 73–74; without such expeditious and complete excavation reports, synthetic studies such as this would be impossible.

[2] *AKKO*, 81–83. The five graves contained a total of 5 males, 3 females, and one infant. These five graves seem to have been part of a cemetery which the excavators believe may have contained up to 15 graves.

and activity of these individuals may be reconstructed from the goods interred with their bones.

Uncharacteristically abundant goods of a specialized nature were found buried with the deceased. These goods included a large quantity of Late Cypriot Bronze Age ceramic imports, specifically White Slip II and Base Ring II pottery; Mycenaean IIIA pottery; 106 copper and bronze weapons, tools, and implements; clusters of weights; rings, seals, and beads; and bits of gold and silver foil.

The imported Cypriot pottery is significant not only for its abundance but also because of its relatively high quality of form and design, signifying it as early in the WS II and BR II series, and for its apparent uniformity as a collection of immediately contemporary vessels, made and in use within the same few years during the first half of the 14th century B.C.[3] This dating is harmonious with that reached for the Mycenaean imports as well.[4] Moreover, the imported pottery is so abundant that in several of the graves it is more numerous than the local Canaanite pottery.

Among the 106 copper and bronze implements found in and near these graves were 71 weapons which, the excavators hint, represent the personal possessions of warriors, an attribution which remains questionable.[5] These javelinheads, arrowheads, spearheads, and daggers are among the finest examples of the armorer's craft found in Late Bronze Age Canaan, but neither the quality nor the quantity of these weapons necessarily identifies the deceased as warriors, as will be demonstrated below. Together with these weapons, moreover, the excavators recovered a fine bronze Egyptianizing mirror,[6] a bronze trident with parallels throughout the Near East,[7] and a number of strange items whose functions elude interpretation.

Several concomitant factors indicate that the individuals buried near the Persian Garden were involved in commercial activity. The first factor is the homogeneous collection of foreign imports which, contrary to the usual situation in Late Bronze Age tombs, do not span a large segment

---

[3] See Barry M. Gittlen, *Studies in the Late Cypriote Pottery Found in Palestine* (Ann Arbor: University Microfilms, 1977) and "The Cultural and Chronological Implications of the Cypro-Palestinian Trade During the Late Bronze Age," *BASOR 241* (1981) 49–59. I fully agree with the excavators' dating of the cemetery in the early 14th century B.C. (*AKKO*, 36).

[4] V. Hankey, *AKKO*, 45–51. Hankey considers the Mycenaean vessels to have been personal possessions rather than items for trade.

[5] *AKKO*, 36.

[6] See my review in *BASOR* 248 (1982) 73–74.

[7] One may add to the examples cited by the authors E. O. Nagahban, "Maceheads from Marlik," *AJA 85* (1981) pl. 61: fig. 8. The trident depicted is unfortunately not mentioned in Negahban's text.

of the Late Cypriot sequence. The similar homogeneity and contemporaneity of the Mycenaean finds serves to enhance the importance of the close sequential grouping of the Cypriot finds.

The second factor pointing toward the commercial involvement of the deceased is the above-mentioned collection of fine metal implements, probably of relatively contemporary manufacture and representing special-purpose function. Thus, we have two collections of items, collections acquired as part of a sequence of commercial activites.

The rings and seals of Egyptian, Mitannian, and Cypriot influence, spanning perhaps the late 15th as well as the early 14th century B.C., are further evidence of the commercial contacts of the deceased. These items may represent the personal belongings of the deceased rather than items for trade and may well have been acquired at various locales and at various times, unlike the homogeneous collections of metal and ceramic objects.

More than any of the other items, however, the collection of 58 weights found in clusters in the graves illuminate the commercial involvement of the people buried near Akko. The variety of the weights and of the standards represented—most of the known metrological systems of the Eastern Mediterranean in the Late Bronze Age—indicate both multiple-commodity objectives and differing commodity objectives for the bearers of these weights.[8] Therefore, it is perfectly clear that the bearers of these fine ceramics and metal implements were somehow involved in the complex network of international trade during the first half of the 14th century B.C., the era also known to us as the Amarna Age.

What role within the economic system of the Late Bronze Age in the Eastern Mediterranean was played by these individuals? Assuming that they formed a segment of the distribution aspect of the economic system, dealing in finished products, what can we reconstruct of their activities from the wealth of textual data bearing on the Amarna Age? Written documents found at el-Amarna, Ugarit, and Alalakh illuminate, albeit neither as clearly nor as completely as we would like, the functioning of Late Bronze Age commerce and the framework of the ecomonic system in which it operated. We find three basic spheres of economic activity— the urban center, the village, and the pastoral realm—each of which had points of contact with others providing essential social, political, and economic interaction. By a variety of means, the urban centers accumulated enough surplus to be the focus of intrastate and international commerce. One such urban center properly aligned along a conjunction of major caravan routes and having reasonable port facilities was Akko (see map on following page).

[8] See the excellent analysis and review of the comparanda by Edelstein and E. Eran in *AKKO*, 52–62.

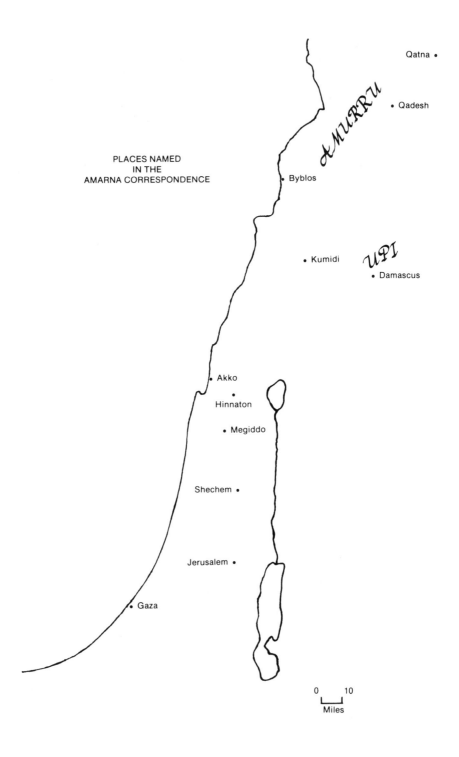

PLACES NAMED
IN THE
AMARNA CORRESPONDENCE

Qatna •

• Qadesh

𝒜𝑀𝒰𝑅𝑅𝒰

• Byblos

𝒰𝒫𝐼

• Kumidi

• Damascus

• Akko
•
Hinnaton

• Megiddo

Shechem •

Jerusalem •

• Gaza

0   10
Miles

Located midway on the caravan route from Gaza to Byblos and intersected by the caravan route from Damascus to the Mediterranean coast, Akko was an important commercial center during the Late Bronze Age. From the Ras Shamra tablets, we know that the Ugaritic fleet often stopped at Akko.[9] From the Amarna Letters, however, we learn much more of the activities of Akko.[10] During the reign of Akhenaten, two kings of Akko are mentioned in the Amarna correspondence: Zurata (EA 8, 85, 88, 232, 245, 290) and his son and successor, Zatatna (EA 8, 233, 234). In EA 234, Zatatna claims that "Akko is (as Egyptian) as Migdol in Egypt."[11] Since Migdol was Egypt's border fortress and military station at her northeastern frontier,[12] did Zatatna intend merely to point out the steadfast loyalty of Akko; or did he wish to claim that Akko was Egypt's last loyal outpost against a hostile northern frontier, equally as important to Egypt's security as the Migdol fortress? That the latter claim was probably intended may be seen in Zatatna's demand that a pharaonic commissioner be dispatched directly from Akhenaten to take Zatatna's prisoner, Zirdamiashda, to Biryawaza, prince of Upi,[13] the region around Damascus.[14]

Despite Zatatna's grandiose equation of Akko with Migdol, elsewhere in the Amarna correspondence Akko seems to be a center of intrigue and byzantine interests. While assuring Akhenaten of his loyalty

[9] RS 18:31 (C. Virolleaud, *PRU V*, p. 78) and UT 2059 (J. Sasson, "Canaanite Maritime Involvement in the Second Millennium B.C.," *JAOS* 86 [1966], p. 137).

[10] J. Knudtzon, *Die El-Amarna Tafeln* (Aalen: Otto Zeller Verlagsbuchhandlung, 1964 [reprint of 1915 edition]). References to the various Amarna Letters follow the EA numbers of Knudtzon.

[11] EA 234:28–30, following Albright in *ANET* 484–85.

[12] Tell Maskhutah or Tell el-Her.

[13] Biryawaza is rendered as "Namiawaza" and also as "Biriamaza" by Knudtzon (*Amarna Tafeln*) followed by S. A. B. Mercer, *The Tell el-Amarna Tablets* (Toronto: Macmillan, Ltd., 1939); as "Piryawaza" by Albright (*CAH*[3] II/2, chap. XX); as "Biryawaza" by E. F. Campbell, *The Chronology of the Amarna Letters* (Baltimore: Johns Hopkins, 1964) following Albright's rendering in *ANET*; and as "Biriyamaza" by A. L. Oppenheim, *Letters from Mesopotamia* (Chicago: University of Chicago, 1967). According to Albright (*CAH*[3] II/2, 101-2, 104, and 111), Biryawaza was the prince of Upi, the area centered on Damascus. In this analysis, Albright is followed by both Campbell and Oppenheim. Furthermore, Oppenheim (*Letters*, 115), in his translation of EA 7, seems to indicate that Biryawaza operates just outside of the area controlled by Egypt.

[14] EA 234:33–35. This evidence for the importance of Akko during the 18th Dynasty seems to support J. Weinstein's contention ("Was Tell Abu Hawam a 19th Dynasty Egyptian Naval Base?" *BASOR 238* [1980], 43–46) that Akko rather than Tell Abu Hawam was a 19th Dynasty Egyptian naval base. Clarification of what this may mean in terms of the material culture of Akko awaits the further excavation and publication of this site by M. Dothan.

(EA 232), Zurata—father of Zatatna and his predecessor as king of Akko—conspired to set free the anti-Egyptian king of Shechem, Labayu. Biridiya, king of Megiddo had managed to capture and detain Labayu at Megiddo. Zurata was to have sent Labayu to Akhenaten by ship, but instead he took Labayu's ransom in silver (a bribe?) and sent him home a free man (EA 245).

Similarly, Zatatna became involved in a jurisdictional dispute over Zirdamiashda, as mentioned above (EA 234). Zirdamiashda had originally been in the custody of Biryawaza, prince of Upi, who had released him into the custody of the pharaonic petty official Shuta, perhaps for transport to Egypt. However, Zirdamiashda escaped and found sanctuary with Zatatna in Akko, and Zatatna refused Shuta's efforts to have Zirdamiashda returned to the custody of Biryawaza, writing that "Akko is (as Egyptian) as Migdol in Egypt, but the king, my lord, has not heard that Shuta has turned against me. Now, let the king, my lord, send his commissioner and fetch [Zirdamiashda]."[15] Since Zirdamiashda escaped to Akko only after his pharaonic guard left Megiddo, it would seem that the poor relations between Megiddo and Akko that prevailed at the time of Zatatna's father continued to affect events in his own time.

The duplicity illustrated above was common in a frontier zone such as the area north of Megiddo, the frontier between the Egyptian and the Hittite spheres of economic interest during the 14th century B.C. Within this frontier zone, one individual stands out for his ability to maneuver and influence events, Biryawaza, prince of Upi. His authority was recognized from Akko and Megiddo in the south to Amurru in the north.[16] In his own letters (EA 194–197), we find Biryawaza accompanied on pharaonic missions by a substantial personal force composed of soldiers, chariots, "brothers" (convenantal allies?), SA.GAZ, and Sutu.[17] We also find him requesting an additional 200 soldiers to help protect pharaoh's loyal cities to the northwest and southwest of Damascus.[18] In short, Biryawaza was the protector of the pharaoh's cities and caravans, in which function he was dispatched on at least one occasion to Mitanni (EA 194).

Biryawaza is specifically described as pharaoh's representative in letters from Akizzi of Qatna (EA 53:34) and Rib-Addi of Byblos (EA 129:82). Thus the position of powerful pharaonic representative accorded Biryawaza in his encounter with Zatatna (EA 234) was commensurate with his

[15] EA 234:28–35, after Albright, *ANET*, 485.

[16] According to the varied references to his activity in the EA texts cited above and below and inferring from the remarks by Campbell, *Chronology*, 124–25. It is noteworthy that Albright, *CAH*[3] II/2, 102, felt that Biryawaza had an important role in the Egyptian administration of Syro-Palestine although he did not define what that role may have been.

[17] EA 195:24–32.

[18] EA 196:34–38.

role further to the north. Moreover, it was plainly within the context of such pharaonic support that Ba᾽lu-UR.SAG (EA 250) asked Akhenaten to commission Biryawaza to subdue the trouble-making sons of Labayu.

Amarna Letter 7 from Burnaburiash II to Akhenaten illuminates yet another facet of the career of Biryawaza. Heretofore, our documentary evidence has depicted Biryawaza as Egypt's loyal representative in Upi, deciding inter-city disputes and maintaining stability in the region and its frontiers by force of personality and military might. In EA 7, however, Burnaburiash has accused Biryawaza of plundering a caravan belonging to Ṣalmu, a merchant in his employ.[19] Although all other references indicate that Biryawaza acted to promote stability and uninterrupted commerce, his wide-ranging activity and territorial interest, stretching from Upi to Akko and northward, to Kumidi and to Amurru, put him in a position to hinder as well as promote caravan traffic between Babylon and Egypt. It would be in character with the mores of the Amarna Age[20] if Biryawaza, dissatisfied with the duties he collected from goods in transit through his territories,[21] and driven by his influence and power, also acted to the detriment of the peaceful flow of international commerce, materially enriching himself while relatively safe from physical repercussions.[22] One wonders if such destabilizing activity lay behind Abi-Milki's denunciation of Biryawaza (EA 151:62) as a friend of the notorious Aziru of Amurru.

In a letter which may follow his complaint of Biryawaza's plundering, Burnaburiash wrote to Akhenaten of the plunder of yet another caravan (EA 8), adding that a full account of the incident could be obtained from Burnaburiash's representative at the court of Akhenaten, an individual whose name is incomplete and unclear but who might be the same Ṣalmu of EA 7.[23] Not only has this latest caravan been plundered,

---

[19] In EA 7:73–75 and EA 11: rev. 8 Ṣalmu is referred to as "my messenger" by Burnaburiash.

[20] One of the least negative interpretations in that of M. Several, "Reconsidering the Egyptian Empire in Palestine During the Amarna Period," *PEQ* 104 (1972) 123–33.

[21] Based upon the textual information from such Late Bronze Age centers as Ugarit and Alalakh, we assume that an important region such as Upi, astride an international trade route, must have levied similar duties.

[22] The negative aspects of Biryawaza's activity are also seen in EA 189 (from Etaqqama to Akhenaten) in which Biryawaza is accused, according to Campbell (*Chronology*, 124), "of complete disloyalty in turning cities into SA.GAZ territory and in burning Etaqqama's city, Qadesh." However, in EA 197:31–32, Biryawaza accuses Etaqqama himself of destroying Qadesh.

[23] The association of the name in EA 8:22 with Ṣalmu is hypothetical. In EA 7:73, Ṣalmu is written with three signs while both Knudtzon and Mercer indicate that they understood two signs in the damaged space in EA 8:22.

but the merchants have been murdered and their silver stolen (EA 8:20–21). In language reminiscent of a covenantal lawsuit,[24] Burnaburiash demands that Akhenaten take action against the perpetrators of this crime for Canaan is his, Akhenaten's land (EA 8:22–29).

Burnaburiash clearly identifies Zatatna, king of Akko and old nemesis of Biryawaza, as the perpetrator of this robbery and murder (EA 8:19). Moreover, the plot seems to have been carried out in cooperation with another Canaanite king, Shumadda,[25] in Hinnaton (EA 8:17), that city between Akko and Megiddo from which Zurata, Zatatna's father, set free the infamous Labayu (EA 245:32). Not only does Burnaburiash claim that Zatatna slew his merchants and stole their silver, an accusation that his personal messenger will confirm with specifics (EA 8:22–24), but Burnaburiash demands that Akhenaten summon Shumadda and Zatatna to Egypt to testify (EA 8:40–41).

But what of the evidence: outside of the testimony of Burnaburiash and that of his messenger, where is the evidence of this foul deed, the evidence necessary to convince Akhenaten? The evidence which supports the accusations of Burnaburiash may indeed rest with the bones of the nine individuals buried near the Persian Garden, just north of Akko. Although we cannot prove the connection beyond the shadow of a doubt, there is a body of evidence which supports the assumption that these may be the bones of those very merchants, and members of their families, robbed and murdered by Zatatna and his co-conspirators. Included among the evidence is the proximity of this small cemetery to Akko, 2.5 km to the south. There being no other settlement nearby, one wonders what reasons lie behind the situation of a burial ground in this spot. Moreover, despite the wealth interred with the bodies and the careful arrangement of the objects in the graves, the graves themselves were rather poor, hastily dug pits in the sand.[26]

Perhaps the strongest evidence in support of our correlation lies in the secondary character of these burials.[27] That the bodies were at least beginning to decompose when buried in these sand pits is indicated by the disarticulated condition of the skeletal remains. Even the best articulated skeleton, that in grave B3 is slightly scattered and missing its pelvis.[28] Moreover, the Minoan style larnax which accompanied burial C2

---

[24] Compare EA 8:8–34 with, for example, Deuteronomy 32, Isa 1:2–3, Jer 2:4–13, and Mic 6:1–8.

[25] On Shumadda see also EA 49:2 and EA 224:3.

[26] Burial in pits dug into the earth or sand are common in the coastal plain region in the Late Bronze Age. These Persian Garden graves seem simple in construction and perhaps even hastily dug.

[27] Since photographs and plans of the burials make it perfectly clear that they were secondary burials, one wonders why the excavators never considered this possibility in print.

[28] *AKKO*, fig. 3.

may indicate the recovery and burial of fragmentary remains.[29] If these bodies had indeed lain exposed for some time and had begun to decompose prior to this interment near the Persian Garden, such exposure to the elements together with burial in the sand would explain the poor preservation of the skeletal remains which has hampered analyses of the cause of death.

The final piece of evidence linking the Persian Garden remains with the merchants of Burnaburiash is the clearly mercantile aspect of the grave goods: the weights of the various international standards, the fine Mycenaean and Cypriot pottery, the rings and seals from north Syria, Egypt, and Cyprus, and the important collection of copper and bronze weapons, tools, and utensils. Although, as indicated above, the excavators claimed that the 71 weapons indicated a military function for at least a few of the deceased, these weapons were clearly meant for trade. Confirmation of my position commes from UT 2056, an important Ugaritic mercantile text which mentions a ship's origin (Alashia), its destination (Ugarit), and its cargo: crude copper and finished copper products including weapons and agricultural tools.[30] Similar items have been recovered from the Cape Gelidonya wreck, although neither the quality nor the quantity of the weapons and tools is comparable.[31] Finally, the javelinheads and arrowheads were found grouped together in bundles which the excavators suggested were the result of being contained in quivers.[32] However, being bundled together is precisely the attitude one would expect for trade goods in transit. Clearly, the quality, quantity, international character, and final deposition of the grave goods indicates that the deceased were involved in commercial activity.

In view of the evidence in the case, the location of the graves, the small population of the cemetery, the secondary nature of the burials and the apparent haste in which they were buried, and the clearly mercantile activity of the deceased, there is ample reason to suggest that the individuals discovered buried near the Persian Garden may be the very merchants of Burnaburiash mentioned in EA 8. But if indeed these are the merchants robbed and murdered by Zatatna of Akko, why are they found buried with such elaborate grave goods? This serious objection

[29] *AKKO*, fig. 6, pl. XV:10, and p. 19.

[30] See E. Linder, "Ugarit: A Canaanite Thalassocracy," in G. D. Young (ed.), *Ugarit in Retrospect* (Winona Lake: Eisenbrauns, 1981) 37. Similar information comes from EA 13:15–25; 14: col. II:75–88 and col. III:1–10; 22: col. IV:17–33; 25: col. IV:56–62; and 333:12–13.

[31] See G. Bass, "The Cape Gelidonya Wreck: Preliminary Report," *AJA* 65 (1961) 271–74. Hordes of copper and bronze objects have been found in a number of Late Bronze Age tombs among which some of the most notable are Tombs 101, 102, and 119 at Tell es-Sa^{c}idiyeh (J. Pritchard, *The Cemetery at Tell es-Sa^{c}idiyeh, Jordan* (Philadelphia: The University Museum, 1980).

[32] *AKKO*, 34.

may be answered by reference to the nature of secondary burial and to the nature of the robbery as reported in EA 8. The goods interred with the bodies were those neglected by the robbers or the personal belongings of the deceased which were not with them at the time of the murders. It is important to recall that while Burnaburiash often made extensive lists of the types and quantities of the gifts and goods travelling in his caravans, in EA 8 he claimed only that *silver* (*kaspu*, EA 8:21) was stolen from this caravan.[33]

It seems reasonable to conclude, therefore, that in the Persian Garden graves, just north of ancient Akko, we have one of those very rare and exciting links between the often anonymous discoveries of the archeologist and an explicit textual reference. These may be the bones of the merchants of Burnaburiash, robbed and murdered at the hands of Zatatna.

[33] The excavators did, however, report finding a few pieces of silver jewelry and silver foil.

ADAM'S RIB

Hans Goedicke
Dept. of Near Eastern Studies
The Johns Hopkins University

N OT too long ago a well-respected professor of Hebrew and biblical history was quoted as saying, "The last person I would trust to tell me what to believe would be an Egyptologist." The statement is remarkable for two reasons. First, it demonstrates a bias which should not be found with a scholar. Academic inquiry is not a demonstration of beliefs, but an objective search for truth. Those who cannot separate inquiry from belief should separate themselves from academia. The second, equally objectionable, slant in the quoted statement is the denial of the impact of ancient Egypt on the formation, intellectual, spiritual, and political, of Israel. It requires a high degree of myopia to disregard the fact that the early history of Israel is for approximately a millenium closely linked with that of the Nile Valley. Israel's self-understanding of her past assigns a major role in the development to Egypt. The pharaohs were sovereigns not only of the Nile Valley but of Syro-Palestine as well from the sixteenth to the twelfth century. The archaeological record provides telltale evidence for extensive physical and cultural interaction between the two regions.[1]

Despite the available extensive evidence, there is but little concern among those studying the early history of Israel or the Bible for ancient Egyptian evidence which might pertain to their research. In part it is also the shortcoming of the Egyptologists that they do not emphasize and make accessible any pertinent material. Sam Iwry, who with his long association with the late William F. Albright has been imbued by the idea of the ancient Near East as one large integrated area, has always maintained a wide perimeter for his intellectual pursuit. As a token of recognition of many years as colleagues, the potential aspects will be demonstrated by one minute point.

Any discussion about the Torah has to begin with the Creation, of which there are two versions, P and J. There is no commentary which does not compare the Genesis account with the Babylonian Creation

---

[1] Among the numerous phenomena which could be cited in this connection, none is more apparent than the adoption of the Egyptian numerical notation system into early Hebrew writing.

Epic, the *Enuma eliš*, to which a Second Millennium date is commonly assigned, although no extant text antedates the First Millennium B.C. It might, however, be noteworthy for scholars interested in man's ideas about the origins of the Universe and himself that an Egyptian literary text, The Instructions for King Merikare[c],[2] contains an account which displays striking similarities to the biblical account. The text, written shortly after 2000 B.C., is a literary and not a theological composition. Insofar as the Creation is discussed, it would seem to rely on other accounts, which, however, are not preserved. The inclusion in a literary text shows that there was basic consensus about the events at the Beginning of Time. The pertinent section, which is part of an admonition to be religious, follows a wide range of political advice. It reads:[3]

"Well tended is mankind, god's cattle,
    after he made heaven and earth for their sake,
    after he repelled the water-monster,
    after he made breath in desire that their noses live.
His likenesses are they who came forth from his limbs
He shines from heaven for their sake,
    after he made for them plants, cattle, fowl, and fish for consuming it.
He has slain his enemies
    and he has annihilated his children
        for their intention to act rebellious."

The formulation lacks the concise structuring into seven steps, so familiar from Genesis. "Seven" is a recurrent structure in Egyptian religious formulations: there were 7 sacred ointments, 7 truths, 7 funerary offerings, 7 uraei or 7 Hathors.[4] Despite this frequency, it does not occur in Egyptian cosmology proper, in addition to the wide distribution of seven as a structural element. Needless to say, no direct link with the biblical account can be established, as ideas and images move in subtle ways.

According to Gen 2:7 man was formed from "clods consisting of soil." For an alluvial society like that of ancient Egypt the potter's mud

---

[2] The best edition of the text is by Wolfgang Helck, *Die Lehre für König Merikare*, Kleine Ägyptische Texte (Wiesbaden: Otto Harrassowitz, 1977). Earlier editions are: Vladimir Golenischeff, *Les papyrus hiératiques nr. 1115, 1116A et 1116B de l'Ermitage Impérial à St. Pétersbourg*, 1913, pls. 9–14; Aksel Volten, *Zwei altägyptische politische Schriften*, Analecta Aegyptiaca IV, (Copenhagen, 1945).

[3] Translation by Miriam Lichtheim, *Ancient Egyptian Literature: A Book of Readings*, Volume I, (Berkeley and London, 1973) 106.

[4] Hermann Kees, *Der Götterglaube im alten Ägypten* (Leipzig, 1941) 158f.; Kurt Sethe, *Von Zahlen und Zahlworten bei den alten Ägyptern* (Strassburg, 1916) 33f.

was the ubiquitous substance for shaping things, and man was no exception. There are numerous representations of the god Khnum, the artist and demiurge in the Egyptian religion, seated at the potter's wheel on which he fashions a human being.[5] The material used for fashioning is clay, in Egyptian *imw*.

While the Egyptian creation accounts make no difference between male and female, Gen 2:21f. contains a special story about the origin of women as "God Yahweh cast a deep sleep upon the man and, when he was asleep, he took one of his ribs and closed up the flesh at that spot. And God Yahweh fashioned into a woman the rib that he had removed from the man." This account of Eve's origin from Adam's rib is one of the most influential idiosyncracies of the Bible, but also a major riddle. The dispute about the number of ribs of man and woman raged for centuries in academic circles and is by no means settled among laypeople. Even today the notion that men have one rib more than women can be encountered quite commonly. One of the great anatomical breakthroughs was the proving of the equal number of ribs for both genders. The events leading to this recognition triggered concern for anatomical studies and had a vital impact on the development of medicine altogether.

If there is no anatomical difference between male and female as far as the number of ribs is concerned, what is the possible origin and meaning of the biblical statement about Adam's rib? Despite my efforts I have not been able to find an answer to this question in the numerous commentaries on the Book of Genesis. They all seem to pass over this curious expression wordlessly. As there is no physiological basis for it, a metaphorical usage would seem a likely assumption. What, however, could it indicate? I am not aware of any specific symbolic meaning attached to the rib. There is not even a case for a sexual symbolism, as Adam is certainly not involved in the creation of Eve. Even more perplexing is the question how to reconcile the fashioning of Eve from the rib of Adam with his being made of clay.

In this quandary it is curious to note that the Egyptian word for "rib" is *imw* and that it is a homophone with the word *imw* "clay."[6] This might be purely accidental, but it could provide an approach for solving the riddle Adam's rib constitutes. In Egyptian the making out of

[5] Helmut Brunner, *Die Geburt des Gottkönigs* (Ägyptologische Abhandlungen 10, 1964) 68ff.; Herbert Ricke, George R. Hughes, Edward F. Wente, *The Beit el-Wali Temple of Ramesses II* (University of Chicago, 1967) 91.37.

[6] Adolf Erman und Hermann Grapow, *Wörterbuch der ägyptischen Sprache I* 78, 2; ibid. 77, 16; cf. also Gustave Lefebvre, *Tableau des parties du corps humain mentionnees par les egyptiens, Supplement aux Annales du Service des Antiquities* (Cahier no. 17, 1952) 27. Samuel Noah Kramer (*History Begins at Sumer* [Garden City, New York, 1959] 146) attempted to explain the connection between "rib" and "Eve" on the basis of a Sumerian pun. Such a connection, however, seems unlikely.

"clay" (*imw*) could be mistakenly taken as making out of a "rib" (*imw*), or Adam's clay could in Egyptian be confused with Adam's rib. What might seem contrived takes on another dimension when realizing that this very conflation can be corroborated for the ancient Egyptians. In the Coffin Texts[7] there is an introduction of the deceased to Osiris as "Your son it is, your infant it is of your own *flesh*" (*imw*) which in two versions is spelled as if it were the word "rib" (*imw*). There is certainly not enough objective proof to promulgate a thesis which might convince an Egyptologist. It might, however, inspire possibilities for future research by those seeking clarity and truth, even at the danger of someone's frail beliefs.

---

[7] Adriaan de Buck, *The Egyptian Coffin Texts*, vol. I, 106, c; cf. R. O. Faulkner, *The Ancient Egyptian Coffin Texts*, Volume I (Warminster, 1973) 21.

ON MAKING OTHER GODS

Cyrus H. Gordon
New York University

A tablet from Ebla[1] records eight minas of silver for fashioning one statue, and fifteen minas of silver to be exchanged for gold to make another statue, as gifts of the King for the Temple of Hada.

Making effigies of gold and silver was so usual throughout Near East antiquity that it evoked a specific prohibition: "You shall not make for yourselves gods of silver and gods of gold" (Exod 20:23). It was not only their pagan neighbors who were casting such molten images, but also the Israelites themselves. The episode of the Golden Calf is too notorious to require further comment. Less publicized is Judg 17:1–6 which narrates how a Yahwistic household in the hills of Ephraim converted two hundred (shekels) of silver into an idol for worship in the family shrine.

There is an Aramaic stela from the Arabian oasis of Tēmā (5th–4th centuries B.C.) authorizing the introduction of a new god with a cult under a new hereditary priesthood with a permanent yearly endowment in the name of the already established triad of local deities that had constituted the Tēmā pantheon. The new deity is called ṢLM of HGM; he has his own temple, and his own priest, ṢLMŠZB, son of Petosiris.[2]

This permissiveness in adding new gods is not strange in the annals of paganism, but neither is the reaction to it. In the Apology of Hattusilis III (13th century B.C.), the absolute, uncompromising loyalty of the emperor and his successors to their protective deity, Ishtar, is a cardinal element in the covenant between the royal line and the deity credited with establishing the dynastic throne.[3]

We must avoid the pitfall of requiring consistency. Ebla had a numerous pantheon and yet it cherished a hymn to "The Lord of Heaven and Earth" who can only be the single, monotheistic, master of the universe.[4]

---

[1] Giovanni Pettinato, *The Archives of Ebla* (New York: Doubleday, 1981) 169.

[2] Text 228 in H. Donner and W. Röllig, *Kanaanäische und aramäische Inschriften* (Wiesbaden: Harrassowitz, 1962 and later editions).

[3] Cyrus H. Gordon, *Forgotten Scripts: Their On-going Discovery and Decipherment* (New York: Basic Books, 1982) 199–207; note especially the final section of the *Apology* on p. 207.

[4] As noted by Pettinato, *Archives*, 244, 259–260.

The Nuzu/Kirkuk tablets (ca. 1400 B.C.) indicate that the household gods were taken quite seriously in last wills and testaments. The chief heir alone was to take possession of the gods.[5] Genesis 31 embodies this institution too. Loyalty to the household gods was so important that a Nuzu tablet spells out the prohibition against making new household gods. Specifically only the chief heir is to inherit the father's household gods. The other sons are to direct offerings and prayers to those same gods and are not to make other gods.[6] The function of this prohibition is clear: it is to keep the family united and to prevent its being split up cultically.

Jeremiah (2:27) knows of devotees "who say to the tree 'thou art my father' and to the stone 'thou hast borne me.'" "Tree" ($^{\varsigma}s$) is masculine, while "stone" ($^{\jmath}bn$) is feminine; thus the genders are right for fatherhood and motherhood, respectively. There were people who claimed descent from sacred trees and stones, so that such claims can refer to supposed parenthood from specific trees and stones. It is conceivable, too, that Jeremiah's words apply also to idols of wood and stone. Either interpretation could be bolstered with copious examples from ancient Near East usage.

The prohibition in the Decalogue against making idols can be, and has been, interpreted in different ways. Since the text states "thou shalt not bow down to them nor serve them" (Exod 20:5 = Deut 5:9), it could be interpreted as permitting images provided that one does not worship them. It can also be understood as outlawing three-dimensional idols (for *psl* in Exod 20:4 = Deut 5:8 designates sculpture only) but not two-dimensional icons such as drawings, paintings, and mosaics. In view of the setting, the prohibition is covenantal: "Thou shalt have no other gods over and above me" (Exod 20:3 = Deut 5:7) because "I am Yahweh, thy God, who brought thee out of the land of Egypt, from the house of bondage" (Exod 20:2 = Deut 5:6). The Hebrews owe Yahweh uncompromising loyalty because it was He who redeemed them out of slavery into freedom.

We have collocated several sources from the world of the Old Testament, giving both sides of the question: Should new gods be made or not made? The permissive attitude has been illustrated from Early Bronze Age Ebla to Iron Age III Tēmā. Prohibitions against it range from the Nuzu tablet precluding the manufacture and worship of new household gods to the Decalogue requiring Israel to serve only Yahweh and to refrain from worshiping any graven image.

---

[5] Cyrus H. Gordon, *"Erēbu* Marriage," in *Studies on the Civilization and Culture of Nuzi and the Hurrians (In Honor Of Ernest R. Lacheman)* (Winona Lake, IN: Eisenbrauns, 1981) 155–60; note pp. 156–57.

[6] Karlheinz Deller, "Die Hausgötter der Familie Šukrija S. Ḫuja," in *Studies on the Civilization and Culture of Nuzi*, 47–76; note pp. 73–74.

Obviously, these few examples do not exhaust the subject, but they aim at opening fresh approaches to a pervasive aspect of the Judeo-Christian tradition. One of the products of this collocation emanates from the bearing of the Nuzu prohibition against making new gods on the Decalogue. The Nuzu document is designed to hold the family together. By the same token, the Decalogue prohibition against making new gods aims at holding the nation together.

The cohesion of the Hebrews resulted to a great extent from the ideology of the Pentateuch: unified tribes claiming descent from one father, sharing one history and one destiny, under one God.

THE MEANING OF *TKWNH**

Jonas C. Greenfield
Dept. of Semitic Languages
The Hebrew University, Jerusalem

T HE Hebrew element in the vocabulary of the Aramaic texts from Elephantine is surprisingly limited. There are such obvious Hebraisms as ʿdh "community, assembly" (*CAP* 15:22; *BMAP* 7:21), *khn* "priest" (*CAP* 30:1), *ṣdqh* "merit" (*CAP* 3:27) and *škn* "dwell" (*BMAP* 12:2) used of God's dwelling in the temple at Elephantine. The paucity of such terms in the legal documents is noteworthy. The term *tkwnh* is a rare exception.[1] It occurs three times in Biblical Hebrew and in two of the Elephantine papyri (*CAP* 15:6; *BMAP* 7:5, 15, 22, 27).[2] The first text *CAP* 15 is the "marriage contract" drawn up between Mibtaḥia daughter of Maḥseiah and Eshor son of Ṣeḥo. In it the groom declares: *hnʿlt ly [brtk] mptḥyh bydh ksp tkwnh krš 1 šqln 2 bᵓbny mlk*ᵓ "Miptaḥia your daughter brought into me in her hand *ksp tkwnh* (of) 1 karsh, 2 shekel royal weight."[3] As long as this was the only known occurrence of the phrase *ksp tkwnh* it was variously rendered and it was indeed difficult to decide on an accurate meaning. Cowley interpreted it as "cost of furniture" but this translation was patently wrong.[4] With the publication of *BMAP* 7 by Kraeling the use of *tkwnh* was clarified. This text is the

---

* Abbreviations: *CAP*—A. Cowley, *Aramaic Papyri of the Fifth Century* B.C. (Oxford, 1923); *BMAP*—E. G. Kraeling, *The Brooklyn Museum Aramaic Papyri* (New Haven, 1953); *Porten-Greenfield*: B. Porten-J. C. Greenfield, *Jews of Elephantine and Arameans of Syene, Fifty Aramaic Texts with Translations* (Jerusalem, 1974).

[1] A seeming exception is ʿrbn "security, pledge" (*CAP* 10:9, 13, 17; *BMAP* 11:10) from Heb. ʿērābōn. The correction to Kraeling's *bʿd bny* was first suggested by H. L. Ginsberg (*JNES* 18 [1959] 148, and has been generally accepted, cf. *Porten-Greenfield*, 66. But ʿrbn "security" is known also from Ugaritic and the term was in all likelihood borrowed from "Canaanite" rather than specifically from Hebrew.

[2] The word *tĕkūnā* occurs in Nah 2:10; Ezek 43:11; and Job 23:3; this discussion deals *only* with the occurrence in Nah 2:10, the understanding of the other verses, especially Ezek 43:11, may profit from it.

[3] *Porten-Greenfield*, 20–21; for the background of this text, see B. Porten, *Archives from Elephantine* (Berkeley, 1968) 235–63.

[4] *CAP*, 47.

marriage contract drawn up for the manumitted handmaiden Yehoyish-maᶜ and Ananiah son of Haggai.[5] In it there is a statement similar to that of *CAP* 15:6, for Ananiah states: *hnᶜlt ly yhyšmᶜ ᵓḥtk lbyty tkwnh zy ksp kršn 2 šqln 2 ḥlrn 5* "Yehoyishmaᶜ your sister brought into me, to my house a *tkwhn zy ksp* 2 karsh, 2 shekel, 5 hallur."[6] Elsewhere in this document the *tkwnh* is referred to either in the Aramaic determined from *tkwntᵓ* "the *tkwnh*" or as *tkwnth* "her *tkwnh*." It was clear from *BMAP*, as Kraeling had seen, that a sum of money was meant and he therefore translated it as "substance of silver."[7]

J. A. Fitzmyer, reviewing the earlier interpretations has called it "dowry sum" and commented that it almost certainly represents a sum of money or an amount of silver distinct from the other items and from the *mhr*; it was the dowry sum in the strict sense.[8] Fitzmyer is right that the *ksp tkwnh* did not include the value of the real items listed in the document as "brought in" by the bride. He provides a careful calculation to prove this. Yet, calling it a "dowry sum" begs the question since we do not learn from either text if the husband has the right to use this *tkwnh*, which is a very important matter in the classification of a sum as a dowry.[9] Therefore, the translation "dowry sum" is not satisfactory here. Two other translations of the term should be noted here, the first that of H. L. Ginsberg who translated *tkwnh zy ksp* in *BMAP* 7 simply as "a cash sum"; the other is that of P. Grelot "une somme en numeraire."[10] I believe that these translations are essentially correct, but how does one explain the usage?

Comparison with *tĕkūnā* of Nah 2:10 may prove enlightening. It has been widely assumed that Biblical Hebrew *tĕkūnā* should be compared with *tĕrūmā*, *tĕbūnā*, and *tĕqūmā* and thus the root was taken to be *kwn* even though this did not advance the interpretation of the word.

---

[5] For the background of this text see Porten, *Archives*, 200–234.

[6] *Porten-Greenfield*, 52–53.

[7] *BMAP*, 205 and also 209; see also Hoftijzer, *DISO* 308.

[8] Cf. J. A. Fitzmyer, "A Restudy of an Aramaic Marriage Contract (AP 15)," reprinted with revisions in *A Wandering Aramaean* (Missoula, 1979) 243–47; for *ksp tkwnh* see 255.

[9] For a discussion of the use of the funds brought in as the *tkwnh* cf. Y. Muffs, *Studies in Aramaic Legal Papyri from Elephantine* (Leiden, 1969) 60–61 and 198 and also E. Bickerman in the revised version of "Two Legal Interpretations of the Septuaginta" in his *Studies in Jewish and Christian History I* (Leiden, 1976) 201–24, esp. 204. Bickerman sees the husband as a mere trustee but this is surely not correct; see below.

[10] H. L. Ginsberg in *ANET*[3], 548; P. Grelot, *Documents araméens d'Égypte* (Paris, 1972) 193. Y. Muffs, (*Studies*, 51) records the semantic parallel suggested by M. Greenberg with rabbinic *mĕzummānīm* "ready cash." This presumes the *use* of coins, but these were not in common use at this time in Egypt. See below, n. 16.

I would propose that the well-attested verbal root *tkn*, whose meaning is "to measure, weigh" is at the base of *těkūnā* and that this is a feminine passive participle with nominal usage. The verb *tkn* occurs frequently in the *qal, nif ᶜal* and *pi ᶜel*, it is found in parallelism with *mdd* and other verbs used for specific types of weighing and measuring (Isa 40:12). Thus the exact number of bricks is *token* (Exod 5:18) and *matkonet* is used for various types of tallies, measurements and proportions.[11]

The use of the pu ᶜal participle *mětukkan* in 2 Kgs 12:12 is of prime importance for understanding the use of this verb. In vv 7-17 we read of Jehoash's efforts to repair the temple. In v 10 we learn of the plan to have the "guards of the threshold" collect the silver for the repair of the temple and to put that silver in an *ʾărōn* whose lid had a hole bored in it, set near the altar. In v 11 we are told that when this *ʾărōn* was full the royal scribe and the high priest came and performed a task described in the text as *wyṣrw wymnw ʾt hksp*. The MT vocalised *wyṣrw* as *wa-yāṣūrū* "and they tied," made more explicit in some translations as "and they tied in bags." Some modern translations, in order to avoid an assumed *hysteron proteron* translate these words as "and they counted and tied up in bags the money" (*RSV*, but thus already the Peshitta). These translations share with the LXX, targum, and Peshitta the anachronistic assumption that money was being counted rather than silver being weighed. But this is a "modern" way of seeing things, possible only after the spread of coinage and the acceptance of coins at their face value. It is possible that the reading of the consonantal text as *wa-yāṣūru* developed under similar circumstances.

It was O. Eissfeldt, following an insight of C. C. Torrey, who argued that *wyṣrw* should be vocalized *wa-yiṣru* "and they cast," that is they cast the various sorts of silver—lumps, fragments, trinkets—into usable form in some sort of bullion for payment to the workmen and for the materials needed for the repair of the temple.[12] This idea has been generally accepted and has been incorporated into various recent translations (*NEB, NAB, Bible de Jerusalem*). In v 12 this silver is then called *mětukkan* which has usually been translated "weighed out." This is literally correct but it does not provide the needed nuance. In this verse *ha-kesef ha-mětukkan* would be the silver which had been measured out (after the casting) and whose value had been established and was thus readily available and dispensible.[13] In 2 Kgs 22:3-11 a similar incident concerning

[11] The verb *tkn* is also found with related meanings in the Qumran texts.

[12] C. C. Torrey developed this idea in two articles: "The Foundry of the Second Temple at Jerusalem" *JBL* 55 (1936) 247-60, and "The Evolution of a Financier in the Ancient Near East" *JNES* 2 (1934) 295-301. Eissfeldt's article of 1937 "Eine Schmelzstelle am Temple zu Jerusalem" is reprinted in his *Kleine Schriften* II (Tübingen, 1963) 107-9.

[13] After the silver had been cast, which also served to guarantee its "purity" as *kesep ṣārūp*, it could be "counted," that is, weighed, and recorded. Hoards

repairs to the temple in the reign of Josiah is reported.[14] Silver collected by the "guards of the threshold" was melted and used for payments and purchases. A. L. Oppenheim has shown that similar techniques were used in Babylonian temples in the neo-Babylonian and Persian periods.[15] The containers into which the silver—"miscellaneous cuttings, rings, wires, objects, etc."—was deposited were called *arannu* (Biblical Hebrew *ʾărōn*) or *quppu* (Mishnaic Hebrew quppā). These were then removed by the temple authorities and it was the job of the temple foundry to smelt all of it into silver ingots. Torrey pointed out that Herodotus (Book 3, chap. 96) had reported that Darius I had the tribute brought to him in various precious metals melted down into a form that could subsequently be used for diverse purposes.

Let us now turn to *těkūnā* of Nah 2:10. The line reads: *bozū kesef bozū zāhāb / wě ʾēn qeṣe la-těkūnā / kābod mikkol kělī ḥemdā*. The recent *NJPS* translation almost supplies the needs of the passage:

> "Plunder silver! Plunder gold!
> There is no limit to the treasure,
> It is a hoard of all precious objects."

But "treasure" for *těkūnā*, found also in other translations, repeats ancient wisdom since the Targum had already offered *ʾōṣārayyā* for *těkūnā*. What then is the *těkūnā* in this verse? I think that the writer was simply listing the forms in which silver and gold were to be found stored in the royal palace at Nineveh: either in the form of *těkūnā*—that is gold and silver melted down, weighed, and ready for use—or in the form of precious vessels which originated either in tribute and gifts or in spoils, booty taken from many nations.

---

from various periods have been found in different parts of the Near East. These are listed at the end of the article by C. M. Kraay and P. R. S. Moorey, "Two Fifth Century Hoards from the Near East," *Revue Numismatique* (1968) 181–235. Relevant to the period under discussion is a hoard from Engedi for which see now *Inscriptions Reveal*[2] (Jerusalem, 1973) 52 (English) and 112 (Hebrew), and the Eshtemoʾa hoard for which cf. Z. Yeivin, *Qadmoniot* 5 (1971–72) 45–46 and *Inscriptions Reveal*[2] 110–11 (Hebrew) and 52 (English). The contents of these hoards would be typical of the "silver" that would be put into an *ʾărōn*.

[14] Cf. Eissfeldt, "Schmelzstelle," 109. There is no reason to believe that a change had taken place in the treatment of the silver collected for the repair of the temple in the period between the reigns of Joash and Josiah. Although scholars have assumed that this passage was influenced by the narrative of the repairs made by Joash, it is independent in its use of terminology.

[15] Cf. A. L. Oppenheim, "A Fiscal Practice of the Ancient Near East," *JNES* 6 (1947) 116–20. The continuation of this practice into the Arsacide period has been noted by G. J. P. McEwan, *Iraq* 43 (1981) 131–32c, cf. text AB 245 (136–38).

To return to Elephantine—the *tĕkūnā* in these two marriage documents refers to the specifically weighed "cash" that the bride brought
with her as part of her dowry from her father's house. In the Persian
period the *tĕkūnā* could have been either in the form of silver ingots, or
the like, or even of silver coins, but even these were not counted at their
face value but were weighed.[16] In all likelihood the *tĕkūnā* was placed at
the husband's disposal but had to be returned in full value in case of
divorce.[17]

[16] In the hoards from the Persian period discussed by Kraay and Moorey
(above, n. 13) there are coins, whole and fragmentary, pieces of jewelery of all
sorts, pieces of ingots, etc. The same is true for a hoard from Iraq, published by
E. S. G. Robinson, "A 'Silversmith's Hoard' from Mesopotamia," *Iraq* 12 (1950)
44–50; see also C. M. Kraay, *JHS* 84 (1964) 76–91. (I am indebted to Prof. D.
Barag for these and other references.) These scholars are of the opinion that in
most of the Persian Empire coins were valued primarily for their weight. Cf. too
the older opinions assembled by B. Porten (*Archives*, 69, n. 43) concerning Egypt
in particular.

[17] Cf. the discussion of the dowry in M. A. Friedman, *Jewish Marriage in
Palestine*, Vol. 1 (Tel Aviv, 1980) 288–93.

CULT AND PRAYER

Menahem Haran
Dept. of Bible
The Hebrew University, Jerusalem

I

I N antiquity, the functions of priesthood were by no means restricted
to cult. Thus, biblical priests engaged, among other things, in
divination—though, in contrast to prophets, who foretold the future in
ecstatic manner and poetic language, priests would reveal the divine will
with the help of "implements" (*urim* and *thummim*, lots), or would
perform ordeals to resolve doubtful cases (as is exemplified by the law
concerning a wife suspected of adultery in Num 5:11–31). As guardians
of ritual purity, the priests would also fulfil the role of "physicians," in
which cases purity would be achieved through purging or by apotropaic
rites meant to exorcise the demonic powers of defilement or prevent their
return to a cleansed body (a truly secular medicine was hardly to be
found in the ancient Near East). Priests, in addition, functioned as
judges, and they also were instructors of the people, in that they would
impart "teachings," *tôrôt*, to those who inquired.[1] Central to all these
activities, however, remained the fundamental responsibility of caring
for the cult as such—for the constant and orderly service of God. Priesthood, in essence, is the most exalted and fullest manifestation of divine
service in ancient Israel. There was no real service of God in biblical
times but with the agency of priesthood.

The task by which the priests are singled out from among all
other functionaries is indicated by the epithet reserved for them in
the biblical diction: *mešārĕtê Yahweh*, "servants [or attendants] of the
Lord," *mešārĕtê ʾĕlohîm*, "servants of God" (Isa 61:6; Jer 33:21–22;
Joel 1:9, 13 *et al.*). They are also depicted as "standing before the Lord
to serve him" (Deut 10:8; 17:12; 18:5, 7 *et al.*), "drawing near to the Lord
to serve him" (Ezek 40:46; 43:19; 44:15), "drawing unto his table to serve
him" (Ezek 44:16), in all of which cases the verb *šrt*, "to serve," is employed. This is not merely a stereotyped phrase but an actual expression

---

[1] For the priesthood's functions in general see my remarks in *Encyclopaedia
Miqraʾît*, vol. IV, cols. 22–29.

87

of the priest's functional idiosyncrasy—a remnant of a primary historical comprehension of the task as fossilized in linguistic usage.[2]

The only place where the priest could carry out his appointed task
as a servant of God was the temple. Outside the temple he could perform
some of his other duties or attend to certain of the cult objects (such as
the ark, the ephod, a censer with incense) which were at times taken out,
but his principal role as God's servant could not come to fruition.

In Biblical Hebrew, however, the institution which the English language designates as "temple" (from the Latin *templum*) and in which
the priest performed his basic task as a divine servant, bore some descriptive epithets,[3] but its fundamental, defining term was "house of the
Lord," *bêt Yahweh*, or "house of God," *bêt ʾĕlohîm*. The most well-
known houses of God in Israel were the two built in Jerusalem and
became central religious symbols even for later generations. But these
were preceded by a dozen earlier houses of God erected at various sites
throughout the country (such as Shiloh, Bethel, Dan, Gilgal in Ephraim,
Mizpah in Benjamin, Hebron) and some of which originated in the
beginning of the period of the Judges or even in the Israelite settlement
in Canaan.[4] When Solomon built the First Temple in Jerusalem some
early houses of God had already declined and faded away.

The term "house of God" clearly designated the institution's primary function, which was exactly what the term implies—a house for
the god, his dwelling place. Just as every temporal king, and indeed any
man, has his own domicile, so the divine king, in whose shadow the
community takes refuge, has a residence of his own. And just like in
every luxurious house so in this dwelling place the master of the residence is provided with all his "needs": bread set on the table, incense for
smelling, lamps for light, flesh of burnt- and peace-offerings, grain- and
drink-offerings presented on the outer altar—the altar which in the
fossilized cultic language is still referred to in the Bible as "the Lord's
table" (Ezek 44:16; Mal 1:7). In this dwelling place, then, the master of

---

[2] The prophet's conventional epithet is, in contrast, "slave [or servant], *ʿebed*,
of the Lord" (1 Kgs 14:18; 15:29; 2 Kgs 9:33; 10:10; Isa 2:3 *et al.*) and this is Moses'
title outside P (Num 12:7–8; Deut 34:5; Josh 1:1–2 *et al.*). Prophets in general are
referred to as "my slaves, *ʿabāday*, the prophets," "his slaves, *ʿabādāw*, the
prophets," where the inflected noun for "slaves" is always directed to God
(2 Kgs 9:7; 17:13, 23; Jer 7:25; 25:4 *et al.*).

[3] Such as *miqdāš*, "(place of) holiness;" *bêt hammiqdāš* (only in 2 Chr 36:17),
"house of holiness"; *bêt zebûl*, "lofty house" and some other poetic appellations;
also *hêkal Yahweh*, "the Lord's palace." See my book *Temples and Temple-
Service in Ancient Israel* (Oxford, 1978; reprinted, Winona Lake, 1985) 13–15.

[4] For a complete and detailed listing of these temples see in my aforementioned book, 26–42, where I also pointed out that defining the archaeological
discovery in Arad as a "royal Judahite temple" is a mere conjecture (on the latter
point see further my observatins in the quarterly *Beth Mikra* 76 [1979] 103–5).

the residence has his own servants, the priests, who care for his necessities and keep the house in order—just like any reigning monarch has in his palace servants and retinue surrounding him constantly and performing his orders.

It should be pointed out that, in fact, biblical religion was long since freed from such a crude comprehension of the nature of God. Even the conception of the divine in the pre-biblical Near Eastern religions had already been rid of such physical limitation. Nonetheless, neither biblical religion nor those that preceded it ever thought of abandoning the cultic clichés and practices associated with the house of God—even though the institution itself had certainly emerged in a most distant past, at a time when man first started to use built-up houses as his abode and to conceive of the divine forces as possessing personal and distinct character. To put it differently, it was not biblical religion that invented the house of God—this institution came to it ready-made, with its identifying marks clearly discernible.[5] It is a good general rule that all religions in history do not usually create their institutions *ex nihilo*, but inherit them from earlier stages and, at times, try only to infuse them with a new spirit or to afford them a special meaning. After all, the modes of worship associated with the house of God might not be much more anthropomorphic than the practice of prayer, which is also just an inheritance from the hoary past.

II

From this aspect, there is a fundamental difference between the temple and the synagogue, which constitutionally is only a gathering place of the community for liturgical purposes, that is, for public prayer (like any religious experience, prayer is also preferably a communal matter, even though it may be performed by individuals). The synagogue is not exactly a "substitute" for the temple; rather, it is an entirely new institution, which without exaggeration may be considered one of the greatest innovations in the history of religions.[6] In contrast to the house of God, where a layman could come only as a guest and linger in the outer court, being denied access to the inner cultic sanctity which remained the sole prerogative of priests—the synagogue is a democratic

---

[5] On the comprehension of the temple as a divine dwelling place in ancient Near Eastern religions, see, e.g., H. H. Nelson, A. L. Oppenheim *et al.*, "The Significance of the Temple in the Ancient Near East," *BA* 7 (1944) 44, 58–59, 66–68.

[6] This has been acknowledged by scholars of the history of religions. See, e.g., C. H. Toy, *Introduction to the History of Religions* (Cambridge, 1913) 546; G. F. Moore, *History of Religions* II (New York, 1919) 62–63; likewise F. V. Filson, in *BA* 7 (1944) 83–84.

institution in its character (as far as the concept "democracy" is applicable in this context). Its first appearance took place during the Second Temple times, apparently toward the end of the Persian period. In any case, by Hellenistic times it was already a well-established and accepted institution.[7] Mishnaic traditions report that even on the Temple Mount itself, in the inner courtyard, there was a synagogue (*m. Yoma* 7:8; *Taʿan* 2:5; *Soṭa* 7:7–8). This is only one of the indicators of the fact that the Second Temple times were a transition period in the history of Judaism, as during that period Judaism reached the stage at which it could practically give up the institution of the house of God altogether (something that was impossible after 586 B.C.E., when restoration of the temple service was still absolutely essential for Israel's survival as a national group). Consequently, when the Second Temple fell, Judaism could absorb the blow without collapsing. The temple was thus turned into an eschatological symbol, to be resurrected only at the end of days, while for the ongoing daily life new frameworks and channels of communal activity were found.

Within the context of synagogue liturgy, in contradistinction to temple service, the priest has no real function. All his roles in the synagogue are only ornamental touches, reminiscent of a historical phase that preceded the emergence of the new institution. Proof of this is the fact that when no priest is present, liturgical activity can proceed without him. With the emergence of the synagogue (all the more so, with the destruction of the Second Temple), the substantial role of the priest came to an end.

Yet, even though the synagogue is mainly a gathering place for praying, prayer itself, far from being the synagogue's creation, originated in much earlier periods and, like sacrifice, is one of the earliest manifestations of human spirit. Prayer was also prevalent in the temple courts, and it is no mere coincidence that on one occasion the epithet "house of prayer" is applied to the temple by one of the prophets (Isa 56:7). In Solomon's prayer, a Deuteronomistic casting, the temple is also described as a place of prayer, while sacrifices are not even mentioned (1 Kgs 8:22–53). In the temple, however, prayer was considered a gesture

---

[7] Precisely because of its being prevalent and typical of Jewish life, the old-time writings take it for granted that the synagogue is as old as Judaism and that it was Moses who initiated it. This premise is shared not only by the midrash (*Yalqûṭ Shimʿônî*, par. 408) and the targum (*Pseudo-Jonathan* on Exod 18:20) but also by Philo (*Vita Mosis*, II, 215–16), Josephus (*Contra apionem* 2:17), and the NT (Acts 15:21). Some medieval commentators also thought along this line. However, this should not be taken as evidence for the antiquity of the institution. In fact, we have no solid proof of the existence of synagogues before the Hellenistic period (but this does not eliminate the possibility that the first spores of this institution could have already emerged toward the end of the Persian period).

of secondary order. There it was a substitute for sacrifice, a kind of "offering of the poor": *a priori*, a visitor to the temple was expected to bring an oblation to the Lord—a burnt-, peace-, or grain-offering, but in case he came empty-handed he was at least supposed to utter a prayer, which would be in the nature of substitute. Such an understanding of prayer as being secondary to sacrifice finds explicit expression in the Book of Psalms, the collection of the Jerusalem Temple prayers (at least a part of which are rooted in the conditions of the First Temple period). Thus we find a suppliant asking that his prayer "be taken like incense" before the Lord and his "upraised hands" (that is, the palms raised upward in a customary gesture of prayer) like an evening grain-offering" (Ps 141:2). When the psalmist says "accept, O Lord, the free-will offering of my mouth" (Ps 119:108) he actually awaits that his words will be as acceptable as a free-will sacrifice. When he declares that "sacrifices to God are a broken spirit" and proclaims that God "will not despise" the contrite and crushed of heart (Ps 51:19), he has no intention of renouncing sacrifices as such but merely indicates the fact that "a broken spirit" is all he can offer and sets forth his hope that this spirit will count for him as if it were a sacrifice.[8]

Within the framework of temple service, therefore, sacrifice could not usually be done without (even though certain offerings were brought as a matter of choice), while prayer was optional. The decisive fact is that whereas bringing offerings is frequently referred to in the Pentateuch as a categorical obligation, both in the priestly legislation and outside, there is actually no mention of a requirement to pray to God. The Rabbis were able to derive such a commandment from the Torah only indirectly, by explaining the verse "and to serve him with all your heart" (Deut 11:13) as referring to prayer (*Sipre Eqeb* 41).[9] In the biblical period itself, prayer belonged to the periphery of cult and in fact was

---

[8] Consequently, one cannot argue to the contrary by resorting to the previous verse: "You do not want me to bring peace-offerings, you do not desire burnt-offerings" (Ps 51:18), which seems to renounce burnt- and peace-offerings altogether. The fact of the matter is that this is only a kind of preliminary assertion made by the supplicant, who has already turned to the Lord requesting "open my lips and let my mouth declare your praise" (Ps 51:17) and thereby has already said by way of apology that, in any case, all he intended to do was only to praise his God with mouth and lips. It is in line with this tendency to pronounce the importance of prayer, not to deny the substantiality of sacrifices as such, that we must also understand statements of this kind occurring in some other psalms. Thus, my formulation of this matter comes close to that of Y. Kaufmann, *Tôlĕdôt Ha-ʾEmûnāh Ha-Yiśreʾelît* vol. II, 510, 671–74 (though it is not exactly identical with his).

[9] They took the adverbial phrase *bĕkol lebabkem*, "with all your heart" not to mean "with your utmost devotion" (as it does) but to convey a sense of instrumentality, that is, "by means of, through the agency of, your heart."

not a part of cultic activity. Its place was outside the priestly circle, which within the temple precincts held sole responsibility for all cultic matters.[10]

In this wise I have also indicated my own position concerning an important question in the study of psalmodic poetry. In certain psalms one can discern strophes containing what appears to be an answer to the petitioner's pleas, a sort of "divine response" (see, e.g., Pss 60:8–11; 85:9–14; 121:3–8). In royal psalms one can observe some indications to the effect that an oracle has been delivered to the king (e.g., Pss 2:7–9; 20:7; 21:5; 110:1, 4), while in some psalms (e.g., Pss 15; 24:3–6) we hear the sound of stern moralizing teaching. Now there are those who suggest that in such cases we come across intimations, or quotations, of words of "cultic" functionaries whose task it was to convey divine answers to petitioners and who actually were priests (while others assume that in some cases those functionaries were special cult-prophets who had their own role in the temple service). To my mind, in all these instances we can speak not of cult in the strict sense of the word but only of certain liturgical mannerisms, the place of which, as already stated, was in the temple courts, outside the actual cultic circle. There does not seem to me to be sufficient proof that some of those functionaries (conjectured in themselves) were in fact priests, and there are no grounds for claiming that under the prevailing conditions of the First Temple period, priests ever engaged in prayer.

[10] As I see it, Kaufmann (*Tôledôt Ha᾽Emûnāh*, vol. II, 476–78) was, then, quite right in describing the priestly temple service in the Bible as "a soundless worship."

MARGINAL NOTES TO THE BIBLICAL LEXICON

Moshe Held†

The Jewish Theological Seminary of America

I HEBREW חוד, חידה = AKKADIAN ḫâdu (ḫiādu), ḫittu

BIBLICAL scholars, medieval and modern alike, have long recognized that the widely attested Hebrew substantive חידה[1] and the rare expression חוד חידה[2] denote "riddle" and "to propound a riddle" respectively. The etymology of our Hebrew vocable, however, is more problematic and to this day remains unsettled. Ever since Lagarde's *Notes on the Greek Translation of the Book of Proverbs*[3] biblical scholars, with but a very few exceptions,[4] have adopted the view whereby Hebrew חידה is to be derived from the Aramaic אחידה and Syriac אוחדתא respectively.[5] In other words, the Hebrew loan word חידה, not unlike its Aramaic

---

[1] The substantive חידה is attested seventeen times in Biblical Hebrew, the earliest occurrences being Num 12:8; Judg 14:12–19 (eight times) and I Kgs 10:1.

[2] The denominative verb חוד is attested four times in Biblical Hebrew: Judg 14:12, 13,16; Ezek 17:2. The Targum and Peshitta render the Hebrew expression חוד חידה by חוד חודיתא and אחד אוחדתא respectively. The medieval translators (e.g., Saadia) and lexicographers (e.g., Ibn-Janāḥ), however, employ the very general expressions *ḥaddaṯa/aḫbara ḥadīṯan/qiṣṣatan* "to tell/relate a tale/story." Note, however, that the semantic Arabic equivalent of Hebrew חוד חידה is *ḥājā ᵓuḥjiyyatan/luġzan*. For the former, cf. e.g., Saadia on Num 12:8 (אחאדית); Ps 49:5 (מתל//חדית); 78:2 (אמתאל//אחאדית); Prov 1:6 (מתל//אחאדית); Dan 8:23 (אחאדית); Ibn-Janāḥ, *Kitāb al-uṣūl* (ed. Neubauer; Oxford, 1875) 214 (קצץ ואכבאר "tales and narratives"). For the latter, see Lane, *Arabic-English Lexicon* I/2, 523; *ibid.*, I/7, 2664.

[3] P. de Lagarde, *Anmerkungen zur Griechischen Übersetzung der Proverbien* (Leipzig, 1863) 73.

[4] See *BDB*, 295a, 1092a; König, *HAW zum AT* (Leipzig, 1922) 105b (Note, however, that Hebrew חוד has nothing to do with Arabic *ḥāda* "to turn aside"!).

[5] For earlier literature, cf. e.g., E. Kautzsch, *Aramaismen* (Halle, 1902), 30–31; *GB*,[17] 226a; J. A. Montgomery, *Daniel* (ICC, Edinburgh, 1927) 260–61. For more recent literature, cf. e.g., W. Rudolph, *Esra und Nehemia* (HAT, vol. XX, Tübingen, 1949) 138; M. Wagner, *Aramaismen* (BZAW 96, Berlin, 1966), 55–56 (No. 100–1); *KBL*[3] 283b, 296b.

counterpart אֲחִידָה, goes back to the root אחז־אחד, and allegedly denotes "that which is 'held in' or 'fast'"[6] (Passive participle from אחד־אחז!). The uncritical acceptance by a majority of modern Biblical scholars notwithstanding, this widely accepted philological interpretation carries little conviction and is untenable on several counts. First, if Hebrew חידה is indeed a very early loan word[7] from Aramaic אחז־אחד one would expect in early Hebrew the form חיזה (not חידה!) since Proto-Semitic ḏ > z in Old Aramaic and only in Late Aramaic does ḏ > d.[8] Second, the alleged semantic rationale whereby the meaning of חידה "enigma," ultimately derives from אחז־אחד connoting "to fasten, to bar (gates)" (Neh 7:3) is far-fetched and unconvincing.[9] Third, the Aramaic vocable אֲחִידָה "riddle" (Dan 5:12) can hardly be labeled as "typical of the Aramaic wisdom [literature],"[10] since its attestation in Aramaic wisdom literature is altogether problematic.[11]

It would appear that biblical scholarship has hitherto overlooked the fact that the Akkadian substantive ḫittu (< *ḫidtu) and the verb ḫâdu (< ḫiādu) may shed some light on the problem under consideration. In fact, one may surmise that we are confronted here with a case where the Akkadian and Hebrew vocables are bound to elucidate one another. While there is no denying that ḫittu and ḫâdu are attested, for the most part, in lexical texts, the fact remains that the meaning of our Akkadian vocables can be ascertained with a fair degree of certainty. Thus, in the lexical text Izi-išātu Tablet V:31–33 we read: I.BI.LU = ḫittu; I.BI.LU = tēltu; I.BI.LU.DUG₄.GA = ḫiādu.[12] The Akkadian Dictionaries take ḫittu and ḫâdu to denote "utterance" and "to make an utterance" respectively.[13] It stands to reason, however, to assume that the meaning of our vocables may be more precisely defined as "riddle" and "to make an enigmatic utterance" respectively. This assumption gains much in probability when it is realized that the sequence I.BI.LU = ḫittu, tēltu is to be equated with the Hebrew מָשָׁל־חִידָה "proverb-riddle" attested five times in Biblical Hebrew.[14] Observe that the equation of Akkadian tēltu with Hebrew מָשָׁל

[6] Montgomery, *Daniel*, 260; cf. already, Kautzsch, *Aramaismen* 31.

[7] See Kautzsch, *Aramaismen*, 31; Montgomery, *Daniel* 260.

[8] See H. L. Ginsberg "The Northwest Semitic Languages," *The World History of the Jewish People* (Vol. II: ed. B. Mazar: Tel Aviv, 1970) 122.

[9] Contrast Kautzsch, *Aramaismen*, 31; Montgomery, *Daniel*, 260; Rudolph, *Esra und Nehemia*, 138; Wagner, *Aramaismen*, 55.

[10] Montgomery, *Daniel*, 260.

[11] Observe that אחדי in Aḥiqar 99 (A. Cowley, *Aramaic Papyri* Oxford, 1923) 215 may perhaps be rendered "secrets" (see H. L. Ginsberg, *ANET*³ 428b), but its equation with Hebrew חיאה "riddle" can in no way be viewed as substantiated.

[12] *MSL* 13 (1971), 161; cf. Izi J i:5 AŔ.RI = ḫittum (*MSL* 13, 212); note also Nabnitu v:11 [I.BI.L]U = ḫittum.

[13] See *CAD*, Ḫ, 28a, 208b; cf. *AHw*, 342b, 350a.

[14] Ezek 17:2; Hab 2:6; Ps 49:5; 78:2; Prov 1:6.

is fully corroborated by juxtaposing the Old Babylonian (Mari) formula *kīma tēltim ullītim ša ummāmi* "As the ancient proverb which says"[15] with its Hebrew counterpart כאשר יאמר משל הקדמני "As the ancient proverb says."[16] It will be recalled that the Akkadian formula is employed by Šamši-Adad to introduce his widely quoted but as yet not fully understood proverb concerning the bitch (*kalbatum*) and her litter of blind puppies (*huppudūtum*).[17] In a similar vein, the Hebrew formula is employed by David to introduce his equally problematic proverb concerning wicked deeds emanating from wicked men (מרשעים יצא רשע וג') during his encounter with King Saul.[18] A glance at these two formulas makes it abundantly clear that they are identical in every respect. In other words, the Hebrew כאשר יאמר משל הקדמני is to be equated with, and is in no way different in meaning from the Akkadian *kīma tēltim ullītim ša ummāmi*. Thus, since *tēltu* is the exact semantic equivalent of משל, it stands to reason that Akkadian *ḫittu* is likewise the exact equivalent, both semantically and etymologically of Hebrew חידה. Furthermore,

---

[15] ARM I, 5:10-11. As far as can be ascertained this formula is unique in Akkadian literature, its closest parallel being *kīma ša tēltim ša <ummāmi>* "Like the proverb which <says>" (ARM X, 150:8-9); note also *ABL* 403:4-5, 13-14 *ina tēlte (tēltimma) ša pî (nišī šakin umma* "In the popular proverb it says"; see W. G. Lambert, *BWL* (Oxford, 1960) 281.

[16] I Sam 24:14; note that many scholars (cf. e.g., H. P. Smith *Samuel* [ICC, Edinburgh, 1899] 219; W. Nowack, *Samuel* [HKAT, Göttingen, 1902] 122; M. H. Segal, *Samuel* [In Hebrew; Jerusalem, 1956] 191) read הקדמנים "the ancients" in the plural, the omission of the final מ being due to a haplography before מרשעים. Indeed, such a reading is now attested in 4Q Samᵃ. The Old Babylonian (Mari) formula, however, surely points in the direction of כאשר יאמר ה[מ]משל הקדמני "As the ancient proverb says"!

[17] See the illuminating remarks of W. L. Moran, "Puppies in Proverbs—From Šamši-Adad I to Archilochus?" in the H. L. Ginsberg festschrift (*EI* 14, Jerusalem, 1978) 32*ff.

[18] This proverb is problematic indeed and can hardly be viewed as a proverb in the strict sense. The silence of many scholars notwithstanding (cf. e.g., S. R. Driver, *Notes on the Hebrew Text of Samuel* [Oxford, 1913] 194), the MT seems to contain the moral of a proverb rather than the proverb itself which must have been accidentally omitted. It is not excluded that some such proverb is to be sought in the parallel text (I Sam 26:20). Following the suggestion of Wellhausen (*Samuel*, GoRttingen, 1871) 130, most scholars omit 24:14 as a late interpolation (cf. e.g., K. Budde, *Samuel* [SBOT VIII, Leipzig, 1894] 71; O. Thenius, *Samuel* [Leipzig, 1898] 104, and many others). Such an arbitrary solution, however, can hardly be sanctioned today. There is surely little gain in pursuing arbitrary emendations such as the one put forth by Tur-Sinai (*Lesh* 22 [1958] 6; idem, *The Plain Meaning of the Biblical Text*, Vol. II [In Hebrew, Jerusalem 1964] 177). Here it will suffice to note that his attempt to discard the expression משל הקדמני is refuted by its Old Babylonian forerunner *tēltum ullītum*, discussed in this paper.

Sumerian I.BI.LU.DUG₄.GA (= ḫiādu)[19] may be literally rendered into Akkadian as *ḫitta qabû. Since Sumerian I.BI.LU and DUG₆.GA equal Akkadian ḫittu and qabû respectively, such a rendering can hardly be off the mark. Thus, the Akkadian ḫiādu = *ḫitta qabû calls to mind the semantically equivalent Hebrew expression הגיד חידה[20] = Aramaic אחוי אחידה[21] (= Arabic aḫbara 'uḫjiyyatan).[22] As far as can be ascertained, the substantive ḫittu "riddle" is nowhere in evidence outside of the lexical texts. Note, however, that the verb ḫâdu "to make an enigmatic utterance" is attested in a Standard Babylonian prayer to Marduk published by W. G. Lambert.[23] Thus, apuḫḫu[24] anūnu[25] ḫattu pirittu ṭardūšumma unassû nizmassu iḫtīdamma[26] marṣāku ibakkīka should probably be rendered as follows: ". . . fear, panic, terror are dispatched against him and so make his wish remote; He relates to you perplexingly:[27] 'I am miserable' while shedding tears to you."[28]

---

[19] Izi-išātu V:33 (MSL 13 [1971] 161).

[20] Judg 14:12, 14, 15, 16, 17, 19.

[21] Dan 5:12; cf. חוי חודיתא (Targum on Judg 14:12 ff.).

[22] Note that Saadia renders אחוית אחידן in Dan 5:12 as ירוי אלאחאדית "who relates tales"; see above note 2.

[23] AfO 19 (1959–60) 58, ll. 127–29.

[24] The substantive apuḫḫu is attested only here and its exact meaning cannot be determined with any degree of certainty. Context and parallelism, however, call for some vocable denoting "dismay," "consternation" or the like; see AHw 62b; CAD A/II 205a; contrast Langdon (OECT 6 62, n. 5) whose etymology and rendering must be rejected.

[25] Cf. the expression anūna kullumu "to make S.O. experience fear" attested in a Standard Babylonian prayer to Ištar (AfO 19 [1959–60] 51, l. 74); see AHw 55b; CAD A/II 150a.

[26] Whether the identical cluster iḫ-ti-dam-ma in the great Hymn to Nabû (ZA 4 [1889] 239, l. 38) belongs here (Lambert, AfO 19 [1959–60] 58, note on line 129; AHw 342b, sub. ḫiādu) remains uncertain mainly because of the lacunae in the text. It should be noted that von Soden (ZA 61 [1971] 56, l. 151) is now inclined to read our cluster as iḫtīṭamma (from ḫiāṭu/ḫâṭu "to trace, examine, investigate"). Nevertheless, one cannot help feeling that the context and tone of this segment of the Hymn clerly point in the direction of a derivation from ḫiādu/ḫâdu "to relate perplexingly."

[27] Observe that renderings of our verb such as "to mutter" (Lambert, AfO 19 [1959–60] 58), or "to utter" (AHw 342b) are imprecise. On the other hand, Langdon's reading and translation iḫ-ti-ṭam-ma (from ḫaṭû) "he sinned" (OECT 6, 63, l. 10) are untenable; Correct the translation given in CAD B, 37a, meaning 2, accordingly.

[28] After this study was completed, I noticed that W. G. Lambert (AfO 19 [1959–60] 58, note on line 129) correctly observed that the verb ḫiādu is "perhaps related to the Hebrew ḥîdah, ḥûd." I wish to give full credit to Prof. Lambert who has anticipated me on this point.

II HEBREW מִיץ (PROV 30:33) = AKKADIAN *māṣu*

Biblical scholars, medieval and modern alike, have long recognized that Hebrew attests to three roots 1) מצץ, 2) מצה, 3) מיץ. While the meaning and etymology of מצץ "to suck" and מצה "to drain" are fairly well established, the meaning and etymology of מיץ in Prov 30:33 have constituted thorny problems to ancient and modern scholars alike. The verb מצץ "to suck, draw" is on all counts recognized in the moving and tender prophecy in Isa 66:10–11: "Rejoice with Jerusalem and be glad for her, all you who care for her! Join in her jubilation, all you who mourned over her" למען תינקו ושבעתם משד תנחמיה למען תמצו והתענגתם מזיז כבודה "That you may suck from her breast consolation to the full, that you may draw from her teat[1] glory to your delight." The synonymity of ינק-מצץ is supported by etymology and is further corroborated by the parallel text in Isa 60:16.[2] It has long been recognized that the very same pair *ynq//mṣṣ* is attested in Ugaritic[3] where the poet states concerning Keret's son Yaṣṣib: *ynq ḥlb a[t̠]rt mṣṣ t̠d btlt [ᶜnt]*[4] "who shall suck the milk of Ashera, draw from the breasts of Maiden Anath."[5] The

---

[1] To judge by context and parallelism, a vocable denoting "breast" or "udder" is desiderated. The interpretation of some of the medieval scholars whereby זיז is a synonym of זיו "splendor" (cf. Qimḥi זיו מקומו לפי עניינו) is merely an intelligent guess. The widely accepted rendering of זיז is as "abundance" (see the commentaries) may likewise go back to the medievals (cf. Targum מחמד יקרה; Saadia מן לדיד כרמהא). Note, however, that the alleged Akkadian *zāzu denoting "abundance" is the result of a misreading (see H. Cohen, *Biblical Hapaxlegomena* [SBLDS 37; Missoula, 1978] 89, n. 220). The reading ביז (< Aramaic ביזא "breast") is gratuitous in view of the Akkadian (Neo-Assyrian) *zīzu* "teat"; see the detailed remarks by Cohen, *Biblical Hapaxlegomena* 46 and cf. Streck, *Assurbanipal* (Leipzig, 1916) 348, 1. 8 *erbi zīzēša ina pîka šaknā 2 tenniq 2 taḫallip ana panīka* "Her (Ištar depicted as a cow) four teats are placed in your mouth (Assurbanipal's), you suck at two, and two you milk for yourself."

[2] Whether the problematic המץ in Isa 16:4 belongs here (cf. Ibn-Janāḥ, *Kitāb al-uṣūl* [ed. A. Neubauer: Oxford, 1875] 373, 386) is uncertain. In parallelism with שדד and רמס one surely expects here חמץ or חמוץ "despoiler, marauder"; cf. חומץ in Ps 71:4 (see F. Perles, *Analekten* [München, 1895] 69–70; B. Duhm, *Jesaja*[5] [Göttingen, 1968] 129) and Akkadian *ḥamāṣu* "to strip off (clothes)," "to rob, despoil" (= Hebrew פשט!); note particularly the West Semitic form *ḥamūšam iḥmuṣ* "he despoiled greatly" in Yaḥdunlim's Šamaš inscription (*Syria* 32 [1955] 14, ii:19).

[3] See *Lesh.* 18 (1953) 148, § § 15.

[4] III K 2:26–27; see *Lesh.* 18 (1953) 146, § 6.

[5] Cf. En. el. I:85–6: *ītenniqma* (var. *ultenniqšūma*) *ṣerrēt ištarāti tārītu ittarrûšu pulḫāta ušmallī<šu>* "He (Marduk) used to suck the breasts of Goddesses, a (divine) nurse that was guiding him covered <him> with awesomeness."

distribution for *mṣṣ* is as follows: Akk. *naṣābu(m)*;[6] Ug. *mṣṣ*; Aramaic-Syriac מצץ; Arabic *maṣṣa/imtaṣṣa*.

The verb מצה "to drain" is attested seven times in Biblical Hebrew,[7] including three occurances in similar contexts dealing with draining (a drink or a cup) to the dregs; all three verses exhibit the sequence of שתה//מצה.[8] The most celebrated occurrence is attested in Isa 51:17ff. in a most eloquent, prophetic literary piece assuring Jerusalem that she will never again drink the cup of the Lord's poisonous draught which she has drained to the dregs: התעוררי התעוררי קומי ירושלם אשר שתית מיד ה' את כוס חמתו את קבעת [כוס[9] התרעלה [שתית] מצית "Gather strength, gather strength![10] Arise, O Jerusalem, you who from the Lord's hand have

---

See already, H. L. Ginsberg, *The Legend of King Keret* (*BASOR* Sup. St. 2–3; New Haven, 1946) 41; idem, *BASOR* 97 (1945) 9.

[6] See *AHw* 755a; cf. *CAD* N/II 33; note particularly the sequence of *šizba enēqu-šizba naṣābu* "to suck milk"-"to draw milk" in Ḫḫ Tab. 13:343–44 (see *MSL* 8/I [1960] 49). It should be noted in passing that the Arabic etymology suggested by von Soden for our vocable is problematic since *naḍaba* denotes "to be absorbed," "to dry up" and the like, but seems to have nothing to do with the notion of "to suck" (= *raḍiᶜa, maṣṣa* in Arabic).

[7] Lev 1:15; 5:9 ("to drain out blood"; note Saadia's ימצי "he will remove" for the expected ייעצר!); Judg 6:38 ("to drain out dew"). Whether ימצה in the problematic verse Ps 73:10 belongs here is uncertain (see the commentaries). Note that many scholars are inclined to derive our verb from מצץ (cf. e.g., H. Gunkel, *Die Psalmen* [Göttingen, 1926] 311, 318 and see most recently M. Dahood, *Psalms II* [AB XVII; Garden City, 1968] 190; cf. *KBL*³ 590b) while others, following LXX, would derive it from מצא (cf. e.g., B. Duhm, *Psalmen* [KHC XIV; Leipzig, 1899] 190).

[8] Isa 51:17; Ezek 23:34; Ps 75:9.

[9] For the correct explanatory gloss כוס defining the rare and poetic קבעת, see H. L. Ginsberg, *JBL* 62 (1943) 111; cf. most recently H. Cohen, *Biblical Hapax-legomena* 85, n. 200. It stands to reason that שתית in v. 17c is likewise an explanatory gloss defining the rare verb מצית; cf. מצה//שתה in Ezek 23:34 and Ps 75:9.

[10] Read, with H. L. Ginsberg (oral communication) התעודדי for MT התעוררי; cf. the same sequence קום-התעודד (in reversed order) in Ps 20:9; observe that Ginsberg's suggested reading gains much in probability in view of the very same sequence *ᶜdd-qwm* attested in Ugaritic (II AB 3:11–13; see Cassuto, *Biblical and Oriental Studies*, Vol. II [Jerusalem, 1975] 55 and contrast most recently J. C. L. Gibson, *CML*² [Edinburgh, 1978] 58 whose reading, etymology and translation must be rejected by any serious student of Ugaritic). It may be noted that the Ugaritic verbs *ᶜwd* and *ᶜdd* must strictly be kept apart (contrast C. H. Gordon *UT* [Rome, 1965] 19.1819 and 19.1832). The former, a Hitpolel from *ᶜwd* and a synonym of *qwm*, denotes "to stand erect," while the latter, an ע"ע verb and a synonym of *lʾk* (II AB 7:45–47; cf. III AB B:22, 26, 28, 30, 40–41, 44) denotes "to send (a message), to dispatch (a delegation)"; see H. L. Ginsberg in *EI* V (Mazar Volume; Jerusalem, 1958) 62*b and cf. my remarks in *EI* IX (Albright Volume; Jerusalem, 1969) 72*, n. 15. In view of our observations it becomes abundantly

drunk the cup of His poisonous draught,[11] you who have drained to the dregs[12] the chalice[13] [the cup] of venom." The interdialectal distribution

---

clear that Hebrew (עודד(התֹ) cannot be etymologically equated with the Ugaritic verb ǵdd (V AB B:25-26; contrast C. H. Gordon, *UT*, 19.1947). For the latter verb see U. Cassuto, *The Goddess Anath* (Jerusalem, 1971) 88-89, 119-20. While Cassuto's interpretation is certainly correct, his Arabic etymology (ǵadda "to be swollen") remains conjectural. Note, however, that context and parallelism reveal that Ugaritic ǵdd is semantically to be equated with the Akkadian verbs elēṣu and ḫabāṣu both denoting "to swell" and "to rejoice, be elated" (see *CAD* E 88b). It should further be noted that Ugaritic ǵdd has nothing to do with the problematic התעררתי in Job 31:29 (contrast *BHS* Job and Prov 33) where the correct reading is, in all probability, התרעעתי "I exalted"; cf. Targum יכבית and see the commentaries (e.g., S. R. Driver, *Job*, II [ICC; Edinburgh, 1950] 226f.; N. H. Tur-Sinai, *Job* [Jerusalem, 1957] 444-45).

[11] Note that the primary meaning of חמה (= Akkadian *imtu*) is "poisonous foam" which comes to denote "wrath, anger." This semantic development becomes readily apparent when viewed in the light of Akkadian *imtu*, the primary meaning of which is poisonous foam forming at the mouth of a raging god, demon or animal (see *CAD* I 140-41). For a similar case in point, cf. Hebrew קצף "foam" (Hos 10:7) which likewise connotes "wrath, anger." (See H. Cohen, *Biblical Hapaxlegomena*, 24-25 and cf. my remarks in *EI* 16 [Orlinsky Volume; Jerusalem, 1982] 84, n 82). Here it will suffice to juxtapose the following Hebrew expressions with their Akkadian counterparts: 1) Hebrew חמת תנינים/חמת נחש "snakes' venom/vipers' venom" (Ps 58:5; Deut 32:33) = Akkadian *imat bašmi/imat ṣēri* (e.g., Erra I:38; LKU 33:23); 2) Hebrew שפך חצה "to pour out venom/wrath" (e.g., Isa 42:25; Jer 10:25 = Ps 79:6) = Akkadian *imta tabāku/salāḫu* (e.g., J. Büllenrücher, *Nergal* 24, ll. 30-31; R. Borger, *Asarhaddon*, 87, l. 12); 3) Hebrew השקה חמה "to give to drink venomous draught" (Jer 25:15) = Akkadian *šaqû ša imti* (Nabnitu L:271-72; see *CAD* I 139a, lexical section); 4) Hebrew מלא חמה "to be filled with venom" (Isa 51:20; Jer 6:11) = Akkadian *imta malû/mullû* (e.g., En. el. II:22; Šurpu VII:21-22).

[12] It is amazing that a majority of the medieval philologists, whose ears were particularly attuned to matters of balance and parallelism, should fail to realize that קבעת is but a poetic synonym of כוס. It would seem that etymology had led astray luminaries such as Saadia, Rashi, Ibn-Janāḥ, Ibn-Ezra and Qimḥi. There is no denying that some of them attempted to relate our קבעת to the Late Hebrew קבע "to settle." In other words, קבעת, according to this derivation, denotes the dregs that settle to the bottom of the cup! Thus, while Saadia (Derenbourg, *Version Arabe D'Isaïe* [Paris, 1896] 79) and Ibn-Janāḥ (*Kitāb al-uṣūl* 624) merely render קבעת as תֹפל "dregs" and תֹפל ודרדֹ "dregs and lees" respectively, Ibn-Ezra clearly states that קבעת אין רע לו ויא' השמרים שיקבעו למטה "The word קבעת is a hapax legomenon; some take it to denote the dregs that settle (קבע = "to settle") to the bottom [of the cup]" (see his commentary on Isa [ed. M. Friedländer; London, 1873] 88). So too, Rashi states: קבעת אלו השמרים הקבועים בתחתית הכלי "The word קבעת denotes the dregs that are ומצית יורה עליו כמה שנאמר שמריה ימצו fixed to the bottom of the container as is indicated by the verb ומצית and is corroborated by שמר יה ימצו (Ps 75:9)." Nevertheless, J. Skinner (*Isaiah*, vol. II

for *mṣy* would seem to be as follows: Akk. *nazalu;*[14] Ug. X; Aramaic-Syriac מצי (עצר); Arabic *ᶜaṣara/našafa.*[15]

A glance at the various Biblical lexicons reveals that scholars are perplexed regarding the etymology and meaning of the isolated מיץ in Prov 30:33. As a matter of fact, not a single modern Biblical dictionary or commentary suggests the correct etymology and exact meaning of our vocable. It is sad to note that this state of affairs prevails despite the fact that such an etymology and interpretation had been proposed some twenty-five years ago.[16] It would appear that the misconceptions and erroneous etymologies surrounding the isolated מיץ are due to the following three factors. First, Biblical scholarship has failed to recognize that the isolated verb מיץ is neither etymologically nor semantically related, in any way, to the verbs מצץ "to suck" or מצה "to drain."[17] Second, Biblical scholarship has, wittingly or unwittingly, overlooked the basically sound

---

[CBSC; Cambridge, 1906] 113) is not justified in asserting that "'dregs' is a mistaken Jewish (sic.) rendering of a word קבעת found only here and in v. 22." For it is a fact not to be overlooked that *Tg. Jonathan* indeed renders קבעת correctly as פיילי namely "bowl" (< Greek φιάλη); cf. also *Tg.Ps.-J* Judg 5:25 (גברייא בפיילי) and Amos 6:6 (בפילוון דכסף) and see Qimḥi, *Lexicon* (Berlin, 1847) 320a. As a matter of fact, Rashi (cf. also Qimḥi, *loc. cit.*) refers to the rendering of the Targum, but he too opts for the misleading etymological interpretation noted above. Observe, however, that another Biblical scholar of the French school, namely Eliezer of Beaugency (12th century) had correctly noted that קבעת must denote a container of some sort. In his own words קובעת מלשו' קובע דבר חלול ועמוק ובית קבול "The word קבעת is related to קובע, something hollow and deep, and a receptacle" (his commentary on *Isaiah* [ed. J. W. Nutt; London, 1879] 124). For a similar interpretation, see S. D. Luzzatto, *Commentary on Isaiah* (reprint; Tel Aviv, 1970) 351.

[13] For the pair *ks//qb ᶜt* in Biblical Hebrew and in Ugaritic, see U. Casutto, *Biblical and Oriental Studies*, Vol. II, 50; on the Canaanite *qb ᶜt* "chalice" and its alleged cognates in Egyptian and Akkadian, see H. Cohen, *Biblical Hapaxlegomena*, 86–87, nn. 205, 208.

[14] See *AHw* 771b; *CAD* N/II 134–35. Note that *nazālu* is attested in contexts dealing with draining of waters only (= Arabic *nazaḥa*). Whether this Akkadian vocable could be employed in contexts dealing with draining a cup remains uncertain.

[15] Cf. Saadia's rendering of מצית in Isa 51:17 as נשפתיה "you sucked it up"; see Derenbourg, *Version*, 79.

[16] See my remarks in *JAOS* 79 (1959) 171.

[17] Contrast the standard Hebrew Lexicons; cf. e.g., *GB*[17] 420 (מיץ), 452a (מצה) and 454a (מצץ); *KBL*[3] 547 (מיץ), 587b (מצה) and 590b (מצץ). Note that the contamination of מיץ-מצה-מצץ is already in evidence among the medieval Hebrew philologists; cf. Saadia's translation of Ps 75:9 ישתו כל רשעי ארץ אך שמריה ימצו as חתّٰي ימצّونהא ויקינא גّמיع טלחא אלארץֹ ישרבון מן דר(א)ּٰהא "Surely the wicked of the earth shall drink from its dregs until they suck it out" (מצץ!) (see his translation of the *Psalms* [ed. Qapeḥ; Jerusalem, 1966] 180); cf. also Ibn-Ezra's commentary

interpretation of our vocable by the two giants of medieval Bible scholarship, namely, Saadia Gaon and Ibn-Janāḥ. Indeed both make it abundantly clear that the Hebrew מִיץ in Prov 30:33 denotes "churning (milk)" and is thus to be semantically equated with the Arabic *maḥaḍa* similarly meaning "to churn (milk)."[18] Third, Biblicists[19] and Assyriologists[20] alike, have failed to note that the rare Akkadian verb *mâṣu* "to churn milk"[21] is to be equated both semantically and etymologically with Hebrew מִיץ and that the Akkadian and Hebrew vocables are bound to elucidate each other. As to the contribution of the medievals, it will suffice to quote here Saadia's rendering of Prov 30:33 on the one hand, and Ibn-Janāḥ's utterly convincing philological interpretation, on the other. Thus, Prov 30:33 in Saadia's Arabic translation reads as follows:[22]

פאנה כמא אן מכ֗ץ אללבן יכרג֗ זבדא ומכ֗ץ אלאנף יכרג֗ דמא כד֗אך מכ֗ץ אלגצ֗ב יכרג֗ כֿצומֿהֿ "For as the churning of milk produces ghee, and the churning of the nose produces blood so the churning of wrath produces strife."[23] Ibn-Janāḥ's philological comment is worth quoting here, albeit in an abbreviated form: מעני מיץ חלב מכ֗ץ . . . ואעלם א֗ן אצל אלמכ֗ץ אנמא הו תחריך אללבן פי אלממכ֗ץ פאסתעיר פי גיר אללבן אתֿסאעא "The meaning of מִיץ חלב is churning (milk) . . . be cognizant (of the fact) that the essence of churning is rather the stirring of the milk in the churn and (only) by

---

on Isa 51:17 (שרשים!) מצית מגזרת למען תמצו ואם הם שנים בנים (בנינים) "The verb מצית should be compared with תמצו (Isa 66:11) despite the fact that they are of different roots (text: "conjugations" which is obviously a scribal error) (see his commentary on *Isaiah* [ed. Friedländer] 88); note also Qimḥi, *Lexicon* 191a (מיץ) and 199b (מצה); Alfasi, *Kitab Jami Al-Alfaz* II (ed. S. L. Scoss; New Haven, 1945) 225 (מץ).

[18] See Lane, *Arabic-English Lexicon* I/7, 2693; cf. *JAOS* 79 (1959) 171, nn. 42, 43.

[19] It will suffice to note here that Akkadian *mâṣu* is nowhere in evidence in the latest edition of Koehler-Baumgartner, *Hebräisches und Aramäisches Lexikon zum AT* (see *KBL*³, vol. II [Leiden, 1974] 547 [מיץ]).

[20] It comes as no surprise that *CAD* (M/I 350b) offers no etymology for *mâṣu* since that dictionary rarely posits any etymology. It is remarkable, however, that Hebrew מיץ is wanting from von Soden's dictionary since it abounds in etymologies of all sorts, our verb *mâṣu* being no exception (see AHw 621b with a misleading Ugaritic etymology!).

[21] *AHw* 621b; 726a; *CAD* M/I 350b; *CAD* N/I 220a.

[22] J. Derenbourg-M. Lambert, *Version Arabe des Proverbes* (Paris, 1894) 195 = J. Qapeḥ, *Saadia's Translation of Proverbs* (Jerusalem, 1976) 262.

[23] It is instructive to juxtapose Saadia's rendering of Prov 30:33a with those put forward by the two celebrated recent translations of the Hebrew Bible. Thus, the NEB (1970) renders כי מיץ חלב יוציא חמאה as "For wringing out the milk produces curd" while the NJPS (1982) has: "As milk under pressure produces butter." It must be candidly stated that both of these translations are found wanting when weighed against the one of Saadia.

extension is it metaphorically employed of matters other than milk."[24] While there is no denying the fact that Akkadian *mâṣu* "to churn (milk)" is, for the most part, attested in lexical texts only, the fact remains that its meaning is now firmly established and fully corroborated by its Hebrew counterpart.[25] Thus, in the Old Babylonian Lexical text Proto-Ea (*MSL* 2 [1951], p. 146 IV: 39–40) we read: du-un = BÚR = *nâšu*[m]; du-un = BÚR = *mâṣum*.[26] So too, Diri Tablet II, I:48, 58 du-du = BÚR.BÚR = *mâṣu*; du-du = BÚR.BÚR = *nâšu*.[27] These equations of the Sumerian DUN with the Akkadian verbs *mâṣu* and *nâšu* "to churn" and "to shake" respectively are hardly surprising when it is borne in mind that the process of churning milk in primitive cultures involves shaking.[28] This assertion is buttressed by Arabic *maḥaḍa* which likewise denotes both "to churn" and "to shake."[29] Not unexpectedly the lexical texts also attest to the maqtal>naqtal *namāṣu* denoting "churn, churning jar." Thus, Hg. Tablet II:70 reads: DUG ^šá-ki-ir URU×GU = *šakirru* = *namāṣu ša šizbi*.[30] It is quite clear that *namāṣu* is the semantic equivalent of the Arabic maqtal *mimḥaḍun/mimḥaḍatun* "churn."[31] As far as can be ascertained, the verb *mâṣu* "to churn (milk)" is, outside of the lexical texts, attested only in a Standard Babylonian bilingual Hymn to Enlil published by Reisner.[32] Thus, UMUN ^dMU.UL.LÍL.LA GA NU. DUN.DUN DUG.ŠAKIR.RA I.BÍ.IN.DÉ *bēlum* ^dMIN *šizibbi lā mâṣi ina šakirri tašpuk* "O Lord Enlil, you have poured into the churning jar[33] milk which cannot be churned." At this point is should be noted that the lexical text Ea Tablet VIII/2 :158–61[34] attests to the following equation: du-u = BÚR = *daʾāpu* = du[ʾʾupu] = *mâṣu* = nâ[šu] "Sumerian 'dun' is to be equated with the Akkadian verbs denoting 'to press,' 'to compress,' 'to churn' and 'to shake.'" It stands to reason that this equation may shed light on the expression אף מיץ in Prov 30:33b. For while מיץ חלב is to be equated with Akkadian *mâṣu ša šizbi* "churning milk," one is on shakier ground concerning מיץ אף. It will be recalled that Saadia renders מיץ אף

---

[24] *Kitāb al-uṣūl* 373 = *Sepher Haschoraschim* (ed. W. Bacher; Berlin, 1896) 260; cf. Alfāsi, *Kitāb Jāmiᶜ Al-Alfaẓ* II 205.

[25] See *JAOS* 79 (1959) 171.

[26] See now *MSL* 14 (1979) 121.

[27] B. Meissner, MAOG 3/3 (1929) 6, I:48, 58; cf. Proto-Diri 90: BÚ.BÚR = *mâṣum*.

[28] See n. 25 above.

[29] See n. 18 above.

[30] *MSL* 7 (1959) 110; cf. *JAOS* 79 (1959) 171, n. 44.

[31] See *Kitāb al-uṣūl* 373 (מיץ); cf. Lane, *Arabic-English Lexicon* I/7 2695.

[32] SBH 130 (No. I): 12–13; for the transliteration and translation, see *JAOS* 79 (1959) 171, n. 44.

[33] On the Sumerian loan-word *šakirru* "jar" see B. Landsberger, *MSL* 2 (1951) 117, P4; cf. *MSL* 9 (1967) 191, 1. 249; see now *AHw* 1140a.

[34] See now *MSL* 14 (1979) 501.

as מכץ אלאנף while Ibn-Janāḥ asserts that מיץ "to churn milk" may metaphorically be extended to include matters other than milk.[35] Indeed, the Akkadian evidence would seem to point in the direction of מיץ אף connoting pressure applied to the nose. This assumption may gain in probability when we note that *daʾāpu-duʾʾpu* "to press, to compress" and *nâšu-nûššu* "to shake, to dislodge" are not infrequently attested in contexts dealing with pressure applied to various parts of the body, or dislocation thereof, such as *irtu* "chest,"[36] *šinnu* "teeth"[37] and, most significantly, *appu* "nose."[38] Thus, Prov 30:33 may be rendered as follows: "For as the churning of milk produces ghee, and the pressing of the nose produces blood, so the stirring up of wrath[39] produces strife."[40]

[35] Observe that Alfāsi (*Kitāb Jāmiᶜ Al-Alfāẓ* II 205) interprets מיץ (חלב) as מכֹץ "churning (of milk)," מיץ (אף) as עצר "compressing (of the nose)" while מיץ (אפים) he takes to denote חרכֹה "stirring up (of wrath)."

[36] Cf. e.g., Maqlû I: 98 *irta daʾāpu* "to compress the chest//*eṣenṣēra kapāpu* "to bend the spine"; for other references see *CAD* D 1.

[37] Cf. e.g., STT 279:1 *šinnāšu nuššāma dama iḫillā* "His teeth are dislodged and do exude blood"; for other references see *CAD* N/II 115, meaning 5.

[38] See S. Parpola, *LAS*, No. 252 (ABL 108) r. 7–13 *lippī . . . ina muḫḫi naḫnaḫete ša appi ummudū naḫnaḫutu udaʾʾupū ištu pani damū uṣṣūni* "They lean the tampons against the cartilage of the nose compressing the cartilage (of the nose) and that is why the blood keeps running."

[39] Observe that many modern scholars view Prov 30:33c as a gloss (cf. e.g., Müller-Kautzsch, *Proverbs* [SBOT XV; Leipzig-Baltimore, 1901] 68; R. B. Y. Scott, *Proverbs* [AB 18; Garden City, 1965] 182). Such an arbitrary solution, however, does not seem to recommend itself; cf. A. B. Ehrlich, *Randglossen*, vol. 6 (Leipzig, 1913) 173–74.

[40] See n. 35 above.

A DIFFICULT CURSE IN AQHT (19 [1 Aqht] 3.152-154)

Delbert R. Hillers
Dept. of Near Eastern Studies
The Johns Hopkins University

A FTER burying his son, Aqhat, the distraught father visits those places where he suspects the lad met his end, and curses each. Though many details of the passage remain obscure, the curses on the last two towns are intelligible in their main lines. In the imprecation against *Mrrt-tǵll-bnr*, the personified place is thought of as a plant, whose root and top are to perish.[1] *Ablm* in turn is to be made blind.[2] But the curse on the first place visited, *Qr-mym*, is more difficult, and probably even the general sense has so far escaped us.

152. - - - - - *ylkm.qr.mym.d*⸢*lk*⸣
153. *mḫṣ.aqht.ǵzr.amd.grbtil*
154. ⸢*nt.brḥ.p*⸤*lm.h.*⸤*nt.pdr* [.*dr*]

"Woe to you, Qor-maym,[3]
For by you was slain Aqhat the hero.
(May) - - - - - - - - - - - - - -
Now, yesterday, and forever;
Now and forevermore."[4]

---

[1] For this curse, cf. e.g., Eshmunazor (*KAI* 14) lines 11–12 and H. L. Ginsberg, "'Roots Below and Fruit Above' and Related Matters," in *Hebrew and Semitic Studies Presented to G. R. Driver*, ed. D. W. Thomas and W. D. McHardy (Oxford: Clarendon, 1963) 72–76.

[2] Cf., e.g., Sefire I (*KAI* 222) 39.

[3] Probably "Well of Water."

[4] Translation of *brḥ* as "yesterday" follows the implied suggestion of W. F. Albright, "The Psalm of Habakkuk," in *Studies in Old Testament Prophecy*, ed. H. H. Rowley (Edinburgh: T. & T. Clark, 1946) 2–3, n. 9, where Albright maintains that Ugaritic *brḥ*, as an epithet of *Ltn*, means "primeval." Note also Arabic *al-bārihata* "yesterday." Of course it is incongruous to have a curse, which can only take effect in the present and future spoken of as effective in the past ("yesterday") as well, but this is evidently a formula, a fixed temporal designation dividing time into three parts; similar phrases are common in world literature, as "Yesterday, today, and forever" (Heb 13:8).

The line left untranslated should contain a curse, but no rendering has proved generally convincing, though Gaster's (incorporating the ideas of others) is popular and may serve as a means for exposing the difficulties: "Always as a refugee, seeking sanctuary at shrines."[5] Gaster accepts in principle the rendering of Virolleaud for *gr bt il:* "l'hôte de la maison d'El."[6] Unable to parse *amd*, he emends to *t!md* "always," and explains the sense of the whole as follows. The city, as a collective murderer, is to flee continually like a client of the sanctuary. This is, then, a reference to asylum, for which Gaster cites numerous parallels.

Several objections to such a rendering readily occur. First, the resultant curse seems to be without parallel in the body of ancient maledictions. There are, of course, curses of a singular or unusual nature, but in general ancient curses were of standard types, and the same sentiment recurs in different texts, often over many centuries. In the case of a difficult curse, it would be more satisfying to discover a sense that is commonplace, not unique. A second, more serious, objection is that to be a sojourner in the house of a god would, if anything, have been a blessing. Note the Phoenician personal names *grb ᶜl, grmlk, grmlqrt* and *grᶜštrt*, and such biblical passages as Ps 23:7; 15:1, and 61:5 "May I sojourn (*ᵓāgûrāh*) in thy tent forever." The word *brḥ*, which Gaster takes as a verb "flee," thus harmonizing with and supporting his interpretation of the whole curse, occurs with the second malediction also, and is evidently part of a formula for time; it cannot help determine the sense of the first curse. Thus Gaster's rendering, though more plausible than some others, fails to be totally convincing.

Read, for the latter part of the line, *grbt il* "the leprosy of El." There are no word-dividers or spaces in the text to oppose this collocation of letters; the usual printing as *gr bt il* is interpretive. Derivatives of *grb* to denote some sort of skin-disease are widespread in Semitic. In Deut 28:27 a related form occurs in a curse. The Ugaritic form with *t* proposed here, namely *grbt*, suggests perhaps a *qaṭṭalt* pattern (**garrabtu*), as common in names of diseases in Biblical Hebrew.[7] The translation "leprosy" is not meant to suggest any specific disease; it is merely conventional.

As is typical in phrases of this sort, consisting of a noun in construct before a word for "God," it is difficult to decide whether the final divine element is to be taken as producing a kind of superlative, or actually designates a deity.[8] Is it "a terrible leprosy" or as above "the leprosy of El"?

Several parallels favor the latter view, and in addition lend plausibility to the general understanding of the line defended here. In an Akkadian

---

[5] T. H. Gaster, *Thespis* (Doubleday: Garden City, NY, 1961) 365–66.

[6] Charles Virolleaud, *La légende phénicienne de Danel* (Paris: Geuthner, 1936) 167, n. 1.

[7] See Bauer-Leander, *Historische Grammatik*, 467–77.

[8] See D. Winton Thomas, "A Consideration of Some Unusual Ways of Expressing the Superlative in Hebrew," *VT* 3 (1953) 209–24.

cultic commentary (see *AHw* and *CAD* s.v. *garbu* and *garbānu*) occurs the phrase *garabānu ša ina nāri uṭabbû ga-ʳribꞁ ᵈA-nim* "The leper whom they immerse in the river is the leper of Anu." As von Soden pointed out, there is a play on words here, but this would not seem to invalidate the legitimacy of the phrase "leper of Anu." The whole text is, however, obscure in nature.[9]

Note also now a curse in the recently discovered Akkadian-Aramaic bilingual inscription from Tell Fekheriyeh, dating to the 9th century B.C.[10] Line 23: *wmwtn : šbṭ : zy nyrgl : ʾl : ygtzr : mn : mth* "And may pestilence, the plague of Nergal, not be cut off from his land." The phrase that is of interest in this connection is "the plague (rod = disease) of Nergal." A disease is identified (in a curse) as associated with a specific deity—a point of similarity to the curse in Aqht as interpreted here. This is not unlike the locutions in Akkadian medical texts, where certain symptoms are identified as pointing to the "hand" (*qât*) of a specific god, or the "rod" (*ḫaṭṭu*) or "blow" (*miḫṣu*) of a deity.[11]

The final phrase in the curse from Aqht, then, may be taken to mention "leprosy of El." The associated word *amd* or *ṭ!md* remains obscure to me, but similar curses perhaps suggest the direction in which a solution is to be sought. In curses having to do with leprosy, the usual form of words is somewhat as in the following example: "May the great lord Sin who dwells in Harran, clothe Matiʾilu, his sons, his officials, and the people of his land in leprosy as in a cloak."[12] The notion of *clothing* constantly accompanies the curse of leprosy, and thus it may be suggested that *amd* or *ṭ!md* is a volitive form of a verb meaning "clothe," perhaps from a root *mdd* or *mdw/y*; note Ugaritic *md* "garment, covering," with Biblical Hebrew cognates.

If this possibility is incorporated the resulting translation is: "May you be *clothed* with leprosy of El!"[13]

---

[9] I am grateful to my colleague, Prof. Jerrold Cooper, for counsel on this text and assistance with other Akkadian materials.

[10] First edition by Ali Abou Assaf, "Die Statue des HDYSᶜY, König von Guzana," *Mitteilungen der Deutschen Orient-Gesellschaft*, No. 113 (Berlin, 1981) 3–22.

[11] See *AHw* and *CAD* s.v. *ḫaṭṭu* "staff" and René Labat, *Traité akkadien de diagnostics et pronostics médicaux* (Leiden: Brill, 1951) xxi of the introduction, and *passim* in the texts.

[12] From an 8th-century Akkadian treaty (Matiʾilu with Ashurnirari V), trans. Erica Reiner, *ANET³*, 533. For numerous parallels see D. R. Hillers, *Treaty-Curses and the Old Testament Prophets* (BibOr 16; Rome: Pontifical Biblical Institute, 1964) 15–16.

[13] When this understanding of the Aqht text occurred to me, years ago, I told W. F. Albright of it and he informed me that the same idea had occurred to him. I mention this not only to give proper credit, but in the belief that Samuel Iwry will be pleased at this recollection of a beloved teacher.

CAIN, THE ARROGANT SUFFERER

Herbert B. Huffmon
Drew University

T HE story of Cain and Abel is dramatic and powerful, with many dimensions. An especially striking feature of the story is its truncated character. Commentators typically refer to its terse, telescoped, incomplete style. So many possible questions are left unanswered, so many conceivable lines of development are passed over, that the story remains elusive to us. It is not just a matter of the old question as to the source of Cain's wife. The story gives only selected highlights, seeking to concentrate our attention on a few issues. What this paper undertakes is far from an overview of the Cain-Abel story. Rather, it offers an interpretation of one specific dimension of the story, namely, the sacrifices of Cain and Abel, God's response to those sacrifices, and Cain's response in turn to God's rejection.

The Cain-Abel story represents the Yahwist's further unfolding of the drama of human history. Following upon the easy style of divine-human communication in the Garden, it presents some of the difficulty now involved in interchange with God through sacrifices. Genesis 2–3 having stressed the special union of man and woman, Genesis 4 proceeds to depict the conflict found within the human community, even—or especially—between brothers. Our story also notes the basic occupational contrasts of shepherd and farmer and leads on to the building of a city. Indeed, some commentators see God's favorable response to Abel's sacrifice, rather than Cain's, as indicating a preference for the nomadic, pastoral life as opposed to agricultural pursuits. Reference is made to the so-called "nomadic ideal" in Israel, and, e.g., Skinner argues that the narrative assumes that only animal sacrifice is acceptable, vegetable offerings being introduced only "after the adoption of agricultural life" in the settlement period. Even in the early days of the settlement, Skinner suggests, Israel may have held that "the animal offerings of their nomadic religion were superior to the vegetable offerings made to the Canaanite Baals."[1] But the occupational contrast is historically unrealistic and seems unrelated to the different responses to the sacrifices. There is no

---

[1] J. Skinner, *Genesis* (ICC; 2d. ed.; Edinburgh: T. & T. Clark, 1930) 105–6.

suggestion of a denigration of the agricultural life, precisely the occupation of the man in God's garden and following expulsion from the Garden (Gen 3:17-18). The story does not stress a competition between the shepherd and the farmer. There is no real parallel to the Sumerian text variously called "Inanna Prefers the Farmer" or "The Wooing of Inanna," in which the shepherd Dumuzi and the farmer Enkimdu compete for the favors of Inanna, with somewhat uncertain results.

Likewise, the contrast in the offering material—"the fruit of the ground" from the farmer, Cain, and "the firstlings of the flock," especially "their fat," from the shepherd, Abel—does not seem to be decisive. Many commentators have stressed the "choice" nature of Abel's offering over against the less selective offering from Cain. For example, Speiser refers to "the unstinted offering on the part of Abel and the minimal contribution of Cain."[2] But although Cain may not have followed "later" ideas about sacrifice, the Genesis text shows no obvious intention to subordinate an offering "from the fruit of the ground," or to infer the offering of an inferior agricultural product.

The first significant differentiation in the text is the note that "God had regard for (wayyiša^c . . . $^{\circ}el$) Abel and his offering, but for Cain and his offering He did not have regard (lō$^{\circ}$ šā^{c}â)" (Gen 4:4b–5a). This is the first evaluative statement and it points to the essential question. That question does not concern the contrasting occupations—farmer/shepherd—nor offering material—animals and animal products/plants—but the nature of the sacrificial act, including especially the divine response to the sacrificial act and subsequently the human reaction to that divine response. In Genesis 4 the divine response is to favor Abel but not to favor Cain. Cain's subsequent response is to get angry, murderously angry. The text does not indicate why Abel's offering was favored nor why Cain's was not. In the Targum Neophiti, Cain and Abel converse. Abel says that his offering was better and the world is just; Cain says that the world has no moral order, no just retribution (i.e., the world is capricious).[3] This expansion points to a fundamental issue in the text.

In his anger Cain indicates that God is judged unfair. It is widely assumed that Cain lacked the proper attitude in his sacrifice, and the story does not rule out that possibility, but his anger suggests rather that Cain was unaware of any deficiency in his sacrifice or in his attitude, at least in comparison with his brother. Cain cannot accept the fact that one sacrifice was acceptable and the other was not. In other words, Cain represents the idea that sacrifice should be automatically effective. It may

[2] E. A. Speiser, Genesis (AB; Garden City: Doubleday, 1964) 30. For a recent survey of opinions, see J. Goldin, "The Youngest Son or Where Does Genesis 38 Belong?" JBL 96 (1977) 32–33, n. 36.

[3] The Palestinian Targum to the Pentateuch, Codex Vatican (Neofiti 1) (Jerusalem: Makor, ca. 1979) pl. 9.

be precisely this idea of sacrifice that God rejects in rejecting Cain's offering.

A side issue is the question of how Cain and Abel could know whether an offering was acceptable or not, for the text does not tell us. Some manifest sign has been suggested by many commentators, and one tradition, found at least as early as Theodotion's text and cited favorably by Rashi, affirms that heavenly fire consumed Abel's offering, leaving Cain's unkindled, like the angelic kindling of Gideon's sacrifice (Judg 6:19–24). Again, there may have been some accompanying circumstance, such as the ascent of the smoke or the aroma of the sacrifice that signaled acceptance or not. However, the most persuasive suggestion is that Cain and Abel would judge the acceptability or non-acceptability of the offering by the course of subsequent events. For example, Cassuto, following Brock-Utne (and an old tradition),[4] says that "after the offerings had been made, the Lord bestowed blessing and fertility upon Abel's flocks, but not upon the field of Cain."[5] This is in accord with common expectations, as illustrated by the teaching of the Wisdom of Amenemope: "When he rises you shall offer to the Aten, saying, 'Grant me prosperity and health.' And he will give you your necessities for life, And you will be safe from fear" (10, 12–15).[6]

But however one might be able to tell that an offering was not acceptable, the more basic question is how one responds to such a discovery of disfavor. Cain's response was to become angry. Another possibility, for those who take the discovery more in stride, is to seek redress by appealing to the god's more narrow self-interest. This response is illustrated by an appeal to the Storm God of Hatti in one of the Plague Prayers of King Mursilis: "Suffer not to die the few who are left to offer loaves and libations!"[7] After all, where would the deity be without loaves and libations? Yet for the pious adherent the response is somewhat different. Such a person undertakes to find out wherein the god(s) were offended so that he can make amends. This kind of response is amply illustrated in the Hittite royal prayers. For example, in the Plague Prayers of Mursilis, the disfavor made manifest in the plague leads to the plea, "Now, O Gods, whatever sin you see, either [let] a man of god

---

[4] A. Brock-Utne, "Die religionshistorischen Voraussetzungen der Ḳain-Abel-Geschichte," *ZAW* 54 (1936) 210–12. He correlates the differential treatment with climatic factors. See also Lekach Tov and Haᵓamek Davar (cited by M. Zlotowitz, *Bereishis* [New York: Mesorah, 1977] 145), to which Calvin could be added, for this opinion.

[5] U. Cassuto, *Genesis, Part I: From Adam to Noah* (Jerusalem: Magnes, 1961) 207.

[6] Translated by W. K. Simpson, in Simpson, ed., *The Literature of Ancient Egypt* (new ed.; New Haven: Yale University, 1973) 250; cf. *ANET*, 423a.

[7] Ph. H. J. Houwink ten Cate, "Hittite Royal Prayers," *Numen* 16 (1969) 98.

come and declare it or [let] the old wives, the seers [(or) the augurs determine it] or let men see it in a dream. Then we will [. . . make amends], and, O Gods, take pity again upon the land of Ḫatti."[8]

Cain's response, instead of anger, should have been the careful attempt to find out what error of commission or omission was causing interference with the appropriate positive relationship with God. Cain should have reacted as Saul did when, on the occasion of the rash imposition of a ban, which, unknown to Saul but well-known to the people, had been violated by Jonathan, he discovered that God would not answer further queries and resorted to searching out what the trouble was (1 Samuel 14).

Cain's experience, on this momentous occasion of the first recorded sacrifice, is meant to illustrate some basic questions in Israelite piety. First, sacrificial offerings are not to be seen as effective in and of themselves—as controlling God, as automatically accepted. Communication with God now presents some difficulties. Second, the response to the awareness of divine disfavor should not be anger, but pious searching of the circumstances.

The rather elusive Gen 4:7, described by Procksch as "the most obscure verse of the chapter, indeed of Genesis,"[9] relates to the issue raised earlier. Was Cain's offering flawed by an improper intentionality on his part, though the text does not explicitly make that point, or was the failing really his angry response to the discovery of rejection, a point that the text does clearly make? We can perhaps interpret the verse as "If you do rightly, you will gain acceptance, and if you do not do rightly it is because of the power of sin, though you can overcome it." But following, as it does, upon the report of Cain's anger, the sense might be, "If you do rightly" (i.e., in your response to disfavor) or "If you do rightly" (i.e., knowing that sacrifices are not automatically effective). Thus the stress need not be on Cain's (and Abel's) inward state of mind nor on the care or lack of care in selecting the offering. The point may well be that God is somewhat uncontrollable and unpredictable, a bit capricious and hidden.[10] Cain, then, may be liable for his lack of proper response to God's clear rejection of the offering, and in this interpretation the emphasis is more upon Cain's exterior behavior and lack of positive

[8] O. R. Gurney, *Hittite Prayers of Mursilis II* (Annals of Archaeology and Anthropology, 27; Liverpool: University of Liverpool, 1940) 26–29, 90, 142. For a similar sentiment see the text translated by A. Goetze in *ANET*, 497–98.

[9] O. Procksch, *Genesis* (KAT, 1; Leipzig: A. Deichertsche Verlagsbuchhandlung, 1924) 47.

[10] G. von Rad (*Genesis* [OTL; Philadelphia: Westminster, 1961] 101) and W. Zimmerli (*I Mose 1–11* [Zürcher Bibelkommentare; Zürich/Stuttgart: Zwingli, 1967] 212) emphasize God's freedom to accept or reject without reason.

action. Cain and Abel are perhaps being tested by God, and Cain just does not respond as a pious man should.[11]

For the Yahwist, the initial sacrifice with Cain and Abel may have been seen as a real contrast with Abraham's challenging sacrifice in Genesis 22. Abraham responds to the test with true piety; Abraham trusted that God would provide. When Cain and Abel were tested Cain failed. Sacrifice is not effective in and of itself; God's freedom is not so easily curtailed. And when God's pleasure is made clear, the appropriate response of a pious adherent is also clear.

[11] P. A. Riemann ("Am I My Brother's Keeper?" *Int* 24 [1970] 482-91) emphasizes Cain's lack of piety in his famous response to God.

ORIGINALS AND IMITATIONS IN BIBLICAL POETRY:
A COMPARATIVE EXAMINATION OF 1 SAM 2:1-10 AND PS 113:5-9

Avi Hurvitz
Dept. of Bible
The Hebrew University, Jerusalem

I

T HE purpose of this study is to combine the insights of two different scholarly approaches which all too often are pursued without sufficient awareness of each other. The first deals primarily with grammar and belongs to the discipline of linguistics; the second, which is concerned with style, is included within the realm of literary criticism. In our specific case—the comparative study of 1 Sam 2:1-10 and Ps 113:5-9—the basic questions posed by each approach are as follows:

(1) The linguistic-grammatical—how can we distinguish, methodologically, between *archaic* (= authentic) language and *archaizing* (= artificial) style? In other words, how can we determine whether seemingly ancient linguistic elements in a given biblical text are genuine survivals of an older period, or deliberate imitations, the artificial creations of later generations?[1]

(2) The literary-stylistic—what is the interrelationship, in terms of dependency and priority, between the clsoely related texts of 1 Samuel 2 and Psalm 113? Are these texts, with their many verbal affinities, directly dependent on each other, or do they reflect, each in its own way, a common source underlying them both? In any case, which of the two texts is earlier?[2]

---

[1] Cf., for instance, GKC §91*l*(3) (a discussion of the ending מוֹ- ["an indication of archaic language" or "revivals . . . consciously and artificially used"?]).

[2] Cf. the standard commentaries on the book of Psalms, many of which suggest that Psalm 113 borrowed from or has been influenced by 1 Samuel 2 (for instance, J. Olshausen, *Die Psalmen* (KeH; Leipzig: Hirzel, 1853) 427-28; F. Hitzig, *Die Psalmen*, vol. II (Leipzig und Heidelberg: Winter, 1865) 331; H. Ewald, *Commentary on the Psalms* (London-Edinburgh: Williams and Norgate, 1881 [= *Commentary on the Poetical Books of the Old Testament. Division*

The renewed interest in these problems must undoubtedly be credited to Prof. D. N. Freedman's recent article on "Psalm 113 and the Song of Hannah."[3] In this instructive study, the thesis is put forward that "Psalm 113 is the more archaic of the two, and belongs to an earlier phase of Israelite prosody."[4] Freedman's arguments in favor of this view are not all of a piece, ranging as they do from considerations of prosody and style to those of history and religion. To be sure, most of his article is devoted to a literary-textual analysis (literary structure, metrical patterns, textual reconstructions). Yet, the linguistic aspect has also played a considerable role in his reasoning and judgment. This is obvious particularly from the fact that in arguing for the relative earliness of Psalm 113 he more than once[5] adduces evidence of 'archaisms' to prove his point.

We also consider the issue of 'archaisms' to be of major importance in any attempt at determining the relative dating of 1 Samuel 2 and Psalm 113. However, we believe that it is 1 Samuel 2, rather than Psalm 113, which is the older composition. Our conclusion is based specifically on the linguistic nature of some of the so-called 'archaisms' encountered in Psalm 113.

II

The Hebrew Grammars note that certain endings attached to some nouns in BH—e.g., אֹסְרִי לַגֶּפֶן, חַיְתוֹ אָרֶץ (Gen 1:24), בְּנוֹ בְעֹר (Num 24:3), עִירֹה ... בְּנִי אֲתֹנוֹ (Gen 49:11), שֹׁכְנִי סְנֶה (Deut 33:16), אֹהַבְתִּי לָדוּשׁ (Hos 10:11)—may reflect petrified survivals of obsolete case-endings.[6] Another theory suggests that the morpheme -ō, and possibly -ī as well, represents

---

I, vol. II] 300–301; A. F. Kirkpatrick, *The Book of Psalms. Books IV and V.* (CamB; Cambridge: Cambridge University, 1903) 687–79; C. A. and E. G. Briggs, *A Critical and Exegetical Commentary on the Book of Psalms*, vol. II (ICC; Edinburgh: Clark, 1907) 388; H. Herkenne, *Das Buch der Psalmen* (HS; Bonn: Hanstein, 1936) 370–71; W. O. E. Oesterley, *The Psalms* (London: S.P.C.K, 1953) 469. Cf. also J. T. Willis, "The Song of Hannah and Psalm 113," *CBQ* 35 (1973) 139–54. The final conclusion of this detailed study is that the texts are, in fact, contemporaneous ("both Songs were ultimately influenced by a common milieu" [154]).

[3] *Eretz-Israel*, vol. 14 (Jerusalem: Israel Exploration Society, 1978) [= H. L. Ginsberg Volume] 56*–69*).

[4] Ibid., 56*.

[5] Ibid., 57*, n. 1; 59*; 60* (and 69*).

[6] Cf. GKC §90 (especially paragraph K, the passage printed in italics); P. Joüon, *Grammaire de l'hébreu biblique* (Rome: Institut Biblique Pontificial, 1923) §93. The biblical occurrences of the -ī and -ō endings are readily available in D. A. Robertson, *Linguistic Evidence in Dating Early Hebrew Poetry* (Missoula: Society of Biblical Literature, 1972) 69–77.

an original pronominal (possessive) suffix of the 3rd m.s.[7] In recent years two other theories have been put forward as to the possible origin of the *hireq compaginis*. The first one, in light of parallels adduced from the Amarna letters seeks to interpret this final -ī as an unrecognized ending of the infinitive absolute;[8] the second explains the vowel as a reflection of "an archaic state of affairs in which nouns in the neutral or absolute positions ended in -ī."[9] Be that as it may, the general concensus among scholars is that these forms, whatever their original function, are archaic relics within the language. This view, based in the first place on an analysis of *Biblical Hebrew*, is further confirmed by the fact that from the viewpoint of *biblical literature*, the -ō and -ī endings are prevalent particularly in poetic contexts; these, as is well known, often tend to preserve exceedingly ancient elements.[10] It is to be noted, however, that none of the distinctively early poetic compositions contained in the Pentateuch and the Former Prophets provides us with even a single case of these archaic endings attached to a word which employs at the same time the definite article. Forms like הַיֹּשַׁבְתִּי עַל מְבוֹאֹת יָם (Ezek 27:3 [K; Q: הַהֹפְכִי הַצּוּר אֲגַם מָיִם]),—contrast Jer 10:17 יֹשַׁבְתִּי בַּמָּצוֹר [K; Q: יֹשֶׁבֶת]),—(Ps 114:8), הַיֹּשְׁבִי בַּשָּׁמָיִם (Ps 123:1—contrast Ps 2:4: יוֹשֵׁב בַּשָּׁמַיִם; Isa 40:22: הַיֹּשֵׁב עַל חוּג הָאָרֶץ) appear in the Book of Ezekiel, from the exilic period, and are found in some Psalms whose antiquity is doubtful,[11] but they are never encountered in any of the texts which belong either to the unequivocal corpus of classical biblical literature in general[12] or to "Ancient Yahwistic Poetry" in particular.[13]

---

[7] Cf. H. Bauer-P. Leander, *Historische Grammatik der hebräischen Sprache* . . . (Halle: Niemeyer, 1922) §65i, m.

[8] Cf. W. L. Moran, "The Hebrew Language in its Northwest Semitic Background," *The Bible and the Ancient Near East: Essays in Honor of W. F. Albright* (ed. G. E. Wright; Garden City: Doubleday, 1961; reprinted, Winona Lake: Eisenbrauns, 1979) 60.

[9] Cf. C. Rabin, "The Structure of the Semitic System of Case Endings," *Proceedings of the International Conference on Semitic Studies 1965* (Jerusalem: The Israel Academy of Sciences and Humanities, 1969) 195.

[10] GKC, §2q, s; Bauer-Leander, §2n n. 1; Joüon, §3d. Cf. also D. N. Freedman, "Archaic Forms in Early Hebrew Poetry," *ZAW* 72 (1960) 101–7.

[11] Cf. the standard commentaries on Psalms. See also GKC §90m; S. R. Driver, *A Treatise on the Use of the Tenses in Hebrew* (3d ed.; Oxford: Clarendon, 1892) 240.

[12] The form הָהֹלַכְתִּי mentioned in GKC §90n is a slip of the pen; the correct version is הֹלַכְתִּי (2 Kgs 4:23 [K; Q: הֹלֶכֶת]), without the definite article.

[13] Cf. F. M. Cross and D. N. Freedman, *Studies in Ancient Yahwistic Poetry* (Missoula: Scholars Press, 1975). According to this book (5–7), the most representative compositions from "The corpus of ancient Yahwistic poetry" are the following: The Blessing of Jacob (Genesis 49), The Song of the Sea (Exodus 15), The Oracles of Balaam (Numbers 23–24), The Blessing of Moses (Deuteronomy

These findings should come as no surprise if we consider them in light of the nature and history of the definite article in general. The definite article was gradually introduced into various Semitic languages only at a relatively later stage of their development,[14] a process which is clearly visible within the biblical texts themselves. Only with the passage of time is the use of the definite article intensified until it becomes a prominent element in BH; thus early biblical poetry, with its rare and random use of the *h*-, reflects in this regard a much more primitive phase of the Hebrew language.[15]

Furthermore, certain linguistic "fossils" preserved in the Bible bear witness to the fact that the classical language avoids using ancient, extremely outdated forms alongside the increasingly employed morpheme *h*-. Thus, for example, the poetic expression חיתו ארץ (Gen 1:24) is interchanged, within the same paragraph, with חית הארץ (Gen 1:25); but nowhere do we find in biblical literature a mixture of the two, resulting in חיתו הארץ*.[16] Note, further, that the verse רֹעִי האליל עזבי הצאן—the only extra-Psalter example in biblical literature comparable to the hypothetical combination חיתו* הארץ—is found in the book of Zechariah (11:17), which, of course, represents the post-classical phase of biblical literature. (In the book of Psalms we find an additional example in ההפכי הצור 114:8.) Another case in point is the poetic word שָׂדַי, which is found 13 times in BH and which reflects the original,[17] and hence, the more archaic, pattern of the noun שָׂדֶה. *Śāday* never takes the definite article; cf., for instance, Ps 96:12: "let the field (*śāday*) exult, and everything it it!" However, in the parallel text of this Psalm, 1 Chr 16:32, the resolution of the final diphthong of *śāday* coincides with the introduction of the definite article: "let the field (*haśśādê*) exult, and everything

---

33), The Song of Deborah (Judges 5), The Lament of David (2 Samuel 1), The Song of David (2 Samuel 22 = Psalm 18).

[14] Cf., for instance, S. Moscati, *An Introduction to the Comparative Grammar of the Semitic Languages* (Porta linguarum orientalium, 6; Wiesbaden: Harrassowitz, 1964) §12.77.

[15] Cf. the references quoted above, n. 10.

[16] Adducing the above mentioned variants of חיתו ארץ/חית הארץ, H. Bauer has suggested that the -*ō* is an anticipating pronominal suffix (cf. above, n. 7) which serves semantically as the (older) equivalent of the (later) definite article (see in detail *ZDMG* 68 [1914] 597–99). For purposes of the present discussion it is immaterial whether we accept or reject this theory (against it cf., for instance, U. Cassuto, *A Commentary on the Book of Genesis*, Part I [Jerusalem: Magnes, 1961] 54). Our main concern here is the *form*, not the supposed *meaning*; as far as grammatical form is concerned, there is no question but that the -*ō* is an archaic remnant which gradually disappeared from the common language (cf. the references quoted above, n. 10).

[17] Cf., for instance, BDB 961a.

in it!" Again, a mixed form הַשָּׂדַי* is unheard of in BH, so evidently the archaic ending -*ay* on the one hand, and the definite article on the other, are in fact mutually exclusive.[18] Finally, mention should be made here of yet another poetic[19] termination, the feminine ending -*tā*, which is likewise common in biblical literature without the definite article; for instance, אֵימָתָה (Exod 15:16 [the Samaritan[20] has אימה]), יְשׁוּעָתָה (Ps 3:3), עוֹלָתָה (Hos 10:13), עֶזְרָתָה (Ps 94:17), עֵיפָתָה (Job 10:22). The peculiar composite form הַמְזִמָּתָה is encountered in the Bible only in Jeremiah (11:15), a book which represents the dawn of the exilic period.[21]

Clearly, then, extremely archaic forms like שָׂדַי, חיתו (אֶרֶץ־), and אֵימָתָה were felt in classical BH to be incompatible with the definite article, representing the far more "modernistic" trends of BH in its later phases. In all of these cases the *addition* of the definite article coincides with the *omission* of the outdated ending.

III

Psalm 113 abounds in forms which belong in the category of *hireq compaginis*. Out of a total of 9 verses which make up the chapter, no fewer than 5 contain words terminating in -*ī*:

---

[18] It is interesting to note that חיתו שדי of Isa 56:9 is modified in 1QIsaᵃ to חיות שדה rather than חי(ו)ת השדה. The version of the scroll thus exhibits a familiar tendency of the later period to get rid of antiquarian forms (cf. E. Y. Kutscher, *The Language and Linguistic Background of the Isaiah Scroll (1Q Isaᵃ)* (STDJ VI; Leiden: Brill, 1974) 387. The Samaritan version חית הארץ instead of חיתו ארץ in Gen 1:24, is also interpreted by Kutscher as reflecting this linguistic process [ibid.]). However, for one reason or another, the further stage of development observed above, i.e., the introduction of the extra *h*-, did not take place in 1QIsaᵃ.

[19] Cf., for instance, GKC §90g.

[20] Cf. above, n. 18.

[21] If one accepts המזמתה in Jeremiah as a corruption, as suggested by many scholars (cf. the commentaries and the dictionaries), then of course even this single and isolated example must be disregarded.

Another word which ought to be considered in this connection is הַמָּוְתָה (Ps 116:15). To be sure, the *t* of *hammāwtā* is part of the root, unlike the *t* of המזמתה (= המזמה) which represents an external grammatical morpheme (the feminine ending), and consequently, one could argue that *hammāwtā* is irrelevant for the present discussion (which deals with forms like *hamzimmātā*). However, since both *hamāwtā* and *hamzimmātā* do exhibit the very same "ornamental device of poetic style" (GKC §90m), i.e., a final -*tā* attached to a noun having the definite article, some connection between the two cannot be excluded after all; cf. S. R. Driver, *Treatise*, 240 ["the later poets loved these quaint forms"]).

Ps 113:5:	Who is	like the Lord	our God,
[1 Sam 2:2:	There is none . . . like the Lord . . . like our God.]		

Who is seated on high (המגביהי לשבת),

[------   ]

Ps 113:6:	who looks far down	(המשפילי לראות) . . .
[1 Sam 2:7:	he brings low	(משפילי [22]), he also exalts.]

Ps 113:7:	He raises	(מקימי)	the poor from the dust,
[1 Sam 2:8:	He raises up	(מקים)	the poor from the dust;]

and lifts the needy from the ash heap,

[he   lifts the needy from the ash heap,]

Ps 113:8:	to make them sit	(להושיבי)	with princes,
[1 Sam 2:9(8):	to make them sit	(להושיב)	with princes . . .]

Ps 113:9:	He gives	(מושיבי)	the barren woman
[1 Sam 2:5:		------	The barren]

a home, making her the joyous mother of children.

[has borne seven, but she who has many   children is forlorn.]

מקימי and מושיבי, without the definite article, are in perfect harmony with the older accepted patterns of BH and may, consequently, be viewed as genuine archaic features. המגביהי and המשפילי, in contrast, exhibit a hybrid form unattested in the golden age of biblical literature. As we have seen, this type of *forma mixta*—echoing "in missbräuchlicher Weise"[23] a distorted old usage—represents a "degenerate" language which is worlds apart from classical BH. Our conclusion is, therefore, that at least some of the apparent 'archaisms' encountered in Psalm 113, namely *hammagbīhī* and *hammašpīlī*, must be viewed instead as 'neologisms'. These forms betray a linguistic background indicative of a relatively late period in BH, a period which witnessed the loss of a *Sprachgefühl* for genuine classical forms and their replacement by in-

---

[22] Although in both verses we have the same *form* of the participle, the *meaning* of (אף מרומם משפיל) is different from (המשפילי לראות). In the first case the correct rendering is "lays law, sets in a lower place" (BDB 1050a; KB, 1005); in the second it is "looks down from his height" (KB, 1005), ". . . stoops to look" (M. Dahood, *Psalms III* [AB; Garden City: Doubleday, 1970] 130 ["an elative, not causative"; 131], "seeing what is below" (*The Book of Psalms* [Philadelphia: The Jewish Publication Society of America, 1972] 118). The syntactical pattern of משפיל לראות is the same as מיטיב לנגן (1 Sam 16:17) or מרבים העם להביא (Exod 36:5); cf. GKC §114n, n. 2 (here I differ from Freedman's interpretation which renders Ps 113:5-6: "Who elevates some to a seat of honor/ Who abases others in the sight of all"[59*]. However, once again [cf. above, n. 16], it is the form, not the meaning, which is vital for our discussion).

[23] Bauer, *ZDMG* 68 (1914) 599.

terior pseudo-archaisms.[24] In other words, not only are these forms incompatible with BH of "the pre-monarchic period,"[25] but they can
scarcely be attributed even to the pre-exilic era.[26]

We therefore suggest that the whole thesis arguing that Psalm 113 is
early be reexamined. This would of course involve a reexamination of
various criteria employed in Freedman's study, for instance, the suggestion that "elaboration" and "more complex patterning" are necessarily later characteristics than a "simple structure."[27] In any event, there
is one conclusion which does seem clearly established: the appearance of
המגביהי, המשפילי (and possibly,[28] להושיבי) in Psalm 113 casts grave doubt
on the assumption that this Psalm, in its *extant*[29] version, is an archaic
composition antedating 1 Samuel 2. As noted above, the genuineness
and antiquity of these forms are highly questionable; in fact, they should
be considered pseudo-classicisms indicative of a relatively late linguistic
phase in the historical development of BH.

[24] This explanation seems to us also to fit best the peculiar להושיבי (v 8)—a
form (infinitive construct + ī) which has no parallels whatsoever in the entire
Bible. According to M. Dahood, however, the final *yod* represents here the suffix
of the 3rd m.s. (*Psalms III*, 132, 376; against this view of Dahood cf. F. M. Cross,
Canaanite Myth and Hebrew Epic [Cambridge: Harvard University, 1973] 140,
n. 96).

[25] Freedman, *Eretz-Israel* 14, 69*.

[26] Robertson (*Linguistic Evidence*) also fails to make the necessary distinction between the forms of the *hireq compaginis* which appear with the definite
article and those which do not (p. 76).

The reader will have noted throughout the article that our chronological
discussions were invariably stated in relative rather than absolute terms. The
avoidance of concrete dating was deliberate, for we lack sufficient linguistic
evidence to link unequivocally the linguistic phenomenon discussed here with a
particular historical age. Yet, from what we know about the history and development of BH, it seems best to identify "the relatively late period" referred to
above (p. 120) with "the exilic/post-exilic period" (cf. our study "The Date of
the Prose-Tale of Job Linguistically Reconsidered," *HTR* 67 [1974] 33). Note,
further, that the three deviations from classical standards adduced above from
biblical compositions *outside* the Book of Psalms—עזבי הצאן, היושבתי, המזמתה—
are found, respectively, in Jeremiah, Ezekiel, and Zechariah, all of which reflect
the exilic/post-exilic period.

[27] Freedman, *Eretz-Israel* 14, 64*. This line of reasoning has been rejected by
various scholars (cf., for instance, A. R. Johnson, "The Psalms," *The Old Testament and Modern Study* [ed. H. H. Rowley; Oxford: Clarendon, 1951] 181); consequently, it cannot serve as a dependable criterion for dating.

[28] Cf. above, n. 24.

[29] Any reconstruction of Psalm 113's original text is, of course, a matter of
pure speculation. This becomes readily apparent upon comparing the textual
discussions of D. N. Freedman (above, n. 3) with those of his predecessors.

STUDIES IN NEO-ARAMAIC LEXICOLOGY

Georg Krotkoff
Dept. of Near Eastern Studies
The Johns Hopkins University

THE widely dispersed dialects of Neo-Aramaic (NA), which survive in various mountainous retreat areas of the Near East, represent a living reservoir of Semitic and non-Semitic speech elements of considerable interest for both Semitic and Iranian lexicology.

The interest for Iranian (mainly Kurdish) studies lies in the fact that the numerous borrowings from Kurdish into NA provide a welcome supplement to existing Kurdish dictionaries, which do not yet adequately account for the vast and varied vocabulary of the Kurdish linguistic area.

Even the relatively small corpus of texts in an NA dialect from Iraqi Kurdistan[1] collected by this writer contains a surprising amount of heretofore unrecorded vocabulary. A large number of these words which cannot be found in available reference works may be presumed to be Kurdish on the basis of probability and phonetic appearance. Examples of such words are: *ajibarruk* f. 'mole-cricket'; *dambuš* 'a tall grass used for binding'; *sinnik* 'an agricultural pest'.

Other Kurdish loan words, even if positively identifiable, may exhibit considerable differences from their prototypes as found in the dictionaries.[2] The most salient case is *iṣṣir* f. 'frost' vs. *sur*. The differences are either due to inexplicable sound changes or to morphological adjustments to the structures of NA. The following examples will illustrate

---

[1] G. Krotkoff, A *Neo-Aramaic Dialect of Kurdistan* (American Oriental Series 64, New Haven, 1982). This is a description of the dialect of the village Aradhin near Amadia, Iraq. Quotations from this book are given here in a slightly simplified transcription. In those languages in which the voiceless velar fricative is not an allophone of *k*, it is written *x*.

[2] The following Kurdish dictionaries were used:
Ch. Kh. Bakayev, *Kurdsko-russkiy slovar'* (Moskva, 1957).
I. O. Farizov, *Russko-kurdskiy slovar'* (Moskva, 1957).
K. K. Kurdoyev, *Kurdsko-russkiy slovar'* (Moskva, 1960).
Kurdish dictionaries based on the dialect of Suleymania proved useless for our purposes. The spelling used in above dictionaries was slightly adjusted to avoid conflicting use of symbols.

the different degrees of change and adaptation: *kučča* 'bunch of grapes' vs. *gūšī; juwwāla* f. 'sack, bag' vs. *čawal; kawāza* 'pitcher' vs. *kūz; piška* 'bud' vs. *biškož* 'button, bud'; *piškille* 'dung of sheep' vs. *biškul; homa* 'only' vs. *hema; pista* 'a skin (as container)' vs. *post; gira* 'hill' vs. *gir; lašša* 'body, carcass' vs. *lāš; simma* 'hoof' vs. *sim; tarra* 'fresh' vs. *ter; tarrāša* 'bush, thicket' vs. *teraš; qundarta* f. 'shoe' vs. *kondere* (here and in the two following examples the feminine gender of the Kurdish word caused the addition of a feminine ending in the loanword); *sīrikta* f. 'garlic' vs. *sīrik; tarrikta* 'travel bag' vs. *terki; zōpa* 'stove' vs. *sobe* (<Turkish *soba*).

The texts from Aradhin yielded also highly interesting Semitic lexemes.[3] Perhaps the most surprising to have escaped Maclean's and all other lexicographers' attention is the prominent agricultural term *miššāra* 'paddy, bed, subdivision of a rice or tobacco field'. For the important activity of dividing a field into paddies the denominative verb *mamšōre* has been formed. The noun of action is *mamšarta*.

This term can be traced through older Aramaic *mešārā*[4] to Akkadian *mūšarum*,[5] where it is most likely the reflex of Sumerian *mu-sar* 'garden'.[6]

---

[3] In the following discussion repeated reference will be made to the following works:

C. Brockelmann, *Lexicon syriacum* (2nd ed. Halle, 1928).

G. H. Dalman, *Aramäisch-neuhebräisches Wörterbuch* (Frankfurt, 1901).

I. Garbell, *The Jewish Neo-Aramaic Dialect of Persian Azerbaijan* (The Hague, 1964).

M. Jastrow, *A Dictionary of the Targumim, the Talmud Babli and Yerushalmi* (London-New York, 1903; reprint: New York, 1950).

St. A. Kaufman, *The Akkadian Influences on Aramaic* (University of Chicago, 1974).

St. Lieberman, *The Sumerian Loanwords in Old-Babylonian Akkadian* (Harvard Semitic Studies 22, 1977).

A. J. Maclean, *Dictionary of the Dialects of Vernacular Syriac* (Oxford, 1901; reprint: Amsterdam, 1972).

R. Macuch und E. Panoussi, *Neusyrische Chrestomathie* (Wiesbaden, 1974).

Th. Nöldeke, *Grammatik der neusyrischen Sprache am Urmia-See und in Kurdistan* (Leipzig, 1868).

A. Salonen, *Agricultura mesopotamica* (Helsinki, 1968).

J. P. Smith, *A Compendious Syriac Dictionary* (Oxford, 1903).

R. P. Smith, *Thesaurus syriacus* (Oxford, 1879–97).

W. von Soden, *Akkadisches Handwörterbuch* (Wiesbaden, 1959–81).

A. Wahrmund, *Handwörterbuch der arabischen und deutschen Sprache* (Giessen, 1877).

[4] Dalman 224a 'Beet', Jastrow 779b 'bed'. For Old Syriac (OS) Brockelmann 408a records *mšārtā* 'arvum, area'. Arabic preserves this word as *mašārah* 'Theil des Ackers' (Wahrmund II 804a).

[5] Von Soden 681b (also *muš/sa(r)rū*) 'Beet'. The possibility of a loan from Sumerian is indicated with a question mark. The *Chicago Assyrian Dictionary* v.10/II separates *musarû/mušarû* 'garden' (233) from *musarū/mūšarū* pl. *tantum*

The semantic and phonetic stability of this lexeme is remarkable, and one should not be deterred from accepting its continuity in this area by the fact that on occasion it became associated and confused with derivatives from the roots *yšr 'to be straight', whence the meaning 'plain' (Jastrow 779b),[7] and *šry 'to untie', whence the meanings 'camp' and 'habitation' as in OS mašryā and mašrīṯā (J. P. Smith 309a).[8]

The low dam or wale which encloses a paddy is called banxa. It is not attested in either NA or OS, but there is a likely connection with JA binkā. The latter is translated by Dalman (56a) 'Furche' (= furrow) and considered by him a foreign word. He apparently normalized it from a Talmudic hapax legomenon, the plural binkē 'cavities dug around the vine to receive the water' (Jastrow 177b). Dalman's translation seems more appropriate than 'cavities', and it is easy to see how the designation for a furrow or a shallow ditch may also imply the little dam formed by the excavated earth, since both are complementary and in fact the two sides of the same coin. The further etymology of banxa remains unclear.

A very interesting group of words, not all new, is connected with the plow and the yoke. The plow itself appears in Aradhin in the variant bḏāna. Maclean lists ptānā, pdānā, and bdānā. All of these are reflexes of OS and JA paddānā 'yoke, plow',[9] but the spirantization of the d in Aradhin goes beyond the regular morphophonemic expectations. The colter of the plow was originally nothing more than a metal point. Its name sikṯa (OS and JA sikkəṯa, sikṯa) derives ultimately from Akkadian sikkatum 'peg, nail' (Kaufman 91). The moldboard of the modern plowshare has obviously no ancient name and is referred to in our text as parra 'wing' (<Kurdish per 'feather, wing'). The plow assembly also contains the beam mašāna, a word not recorded anywhere, but with a very close equivalent in Iraqi Arabic: mišān.[10] An older Aramaic or even Akkadian etymon is therefore very likely. At the rear end of the plow is

'a technical term for planting a field' (262). This term could very well mean 'by subdividing into paddies'.

[6] The Sumerian origin was already noted by H. Zimmern (Akkadische Fremdwörter als Beweis für babylonischen Kultureinfluss, Leipzig, 1915, 40) and is still maintained by Lieberman (no. 485). F. Schulthess discussed the word at length in ZA 19 (1905/6), 128f.

[7] The present discussion supercedes the etymology given in A Neo-Aramaic Dialect (s. note 1).

[8] Cf. Kaufman 74. In Drower/Macuch, A Mandaic Dictionary (Oxford, 1963, 279f.) the gloss for mšara is 'district, zone, habitation, abiding place'. In the last of the ten documented contexts, however, it is rendered 'garden-bed'. This shows how one lexeme may owe its semantic content to entirely different origins.

[9] The semantic connection with Akkadian padānu 'way, path' still begs to be elucidated.

[10] Cf. B. Meissner in Mitteilungen des Seminars für Orientalische Sprachen, v. 5, 168 (Berlin, 1898).

the handle *kawša*, which is also a new addition and which probably derives from the verb *kbaš* 'to squeeze, seize, crush', an appropriate etymon if one considers that in primitive plowing considerable force must be exercised by the plowman. The beam is attached to the plow by two pegs, *xāpe* (sg. *xāpa*), whose cognates are JA *ḥāpā* or *ḥippā*, and Mishnaic Hebrew *ḥāp* (Dalman 148a 'Zapfen', Jastrow 490a 'pivot').

The connection from the beam to the yoke is made by the special connector *qaṭrīwa*, most likely a derivative from the verb *qṭar* 'to tie'. Maclean records only its Azerbaijani equivalent *bōṣa* (36b), but the word is again found in JA as *qaṭrəbā* (Dalman 359b) or *qṭarbā* (Jastrow 1353a). The yoke *nīra* consists in turn of two parts which are called either *katīra* (no known connections) or *kalāma*. Maclean lists the latter as *klīmā* or *klāmā* (133b), while Brockelmann records an apparently unique occurrence in OS of a *klāmā* 'frenum (bovis)' (329b, corrected from *kālmā* of the first edition 158b).

The extraordinary tenacity of agricultural terminology is illustrated by the two terms *māra* 'spade, hoe' and *rušta* 'shovel, spade'. The former has a well documented history: Sumerian *mar*, Akkadian *marru*, OS *marrā*, Arabic *marr*.[11] The latter is obviously related to *rūša* 'shoulder' (*ruyša* in dialects from Iran). The OS cognate *rapša*, as well as the Aramaic loanword in Arabic *rafš* (Wahrmund I 778), combine the meanings 'shovel' and 'shoulder blade'. J. P. Smith's gloss (548a) reads: a) a winnowing-fan. b) the shoulder-blade. Semantic logic would require a reverse order of these items since it is, no doubt, legitimate to say that the scapula of large animals was the ideal instrument for winnowing and shoveling loose materials in a primitive agricultural society.

Akkadian material does not show the above semantic connection clearly, but it does not necessarily contradict it. Furthermore, it seems to provide a common semantic denominator for both terms. According to vSoden 955a–957a *rapšum* is a winnowing shovel, while *rapaštum* is many things, ranging from the pelvic bone and lower back of humans, over thighs of animals to pieces of meat. Remarkable is mainly the fact that the specialized secondary meaning is carried by the unmarked noun, while the marked one has a great variety of meanings including the apparently more primitive ones. That 'shoulder blade' is not among them may simply be due to the limitations of the texts in which this lexeme is preserved. Given the fact that both meanings are recorded for the OS and Arabic cognates (resp. loanwords, s. Kaufman 88), it is hardly possible to visualize the meaning 'winnowing shovel' without a preceding 'shoulder blade'. In addition, the Akkadian verb *rapāšum* with its simple and basic meaning 'to be broad or wide' provides a semantic clue

---

[11] Lieberman no. 466; Kaufman 70; Salonen 118f.; S. Fraenkel, *Die aramäischen Fremdwörter im Arabischen*, 86. Aside from having a cognate in ancient Egyptian (*mr*) this word has also radiated into Western languages.

for the derivation of 'shoulder blade' and 'pelvic bone' from the same root. Both bones immediately stick out from the rest of the skeleton by their broad surfaces. It is therefore, possible to postulate the semantic development: broad—broad bone—shoulder blade—shovel.[12]

Strong contraction, attrition, assimilation, and sporadic sound change pose a special challenge for the etymologist. Thus, the adverb *l-buṭṭuṭ* 'on an empty stomach', in which sense Maclean and Garbell know only the Persian loanword *nāštā*, must derive from the locution *bāt ṭwāt* 'he spent the night fasting' (J. P. Smith 171a),[13] preceded by the preposition *ʿal>l*.

The unpredictability of vocalic changes and of syllabic restructuring is well demonstrated by *tummil* 'yesterday (OS *eṭmal*, JA *itmol*), for which Garbell lists *timmal* and Maclean *timāl*. Sporadic consonantal change (dissimilation) can be seen in *bilbāṭa* 'spark' (OS *beṭbāṭā*) and becomes a real problem if it affects the initial consonant, as in *mubyāna* 'boil, swelling', a descendant of OS *ʿabyānā*. Also *gayigra* 'threshing sled' may be an irregular development from OS *gargərā*.

The insertion of a nonetymological *l* after initial *t* changes NA *ṭa* 'for' to *tla* in Aradhin. The same is the case with *tlawlēṭa* 'worm' (OS *tawlaʿā*, Akkadian *tultum*) for which Maclean (317a) has no less than five variants: *tiwilʿā*, *tiwiltā*, *tāwilṭā*, *tōleṭa*, and *tūliṭa*. This *l* becomes part of the root in the formation of the participial derivative *mtlūla* 'infested with worms'. Similarly, the transformation of the modern European word for car to *trumbēla* is explicable by the insertion of a nonetymological *r* after the initial *t* of *(o)tom(o)bil*. The complete incorporation of the resulting **trombīl* into the language is then sealed by the addition of the nominal ending *-a* and some syllabic adjustment. A completely different development of the same word has been recorded by Garbell (323a): *otmabel*.

Some names of gadgets whose patterning appears Semitic defy, nevertheless, an etymological explanation. A stone roller kept on the flat roofs of houses in Kurdistan for the purpose of periodically compacting and smoothening the raw clay of which they are made is called *mandurta*, while the corresponding verb 'to roll' is *mandōre*. No connection with any known Semitic root can be suggested. Maclean (182b) lists a *mandrulta* 'roll' and indicates Kurdish origin which cannot be substantiated; it may very well be only a variation of *mandurta*. There is a

---

[12] Von Soden does not explicitly acknowledge a connection between *rapšu* 'broad' and *rapšu* 'winnowing shovel'. Salonen (182) considers the latter an epithet which in the course of time has become independent: *marru rapšu* 'broad shovel'>*rapšu*. Although the process of the elimination of the noun in such phrases is known, it seems to be much less likely in this case than the semantic development envisioned in this paragraph.

[13] D. R. Hillers draws my attention to Dan 6:19. We have here a curious literal survival from Biblical Aramaic.

vaguely similar word in Turkish: *merdane* 'roller',[14] but without further information it is not possible at this time to go beyond a mere listing of these words. (See addendum.)

Of the same order is the problem as to how the words *marzaq* and *mazraka* are related. The former is a new addition from Aradhin, while‚ the latter is recorded by Garbell (319a) who claims for it unsubstantiated Arabic origin. That there is a connection seems beyond question in view of the very specialized meaning of both words and their general similarity. They refer to a curved tray with which the baker slaps the flat loaves on the wall of the hot oven.

The well attested NA word for mill *arxe* f. (pl. *arxāṯa*), spelled by Maclean (20b) *irkhī, erkhī*, is the transformation of OS *raḥyā* or JA *riḥyā* in close parallel with *axri* 'excrement' vs. OS *ḥaryā*. The ending -*e*, a frequent marker of the plural, is also an occasional allomorph of the singular ending -*a* without grammatical significance. Other singular words ending in -*e* are *gāre* 'roof',[15] *qrašte* 'ceiling, roof',[16] and *šimme* 'sky'.[17] Since the final -*e* of *arxe* and *šimme* cannot be explained as a purely phonetic development, it is hardly devious to suggest that it is due to the association of the -*e* with the plural, because the sky is often a plural (or dual) word in Semitic and the mill is an assembly of two millstones. It is easy to show that *raḥyā* and its cognates originally meant a single millstone, wherefore mill in Hebrew is expressed by the dual *reḥayim*. Since *arxe* means a whole mill, NA (at least in Aradhin) has acquired a special word of unknown origin for millstone, *katta*. As for *gāre* and *qrašte*, whose common semantic denominator is a 'cover over the head', it may be permitted to speculate that in conection with the word for sky this semantic category has acquired the characteristic -*e*.

To be sure, one would not need to attach too much importance to sporadic occurrences of this kind, except that there is another pair of words in our material, which share the same semantic category and an unusual final vowel. They are *xināqo* 'whooping cough' (<OS *ḥnaq* 'to choke') and *šalqo* 'smallpox'. The second word is obviously a new formation from *šlaq* 'to boil, scald', since the term in OS is *šālāqīṯā*, which could never yield *šalqo* in a regular phonetic development. This suggests a certain morphological attraction between words with meanings of the same category. A systematic collection of names of diseases as well as closer attention to the quality of final vowels in general might throw more light on this tantalizing problem.

[14] Heuser-Şevket, *Türkisch-deutsches Wörterbuch* (Istanbul, 1942), 293.

[15] OS *eggārā* 'roof'. This word is also of great antiquity (Akkadian *igāru*< Sumerian *igar* 'wall') and underwent the semantic change from 'wall' to 'roof' between Akkadian and Aramaic. Lieberman no. 346; Kaufman 57.

[16] Maclean 286b has only *qirša* 'roof'.

[17] Garbell 333b; not recorded in Aradhin, but probably the same. In literary NA the old *šmayya* is used.

On a lighter note, a curious semantic development can be shown regarding the word *ṣawmā* 'fasting, Lent'.[18] To appreciate the meaning of the corresponding adjective *ṣawmāna* 'homely, ugly' one needs to be familiar with the severity and length of the fast in Eastern Christian rites and to imagine the effect which its observance may have on pretty faces. This word is reminiscent of the Russian expression *sd'elat' postnoye l'itso* 'to make a lenten face', which implies a combination of emaciation, austerity, and piety, and for which the famous picture "American Gothic" provides a fitting illustration.

The following remarks will deal with problems presented by previously recorded and well known NA words.

mīla, f. *milta* 'blue, green' (whence the denominative verb *mamyūle* 'to become green') is connected by Maclean (173b) with Persian *mīnā* 'sky', by Macuch/Panoussi (83b) with Persian *mīnā* 'glass, enamel'. It is true that this versatile Persian word has those meanings plus that of azure, blue, and several others, but the difficulty in deriving NA *mīla* from it is both a phonetic one and one of probability. In *mīnā* the meaning blue is only incidental and probably limited to literary use. In contrast to this, the word *nīli* 'blue' (<*nīl* 'indigo') carries this meaning exclusively and is common to Persian, Iraqi Arabic, and Turkish. Oddly, Kurdish dictionaries do not list it, but it is interesting to note that the Kurdish *šīn* means both 'blue' and 'green', just as in NA. Moreover, it combines with an auxiliary verb to express the greening of the grass. Phonetically, it is much more difficult to justify a change of an intervocalic *n* to *l* than that of initial *n* to *m*. For the latter change a certain tendency exists, as can be shown by such variants as *nepuxtā* 'treacle' (Maclean 214a) vs. *mepuxta* (Aradhin) and the popular pronunciation *maṣṭurnāye* for *nesṭornāye* 'Nestorians'.

mṭaʾōle 'to play'. Maclean (171b), and following him Macuch/Panoussi (61b), derive this verb from OS *ṭayyel* 'to perambulate'. Both phonetically and semantically, this etymology is unjustifiable. First, there is no way *yy* could become a glottal stop. Second, going back and forth, even if for pleasure, is not equivalent to playing, and deriving one from the other cannot be done without undue strain.

Since most glottal stops in NA are reflexes of an older ayin, the most likely root must be *ṭʿl* or *tʿl*. Indeed, OS possesses the denominative verb *taʿʿel* 'to fawn, wag the tail' (<*taʿlā* 'fox'; J. P. Smith 617a), and anyone who has witnessed the *play*ful behavior of young foxes cannot

---

[18] The dialect of Aradhin preserves the diphthong *aw* in contrast with the speech of Urmia, where it becomes *ō*. Thus, Lent in Urmia is *ṣōma*, which is part of the compound *mālṣome* (sic) listed by Macuch/Panoussi (85a) and explained as a derivative of Russian *masl'an'itsa* 'carnival'. The impossibility of this should be obvious, and the correct derivation is from OS *maʿal ṣawmā* 'entrance of Lent', namely the days preceding Lent, or Shrovetide.

but connect it in his mind with the notion of play. As to the velarization of the *ṭ*, it is due to the influence of the ayin before its disappearance. This velarization due to an ayin is a frequent but irregular phenomenon in NA and may differ from dialect to dialect. Thus 'fox' is *ṭālā* in Urmia, but *tēla* in Aradhin. That the verb is velarized in both, shows only that it has long been separated from its etymon and has had its own destiny and distribution among the dialects of NA.

bidra 'threshing floor' is a continuation of OS *edrā*, JA *idrā*, already known from Assyrian times as *idru* (vSoden 364b). The prefixed *b* can be explained as a remainder of *bē(ṭ)* in analogy with the numerous other compounds with it (s. Maclean 31). This word was adopted from an earlier stage of Aramaic by neighboring languages which still retain the long *ē*: Iraqi Arabic *bēdar*, Kurdish *bēder*. The shortening of the vowel in NA must be the result of morphophonemic restructuring due to the consonant cluster in the emphatic state.

The three words which may be considered the most characteristic and distinguishing lexical isoglosses of eastern NA, *aqla* 'foot, leg', *nāta/nāṭa* 'ear', and *baxta* 'woman', are also problematic ones with regard to their origin and etymology.

aqla 'foot', which is spelled with an initial aleph and has completely replaced OS *riglā*, invites speculation because it has no obvious Semitic connections. Maclean (19a) makes two alternate suggestions, a rather tortuous derivation from OS *riglā*, or from OS *ᶜaqqel* 'to twist'. Macuch/Panoussi (16a) accept the first suggestion with caution and express it with the following formula: <a[r]glā?, AS *riglā*. Nöldeke (402) had previously rejected a connection with OS *ᶜaqlānā* 'ankle chain', arguing that the latter had to be derived from * *ᶜql* 'to be crooked', the implication being that 'leg' could not possibly be derived from this notion. He also dismissed a derivation from *riglā* as too farfetched.

In spite of all this, the correct derivation can only be from * *ᶜql*, since J. P. Smith and the *Thesaurus* list an *ᶜaqlā* 'shank, leg' resp. 'crus'. Its apparent status as a hapax legomenon only contributes to the astonishment due to the fact that such a rare OS word has become the only expression for foot and leg in eastern NA. The focus of attention must, therefore, switch from phonetic manipulations to questions of semantics.

There are various things that come to mind when one tries to connect the image of a leg with the notion of twisting or bending. They range from bow-legged people to the sight of a muscular leg, which may look almost like a braid. In support of the latter connection one might even cite the Arabic epithet *maftūl as-sāᶜid* 'with a muscular arm' (literally: twisted of arm). But none of these really satisfies. The truth must lie somewhere in the area of snaring or hobbling animals. It is important at this point to bring in the newly recorded word from Aradhin *aqulta* 'snare, trap', whose connection with *aqla* is too appealing to be rejected out of hand. Furthermore, the connection between foot and snare is documented in OS by the denominative verb *šargel* 'to ensnare'. That the semantic process in the case of *aqla* seems to be reversed makes the explanation only a little more difficult, since it is conceivable that the word originated as a kind of pun on the part of the people for whom the connection between foot and snare was familiar. Also the connection between *aqla* and *aqlānā* appears now in a different light, and Nöldeke's objection may safely be laid to rest.

nāta (Aradhin: *nāṯa*) 'ear'. Nöldeke refused to speculate, but expressly rejected a derivation from OS *eḏnā* (402: "schon wegen des a der 1. Silbe nicht [daran] zu denken"). Macuch/Panoussi (946) suggest a solution according to which the truncated plural (*eḏ*)*nāṯā* took the place of the singular. Then the secondary plural *natwāṯā* was formed. In itself this suggestion is not improbable, since cases of plurals becoming singulars and of secondary plurals are known. The limited applicability of this solution, however, becomes apparent if one considers other variants of the word for 'ear'. In addition to the above, Maclean (219b) lists *nāšā* and *nāwiyā*, while Garbell (322b) records the totally unexpected *nahala/ nahalta/nhalta* (pl. *nahalye/nhalye*). In order to judge the last three variants it is important to know that in the dialect described by Garbell *l* is a regular replacement for the spirantized *ṯ* of OS (e.g., *bela* for *bēṯa*). Thus *nahala* would correspond to *nahata/nahaṯa* in other dialects. The *h*, however, requires an explanation, and it is wise at this stage to keep one's options open.

baxta 'woman'. Because this word does not bear any resemblance to designations of females in any known Semitic language, and because phonetically it coincides completely with the Persian and Kurdish *baxt* 'luck, good fortune', some scholars were inclined to equate the two words without further explanations. Thus, the origin of *baxta* is given as Kurdish by Bergsträsser,[19] Tsereteli,[20] and Garbell (299b, with question mark). Nöldeke (402) had seen the possibility, but decided against it with the words: "Für so galant, die Frau geradezu [*baxt*] "Glück" zu nennen, darf man die Neusyrer wohl kaum halten." This remark misses the point in so far as it is not the gallantry of the people, but the need for a euphemism in a society in which direct reference to women is to be avoided, that would have to be made responsible for such a choice. In itself such a euphemism does not seem impossible, but the main objection against it is the total absence in Kurdish sources of any indication that *baxt* may ever refer to women. The euphemism found commonly is *kulfet* (<Arabic *kulfatun* 'charge, responsibility'), which has also currency in NA as *kilpat*, *kelpat*, or *čilpat*.

It was already the author of the *Thesaurus* who connected NA *baxta* with OS *bāḵeṯṯa*, which he translated 'mulier mercenaria', adding to this

---

[19] G. Bergsträsser, *Einführung in die semitischen Sprachen* (München, 1928), 93.

[20] K. G. Tsereteli, *Khrestomatiya sovremennovo assiriyskovo yazika so slovar'om* (Tbilisi, 1958), 028.

various references which connect this word with the notion of weaving. His gloss for *baxta* is: "mulier . . . texendi notione temporis decursu omissa' (527). This information was then cast by J. P. Smith into her entry (45b): "[*bkt*] part.f. [*bāk̲tā*] to weave for hire; hence [*bāk̲ett̲a*] f. pl. [*-āt̲ā*] a hired weaveress, and Neo-Syriac [*baxtā*] pl. [*baxtāt̲ā*] a woman, spinster."[21] Macuch/Panoussi omit the details of weaving and quote as etymon: "AS *bāk̲ett̲ā* mulier mercenaria."

The existence in OS of a word for a female being which is as close to *baxta* as is *bāk̲ett̲ā*, provides us with an etymology much superior to Kurdish *baxt*, some phonetic difficulties in proving the transition from one to the other notwithstanding. These difficulties could be removed by assuming a spontaneous adjustment of the singular to the plural *baxtāt̲a*. The mystery which remains unsolved, however, is how a word of such apparent rarity in older Aramaic could have become the exclusive carrier of the meaning 'woman' in NA. (See addendum.)

Although Syriac dictionaries which list the word *bāk̲ett̲ā* agree on its meaning 'weaveress', they do not offer evidence that the underlying verb was ever used in OS. J. P. Smith's entry [*bkt*] 'to weave for hire' seems to be solely a deduction from 'mulier mercenaria' of the *Thesaurus*. Also the relationship of the root *bkt to Hebrew *bwk, as suggested in the *Thesaurus*, is farfetched and not convincing. Much more solid support for the existence of such a root is provided by the Arabic doublet of cognate verbs *bakata* and *baxata* 'to strike, beat'.[22] If their meaning seems at first unrelated to weaving, an Akkadian parallel shows clearly that a semantic connection between beating and weaving does exist, no doubt due to the beating down of the weft during weaving. The Akkadian verb is *maxāṣu* 'to strike' and 'to weave'.[23]

Much remains to be done in the field of NA lexicology and lexicography. Admirable as Maclean's dictionary is, it is not reliable with regard

---

[21] It is interesting to compare the wording of Maclean's entry (32b): "[*baxta*], esp. U[rmia], (probably for [*bakta*] fem. pres. part. of OS [*bk̲at*] to spin; cf. OS [*bak̲ett̲a*] an hired spinster), f.8, a married *woman*, *wife*." Dean Maclean is clearly influenced by the last word of J. P. Smith's entry ("spinster"), which he takes not as it was intended, but in its technical sense, adjusting everything else from weaving to spinning. Although the imprint date of Maclean's dictionary is two years earlier than that of *A Compendious Syriac Dictionary*, an acknowledgement in the preface to the latter proves that he collaborated in the final stages of its preparation for print and must have been able to see the entry in question at a much earlier date.

[22] Wahrmund I 181a, 242b. The existence of such doublets is indicative of a borrowing. The spirantized variant would then be a loan from Aramaic. The Aramaic inscription Sefire I, face A, line 24, contains a problematic *bkth* (*bbth*?). One of the attempts to explain it makes use of Syriac *bkt* 'to weave' (see J. A. Fitzmyer in *JAOS* 81 [1961] 195). I thank D. R. Hillers for this reference.

[23] Von Soden 580. S. also the discussion of Ugaritic cognates by M. Held in *JAOS* 79 (1959) 169f.

to phonetic detail, and its dialectological information is insufficient to map the isoglosses which unite and separate the various regions. What is needed, are systematic and phonetically adequate vocabularies for all major dialects. To be really useful in comparative studies they must include the same basic range of the lexicon, covering agriculture, plants, animals, parts of the body, household items, basic activities, and crafts. To remain manageable, such word lists can safely exclude all intellectual and religious terms, since these will be predictably close to OS and, therefore, more or less identical. Presently available glossaries depend on given texts and often lack the most common items.[24]

Neo-Aramaic studies have, after a rather marginal existence since the first pioneering works, enjoyed a remarkable revival during the past two or three decades. Their great chance is that they can still mine a living reservoir of language and thus provide a much needed supplement to Arabic dialectology. But time may be running out, and nobody in a position to contribute should delay doing so.

Eastern Neo-Aramaic has been treated as a change-of-life baby[25] of classical Syriac, an attitude based on the impression provided by the heavy overlay of OS in the missionary literature. It is, however, important to realize that the Aramaic of the Targum and the Talmud is equally important for the elucidation of lexical problems of NA. Structurally, NA has achieved its own independent status, but the elements which are now part of its structure derive from different areas in time and space. Some features belong to immediately preceding periods of the history of the language, while others are of great antiquity. This is very obvious in the vocabulary, but applies also to structural elements. As a case in point, the infinitive pattern of Akkadian (palāxu) has experienced a renaissance in NA (plāxa), bypassing the intermediate stages of Aramaic.

The science of language has frequently looked to the natural sciences for its models. They range from the evolutionary tree of Darwinism over weather maps to the recent mathematical and computer generated models. There may be still room for other inspiration. The mixture of predictability and randomness in the various forms of NA and elsewhere suggests a comparison with the sea, in which parts of the water may be at rest while others move according to predetermined streams, into which rivers carry their manifold deposits and mineral solutions, and in which uncounted living beings exist, each according to the laws of its species. Whenever spoken or written specimens of language are studied, they are comparable to specimens of ocean water or polar ice taken at different points and at different depths. Just as ocean water can only be studied in

---

[24] A case in point is the relatively small overlap between the vocabularies of Garbell and Krotkoff. Regrettably, therefore, Garbell's collection has provided only very little comparative material for this study.

[25] Those who know German will rightly suspect that the word actually in the mind of this writer is the much more expressive *Wechselbalg*.

samples, it is impossible to account for all of language. Vast stretches between samples will always remain unknown, but careful evaluation of retrieved information, judicious projection, and, in the case of language, a realistic assessment of human possibilities can help to bridge the inevitable gaps. Historical linguistics may still have something to learn from oceanography and fluid mechanics.

Addendum.　After the manuscript had gone to press, several exchanges with colleagues resulted in new insights.

　　Following a hint from A. Schall, Heidelberg, and upon further scrutiny of the entries *merdane* in the dictionaries of Redhouse and Steingass, the following semantic and phonetic development appears certain: Persian *mardānah* 'male, manly' → 'what belongs to a man' → (in Turkish only?) 'male organ' → 'club' → 'rolling pin' → 'roof roller'. The NA *mandurta* is obviously the result of a metathesis. Other variants of this word were supplied to me by O. Jastrow, Erlangen: Ṭurōyō *mandrūne, mandrūnīye, mandūrīye;* Anatolian Arabic *mandarūne,* with the corresponding verb *mandar, ymandər.*

　　O. Jastrow draws my attention to the fact that in Anatolian Arabic and in Ṭurōyō *baxt* has also the meaning 'honor'. The cited Kurdish-Russian dictionaries do indeed indicate the additional meaning 'honesty' (not 'honor'). For 'honor' the Russian-Kurdish dictionary gives *namûs, merîfet, hurmet.* Thus the meaning 'honor' seems to be only marginal for *baxt* within Kurdish. It is, however, relevant that *hurmet* (←Arabic *ḥurma* 'that which is inviolate or taboo') is another frequent euphemism for 'woman' in this area. Considering these facts, the association of NA *baxta* with Kurdish *baxt* becomes more plausible, and the scales appear to be tipped in favor of the Kurdish etymology. Some doubts may, however, remain due to such unanswerable questions as to why the seemingly marginal *baxt* got the upper hand over other words for 'honor', and due to the lack of evidence for the use of this word for 'woman' in Kurdish. Those in favor of compromises might even consider a mutual reinforcement and a merging of the two strands *baxt* and *baḵeṯta* into the one dominating *baxta.*

PHILIPPI'S LAW RECONSIDERED

Thomas O. Lambdin
Harvard University

1. INTRODUCTION

I N the course of a lengthy and perceptive article on the historical development of the number "two" in Semitic,[1] F. W. M. Philippi devoted two pages to a discussion of the apparent change of PS *i to a in certain phonetic situations in Hebrew, Ethiopic, and Aramaic. Although the efforts to establish this sound change as common Semitic, i.e., in the PS stage, were not successful, Brockelmann did accept the law as applying to both Hebrew and Aramaic when he codified the basic principles of Semitic historical phonology in his *Grundriss*.[2] He was followed in this regard by Bauer and Leander[3] and by Bergsträsser[4] in their still standard treatments of Hebrew historical grammar. Whether or not Philippi's Law is operative in Aramaic must remain an open question, since we are still far from possessing an adequate knowledge of Aramaic historical phonology. The isolated examples adduced are drawn almost entirely from Syriac and are for the most part susceptible of other phonetic or analogical explanations. The Aramaic evidence, at any rate, has no immediate relevance to the problems treated in the following discussion.

Note the following abbreviations: PS Proto-Semitic; TH Tiberian Hebrew according to the MT; BH Babylonian Hebrew; Hex. Hexaplaric transcriptions of Hebrew in Greek letters.

[1] F. W. M. Philippi, "Das Zahlwort Zwei im Semitischen," *ZDMG* 32 (1878), 21–98; esp. pp. 41–43.

[2] C. Brockelmann, *Grundriss der vergleichenden Grammatik der semitischen Sprachen*, I (Berlin, 1908), 147.

[3] H. Bauer and P. Leander, *Historische Grammatik der hebräischen Sprache des alten Testaments* (Halle, 1922), 195.

[4] G. Bergsträsser, *Hebräische Grammatik*, I (Leipzig, 1918), 149.

[5] PS will be used as a cover term throughout this article to designate forms and sounds normally reconstructed for the stage of development preceding the actually attested Semitic languages. In some instances PWS (Proto-West Semitic) or PNWS (Proto-Northwest Semitic) would be a more accurate designation, but to justify the finer distinction in each case would lead too far afield.

135

Philippi's Law, in one form or another, is universally supposed to be operative in TH. Whenever PS[5] *i turns up as *a* in a closed stressed syllable,[6] the law is cited as a sufficient explanation, but because there are three possible reflexes of PS *i in closed stressed syllables in TH, namely *ē*, *e*, and *a*, the exact statement of the law has always proved troublesome. Brockelmann[7] specifies that the vowel shift takes place "in geschlossener, betonter Silbe im Wortinnern und in solchen wortauslautenden Silben, die schon in Urhebr. geschlossen waren." Bauer-Leander: "... in geschlossener Haupt- und Nebendrucksilbe ...," adding that the change does not take place in "Silben, die erst durch den Endvokalwegfall geschlossen wurden."[8] Bergsträsser describes the environment for the change similarly and further specifies that before doubled consonants the process was not completed, resulting in TH *a*, *e*, or *ē*.[9] Brockelmann and Bauer-Leander also make it clear that the law was contravened by analogy in countless instances. The basis for these qualifications will become clear in the following discussion. In general, however, Philippi's Law falls woefully short of what one expects of a "law" in historical phonology: on the one hand, the phonetic environment in which the law applies eludes precise definition; on the other, in many of the categories where the law is said to apply there are more counterexamples than examples.

The present article is an attempt to disengage a real, clearly definable phonetic law from the chaos of conflicting data that confronts us. This requires not only a resurvey of each morphological category in TH where the law is considered applicable, but also a comparison of these with their counterparts in the non-Tiberian traditions of Biblical Hebrew, specifically the texts with Babylonian vocalization[10] and the Hexaplaric transcriptions.[11] Methodologically, BH and Hex. will be viewed as "dialects" developing parallel to TH and not simply as degenerate mappings of the latter onto less precise grids. This approach entails the conceptualization of a Proto-Biblical Hebrew Tradition from which the various traditions, including TH, evolved by a set of explicit, unambiguous rules. For the fundamental insight of this paper I am indebted to the

---

[6] For the purpose of this paper stress is assumed to be on the same syllable of a word as in TH. Stress may indeed have been different at earlier stages of Hebrew, but the need to deal with this problem does not arise in our discussion.

[7] C. Brockelmann, *Grundriss*, I, 147.

[8] H. Bauer and P. Leander, *Historische Grammatik*, 195.

[9] G. Bergsträsser, *Hebräische Grammatik*, 149.

[10] The source for the Babylonian material is P. Kahle, *Masoreten des Ostens* (Leipzig, 1913), 183–99.

[11] The Hexaplaric transcriptions are taken from E. Brønno, *Studien über hebräische Morphologie und Vokalismus auf Grundlage der Mercatischen Fragmente der zweiten Kolumne der Hexapla des Origenes* (Leipzig, 1943). Note that all transliterations marked Hex. are from transcriptions of Hebrew in the Greek alphabet.

work of Brønno and his insistence on the importance of the Hexaplaric transcriptions for the correct understanding of Hebrew historical phonology.[12] Much of the systematization of the material itself derives from the important study of this same problem by my former teacher, F. R. Blake.[13]

2. THE NOUN TYPES *$qatl$ AND *$qitl$

There are four[14] types of nouns in TH corresponding to the PS types *$qatl$ and *$qitl$:

		constr. pl.	
A.	*melek*/*malkî*		*malkê*
B.	*qeber*/*qibrî*		*qibrê*
C.	*nēder (neder)*/*nidrî*		*nidrê*
D.	*sēper*/*siprî*		*siprê*

Type A is universally taken as the normal development of PS *$qatl$, through the stage *$qatel$ (with anaptyxis) to $qetel$ (with assimilation of a to the anaptyctic e).[15] There is no completely uniform view on the development of types B, C, and D. For Brockelmann, Bauer-Leander, and Blake all *$qitl$ forms should have become *$qatl$, yielding type B, i.e., Philippi's Law operated on the stressed unbound form of the stem but did not affect the unstressed bound form. This explanation presupposed a difference in stress between the two forms at the time when the law was operative. The existence of type D, however, necessitates the preservation

[12] Brønno's *Studien* is an exemplary exposition of the Hexaplaric material and merits close study by all serious students of Biblical Hebrew historical grammar. His conclusion (p. 448), ". . . die Formen der SEC beruhen hier darauf, dass das Gesetz PHILIPPIS in der der SEC unterliegenden Tradition keine Gültigkeit hatte . . . ," is drawn from extended discussions of all relevant forms throughout the book. SEC is his abbreviation for the Second Column of Origen's Hexapla.

[13] F. R. Blake, "The Apparent Interchange between a and i in Hebrew," *JNES* 9 (1950), 76–83.

[14] These types are defined by a pairing of the free form with stressed base and the bound form with unstressed base, the latter represented schematically by the noun with the 1st pers. sing. pronominal suffix -$î$. Nouns from roots II-guttural (ʿ, ḥ, h) have been excluded from the discussion since *$qatl$ and *$qitl$ have merged into a single form for these nouns. Nouns from roots II-ʾ have their own phonetic history and are not relevant to the discussion at hand; nouns from roots with original *w and *y in second or third root position have been omitted for similar reasons.

[15] Hex. exhibits only two types, schematically $qatl$/$qatli$ and $qetl$/$qetli$, the first corresponding to TH type A and the second to TH types B, C, and D. There is no segholation (anaptyxis) in the free form. BH exhibits three types: $qátal$/$qatlî$ corresponding to TH A, $qátal$/$qitlî$ corresponding to TH B, and $qētal$/$qitlî$ (?) corresponding TH D. As we shall observe below, individual nouns do not necessarily belong to corresponding types in the different traditions.

of at least some *qitl* forms so that *qitl>*qitel>qētel. Brockelmann attributes this simply to the analogy of the bound form; Bauer-Leander, to the *i* of the plural *qitalīm*. Blake prefers to see qētel as originally the pausal form, corresponding to pausal qātel for type A. There is probably some truth in all these explanations.

The problem of the origin of type B is further complicated by the fact that according to general scholarly consensus some words of type B were originally *qatl/qatlî* and developed the bound form qitlî by "attenuation" of *a>i* in unstressed closed syllables. The change of *a>i* in unstressed closed syllables is an accepted rule in Hebrew historical phonology, but like Philippi's Law, it is usually stated in terms vague enough to allow for the many instances in which it is not to be applied.[16] Blake, however, attempted to define more clearly the circumstances in which the change takes place and referred to it as the qatqát>qitqát dissimilation: a is dissimilated to i in closed unstressed syllables which are followed by a stressed closed syllable also containing a.[17] The rule thus stated is used by him to account for (1) the first syllable of Niphal, Piel, and Hiphil Perfects, (2) the initial syllable of many nouns of the pattern TH miqtāl (e.g., *madbaru>*madbar>midbār), (3) the initial syllable of various other noun forms (e.g., ⁻*ṣadaqat>*ṣadqat>ṣidqat, *dabaray>*dabray>dibrê), (4) the verbal prefixes of the Qal Imperfect (perhaps), and (5) various isolated words not conforming to any standard pattern. The verb forms under (1) will be discussed in detail below. The various items under (3), (4), and (5) are susceptible of other explanations and need not involve qatqát>qitqát at all. The large group of nouns with prefixed m- referred to in category (2), however, is very important for our present discussion.

There are nearly 200 nouns[18] in TH which are descended from earlier *maqtal, *miqtal, or their feminine counterparts in *-t or *-at. The distribution of the prefixes mi- and ma- in TH is dependent almost entirely on the phonetic character of the consonant following the prefix:

(1) ma- occurs before a guttural (ʾ, ʿ, h, ḥ), a doubled consonant, and occasionally before r, l, m, and n.

(2) mi- occurs elsewhere, including most words with r, l, m, and n.

The only area of ambiguity, then, involves r, l, m, and n after the prefix; me- also is found occasionally before these consonants. Otherwise, the

---

[16] For example, G. Bergsträsser, *Hebräische Grammatik*, 146: "In unbetonter geschlossener Silbe ist a unter gewissen nicht mehr bestimmbaren Bedingungen zu i geworden. . . ."

[17] F. R. Blake, "The Apparent Interchange," 77–79.

[18] Nouns from roots with original *y or *w in any root position and from geminate roots are excluded because they do not preserve the requisite shape in their development.

number of exceptions is negligible, and we may assume with some assurance that any distinctions that may have existed between the bases *maqtal and *miqtal at an earlier stage have been completely erased in TH, the forms being redistributed according to purely phonetic criteria. While it is impossible to determine accurately the relative frequencies of the bases *maqtal and *miqtal for any earlier stage by the comparative method, there is a common consensus that a fairly large number of original *maqtal forms are involved in the TH sample. This would indicate that so far as TH is concerned, the qatqát>qitqát dissimilation did not take place before a guttural consonant or a doubled consonant[19] and was inhibited before r, l, m, and n. Of even greater importance for understanding the historical range of this sound change is the fact that most nouns of the pattern miqtāl in TH show up as maqtāl in BH and maqtal in Hex. At least as far as this important group of nouns is concerned, the qatqát>qitqát dissimilation is not a general Hebrew change but is limited to TH.[20]

The presumed pre-Hebrew base of the Niphal Perfect, *naqtal-, offers a phonetic parallel to *maqtal; hence the assumption that it is also an example of qatqát>qitqát: *naqtál->niqtál. There are two difficulties with this explanation. In the first place, the Niphal prefix ni- is shared by all of the Hebrew traditions, perhaps including Samaritan,[21] and therefore belongs to a level earlier than the qatqát>qitqát of the preceding paragraph. In the second place, there is a qualitative difference in the results of the presumed dissimilation: the treatment of the vowel before gutturals (e.g., neᶜĕbar) and doubled consonants (e.g., nittan) is completely different from that of *maqtal>miqtāl (e.g., maᶜăbār, mattān). In general, the Niphal prefix ni- finds a closer phonetic parallel in the Qal Imperfect prefix yi- of the type yiqtal. The similar problem of the Hiphil prefix will be treated below.

If Blake is correct in requiring the specific environment qatqát for the change *a>i in unstressed closed syllables, the commonly assumed change of some forms *qatlî>qitlî would have to be seen as the result of

---

[19] This is supported further by the existence in TH of the pattern qattāl< *qattal (e.g., gannāb, pārāš) and qattelet<*qattalt (e.g., yabbešet) with no dissimilation of the first vowel. The change of a to e before virtually doubled gutturals belongs to a later order of changes, since it is dependent on the presence of qāmeṣ in the following syllable. Contrast ʾeḥād, constr. ʾaḥad; ʾaḥat, pausal ʾeḥāt; lehābāh, constr. lahebet (<*lahhabat, *lahhabt), ʾaḥay, but ʾeḥāw (his brothers), and many others. The he- form of the definite article also exhibits this sound change in TH.

[20] Samaritan Hebrew is in full agreement with BH and Hex. in this regard.

[21] The Samaritan Niphal Perfect niqqå̊tïl has been re-formed on the basis of the Imperfect yiqqå̊tål; there is therefore no sure way to assess the historical authenticity of the prefix ni-.

paradigmatic leveling, with the change beginning in forms like *qatlák and *qatlám.[22] It is worth noting that if the change from *qatlî to qitlî was a frequent one, Philippi's Law is not required at all in explaining the development of *qatl and *qitl nouns in TH: (A) would be the normal development of *qatl, (D) of *qitl, (B) the dissimilated branch of *qatl, and (C) a mixed type resulting through back-information from the ambiguous bound form qitlî.

There is an interesting phonetic correlation among these types in TH that deserves comment.[23] Of the 87 nouns whose second radical is not l, m, n, or r, 72 (83%) have a bound form qitlî; of the 60 nouns whose second radical is l, m, n, or r, 51 (85%) have an unambiguous qetel as their free form. The historical interpretation of these figures is beset with insurmountable difficulties. In the first place, there is no way to establish the quantitative distribution of the forms *qatl and *qitl at any stage of reconstruction prior to the Hebrew itself. Perhaps the most that can be said is that no one, to my knowledge, has suggested that the distinction between the two types of nouns was based originally on the presence or absence of nasals or liquids in the second root position. In the second place, while etymological comparison of individual nouns is possible with a limited number of words, even these lead to immediate contradictions in many cases.

An even more serious problem arises within the Hebrew evidence itself. The relatively minute corpus of Hexaplaric forms available shows almost 50% disagreement with the TH forms qatlî, e.g., Hex. derkhi (TH darkî), Hex. esdi (TH ḥasdî), Hex. nephsi (TH napšî), Hex. selei (TH salᶜî), Hex. reglai (TH raglay).The similar disparity of the Babylonian corpus is well known, e.g., BH dirkô (TH darkô), BH riglêhem, (TH raglêhem) BH ṣilmê (TH ṣalmê), BH baṭnî (TH biṭnî), BH qabrî (TH qibrî). In view of the limited nature of both of these non-Tiberian corpora, even a casual extrapolation suggests a rather horrendous deviation from TH in this set of forms, a deviation which follows no discernible pattern. Thus, it is virtually impossible to control the distribution of these forms both in general Semitic and within Hebrew. It would appear, however, that in TH the presence or absence of l, m, n, or r in second root position has effected a partial redistribution of these forms.

---

[22] These two forms are the immediate antecedents of TH qatlām (with 3rd pers. masc. pl. suffix) and Hex. qatlak (with 2nd pers. masc. sing. suffix). Limitations of space prevent an extended discussion of the development of these forms; qatlāk was an alternate to TH qatlĕkā and may even underlie the irregular spelling (without a final *mater*) of the MT.

[23] Only those nouns whose types are clearly attested in TH alone have been counted here. Nouns from geminate roots, roots II-guttural, II-w, y, and III-w, y were excluded from the count.

The feminine form of many participles and some nouns was marked by the suffix -*t*.[24] For stems ending in -*CiC* and -*CaC* the resultant forms in -*CiCt* and -*CaCt* coincided identically in their terminal segments with the noun types **qitl* and **qatl*, whose development they then share: (A) -*CeCet*/-*CaCtî*, (B) -*CeCet*/-*CiCtî*. For the vast majority of these forms the coexisting masculine form provides a clear indication of the underlying vowel, and as a group they are quite stable, exhibiting no apparent shift from -*CaCtî* to -*CiCtî* or vice versa.[25]

Feminine infinitives of the type *šebet*/*šibtî* (<**šibt*/*šibtî*) from roots I-y and I-n provide a similar phonetic situation. Here again type D is missing. These forms are also quite stable, with no noticeable shifting of -*CiCtî* to -*CaCtî*; as in the case of the words discussed in the preceding paragraph, the underlying vowel is unambiguously present in closely related forms, namely the Imperfect and Imperative (e.g., *yēšēb*, *šēb*) and occasionally an alternate form of the infinitive (e.g., *lēdāh*/*ledet*). It is undoubtedly significant that the feminine forms in -*CiCt* conform to type B and not to type D with but rare exceptions (e.g., *ʾēšet*/*ʾištî* and *təkēlet*).

Nouns of the types **qatl* and **qitl* from geminate roots, schematically represented as **qall* and **qill* respectively, exhibit counterparts to the types A, B, and D above:[26] (A) TH *qal*/*qallî* (e.g., *ʿam*/*ʿammî*), (B) TH *qal*/*qillî* (e.g., *pat*/*pittî* morsel), (D) TH *qēl*/*qillî* (e.g., *hēn*/*hinnî*). There are well over 40 examples of A, if adjectives are included, about eight of B, and about 17 of D. The two nouns *bat*/*bittî* and *Gat*/*Gittî* (place name) have been included in B, although both have a geminate consonant resulting from the assimilation of an **n*: **bint*, **Gint*. Exactly parallel forms, such as the infinitive *tēt*/*tittî* (from **tint*) and *ʿēz*/*ʿizzî* (from **ʿinz*, she-goat), belong to type D.

The evidence for these nouns in non-Tiberian Hebrew is limited. The free forms of type D occur with *a* in BH, e.g., *ʿat* (TH *ʿēt*), *lab* (TH *lēb*), and with epsilon in Hex., e.g., *em* (TH *ʾēm*), *es* (TH *ʾēš*), *leb*/*lebbi* (TH *lēb*/*libbî*).

If we ignore type B and assume that type A remains essentially unchanged, the minimal reconstruction required here is very simple:

---

[24] Participial examples include Qal active, Niphal, Piel, Pual, Hiphil, and Hophal (*qōtelet*, *niqtelet*, *mĕqattelet*, *mĕquttelet*, *maqtelet*, *moqtelet*); nominal examples include the construct and presuffixal forms of many fem. nouns with prefixed *m*-, like *milḥāmāh*/*milḥemet*/*milḥamtî*, and some feminine nouns and adjectives from the base **qattal*-, like *ʾayyelet*, *gaḥelet*/*gaḥaltî*, *ṣammeret*/*ṣammartô* (foliage), *lehābāh*/*lahebet*.

[25] The original forms of some nouns are, of course, uncertain, e.g., *ʾiwwelet*/*ʾiwwaltî* (cf. the adjective *ʾĕwîl*).

[26] The unusual form *kēn*/*kannô* (pedestal) defies classification.

(1) an initial change of *i to *e before final CC and the subsequent simplification of the final consonant produce the Hex. forms; (2) in BH *e merges with a;[27] (3) in TH *e>$ē$ in monosyllabic words but remains e (seghol) in polysyllabic words. The last part of rule (3) is introduced to account for the rare noun types represented by $barzel$<*$barzill$, $garzen$< *$garzinn$, $karmel$<*$karmill$, and $ʾēmet$<*$ʾimitt$<*$ʾimint$. The nouns of type B remain intractable.

3. FINITE VERBAL FORMS

In the final singly closed syllable of nouns and adjectives, including participles, PS *a, *i, *u develop regularly, by a process known as tonic lengthening, into TH $ā$, $ē$, $ō$; BH $ā$, $ē$, $ō$; Hex. a, $ē$, $ō$.[28] In finite verbal forms, however, the development of the same vowels in the same position is TH a, $ē(a)$, $ō$; BH a, $ē/a$, $ō$; Hex. a, e, o.[29] The reason for this divergent development is unknown; in the absence of firm data one may hypothesize that it is due to (1) original differences in stress between the two categories; (2) a time difference in the closure of the syllable in question, which in all cases was originally open, (3) a combination of these two. Because the divergent development of these two sets of form classes is attested to some extent in all subsequent forms of the "Proto-Tradition" which we are attempting to reconstruct, it must be formulated as a rule in the initial stage of that tradition, approximately: (1) in nouns and adjectives PS *$á$, *$í$, *$ú$, + C#>*$â$, *$ê$, *$ô$ + C#; (2) in finite verbal forms PS *$á$, *$í$, *$ú$ + C# *$á$, *$é$, *$ó$ + C#. Subsequent development would require that *a, *e, *o remain unchanged in Hex., would become a, a, $ō$ in BH, and would become a, $ē$, $ō$ in TH. It is important to note that the initial sound change PS *$í$>*$é$ suggested here has nothing to do directly with Philippi's Law as usually stated. At this stage of development the *$é$ should be regarded simply as an allophone of *i or *$ē$ in this particular position.

It is usually assumed that the Piel Perfect originally had an *i in the second stem syllable, i.e., *$qattil$-, but the argument for *$qattal$- is equally

---

[27] This merger, which superficially resembles Philippi's Law in this particular instance, is actually part of a general merger of most *e, regardless of stress or origin, with the phoneme a in BH.

[28] Remember that Hex. does not distinguish between the vowels represented by TH a and $ā$ when an original *a is involved.

[29] By $ē(a)$ is meant "usually $ē$, but occasionally a;" by $ē/a$, "virtually a free variation between $ē$ and a." The principal finite verbal forms involving PS *i are (1) stative Qal Perfects, (2) Qal Imperfects of the type $yēšēb$ and $yittēn$, (3) Niphal Imperfects ($yiqqātēl$), (4) Piel Perfect ($qittēl/qittal$) and Imperfect ($yĕqattēl$), and (5) some forms of the Hithpael.

persuasive.[30] If the original was *qattal-, the development of qittal- involves only the dissimilation qatqát>qitqát according to the accepted view; the 3rd pers. masc. sing. form qittēl will have acquired its ē from the Imperfect. If we begin, however, with *qattil-, Philippi's Law is customarily invoked to explain *qattil->*qattal-, and then as above. As was emphasized in the preceding section, the clearly definable qatqát>qitqát dissimilation represented by *maqtal>miqtāl cannot be called upon to explain anything outside of TH. The i in the first syllable of the Hebrew Piel is found in all of the traditions considered here[31] and must therefore, if we adhere strictly to our method, be reconstructed as such for our Proto-Biblical Hebrew Tradition. As for the vowel of the second stem syllable, the Hex. Piel forms, schematically *qettel/qetteltha, unambiguously require *qittil-[32] and not *qittal- as a starting point. If we assume an initial change of *qittíl- to *qittél-, we immediately have the source of the Hex. forms;[33] *qittél is also the immediate source of BH qittal by the simple rule that *e merges with the existing phoneme a in BH.[34] *qittél>qittēl in TH. In the inflected forms where a suffix beginning with a consonant is added to the stem, e.g., 2nd pers. masc. sing. *qittéltā, a further change is required in TH: *éC₁C₂(V)>áC₁C₂(V), i.e., *qittéltā> qittáltā. This is the only place in the system proposed here where Philippi's Law surfaces in a recognizable form.

A full discussion of the Hiphil, the stative Qal, and various Imperfect forms with ē in the final stem syllable would only duplicate the preceding discussion. The Hiphil Perfect is further complicated by the fact that the long î of the Hollow verbal system had already been introduced analogically into the 3rd pers. forms of the Perfect of the regular triliteral paradigm by the beginning of our Tradition. The development sketched above will apply, therefore, only to the 2nd and 1st pers. forms of the Hiphil Perfect. The i of the Hiphil prefix, like that of the Niphal Perfect prefix and the first syllable of the Piel Perfect, belongs to the initial stage of our Tradition and, like the ni- of the Niphal, finds its closest parallel in the yi- prefix of the Qal Imperfects of the type yiqtal.

[30] The D (Piel) and C (Causative, Hiphil) bases in Arabic and Ethiopic reflect original *qattala and *ʾaqtala respectively, while Aramaic reflects *qattila and *ʾaqtila.

[31] I am aware that Samaritan preserves what appear to be clear reflexes of Piel *qattil- and Hiphil *haqtil-. I must confess, however, that I find it hard to accept the authenticity of the verbal system in Samaritan Hebrew, which seems to be completely amalgamated with that of Samaritan Aramaic whenever the consonantal spelling permits it.

[32] And similarly for the Hiphil, Hex. (h)eqtil/(h)eqteltha.

[33] Since there is no distinction in Hex. between *e and *i, both appearing as Hex. e, even the change of *qittíl->*qittél- is not required for Hex.

[34] See note 27 above.

In positing all of these forms as original to our reconstructed tradition, I do not mean to imply that their i's are all of the same origin. The yi- of $yiqtal$ is certainly PNWS and probably PS.[35] For the remaining i's it is tempting to propose an earlier version of $qatqat$>$*qitqat$, but because the vowel of the second syllable of the earlier Piel and Hiphil forms is indeterminate, and because the rule would have to be stated in such a way as to leave $*maqtal$ and nominal $*qattal$ untouched at this stage, it is difficult to see what the substance of a general rule would be. The Piel form $*qittil$- may ultimately be the result of an *assimilation*, i.e., $*qattil$->$qittil$-, but this is not easy to substantiate.[36]

4. SUMMARY

By approaching Hebrew historical phonology by first trying to distinguish between sound changes that lie within the developing Biblical Hebrew Tradition and those that lie at the beginning of, or before, the development of that Tradition, we have seen that the customary statement of both Philippi's Law and the $qatqát$>$qitqát$ dissimilation rule includes changes that are in fact scattered over a broad spectrum both chronologically and "geographically." The following set of sequenced rules seems to be the simplest that accounts for the greatest amount of the data:

(1) $*iC\#$>$*éC\#$ in finite verbal forms; $*iC\#$>$*\acute{e}C\#$ elsewhere.
  $*iCC(V)\#$>$*éCC(V)\#$ (the two C's may or may not be identical).
(2) $*-CC\#$>$*-C\#$ if the two C's are the same (geminate consonant).

Hex requires no further rules; $*e$ is written as epsilon.

(3) $*-C_1C_2\#$>$*-C_1eC_2$ (anaptyxis).

Babylonian requires only the further rule that $*e$ merges with already existing a. The remaining rules apply only to TH and are not sequenced:

(4) $*é$ + (m, n, l, t)$\#$>$é$ in polysyllabic nouns; $*éC\#$>$\acute{e}C\#$ elsewhere.
  $*éCCV\#$>$áCCV\#$
  $*éCeC$=$éCeC$.

Variation within the paradigms between $\bar{e}$ and a in finite verbal forms can be explained easily by analogy; the rules at least provide a way (right

---

[35] A full discussion of the Barth-Ginsberg Law involved here would take us too far afield.

[36] The closest parallel is with adjectives of the pattern $qittēl$ (e.g., $gibbēn$, $^{c}iwwēr$, $^{ɔ}illēm$), which must ultimately derive from a base $*qattil$.

or wrong) for distinguishing between the "correct" form and the analogical one. Apart from forms derived from roots with gutturals in third root position, which require a modified set of rules, the only forms specifically not covered by the preceding rules are (a) segholate nouns of type D ($q\bar{e}tel/qitl\hat{\imath}$) and (b) nouns of the type $qal/qill\hat{\imath}$. It is ironical that $bat/bitt\hat{\imath}$, the word most frequently given as the prime example of Philippi's Law, belongs to the small group of words that stand outside the system outlined here.[37]

[37] For the sake of brevity several forms often attributed to Philippi's Law have not been discussed in this paper. The wholesale loss of the Qal Imperfect type *$yaqtil$ is, in my opinion, a morphological and not a phonological problem. A rule accounting for construct forms like $z\check{e}qan$ (from $z\bar{a}q\bar{e}n$) could be included in the rules given above but would require so much qualification as a special case that it would have little appeal. Such forms are probably analogical: $dibr\hat{e}$: $d\check{e}bar$ :: $ziqn\hat{e}$: $z\check{e}qan$. Much more could also be said about the development of the segholate nouns *$qatl$ and *$qitl$, but that must wait for another occasion.

THE WORSHIP OF BAAL AND ASHERAH:
A STUDY IN THE SOCIAL BONDING FUNCTIONS OF RELIGIOUS SYSTEMS

George E. Mendenhall
Dept. of Near Eastern Studies
The University of Michigan

I N a very perceptive article that must have been written shortly before the Japanese attack on Pearl Harbor, William Ernest Hocking observed that a serious problem of civilization lay in the neglect or denial of the human aspects of society in favor of the attempt to explain or ground everything in scientific fact.[1] Since that time the elaboration of science and technology has proceeded with quantum and quarky leaps, while the humanities both in and outside the university scene seem at least to this writer to have become even more primitive. It has already been suggested that one reason for the backwardness of the humanities lies simply in the enormous prestige of the "hard sciences," which has induced scholars in the humanities to attempt most inappropriately to imitate the sciences in the pathetic hope of becoming "scientific."[2] A further stimulus in this direction is to be found in the enormous addition to information about the ancient world since 1945, which has necessitated precisely the sort of specialization that has become so successful in the sciences. There is no doubt, for example, that a scholar's entire

---

[1] "What Man Can Make of Man," *Fortune* (February, 1942) 92–147. Note especially p. 147: "If there were any available fact at once certain enough and valuable enough to hold the devotion of men generally, including our ailing realists, it would by now, one would suppose, be common knowledge. Is it not the absence of such a fact that has begotten our gigantic capacity for consciously adopted myths—the myth of the proletarian revolution, the myth of the pure and dominant Nordic man spread with appalling will to believe by the consumers of Rosenberg's Bible?"

[2] W. Jackson Bate "The Crisis in English Studies," *Harvard Magazine* (September–October, 1982) 46–53: "Practioners of the humanities, when they turned their attention to the procedures of the natural sciences, imitated not their openness but their self-imposed limits of specialization" (p. 48).

lifetime could be spent on the decipherment, publication, and explication of any of the archives recently found, such as those of Ebla, Mari, or Ugarit.

Unfortunately, in a world increasingly obsessed with seemingly insoluble economic, political, and population problems, it is increasingly being called into question whether society feels or even ought to feel any particular obligation or interest in supporting the delving into such totally irrelevant monuments to past failures. It is a main thesis of the present paper to suggest that it is precisely the fact of past failures that should constitute some redeeming social value in the study of the remote past, and in fact we ignore that past to our own peril. This is particularly true of biblical studies, for it is this field that ties the remote past to the present, that ties modern political conflict to the crescendo of religious conflict, and also has constituted the only direct continuity of tradition from the remote ancient Near East to the present day, when that biblical tradition is being seriously challenged by its would-be adherents as well as by its enemies and detractors.

The problem is that the specialists in those ancient fields are faced with such enormous technical problems (and also find unquestionably much satisfaction in dealing with them) in the decipherment and analysis of the ancient artifacts and documents that they seem never to get around to asking questions that in the long run can justify the expenditure of all the scholarly effort. In the problem of "keeping up" with all the new information, and even more with the constant pressure to be ahead of the game in devising "new" methodologies, "new hermeneutics," and new everything, the basic human problems are not dealt with: what is the *value* of the documents and the endeavor? What do they tell us of the human condition of those ancient peoples, and those ancient failures that had to be dug up before we could know anything at all about them? Yet more important, what do the documents tell us about the nature of the historical and cultural process that might enable us to have some transcendent perspective on our own condition, predicament, and prospects?

A major part of the problem lies in the fact that it is emphatically not in contemporary fashion to raise questions of this sort even though almost any text retrieved from the ruin mounds of the ancient world could and should tell us something of these matters. This contemporary fashion results in a curious sort of schizophrenia: every election day, every examination day, we are called upon to make evaluations concerning those things that we regard as important to our individual and corporate well-being, but what the criteria are, what the values are, and whether the operational system is adequate to the total situation are questions that it is not at all fashionable or comfortable to raise. Like the famous Victorian gentleman, we act upon the conviction that "one's metaphysical presuppositions, like one's underclothing should be kept decently hidden." It would seem to be a reasonable assumption that some such attitude has been a constant throughout most of recorded history that we are content to term "civilized."

If this be granted as a probable tendency of those who engaged themselves in producing literary texts, ancient or modern, then it would seem a justifiable conclusion that the interpretation of ancient myths lies on a plane quite different from those currently fashionable, whether of literary or "structural" analysis (whatever that may eventually turn out to be) on the one hand, or of reading a modern mythology of Freudian, Marxist, feminist, or other ideology into the ancient literary works. A very considerable part of the problem, I have long been convinced, lies in the fact that in the world of the humanists, the study of myth and ancient literature was highly developed decades if not centuries ago on the basis of the preserved Greek literary "myths," and on the basis also of very traditional (now, that is) biblical studies. In other words, the basic programming that went into the mind of the humanistic scholar was created long before there was any substantive knowledge about the ancient world, whether biblical or extra-biblical, at all available.

It is therefore not at all surprising that enormous confusion exists concerning the nature of myth, and an equal amount of confusion about the nature of religious systems. There is a beautiful irony in the fact that modern fundamentalist ideology and ancient mythologies share one basic conviction: critical historical method is subversive, vicious, and blasphemous if not treason. At any rate, to engage in historical-critical study of the Bible is sufficient grounds for exclusion from the congregation of the saints in quite a few contemporary religious organizations. It needs emphatically to be pointed out, however, that many political systems of the modern day as well have an equal distaste for historical facts, and it is no accident that George Orwell's *1984* included a hilarious description of political functions of "historians" that is much too close to the truth in many political systems of 1983.

Aristotle has been quoted as saying somewhere (he is not my field of specialization, and I cite him as an authority not because he is fairly old and has survived in some respects, but mainly because it is an intrinsically good idea) that it is the height of injustice to classify together things that do not belong together. The humanistic treatment of myth, the basic ideas about which were formulated in the nineteenth century, together with an amazing amount of other ideological baggage that the civilized world ought to have outgrown decades ago, regards the term as an adequate label for a particular genre, or *Gattung*, of literary productivity, and therefore the term has been applied not only to the classical Greek myths, but also to the much more recently discovered literary works of ancient Babylonia, Egypt, and Canaan. It is only a matter of course, then, that the term would be used to classify into the same literary category various narratives of both the OT and NT in the Bible. It seems that the term "myth" has become virtually a label for any sort of ideological stance, and this contemporary usage is of course linguistically perfectly legitimate. However, when it is used as an explanatory category applied to Babylonian, biblical, and Greek narratives indiscriminately, it is evidence of either incompetence or cultural imperialism, and should cease to be thus used as it is by professors of comparative literature and comparative religion. It is tempting and perhaps even justified to apply an uncomplimentary label to this syndrome.

In the first place, the Greek myths in the form in which they have been preserved probably should not be classified as myths at all in any but a literary formal sense. The narratives have been subjected to a process of "reductionism" that began at least with Plato and Aristotle and ran its course long before the literary works had been composed in their present form. In other words, there is an enormous gap between myth as a mere literary narrative form to which scholars are sensitive, and myth as a narrative presentation of the divine, timeless pattern to which life shapes itself,[3] which is probably the best working, functional definition of myth as a religious system of communication. It is thus not at all on the grounds of similarity of literary form that any significant conclusions can be drawn, for it is similarity of literary form that induces scholars to think they are dealing with the identical phenomenon in the Greek, Ugaritic, and biblical worlds. Already in ancient times at least some people could see that it is the height of naivete to assume that form and function are identical.[4] They could also see the fact that underlying both, and prior to both, is the question of value. In other words, similar literary forms can be driven by radically opposite value systems.

This point can be summarized with the definition of values as determinants of behavior, and not merely verbal labels for the enormous variety of cultural conventions and ensuing forms of behavior, it must be questioned whether there is really an equally large number of such determinants of behavior, once most economic transactions are seen to be determined by the value of reciprocity. However, the biblical NT tradition excludes mere reciprocity from the realm of the religious: "they have received their reward" (Matt 6:3) is the foundation for the distinction between the secular and the sacred in everyday life. The truly revolutionary nature of the biblical tradition is illustrated in this re-statement of the value-based criteria for the definition of the religious, over against

---

[3] C. G. Jung and C. Kerenyi, *Essays on a Science of Mythology* (New York: Bollingen Series 22, 1949) "They [i.e., the myths] form the ground or foundation of the world, since everything rests on them . . . they remain ageless, inexhaustible, invincible in timeless primordiality, in a past that proves imperishable because of its eternally repeated rebirths" (p. 9). It is amusing to see the extent to which this old work relies on modern myths in order to "explain" ancient ones.

[4] Isa 29:13: "This people draws near to me with their lips, but their heart is far from me."

the virtually universal definition of religion as involving "sacred times and sacred spaces."

It has already been hinted above that values are arranged into a system, or a hierarchy:[5] the thief, for example, may not entirely reject the value of reciprocity, for as the saying goes, there is honor among thieves, too. Here the reciprocity-value is a function of a superior value consideration, which is that of the integrity of the group with which the thief identifies himself. It is the group boundary line that turns the reciprocity-value on or off. The same is true, however, of all legal systems: they can function only within the jurisdictional boundary lines of the political system that created them, for law is after all the socially organized administration of society's monopoly of force. If it be recalled that, as pointed out above, law strictly speaking cannot deal with values, but only with overt acts,[6] then it should be clear that a value-based religion such as that of the normative biblical tradition cannot be identified with an administered legal social system.

It is at this point that a most important aspect of the ancient biblical revolution coincides with the modern critical issue of the relation between religion and politics. Contrary to the anachronistic nineteenth century ideology of Gottwald,[7] the biblical revolution was not at all a "class struggle," but a rejection of the idea that a parochial political power system could be identified with the quintessential manifestation of the Ultimate Concern, to use Tillich's useful term as a substitute for "God." In this rejection of the ancient political paganism the ancient biblical religious revolution furnished the foundation for a larger social unity than had ever previously existed—so far as our written records go. To put it another way, the biblical revolution constituted a simultaneous discovery of the fact that there was a transcendent factor in human history that was unifying in its effects, whereas any political power structure must polarize populations across boundary lines—in order to guarantee that the hostility beyond the border is greater than the hostility within the political boundary. It is at this point that the essence of the prophetic protest against Baal-worship becomes comprehensible.

The increasing knowledge of the ancient world has resulted in an increased respect for the sophistication of the populations and organizations that left us the written documents. In spite of the enormous culture

[5] In this respect Tillich's concept of deity as "Ultimate Concern" is a useful operating principle for historical conclusions as to what the hierarchy actually is. "By their fruits you shall know them" (Matt 7:16).

[6] "Justice is an irrational ideal." Similar statements can be found in almost any work on jurisprudence.

[7] Gottwald, by and large, is not really interested in the historical facts of the early biblical society. His system is an anachronistic nineteenth-century ideology that determines his conclusions, entirely analogous to any other fundamentalism in that he wishes to exploit the "authority" of the Bible to support a modern political ideological system.

gap that separates us from them, it is possible to make some reasonable conjectures concerning certain aspects of ancient thought, even though the more intimate workings of the culture may be forever inaccessible to anything but speculation. In this respect, however, it is legitimate to ask whether we really can have very adequate knowledge of such workings of our own society, in view of the dismal failure of both economists and politicians to solve the nagging problems that constantly or periodically afflict us on a global basis.

In sharp contrast to the ideas dominant among scholars only forty or so years ago, the "baalim" can now clearly be seen not to be mere primitive ideas of disembodied ghosts of trees, springs, and standing stones, nor is baal-worship the mere engaging in illegitimate (because foreign) forms of ritual. Baal-worship is far more serious than that, bad as that may be because of the disruptive effects upon social unity that strange rituals may have within the community. In view of the iconography of the "baals" it is only common sense to see in them the hypostatized symbols of the political power structures themselves.[8] It is unfortunate that the system of communication of the ancient Near Eastern societies did not include abstract generalized descriptions of religious symbols in secular terms—and indeed could not without destroying the symbols themselves. Therefore, the description by Thucydides of the Athenian ideology that justified their domination over their neighbors does not have any close parallel in the ancient world outside the Bible, and it is necessary to make the transition from literary form to historical function as a critical method by which to understand the more obscure. Perhaps more to the point is the observation that the driving ideology of

[8] The figure of Baal/Hadad in stride (similar to an Egyptian Pharaoh) with upraised club symbolized the military power of the king. Most clear is the Assyrian reliefs, in which the deity is the mirror image of the king. Mario Liverani has expressed it extremely well: "The inclusion of the imperialistic ideology within the general framework of values of the Assyrian society, brings about what is generally termed its religious character . . . . Conceptual habits prevailing in the scholars' world have tended to lead scholars to treat the religious sphere as if it were autonomous, only to realize quickly that this sphere is in fact an integral part of the political sphere ("sacred" kingship, "holy" war, etc.). I believe on the contrary that if we consider the divinities and the acts of cult as hypostatic expressions of social values, the problem vanishes. . . . A king is not legitimate because of the approval of god Assur; a king, while he rules in Assyria, is always legitimate, and his legitimacy is expressed in religious terms (in fact the less obvious it is, the more it is emphasized). In a broader sense, the divine approval is not the *cause* of the legitimacy of the action, it is clearly its *expressed form.* . . . Assur is precisely the hypostasis of the Assyrian kingship" (*Power and Propaganda: A Symposium on Ancient Empires* [Copenhagen: Akademisk Forlag, 1979] 301). With this compare the statement made recently by a man described as the "guru of religious direct mail": "Nothing is unethical if a man says God told him something. Who can disprove that?"

that Athenian society is not accessible from the reading of their literary "myths," but from a description of their behavior. This is, of course, precisely what characterized the entire prophetic tradition including Jesus of Nazareth: "By their fruits you shall know them:"

> As for the gods, we expect to have quite as much of their favour as you: for we are not doing or claiming anything which goes beyond common opinion about divine or men's desires about human things. Of the gods we believe, and of men we know, that by a law of their nature wherever they can rule they will. This law was not made by us, and we are not the first who have acted upon it; we did but inherit it, and shall bequeath it to all time, and we know that you and all mankind, if you were as strong as we are, would do as we do.[9]

This, I submit, is the naive but therefore honest and unashamed description of "baal-worship" presented as it no doubt was bequeathed to them by the customary ideology of political states since the dawn of history. It is not this that needs to be explained, but its absence in the early stages of that religion we term "Yahwism."

One may note also the Athenians' concept of justice in the same exchange with the Melians:

> For we both alike know that into the discussion of human affairs the question of justice only enters where the pressure of necessity is equal, and that the powerful exact what they can, and the weak grant what they must.

This is an excellent description of an operational, i.e., functional myth, over against the "literary" myths inherited from the past. It is myth that in the first place is attributed both to the remote past, from which it was "bequeathed," and more importantly, it attributes to the gods the same pattern of behavior that is the "rule" on the human level. In modern parlance—and much academic theory—it is the reliable law of human behavior that is appealed to for the justification of the present course of action in which they are not only engaged, but compulsively bound to follow. It is in this sense that myth is a determinant of behavior: it is the unquestionable conviction that this is "the way things are," and therefore they cannot be expected to act in any other fashion. It is only superior force that can stop them, or an equal "necessity" that can induce them to seek "justice." It is quite clear that this historical level of political behavior corresponds to the content of the literary myths, in which the theomachies whether archaic Greek or ancient Near Eastern illustrate the overcoming by superior force of one entity which is usually that which is the sovereign representative of the society that preserved the myth. It is a matter of no concern that the myths of various political

---

[9] Thucydides, *Peloponnesian War*, Book V, chap. 105.

states exhibit very similar content: hardly any other pattern of political behavior was conceivable to those political elites whose ideology the myths reflect. The myth is precisely the verbal expression of the compulsive, locked-in ideology that determined the behavior of those power elites, to whom "to be called a pirate was no insult." It was the source of social status, the source of pride and self esteem to engage in war "for glory, fun and profit"—so long as it was profitable.

What many modern social and intellectual systems have in common with ancient myths is the positing of some transcendent power or Prime Cause that is specific to the phenomenon being investigated or promoted. The difference from ancient myth lies in the fact that the multiplication of divine beings is a phenomenon that has been made ideologically impossible by the two-millennia-long domination of the Judeo-Christian monotheistic metaphysics in Western religion. The functional similarity between modern ideological systems and those of ancient myth-making mentalities has therefore been entirely obscured. The restoration of the similarities can take place through a re-definition that can apply to both cultural systems: a "deity" in ancient or modern ideology is *functionally* a factor operative in human experience or thought which is beyond human control and specific predictivity, and which yet constitutes a value that determines human overt and ideological behavior. The term "god" was used very loosely in ancient times, at least by our modern standards: anything that was important to a group of people could be considered a "god."

Thus, in ancient Rome the inhabitants of a particular apartment house might have a shrine on the first floor dedicated to the "apartment house god" which presumably represented the corporate interests and values of the inhabitants.[10] The similarity functionally to the operation of various corporate interests of the present day should not escape us, merely because of the diversity of language and ritual used to express a very similar interest or value. Thus, the domination of all sorts of abstractions as determinants of ideological or political behavior and decision-making is a constant in human culture, and I have no doubt at all that ancient Babylonians or Romans would be able to recognize as "gods" such abstractions as "archetypes," "genres," "racial traits," "rights," "national defense," "national self-interest," and "the gross national product." The ancient and the modern cultural conventions share this concern for grounding in some transcendent abstraction the "cause" and therefore the authority and absolute "rightness" of that which is being promoted or imposed by force.

The ancient or modern myth-making mentality may be characterized as having the following structure, on empirical grounds that make

---

[10] Ramsey MacMullen, *Roman Social Relations*, 86: "We have the record of a patron deity chosen, its image set up, and prayers offered to it by the tenants of the Bolan building in Rome."

unnecessary any idea that there is some sort of supernatural force which drives human beings to such similarities of conceptual and political behavior. All that is justified and necessary is the observation that in human behavior, similar causes do have similar effects—but there is no non-empirical "force" that invariably determines the process. Otherwise, human society and behavior would be far more predictable and orderly than it obviously is. It should also be pointed out that these characteristics are those condemned as idolatry in the biblical tradition.

1. Since religion is that which bestows social approval and sanction upon that which society regards as important over against the merely trivial, it follows that the myth-making mentality will posit a corresponding metaphysical entity to everything that is important. That metaphysical entity constitutes both the "cause" and the legitimacy for the empirically important, and of course is regarded as "sacred," or "holy." In modern times those terms will not be used outside the context of organized ritual behavior, though the complex of attitudes and reactions determined by that actually held to be holy will continue to operate, but within a totally different range of experience and behavior. The "sanctity" of any given cultural artifact can easily be measured by the intensity of emotional response on the part of its devotees when that artifact is attacked or challenged.

2. That corresponding metaphysical entity is hypostatized. It is often personified and given a name/label, which is of course in ancient times a divine name. In modern times it is often given a (pseudo-) scientific name: "The Oedipus Complex,"[11] "National Interest," "The Holocaust." In this process, it is not the observable facts that are important, but the relationship between the metaphysical entity and the patterns of behavior that it "explains" and justifies (and also frequently enough brings in money). Thus the definition of myth as "the divine, timeless pattern to which life shapes itself."

3. Since what is important in a complex society is increasingly involved with social organization on the one hand, and with increasingly complex political, social, and economic processes on the other hand, abstractions become extremely important in the system of communication. However, abstraction takes two forms: first, is the deification of abstract terms, such as those usually translated with English

[11] The point argued here is that these are operating conventional concepts that have received some acceptance in some circles (now, it seems, mainly people engaged in "literature"), but they are no more empirically, i.e., scientifically, demonstrable than the concepts of God in the Bible. In regard to the other slogans, it is not any empirical reality past or present that is the real concern, and certainly not any understanding of underlying causes or consequences that constitute the reason for their appeal, but rather the slogans' function in persuading persons collectively to support, or at least condone and tolerate, a course of action determined upon by political power structures.

words like "justice," "order," "security," "peace," "salvation,"[12] and the like. This deification of abstractions is well attested at the earliest historical period of nearly every culture of the ancient world, and undeniably has such a strong emotional appeal that it becomes a very effective propaganda weapon for ambitious politicians. Probably most important is the deification of the body politic itself: Assur, Athena, Roma—any deification of symbols of the body politic—and these are the "baals" of OT times.

The second form of abstraction is what I term "abstraction by typical example." It is also a constant in human history. It is the process by which an understanding of a complex of human experience is conveyed through the telling of a story. In the case of mythical narrative it is a set of divine activities and usually conflicts of a more or less violent sort that is told. There may or may not be immediately identifiable empirical referents, and because the narrative is often so closely bound to the particular cultural conventions and situations at the time of formation, the myth may be completely opaque to us.[13] Again, the "truth" of the narrative is just as irrelevant as is the objective, empirical "existence" of the hypostatized mythical entities mentioned above: the only important consideration is the fact that it "works," and in this case belief in the myth is sufficient as an operational factor to guarantee that it will "work," at least for a while. As a modern example we may note the enormous power of the concept of "National Security" as an operational myth that commands unbelievable economic and human resources, when as a matter of fact the armaments can do nothing in modern times but create national insecurity for everyone else outside that national boundary line. If this is true of modern, supposedly civilized populations, it should not be surprising that ancient mythologies tended to emphasize powerfully the divine, cosmic conflict between powers of order—and therefore good—and powers of disorder or chaos—and therefore absolute evil—in which the political boundary line is the definition of the contrast between "order" and "chaos."

4. The fourth characteristic of much myth is its dualistic nature. This follows inevitably from the preceding points. The divine conflict is necessary as a guarantee of the perpetual victory of "ourside" over against the forces of evil. It furnishes—for a time—a transcendent security since

---

[12] It is amusing to note that already in ancient Amorite religion there were at least 18 different gods or divine appellatives that functioned as the subject of the verb $y\underline{t}^c$, 'to save.' The bumper sticker industry could have had a bumper crop.

[13] This position has often been made a dogmatic presupposition, as an excuse for the procedure of reading into an ancient text anything the modern interpreter wishes. The easiest way of doing so is to proclaim that the myth has no empirical referent.

"our god" is always "mit uns." It is amusing also that the powers of
chaos and evil are almost never specifically identifiable in the literary
myths; this is also a great advantage of the abstraction, since in ancient
as well as modern times the enemy of one decade may well be the necessary ally of the next decade. It would therefore be politic not to specify
too narrowly who are the "powers of chaos," for the myth could thus
become too easily "dated" and irrelevant, if not overtly harmful. Besides,
there is always some "Great Beast" somewhere around who can be identified as the absolute evil and thus constantly reinforce the "truth" of the
sacred myth. Once the dualistic myth becomes a widely held cultural
convention it can be counted on to justify, and make almost inevitable,
the sort of conflicts that repeatedly brought civilization to an end. For
this reason, the modern admiration for ancient "paganism" should be
qualified by an awareness of its historical long-range consequences.

It would seem that this compulsion to identify some foreign entity
as the embodiment of absolute evil is the Dead Sea of religion: it is the
only realm of experience in which there is a correlation between the
words of the Sacred Book and historical reality. In most other realms of
experience the "law of increasing abstraction" has become operative. The
import of this observable regularity is that the passage of time and the
constant change in the total social environment creates an increasing gap
between the Sacred Book and the actual life situations of the members of
the social group. The Sacred Book is abstracted from all historical
context, just as the actual life situations of individuals seem irrelevant
to any content of the Sacred Book except for the ritual forms allegedly
sanctioned by it. Actually, in many religious communities there can be
an indignant rejection of the idea that historical reality had anything at
all to do with the origin of the Sacred Book, and thus a violent reaction
against "historical criticism" of it. As a result the sacred tradition is
identified almost entirely with the ritual forms and with the power structure of the associated ritual organization. The rest of time and space, the
non-cultic society and all its activities are correspondingly "secularized"
by the religious tradition. Historically speaking, what actually has happened in such a situation is likely the fact that the "sacred tradition" has
become devoid of any observable social functions other than the preservation of the ritual organization itself. From the point of view of the
"secularized" society, the sacred tradition has itself become trivial since
it no longer appears to deal with anything that is important and seems
merely to act as an unwarranted brake on "progress" and as an irrational
attempt to place unwanted restraints on individual freedoms.

The "worship" of Baal and Asherah is the reduction of human life
and experience to the twin factors of political power and political economy. It is self-evident that the political monopoly of force can exercise
enormous influence and control over everything around it, internally
and externally. It is also obvious in times of success that war can

be enormously profitable, and it needs to be asked whether this rather than some modern psychological theory may not better account for the grotesquely bloodthirsty characteristics of Anat in the Ugaritic myth. However, even apart from the motif of economic advantage derived from successful warfare, there can be little doubt that the satisfaction of beating an opponent tends to become a value that overrides other considerations, especially of morality and ethic.

The transition from the mind-set of ancient pagan mythology that led to the moral and economic bankruptcy of civilization shortly before the time of Moses, to the ethic-centered and historical process theology of the early Israelite religious movement is not the sort of phenomenon that can easily be "explained." After all, if we could adequately explain history, we should be able also to predict it—but this is the province of the charlatans and the modern ambitious politicians searching for the rewards of money, prestige, and power of their modern baals and fertility goddesses.

HEZEKIAH'S SACRIFICES AT THE DEDICATION SERVICES OF THE PURIFIED TEMPLE (2 Chr 29:21-24)

Jacob Milgrom
The University of California, Berkeley

A T the dedication services of the purified Temple, King Hezekiah and the officials of Jerusalem "brought seven bulls and seven rams and seven lambs[1] and seven he-goats as a purification offering for the royal house[2] and for the sanctuary[3] and for Judah" (2 Chr 29:21a). Subsequently, we are told, the king and the congregation[4] performed the hand-laying ceremonial upon the he-goats "to expiate for all Israel, for the king had designated the whole offering and the purification offering to be for all Israel" (v 24). Hezekiah had changed his mind concerning the beneficiaries of the sacrifice from the royal house, the sanctuary, and the people of Judah to "all Israel," a change which is underscored by "the congregation" which performs the hand-laying rite.[5]

The reason for Hezekiah's change of mind begs investigation, but not before we can solve this verse's numerical conundrum. Two questions

[1] The addition *lĕ'ōlâ*, "for a whole offering" is implied.

[2] *Mamlākâ* cannot mean "kingdom," a meaningless abstraction, but connotes "royal household"; cf. W. L. Moran, "A Kingdom of Priests," *The Bible in Current Catholic Thought*, ed. J. L. McKenzie (New York: Herder and Herder, 1962) 7–20.

[3] *Miqdaš*, technically, does not mean "sanctuary," i.e., the Temple, but either denotes the "sacred objects," i.e., the sancta or, as in this case, the "sacred precincts": see J. Milgrom, *Studies in Levitical Terminology* (Berkeley: University of California, 1970) n. 78. The name of Jerusalem's Temple is, of course, *bêt hammiqdāš*, literally, "the House of the Sacred Precinct" (1 Chr 28:10).

[4] *Haqqāhāl* which, in the Chronicler's time, was the technical term for Israel's representatives; see J. Milgrom, "Priestly Terminology and the Political and Social Structure of Pre-Monarchic Israel," *JQR* 69 (1978) 65–81. On purely logical grounds, the hand-laying rite could only be performed by a small, representative group.

[5] Hand-laying, in contrast to all the other preliminary rites permitted to the laity, must be performed by the offerer and not by his proxy.

159

need to be answered: (1) How can each of the 3 original beneficiaries of the sacrifices be assigned the same number of animals, i.e., how can 7 be divided by 3? (2) How can, in Hezekiah's new calculation, such an incongruous number as 21 whole offerings and 7 purification offerings, a total of 28 animals, stand for "all Israel?"

I submit that this two-fold arithmetic problem can be solved by a presupposition suggested (orally) by my colleague, Gerson D. Cohen: the quartet of 7 animals was originally intended for *each* of the beneficiaries. That is to say, 7 bulls, 7 rams, 7 lambs, and 7 he-goats were to be offered up *three times*—first for the royal house, second for the sanctuary, and a third time for the people of Judah. Thus, each beneficiary would have been assigned the same number of animals and sacrifices and the total number of animals was therefore $3(7 + 7 + 7 + 7) = 84$. The solution to the second question is now obvious: $84 = 12 \times 7$. Twelve, of course, is symbolic of Israel's twelve tribes and seven is the number of perfection, attested frequently in Scripture,[6] especially in sacrificial rituals.[7] To be sure, this configuration does not allow each tribe to be the recipient of the same animals, but this was not Hezekiah's intention. The dedication offerings are designated not for the tribes but for "all Israel," and the number 84 stands for the entire Israelite population irrespective of its tribal affiliation.

This proposed solution also unveils the motive behind Hezekiah's change of mind. He was not content to offer sacrifices on behalf of the inhabitants of his own kingdom of Judah. The rededicated temple would henceforth serve "all Israel" and embrace the inhabitants of Northern Israel as well. Northern Israel had ceased as a political entity, its territory having been absorbed into the Assyrian empire. Hezekiah's ambition for Israel's political reunification might have to be suppressed but it could be sublimated in the cultic realm, by making the Temple the central sanctuary for the entire people.[8] Textual evidence of Hezekiah's cultic ambition is contained in the following account of the very first festival to be celebrated in the renovated Temple—the Passover or, more correctly, the delayed Passover (2 Chr 30:2-3; cf. Num 9:1-14). Messengers are dispatched to the inhabitants of Northern Israel inviting them to join in the celebration of the second Passover (v 1); in some tribal areas they are not received too kindly (v 10) but many do come (vv 11, 18).[9]

[6] Cf. Ibn Ezra on Num 23:1.

[7] E.g., seven whole offering lambs on the festivals and twice seven on the Feast of Tabernacles (Numbers 28-29).

[8] The possibility must seriously be entertained that Hezekiah's attempt at cultic centralization was influenced by the book of Deuteronomy (or its core) brought to Jerusalem by refugees from Northern Israel; cf. J. Milgrom, "Profane Slaughter and a Formulaic Key to the Composition of Deuteronomy," *HUCA* 47 (1976) 1-17.

[9] For details, see J. Milgrom, "Did Josiah Ever Rule Megiddo?" *Beth Miqra* 41 (1970) 23-27 (Hebrew).

Thus, the text is justified in stating that "the Israelites who were present in Jerusalem kept the Feast of Unleavened Bread seven days with great rejoicing" (v 21a).[10] But this statement is pregnant with even more significant information. It is alluding to the masses of northern Israelites who settled in Jerusalem following the Assyrian invasions which razed their capital and put an end to their state.

What the text affirms archaeology confirms. N. Avigad has excavated in the Jewish Quarter of the old city a 130-foot stretch of a city wall, 23 feet thick, which dates to the end of the eighth century during the reign of Hezekiah (or, at the latest, in the reign of Manasseh).[11] Avigad's wall and his subsequent Iron Age finds[12] make it certain that the city of Jerusalem about 700 B.C.E. had suddenly tripled or quadrupled in size. According to one estimate,[13] the 44 dunams of David's city and the 130–180 dunams of the eighth century city had become the 500–600 dunams of the seventh century city. Only one factor could cause a rapid territorial expansion of such magnitude: a population explosion. Though the subsequent ravaging of the Judean countryside by Sennacherib (701 B.C.E.) played a role, the major contributory factor must have been the successive waves of refugees who poured into Jerusalem from Northern Israel after its fall in 721 B.C.E. It was, then, the tide of northern Israelites who flooded Jerusalem, not as pilgrims but as permanent residents, that prompted Hezekiah—even before he issued the Passover invitation to Northern Israel—to change the designees of his sacrifices for the Temple rededication service from Judah to "all Israel."

[10] Hezekiah's deferral of the Feast of Unleavened Bread is not in accordance with the Torah, which speaks solely of the deferral of the Paschal sacrifice (cf. *b. Pesah* 56a).

[11] "Excavations in the Jewish Quarter of the Old City of Jerusalem . . . ," *IEJ* 20 (1970) 5–6, 8, 129–34; 22 (1972) 193–98, 200. Most recently, see H. Geva, "The Western Boundary of Jerusalem at the End of the Monarchy," *IEJ* 29 (1979) 84–91.

[12] N. Avigad, "Jerusalem, the Jewish Quarter of the Old City," *IEJ* 25 (1975) 260–61; 27 (1977) 55–56; cf. also R. Amiran and A. Eitan, "Excavations in the Courtyard of the Citadel, Jerusalem 1968–1969 (Preliminary Report)," *IEJ* 20 (1970) 9–10, 16; D. Bahat and M. Broshi, "Excavations in the Armenian Garden," in *Jerusalem Revealed*, ed. Y. Yadin (Jerusalem: Israel Exploration Society, 1975) 56; M. Broshi, "Excavations on Mount Zion, 1971–1972," *IEJ* 26 (1976) 81–82.

[13] M. Broshi, "The Expansion of Jerusalem in the Reigns of Hezekiah and Manasseh," *IEJ* 24 (1974) 21–26.

ESTHER REVISITED:
AN EXAMINATION OF ESTHER STUDIES OVER THE PAST DECADE[1]

Carey A. Moore
Gettysburg College

I T was Professor Sam Iwry who first introduced me at the Oriental Seminary to the Hebrew text of Esther. For me at least, that was a fateful introduction inasmuch as a considerable portion of my subsequent publications has been devoted to that fascinating book. Just as H. Bardtke a couple of years after the appearance of his *Das Buch Esther*[2] felt compelled to update his commentary with an article,[3] so I have wanted to update my two Anchor Bible commentaries on the Hebrew and Greek texts: *Esther: Introduction, Translation, and Notes*[4] and *Daniel, Esther, and Jeremiah: The Additions*,[5] respectively. To a certain extent, I was able to do this in 1982 with the appearance of my *Studies in the Book of Esther*,[6] where I discussed in the Prolegomenon various aspects of each of the anthology's thirty-seven articles, including some published during the past decade. Within the space available here, I would like to continue the task of revisiting Esther.

First, several generalizations are in order. During the past decade students of Esther have by and large ignored certain areas of study. Apart from the articles by R. A. Martin[7] and E. Tov, little significant work has been published on the Greek text of Esther. Tov, in "The 'Lucianic'

---

[1] Although the present article was written prior to the writer's "Esther Revisited Again: A Further Examination of Certain Esther Studies of the Past Ten Years" (*HAR* 7 [1983] 169–86), the latter article was actually published first. Thus the present article should be understood as antedating that article even though, in point of fact, it does not.

[2] KAT, 17/5. Gütersloh: Mohn, 1963.

[3] "Neuere Arbeiten zum Esterbuch. Eine kritische Würdigung," *JEOL* 19 (1965–66) 519–49.

[4] AB, vol. 7B, 1971.

[5] AB, vol. 44, 1977.

[6] The Library of Biblical Studies, ed. H. M. Orlinsky (New York: KTAV).

[7] Fortunately for my Anchor commentary on the Greek Esther, I had access to Martin's work, as well as the fine commentary by H. Bardtke, *Zusätze zu Esther*, Historische und legendarische Erzählungen, Jüdische Schriften aus

Text of the Canonical and the Apocryphal Sections of Esther: A Rewritten Biblical Book,"[8] has argued that the so-called Lucianic text of Esther "is a translation which is based on the LXX but corrects it toward a Hebrew (or Aramaic) text which differed from MT. This text was a midrash-type rewriting of the biblical story."[9] I am not persuaded by Tov's article and have addressed myself to it elsewhere (Moore, *HAR* 7 [1983] 169–86).

Additional light has been shed on the old debate as to why the MT's "Mordecai sat at the king's gate" (2:19 *et passim*) was rendered in the LXX by "Mordecai served in the king's court" (Esth A 2 *et passim*). While the reading in the LXX may have originated in an inner-Greek corruption (i.e., G *pulē*, "gate," being misread as *aulē*, "court"), the rendering may also represent the Greek translator's awareness that the MT's "sitting at the king's gate" could mean that Mordecai was occupying a government post or office.[10]

Nor has the past decade witnessed much interest in scholars' trying to establish the historicity of the Esther story or in using archaeological discoveries to illuminate it.[11] But as might have been predicted, Professor W. F. Albright, who has made so many contributions to his students and their work, made one more, albeit posthumously, in his "The Lachish Cosmetic Burner and Esther 2:12,"[12] by showing that certain carved cuboid limestone "incense burners," supported by four squat legs and with a shallow basin (such as found at Hadramaut, Gezer, Lachish, and Tell Jemmeh), were actually secular cosmetic burners. Women used them

---

hellenistische-römischer Zeit, ed. W. G. Kümmel *et al.*, 1/1 (Gütersloh: Mohn, 1973). Using a statistical analysis of syntax developed earlier in his *Syntactical Evidence of Semitic Sources in Greek Documents*, SBLSCS 3 (1974), Martin demonstrated that Additions A, C, D, and F of the LXX Esther were Semitic in origin while Additions B and E were originally composed in Greek ("Syntax Criticism of the LXX Additions to the Book of Esther," *JBL* 94 [1975] 65–72).

[8] *Textus* 10 (1982) 1–25.

[9] Tov, p. 25. For my views on the "Lucianic" text of Esther, see my "A Greek Witness to a Different Hebrew Text of Esther," *ZAW* 79 (1967) 351–58. See also H. J. Cook, "The A-text of the Greek Versions of the Book of Esther," *ZAW* 81 (1969) 369–76.

[10] See H. Wehr, "Das 'Tor des Königs' im Buche Esther und verwandte Ausdrücke," *Der Islam* 39 (1964) 247–60; O. Loretz, "s'r hmlk—'Das Tor des Königs' (Est 2,19)," *WO* 4 (1967) 104–8; H. P. Rüger, "'Das Tor des Königs'—der königliche Hof," *Bib* 50 (1969) 247–50; and pp. 47–48 of R. Gordis, "Studies in the Esther Narrative," *JBL* 95 (1976) 43–58.

[11] On the general significance of archaeology for Esther studies, see my "Archaeology and the Book of Esther," *BA* 38 (1975) 62–79.

[12] *A Light unto My Path: Old Testament Studies in Honor of Jacob M. Myers*, ed. H. N. Bream, R. D. Heim, and C. A. Moore (Philadelphia: Temple University, 1974) 25–32. Albright had written only the first draft, but Frank Moore Cross kindly edited it for the festschrift.

to burn various kinds of aromatic substances (Heb. *bĕśāmîm*, "spices") to "fumigate" their bodies and clothes so as to make themselves more desirable. Thus "the regimen for women" described in Esth 2:12–13 involved "six months' treatment with oil of myrrh, and six months' fumigation with other cosmetics for women."

Recently, A. R. Millard has shown that Parshandatha, the name of one of Haman's sons (Esth 9:7), is a genuine Persian name, inasmuch as a 5th Century B.C.E. cylinder seal in Aramaic script bears the name "Pharshandath son of Artadatha." [13] My caveat in *Esther* AB 7B–xliv) on being especially cautious in one's use of the onomastic materials in the MT of Esther has been challenged by A. R. Millard in his "The Persian Names in Esther and the Reliability of the Hebrew Text," [14] from which study the reader may draw his own conclusions. In any event, work on Esther in the last decade has not been much concerned with questions concerning the book's historicity or its illumination by archaeological evidence.

Since the appearance of *Esther* AB 7B in 1971, I have been compelled to reverse my views on two basic matters. The one concerns the date Esther was accepted into the Jewish canon. As is well-known, Esther's canonicity was contested by Jews as late as the 3rd and 4th centuries C.E. (see *Esther* AB 7B, xxi–xxv). However, both S. Zeitlin[15] and H. M. Orlinsky[16] have demonstrated that there is not a shred of evidence for Esther's being canonized at the so-called Council of Jamnia (ca. 90 C.E.). Rather, the decision to canonize the book was made no earlier than 140 C.E., at the academy of Ousha (so Zeitlin), and possibly as late as ca. 200 C.E. (so Orlinsky in private correspondence with me later).

The other basic area where I reversed myself concerns the question of the language(s) in which Additions A, C, D, and F of the Greek Esther were originally composed. My earlier view that these Additions "were originally conceived and composed in Greek rather than translated from a Semitic text" [17] was refuted, first in my article[18] and then in my book on the Additions.[19]

---

[13] A photograph of the seal and its impression are on p. 152 of Millard's "In Praise of Ancient Scribes," *BA* 45 (1982) 143–53.

[14] *JBL* 96 (1977) 181–88.

[15] "The Books of Esther and Judith: A Parallel," in M. S. Enslin, *The Book of Judith*, Dropsie's Jewish Apocryphal Literature, 7 (Leiden: E. J. Brill, 1972) 1–37.

[16] "The Canonization of the Hebrew Bible and the Exclusion of the Apocrypha," *Essays in Biblical Culture and Bible Translation* (New York: KTAV, 1974) 257–86.

[17] *Esther*, AB 7B, lxiii.

[18] "On the Origins of the LXX Additions to the Book of Esther," *JBL* 92 (1973) 382–93.

[19] AB 44, 153–252.

Before discussing the area in which much of the best work on Esther has been done in the last decade, I must say a word about one of the new commentaries, namely, G. Gerleman's *Esther*.[20] Although I have written about his commentary elsewhere,[21] a few words are still in order here. According to Gerleman, "All the essential features of the Esther narrative are already there in Exodus 1–12: the foreign court, the mortal threat, the deliverance, the revenge, the triumph, and the establishment of a festival" (p. 11). While scholars like L. A. Rosenthal,[22] M. Gan,[23] and A. Meinhold[24] have detected (and rightly so) certain literary and stylistic influences of the Joseph narrative on Esther, Gerleman saw virtually all "the details of fact" in the Esther story as directly determined by the Exodus story: for example, both Moses and Esther were adopted (Exod 2:9; Esth 2:7); the origins of both Moses and Esther were unknown to their respective kings (Exod 2:6–10; Esth 2:10); both were reluctant to save their people (Exod 3:11; 4:1; Esth 4:11); just as Aaron was Moses' "mouthpiece" (Exod 4:15–16) so was Esther for Mordecai (Esth 2:10; 4:8; 9:20–23); both Moses and Esther repeatedly appeared before their respective kings to intercede for their people (Exod 7:14–12:28; Esth 5:2; 7:2; 8:3); Amalekites were mortal enemies to both Moses (Exod 17:8–16) and Esther (Esth 3:1, where Haman is described as an "Agagite" [cf. 1 Sam 15:8]); both Moses and Mordecai "became great" (Exod 11:3; Esth 10:3). These are but a few of Esther's "details of fact" cited by Gerleman as being inspired by the Exodus story. The Book of Esther, he maintains, is not a godless or profane book; rather, it represents a pronounced and conscious desacralization and detheologizing of a *heilsgeschichtlich* tradition.

While I would never deny that the author of Esther was influenced, both consciously and unconsciously, by the well-known Exodus story, it seems more likely that the demands of effective story-telling technique account for many of Gerleman's "parallels."[25] Moreover, some of Esther's "parallels" with the Exodus story are better viewed as expressions of "twoness" within Esther itself; for example, Esther's two dinners (Esth 5:5

[20] BKAT, 21/1–2 (Neukirchen-Vluyn: Neukirchener, 1970–73).

[21] See my review in *JBL* 94 (1975) 293–96; see also in my *Studies in the Book of Esther*, pp. xlvi–ix, my critique of Gerleman's article, "Studien zu Esther: Stoff—Struktur—Stil—Sinn," BibS(N) 48 (1966) 1–48, in which he first presented his thesis for the commentary.

[22] *ZAW* 15 (1895) 278–84; 16 (1896) 182; 17 (1897) 126–28.

[23] "The Book of Esther in the Light of the Story of Joseph in Egypt" (in Hebrew), *Tarbiz* 31 (1961–62) 144–49.

[24] "Die Gattung des Josephsgeschichte und des Estherbuches: Diaspora-novelle, I und II," *ZAW* 87 (1975) 306–24; 88 (1976) 72–93.

[25] S. Berg also accurately describes and then proceeds to discredit Gerleman's thesis in her *The Book of Esther: Motifs, Themes and Structure* SBLDS 44 (1979); see esp. 6–8.

and 7:10) and her twice risking her life by appearing before the king unsummoned (5:2 and 8:3). And as H. Cazelles has argued,[26] this two-ness, of which only a few examples from Esther have been cited here, is more likely the result of the author of Esther combining two originally separate stories: a "liturgical" text centering around Esther and non-Jews near the time of a new year, and a "historical" text centering around Mordecai, court intrigues, and persecutions of Jews in Susa.[27]

Over the last ten years of Esther studies, the contributions of Robert Gordis and Sandra Berg have stood out above the rest. A scholar and a rabbi, Gordis provided the practicing Jew with an Esther book, complete with introduction, Hebrew text, translation and commentary, as well as the Purim Ma^{c}ariv Service and Purim Blessings and Hymns.[28] He also published two very thought-provoking articles. The first, "Studies in the Esther Narrative,"[29] which tackled and sometimes solved a number of troublesome readings in the MT, is especially noteworthy for its pro-posed solution to what is, ethically speaking, the most troubling passage in Esther, namely, 8:11. According to Gordis, the last five Hebrew words of the verse do not (contrary to popular opinion) represent permission for the Jews to do to others what others would do to them but are an actual quoting of Haman's original edict. Thus, 8:11 should read: "By these letters the king permitted the Jews in every city to gather and defend themselves, to destroy, kill, and wipe out every armed force of a people or a province attacking 'them, their children and their wives, with their goods as booty'." Gordis's rendering, while quite ingenious, is, in my judgment, ultimately unconvincing. For not only does the more traditional view of the passage (i.e., that the Jews were given per-mission to do to others what was to be done to them) fit in better with the blood-and-gore spirit that the author of Esther shows elsewhere in his book,[30] but it is also a splendid expression of the principle of peripety, a principle so basic to the book (see below).

Gordis's second article, "Religion, Wisdom and History in the Book of Esther—A New Solution to an Ancient Crux,"[31] advances the fasci-nating hypothesis that Esther represents a unique literary genre hereto-fore unrecognized in the Bible, namely:

[26] "Note sur la composition du rouleau d'Esther," *Lex tua veritas: Festschrift für Hubert Junker*, ed. H. Gross und F. Mussner (Trier: Paulinus, 1961) 17–29.

[27] H. Bardtke (*Das Buch Esther*, 248–52) viewed this twoness as the result of the author of Esther borrowing three unrelated tales from a Jewish midrashic source (i.e., the Vashti story, a tale about Mordecai, and an account about a Jewish heroine) and combining them into a cohesive story.

[28] *Megillat Esther: The Masoretic Hebrew Text, with Introduction, New Translation, and Commentary* (New York: KTAV, 1974).

[29] *JBL* 95 (1976) 43–58.

[30] Cf. Esth 2:23; 3:6, 13; 5:14; 7:9–10; 9:5–10, 13, and 15–16.

[31] *JBL* 100 (1981) 359–88.

A Jewish author undertook to write his book in the form of a chronicle of the Persian court, written by a Gentile scribe [the author's italics]. A Jew of the eastern Diaspora, seeking to buttress confidence in the veracity of his narrative and thus help establish Purim as a universally observed Jewish holiday . . . writes the book as though it were an excerpt from the official chronicles of "the kings of Medea and Persia" (10:2) (p. 375).

This hypothesis, argues Gordis, explains the absence of any "reference to the God of Israel, to the practices and beliefs of Judaism, to the national history of the Jewish people, or to its ethnic concerns" (375). Gordis goes on to cite an additional twelve reasons why his hypothesis is true, e.g., the gentilic after Mordecai's name ("the Jew") represents the vantage point of the assumed non-Jewish observer; the Jews are always referred to in the third person, not the first; the ancient author concentrates on events rather than motives; the ancient author's predilections for court etiquette (5:4; 9:13) and legalistic terminology (1:22; 3:12). These, in my judgment, are among the less strained examples offered by Gordis in support of his theory.

Lack of space prohibits a point-for-point discussion of Gordis's arguments. But his main thesis is, at least in my judgment, not well-founded. One serious weakness is that he is comparing Esther to something that, to date, has not been found and therefore can only be speculated upon as to approach and contents, namely, historical chronicles (royal or otherwise) for the Achaemenid period (550–331 B.C.E.). Then, too, most of the arguments supporting his hypothesis (i.e., the thirteen points alluded to above) are better explained by a less drastic hypothesis.[32] Finally, S. Berg (see below) offers a much more persuasive theory for why God is not mentioned in Esther. Nonetheless, Gordis's article abounds in thought-provoking suggestions and solutions, some relevant to his central thesis and others to this or that aspect of Esther.

S. Berg's monograph, *The Book of Esther: Motifs, Themes and Structure*,[33] is notable for at least two reasons. First, she performs a detailed, comprehensive, and productive analysis of the narrative and stylistic features of the MT of Esther. Second, Berg does a splendid job of describing and evaluating the recent work on Esther by a number of

---

[32] Gordis rightly maintains that the *Letter of Aristeas* offers a parallel to what he is proposing for Esther: "Aristeas is interested in winning approbation or at least respect from the Gentile world for the Jewish Scriptures in their Greek dress. But his primary goal is to enhance the sacred status of the Septuagint among his co-religionists. . . . Both *Aristeas* and Esther use the device of a non-Jewish writer whose lack of pro-Jewish bias may be taken for granted and thus add credibility to their narratives" (380).

[33] SBLDS 44 (1979).

present-day scholars, including W. L. Humphreys,[34] A. Meinhold,[35] and J. T. Radday,[36] to mention a few.

According to Berg, Esther's dominant motifs[37] of banquets (31-57), kingship (59-72), and obedience/disobedience (72-93) create the book's themes,[38] namely, the Theme of Power (96-98), the Theme of Loyalty to God and Israel (98-103), and the themes of the Inviolability of the Jewish people and Reversal (103-21).

Especially welcome, at least in my judgment, is Berg's demonstration of feasting (and the auxiliary motif of fasting) as the primary motif. Among other things, her literary analysis of this motif throws additional weight on the side of those who argue for the authenticity of Esth 9:20-28 (and even, but to a lesser extent, of 9:29-32). That is, the disputed passage(s) provide a necessary balance for the entire book; for then in the MT there are two separate banquets at the beginning of the story (1:5 and 9), two in the middle (5:5 and 7:1), and two at the end (9:17-18 and 9:20-22). Also especially noteworthy is Berg's view that Esther's literary structure conforms to the principle of peripety, i.e., the unexpected reversal of affairs.[39] Here Berg builds upon the work of M. Fox[40] and Y. T. Radday.[41] In contrast to Fox, however, Berg argues (rightly, I believe) that the peripety actually begins earlier (cf. Esth 2:10, 20 and 4:17, where, with respect to dominance, the roles of Esther and Mordecai are reversed) but becomes apparent only after Esther decides to risk her life for her people (4:13-16). Agreeing with Y. Kaufmann's view that biblical *Weltanschauung* has a dual causality,[42] Berg maintains that:

[34] "A Life-style for Diaspora: A Study of the Tales of Esther and Daniel," *JBL* 92 (1973) 211-23. See Berg, esp. 129-33.

[35] "Die Gattung des Josephsgeschichte und des Esthersbuches: Diaspora-novelle, I und II," *ZAW* 87 (1975) 306-24; 88 (1976) 72-93; see also "Theologische Erwägungen zum Buch Esther," *TZ* 34 (1978) 321-33. See Berg, esp. 72-93.

[36] "Chiasm in Joshua, Judges, and Others," *LB* 3 (1973) 6-13. See Berg, 107-10.

[37] "Dominant motifs," she says, "help to unify the Book of Esther . . . [and] also appear interdependent and provide a balance between the beginning, middle and conclusion of the story" (95).

[38] A "theme" is "reserved for the message or ideas which the author conveyed by his use of motifs. . . . [Themes are] the central, dominant ideas which underlie the narrator's use of motifs, and to which those motifs point" (17).

[39] Cf. Esth 3:1 and 10:3; 3:10 and 8:2a; 3:12 and 8:9-10a; 3:13 and 8:10b-12; and 3:14 and 8:13.

[40] "The Structure of the Book of Esther," in the forthcoming festschrift for I. L. Seeligmann. Professor Fox kindly provided me with a typed copy of that article.

[41] See Berg's critique on 133-36.

[42] Kaufman, *The Religion of Israel* (in Hebrew); Jerusalem: Bialik Institute/Dvir, 1956.

The narrator believed in a hidden causality behind the surface of human history, both concealing and governing the order and significance of events. . . . Because Yahweh's control of history is neither overt nor easily discerned in everyday events, the determination of the shape and dualism of history shifts to human beings. This understanding of the hiddenness of Yahweh in the Book of Esther explains the narrator's emphasis upon individual responsibility for the successful outcome of events. It further provides the logic behind Mordecai's words to Esther in 4:13–14, where he calls upon her to save their people.[43]

In any event, I find Berg's explanation for the "hiddenness" of God more probable and far more convincing than R. Gordis's theory of the "Gentile" scribe.

Evidently working independently of Berg, J. A. Loader arrived at some conclusions very similar to Berg's.[44] According to Loader, God is present and intervenes in Esther, but that presence and intervention are deliberately veiled. This veiling is "a delicate technique with the function of expressing the meaning of the novel on different levels . . . .

Surface	Level i:	The novel should be read as a story of conflict, victory and a commemorating festival (a festal legend).
	Level ii:	It should also be read as a story of God's intervention on behalf of his people (the Exodus model[45] and other religious elements).
Below the Surface	Level iii:	It should, thirdly, be read as a story of human initiative, action and success (the deliberate veiling of God). (Berg, p. 421.)

---

[43] P. 178. Berg's explanation for the "hiddenness" of God is briefly, yet even more clearly, spelled out in her "After the Exile: God and History in the Books of Chronicles and Esther," *The Divine Helmsman: Studies on God's Control of Human Events, Presented to Lou H. Silberman,* ed. J. L. Crenshaw and S. Sandmel (New York: KTAV, 1980) 107–20, esp. 114–20.

[44] "Esther as a Novel with Different Levels of Meaning," *ZAW* 90 (1978) 417–21.

[45] Loader is much impressed with Gerleman's thesis and regards Esther as a new exodus story: "God saved Israel from the Persian predicament as he saved them from the Egyptian predicament. This means that the motif of God's intervention is present in the book but that it is veiled" (Loader, 418). He finds the presence of "veiled" theological/religious elements in such places as 4:14 ("another place"); 3:8 (which Loader understands to refer to the Torah and religious separatism); 3:4–6 (which he thinks makes events coincide with Passover deliberately); and the motif of rest (8:9).

Loader's third level is expressed in what he calls "a chiastic thought pattern" (419): first, Haman prevails over Mordecai and then the reverse occurs; next, the Jews start out being losers and end up being winners; and finally, the days of sorrow and mourning are turned to joy and holiday. "God, then, intervenes but his doing so is concealed. Therefore humans appear as the saviours in our novel. . . . When God intervenes, he does it below the surface—not in a spectacular and ostentatious manner. Human planning and action are not inhibited" (420). In sum, for Loader the "Book of Esther should be read as a story of God's intervention on behalf of his people, but also as a story of human wisdom and initiative. This is shown by the Exodus model and other religious suggestions, in particular the x-pattern of power relations, which are purposely veiled" (421).

To the reasonable suggestion that Loader's Levels ii and iii should be interchanged, C. H. Miller[46] contends that recent research into structural-developmental psychology, especially as worked out by J. Fowler of Emory University, Atlanta,[47] justifies Loader's ordering. "Structural-developmental psychology," concludes Miller, "offers useful categories for penetrating various levels of meaning in the Bible. Esther can be read on three levels, corresponding to a child's literal level, a conventional adult view, and a reflexive, critical level of faith" (148). While a biblical scholar should always welcome from other disciplines confirmation of literary or theological "solutions" in his own discipline, in this particular case I am totally unqualified to judge whether Miller has proven Loader correct. I will say this: whatever the reasons be, over the millennia the Book of Esther has appealed to a very wide audience, ranging from little children to the most sophisticated adults.

Elsewhere I have commented on the recent contributions of A. D. Cohen, R. E. Herst, B. W. Jones, J. C. Lebram, and S. E. Loewenstamm.[48] Finally, there are a number of studies on Esther that, while not discussed here or elsewhere by me, should at least be mentioned, namely, the work of M. E. Andrews, H. Bardtke, S. P. Besser, J. M. Brown, O. Eissfeldt, L. H. Feldman, P. Grelot, B. W. Jones, E. Oikonomos, N. Poulssen,

---

[46] "Esther's Levels of Meaning," *ZAW* 92 (1980) 145–48.

[47] J. Fowler and S. Keen, *Life Maps: Conversations on the Journey of Faith*, 1978, 96–99.

[48] A. D. Cohen, "'Hu Ha-goral': the Religious   Significance of Esther," *Judaism* 23 (1974) 87–94 (see my *Studies in the Book of Esther*, xxvii–xxviii). R. E. Herst, "The Purim Connection," *USQR* 28 (1973) 139–45 (see my *Studies in Esther*, xxxv–xxxvi). B. W. Jones, "Two Misconceptions about the Book of Esther," *CBQ* 39 (1977) 171–81 (see my *Studies in Esther*, lxii). J. C. Lebram, "Purimfest und Estherbuch," *VT* 22 (1972) 208–22 (see my *Studies in Esther*, xxxv). S. E. Loewenstamm, "Esther 9:29–32: The Genesis of a Late Addition," *HUCA* 42 (1971) 117–24 (see my *Studies in Esther*, xxxvi–xxxvii).

D. Tawil, and N. A. van Uchelen.[49] At another time and place I must deal with these articles. But then, Sam Iwry always did assign his students plenty to do!

[49] M. E. Andrews, "Esther, Exodus and Peoples," *AusBR* 23 (1975) 25–28. H. Bardtke, "Der Mardochäustag," *Tradition und Glaube: Das Frühe Christentum in seiner Umwelt; Eine Festgabe für Karl Georg Kuhn*, ed. G. Jeremias, H. W. Kuhn und H. Stegemann. Göttingen: Vandenhoeck & Ruprecht, 1971, 97–116. S. P. Besser, "Esther and Purim—Chance and Play," *Central Conference of American Rabbis Journal* 16 (1969) 36–42. J. M. Brown, "Rabbinic Interpretations of the Characters and Plot of the Book of Esther (as Reflected in Midrash Esther Rabbah)." Rabbinical thesis, Hebrew Union College—Jewish Institute of Religion, Cincinnati, 1976. O. Eissfeldt, "Rechts Kundige und Richter in Esther 1:13–22," *Kleine Schriften* 5 (1973) 31–33. L. H. Feldman, "Hellenization in Josephus' Version of Esther," *Transactions and Proceedings of the American Philosophical Association* 101 (1970) 143–70. P. Grelot, "Observations sur les Targums I et III d'Esther," *Bib* 56 (1975) 53–73. B. W. Jones, "The So-called Appendix to the Book," *Semitics* 6 (1978) 36–43. E. Oikonomos, "A Correction to Esther 1,18a" (in Greek) *Delton Biblikon melēton* 1 (1971) 115–16. N. Poulssen, "Esther uit de grondtekst vertaald en rechtgelegd door," *De Boeken van het'Oude Testament* 6/4; Roermond: R. S. Zonam, 1971. D. Tawil, "The Purim Panel in Dura in the Light of Parthian and Sassanian Art," *JNES* 38 (1979) 93–109. N. A. van Uchelen, "A Chokmatic Theme in the Book of Esther," *Verkennigen in een Stroomgebied Festschrift M. A. Beek*; Amsterdam (no pub.; 1979) 132–40.

RIB-HADDA: JOB AT BYBLOS?

William L. Moran
Harvard University

A MONG the correspondents with the Egyptian court whom we meet in the Amarna letters, none has a sorrier tale, and none tells it more often, than Rib-Hadda of Byblos. He is, as he never tires of assuring the court, the king's loyal servant, Byblos the king's loyal city. However, as he also insists again and again, he and his city are only a small island of fealty in a sea of treason and treachery. The other Egyptian vassals who surround them are not loyal; on the contrary, they are, he constantly claims, ever betraying the king and his interests, ever seeking instead their own. They are, therefore, Rib-Hadda's enemies, united against him, cutting him off, and so he is isolated and suffers for his loyalty. Deserted by his peasantry, whom he cannot feed, he is even, it seems to him, abandoned by his master, the king. Betrayed by his brother, he eventually becomes an exile, and in his last known letter to the king, written from Beirut, he concludes his correspondence of about a decade with the unanswered question, "Why has the king done nothing for me?"[1]

This tale, at least in outline and relieved of repetition, has a certain pathos. But what really happened? *Parti pris* is evident, and no one would accept Rib-Hadda's version of events without question or qualification. But it is the merit of Mario Liverani to have been the first to stress the presence in Rib-Hadda's correspondence of recurring themes and an underlying conceptual pattern that must be recognized and taken into account in any proper assessment of the letters from Byblos as historical sources.[2] This pattern he identifies as one associated with the figure of the "righteous sufferer," one who lives in a tormented present, looks back to a glorious past, and awaits a future that is both imminent and ambiguous, threatening and promising. In the present time Rib-Hadda is a righteous man, that is, loyal to the king—who is innocent

---

[1] *EA* 138:138. The Amarna letters (*EA*) are cited from the edition of J. A. Knudtzon, *Die El-Amarna-Tafeln*, Vorderasiatische Bibliothek, I (Leipzig: Hinrichs, 1915).

[2] "Rib-Adda, giusto sofferente," *Altorientalische Forschungen* 1 (1974) 175–205 (hereafter cited as Liverani); for an earlier, briefer statement, see *Or* NS 42 (1973) 184–86.

but suffering, plotted against and mistreated even by those who should
be his friends. He appeals to the distant god, the king, who is not only a
god in himself but in the role he has in Syro-Palestine—the absolute and
final arbiter of its affairs, who needs only to act and all will be well, the
wicked punished, the righteous man saved and rewarded—but who remains remote and indifferent to the latter's plea for intervention. The
present is also lived in recollection of the past, in memories of a Golden
Age, the good old days when, unlike the present, Byblos housed an
Egyptian garrison and was amply supplied, when, if it was attacked, Rib-
Hadda could count on Egyptian reinforcements, when indeed at the very
sight of an Egyptian the kings of Canaan fled. This present lies, too, at
the verge of a future that will bring either total and irrevocable disaster,
or a restoration of the peace and security of the past. If the king does not
act now, in this final hour, then all will be lost. Rib-Hadda writes in
this final hour—for about a decade. But for just as long he also promises
the happy alternative, should the king intervene, of a better world, the
old world.

Liverani looks for the source of this pattern and considers the possibility of the influence of Mesopotamian wisdom literature. This he does
not reject but considers unlikely, even though, as discoveries at Ugarit
have shown, the Mesopotamian tradition was certainly familiar in some
Syrian courts. Rather, it is the common world of the court—administration, bureaucracy, politics, concern for the king's favor, the envy and
calumnies of others, fidelity to one's duty and denunciation of the
infidelities of rivals, the experience of life in general in this setting—the
world shared by Rib-Hadda, by Byblian and Mesopotamian scribes alike,
the world too reflected in the wisdom literature, that Liverani sees as the
situation out of which came the conceptual pattern both of Rib-Hadda's
correspondence and of the compositions concerned with the problem of
the "righteous sufferer."

Such, in brief and inadequate outline, is Liverani's analysis. It is an
analysis, it seems to me, that is illuminating and, in its general thesis of
the presence in Rib-Hadda's letters of a "schema interpretativo della
realtà," convincing. However, I do not think that his description of the
pattern is adequate or its identification correct. Here I would like briefly
to show why and to propose another "schema interpretativo."

The temporal scheme that Liverani finds cutting across the entire correspondence—a glorious past, a miserable present, an ambiguous future—
seems to me neither as extensive nor, where it may exist, as unhistorical
as Liverani claims. It is the contrast between the present and the past,
the latter allegedly idealized into "una sorta di etaQ dell'oro, di stato
paradisiaco ora perduto"[3] that seems especially doubtful. In its support
Liverani cites or refers to twenty passages in Rib-Hadda's letters, and

[3] Liverani, 192.

in most cases there is no denying that Rib-Hadda looks to the past as a better time.[4] However, what Liverani does not advert to is the fact that of the twenty passages sixteen are found in letters of the time of Amenophis IV, only four in letters of the time of his predecessor.[5] Now, though the correspondence is more extensive, by about a third, in the later period (Amenophis IV), still the imbalance is very striking. Moreover, of the four passages written in the days of Amenophis III, only two really suggest thoughts of a better past, of which neither seems an idealization.[6] In the other two I see no hint of a Golden Age, I detect no "vago sapore paradisiaco" in "May it be pleasing in the sight of the king, my lord, that he give the grain produced in the land of Yarimuta. May what used to be given in Ṣumur now be given in Byblos."[7] This request, which is addressed to the king and then, in essentials, repeated in an accompanying letter to an Egyptian official,[8] suggests nothing more, it seems to me, than reflection on a grave crisis and a certain satisfaction with having found its solution. Grain is available and Rib-Hadda knows where: Yarimuta. In context, therefore, "what used to be given in Ṣumur" is not a sigh for better days, and it savors only of the provincial palace, informed and perhaps contentious, not of paradise. In brief, I do not think that there is one consistent temporal scheme that structures the thought of Rib-Hadda throughout his correspondence. It is only in the time of Amenophis IV that he frequently looks to bygone, better days, a restriction that in itself implies an historical, albeit rhetorical, conception of the past rather than its idealization.[9]

---

[4] *EA* 81:48–50; 85:33–37, 69–73; 86:31–35; 108:28–33; 109:44–46; 112:50–51, 54–56; 114:54–57; 116:61–63; 117:78–82; 118:50–54; 121:11–17; 122:11–19; 125:14–19; 126:18–23; 127:30–33; 129:46–48; 130:21–30; 132:10–18.

[5] *EA* 81, 85–86 (see n. 4) were probably written late in the reign of Amenophis III, though the assignment of *EA* 85–86, it might be noted, is not without its problems; see Edward Fay Campbell, *The Chronology of the Amarna Letters* (Baltimore: Johns Hopkins, 1964) 93–96.

[6] *EA* 81:48–50; 85:69–73. The former passage Liverani mistranslates, "Una volta Ṣumura e i suoi uomini costituivano una fortezza, e davano truppi di guarnigione" (Liverani, 194); render rather, "Formerly Ṣumur and its men were strong (or: there were Ṣumur and its strong men), and there was a garrison with us" (*it-ti-nu* in line 50 is not a form of *nadānu* but the preposition *itti* plus the [Canaanite] pronominal suffix; cf. the passages referred to below in n. 9). That the latter passage ("Moreover, since your father's return from Sidon, from that time the lands have been joined to the ᶜApiru") reflects simply pattern, without specific historical reference (so Liverani, 193, n. 157) is an inference of the allegedly pervasive temporal scheme: on the problem, see also H. Klengel, *Mitteilungen des Instituts für Orientforschung* 10 (1964) 61, n. 19.

[7] *EA* 85:33–37.

[8] *EA* 86:31–35.

[9] That the situation in the time of Amenophis III appears less ideal in contemporary letters hardly proves that Rib-Hadda's later, rosier picture of the

Serious doubts must also be raised concerning Rib-Hadda as the "righteous sufferer." There is no doubt that he thought of himself as righteous, that is, perfectly loyal to the king, and there is no doubt that he thought of himself as a sufferer. It does not follow, however, that he therefore thought of himself as a "righteous sufferer," whether he be of the Mesopotamian or the biblical variety. The first would be repugnant, the second anachronistic.

The repugnance of the Mesopotamian model resides in the fact that in Mesopotamia the "righteous sufferer" is not righteous at all. "Si je suis sans autre raison apparente dans la peine, c'est que je suis puni; et si je suis puni, c'est que j'ai du enfreindre un ordre souverain des dieux. . . . Telle est la théologie fondamentale du Mal, qui s'est maintenue durant toute l'interminable histoire de la vieille Mésopotamie."[10] In the Old Babylonian period this theology may find expression in a simple confession of bewilderment and ignorance of what one has done,[11] or in the acceptance of one's sinfulness, along with its necessary consequences, as another manifestation of *fragilitas humana* common to all men.[12] Later, one may infer from a clear conscience and a life re-examined and found, according to the known rules, faultless, that the gods hold men to the observance of other rules that he cannot know.[13] To these thoughts one

---

period is due to "un inserimento delle sue vicende in un quadro precostituito" (Liverani, 195). Contrary to Liverani's claim (192) that all passages introduced by *pānānu*, "formerly," refer uniformly to a kind of Golden Age, and showing that Rib-Hadda thought in terms of a less simplistic conception of the past, *EA* 104:24–26 reads, "Formerly they (the sons of ᶜAbdi-Aširta) would take cities of your mayors, and you (the king) did nothing." If the past here is better, the beginning of an ever deteriorating situation, it is certainly no Golden Age. In general, Rib-Hadda's better past consists of very specific recollections of fact and much repetition; for example, the success of a military expedition he had pleaded for (*EA* 108:28–33; 117:23–28; 132:10–18; see also *Eretz Israel* 9 [1969] 98), or the presence in the past, and the absence in the present, of a garrison or guard (*maṣṣāru/maṣṣartu*; see *EA* 117:87–88; 121:11–13; 122:11–14; 125:14–15; 130:23–24; cf. 126:22), facts that the Pharaoh's order, "Guard, be on your guard" (*EA* 112:9; 117:84), or—probably another version of the same message—"Guard yourself" (*EA* 121:9; 122:10; 123:30–31; 125:9; 126:31; 130:16–17), gave Rib-Hadda the occasion to recall *ad nauseam*.

[10] J. Bottéro, *Le Problème du Mal en Mésopotamie ancienne*, Recherches et documents du Centre Thomas More, Document 77/7 (Evaux: Centre Thomas More, 1977) 3; see also W. G. Lambert, *Babylonian Wisdom Literature* (Oxford: Clarendon, 1960) 15–16.

[11] J. Nougayrol, *RB* 59 (1952) 243:14.

[12] S. N. Kramer, *ANET*[3], 590:101–2; see also T. Jacobsen, *Toward the Image of Tammuz*, HSS 21, ed. by William L. Moran (Cambridge: Harvard, 1970) 333, no. 32.

[13] Lambert, *Babylonian Wisdom Literature*, 38–41:23–38 (*Ludlul bēl nēmeqi*, tablet 2).

may join a contempt for man as the minion of many moods, a creature that may live gloriously only to die miserably.[14] Or one may make the problem of the mind a problem of the heart, and solve it with reasons of the heart. Instead of wisdom, belief; instead of reflection and argument, a hymn to paradox and contradiction. *Credo quia absurdum.*[15] Attitudes and expressions change; the theology does not.[16]

In his relations with the king and his present sufferings such a conception of evil would hardly appear to Rib-Hadda as either congenial or germane. And as a matter of fact, we have evidence that he shared this common conception. He wrote to the king: "I am old and there is a grievous illness in my body. The king, my lord, knows that the gods of Byblos are *holy*, and the illness is extreme, *as* I have com<*mit*>ted sin(s?) against the gods."[17] Sickness, therefore guilt; nothing could be more conventional. Liverani comments: "(Rib-Hadda) falls into the normal diagnostic procedure of the time, following a deeply rooted conceptual *routine*. But it is not to be transferred to the political situation, which remains without explanation."[18] The assumption that Rib-Hadda was conventional in his religious thought, innovative in the political analogy, I find facile rather than convincing.

Moreover, the figure of the "righteous sufferer," truly righteous or not, ill accords with other recurring features in Rib-Hadda's description of himself. Essential to the latter, it seems, is that he alone is loyal, and that precisely because he is loyal he suffers from the plots and attacks of others.[19] But the "righteous sufferer" never claims that he alone is righteous, nor that he suffers for his righteousness and is isolated for his fidelity to his god.

A truly profound difference between Rib-Hadda and the "righteous sufferer," and again one essential to the figure he describes for the court, is that, unlike the "righteous sufferer," he has a way out of his sufferings that does not depend on the intervention of the "distant god." He can

[14] Ibid., 40–41:39–47.

[15] This is the ultimate position of the author of *Ludlul bēl nēmeqi*, as is evident from the opening hymn now recovered almost entirely (see D. J. Wiseman, *Anatolian Studies* 20 [1980] 102–7); for a revision of the hymn see the writer's remarks in *JAOS* 103.1 (S. N. Kramer festschrift) (1983) 255–60.

[16] For this reason one must assume that in *Ugaritica* V, No. 162, which Nougayrol saw as an early version of *Ludlul bēl nēmeqi* or as deriving with the latter from a common source, the broken introduction or conclusion contained some reference to the sufferer's guilt. An explicit, unyielding declaration of innocence is not found before the book of Job.

[17] *EA* 137:30–33 (in line 33, in favor of reading *ep-*<*ša*>-*ti*, against *epte*, "I confessed," or *epdi*, "I redeemed (by vow)," see our translation of the Amarna letters in the forthcoming volume of *Littératures anciennes du Proche-Orient*).

[18] Liverani, 203.

[19] See Liverani, 179.

simply go over to the other side. This is always the implication when he contrasts his own sufferings as a loyal vassal with the peace and prosperity of his perfidious peers. The possibility of changing allegiance is expressly noted when he reports the tempting pleas of both his family and his fellow-citizens. "Men from Byblos, my own household, and my wife kept saying to me, 'Ally yourself with the son of ᶜAbdi-Aširta so we can have peace between us.' But I refused; I did not listen to them."[20] "The city said, 'Abandon him (the king). Let's join Aziru.' And I said, 'How can I join him and abandon the king, my lord?'"[21]

On one occasion, in separate letters to the king and to an Egyptian official, Rib-Hadda openly threatened rebellion, claiming he could do it with impunity, and also indicating that he was not quite as helpless and cut off as he usually pictured himself, for he had, he claimed, a band of loyal followers. "Moreover, say to Yanḫamu, 'Rib-Hadda is herewith in your charge, and whatever happens to him is your responsibility.' Let not the troops fall upon me. And so I write, 'If you do not tell him this, then I will abandon the city and go off. Moreover, if you do not reply to me, I will abandon the city and go off with the men who are loyal to me'."[22] Earlier in the same letter: "I have written for a garrison and for horses, and they are not being supplied. Send word to me or I will make a treaty with ᶜAbdi-Aširta just as Yapaḫ-Hadda and Zimredda have done, and I will live."[23] To the Egyptian official: "If within two months there are no archers, then I will abandon the city and go off, and my life will be safe."[24]

This is not the language of the "righteous sufferer," who with no alternative can only wail and wait. Life, that good thing that belongs to Liverani's paradise regained, is something Rib-Hadda can have any time he wants. He need only be disloyal and abandon his lord.

But of course he does not. For he is the *arad kitti*, the loyal servant, and it is this figure, I submit, that ideally conceived provides the most comprehensive "schema interpretativo della realtà" in Rib-Hadda's correspondence. In its light he perceived himself; against it he measured himself. Explicit often, implicit at least throughout, the ideal of loyalty unifies the entire correspondence and reveals the nuances and implications of Rib-Hadda's endless claims, requests, and protests.

A detailed examination of this ideal is not necessary here, and a sketch will do. The ideal servant has always been loyal, as has his family.[25] He lives only for his master's interests,[26] and even his ancestral city

[20] *EA* 136:8-15.

[21] *EA* 138:44-47.

[22] *EA* 83:39-51 (for the readings, see translation referred to in n. 17).

[23] Lines 23-27.

[24] *EA* 82:41-45.

[25] *EA* 74:5-12; 116:55-56; 118:39-41.

[26] See Liverani's penetrating description, *RA* 61 (1967) 12-16, of the mentality of the pure functionary displayed by Rib-Hadda and his fellow-vassals.

he protects only because it is the king's, who may be urged to do with it what he please.[27] Whatever is his is the king's, for whom alone he lives.[28] In insisting on his loyalty he in effect abases himself, for as *arad kitti* he is the perfect slave, the pure instrument, renouncing in his relations with his master all autonomy.[29] But if as *arad kitti* he speaks *de profundis*, conscious of his own lowliness and uncertain of royal grace, he also speaks the truth, even the unpleasant truth.[30] And, as we have already seen, just as his loyalty always has been, so it ever shall be, firm and fast, unmoved by blandishment and temptation.[31] He is the *arad kitti*, and the Pharaoh knows this, "knows how long he has been showing me favor because I have no divided allegiance, my only intention being to serve the king, my lord."[32] His role is recognized, appreciated, and at times rewarded; it grounds his confidence, and he lives in hope and expectation.

The figure of the ideal, the perfectly loyal servant is not confined to the letters of Rib-Hadda. The ideal was probably shared by all the royal courts of the time and long before. It is apparent, though fragmentary, in other, less extensive correspondences of other Amarna governors.[33] A most striking illustration, along with related narrative themes, is found in Suppiluliumas' dealings with Ugarit, in which we find the Hittite king writing to Niqmandu, the king of Ugarit, urging him to maintain the peaceful relations of the past between the two kingdoms, now that the neighboring kingdoms of Nuhas and Mukis were in revolt against him. "If you, Niqmandu, heed and observe these words of the Sun, your lord, you will immediately see the favor with which the great king, your lord, will favor you."[34] And Niqmandu did not join the rebellion, and hence the following decree: "The word of the Sun, Suppiluliumas, great king, king of Hatti, the hero. When all the kings of Nuhas and the king of Mukis were at war with the Sun, the great king, their lord, Niqmandu, the king of Ugarit, was at peace and not at war with the Sun, the great king, his lord. And the kings of Nuhas and the king of Mukis urged him, saying, 'Why are you not at war, on our side, against the Sun?' But Niqmandu would not agree to war against the Sun, the great

[27] *EA* 126:44–46.

[28] *EA* 105:81–83.

[29] "I am a footstool for the feet of the king, my lord. I am his utterly loyal servant" (*EA* 106:6–7); cf. also *EA* 116:55–60, which begins with an assertion of loyalty, then states a problem and a request for its consideration, concluding with "Look, I am the dirt under your feet."

[30] *EA* 107:8–11; 108:20–25.

[31] See nn. 20–21.

[32] *EA* 119:39–44.

[33] This statement cannot be elaborated here, but anyone familiar with the Amarna letters can easily recall similar expressions of self-abasement, utter servility, etc., in the letters of other vassals.

[34] J. Nougayrol, *Palais royal d'Ugarit*, IV, Mission de Ras Shamra 9 (Paris: Klincksieck, 1956) 36:14–18.

king, his lord. And the Sun . . . has seen the *kittu* of Niqmandu and accordingly has drawn up this agreement."[35]

The themes are familiar: long-time loyal ally, others disloyal, Niqmandu alone loyal, invitation to join the rebellion rejected, loyalty verified by master. The only real difference between this narrative and what we might call the story of Rib-Hadda's life is in the conclusion: Niqmandu was rewarded, Rib-Hadda was not.

The theme of loyalty demonstrated and/or tested followed by reward is a narrative scheme that also underlies what Moshe Weinfeld has called a covenant of grant, a type of document that he finds from the second millennium down into Neo-Assyrian times and reflected as well in a number of biblical narratives.[36] He argues that it is such a covenant that is given to Noah, Abraham, Caleb, David, and the priesthood of Aaron. More recently, Jon Levenson has pointed to a theme of these grants that Weinfeld overlooked:

> In most of these instances, if not all, there is a contrast between the vassal and some faithless contemporary(ies). In other words, it is not, as Weinfeld states, simply the loyalty of the donee which wins him his covenant, but rather a loyalty unique in his time, a fidelity unparalleled in his context. This context is explicit in the cases of Noah, the only "righteous and pure man . . . of his generation" (Gen 6:9), Caleb, whose confidence contrasts with the faithless cowardice of most of the spies (Numbers 13–14), and Phinehas, whose active zeal stands out against a community paralyzed with grief (Numbers 25).[37]

The relevance of Levenson's observations for Rib-Hadda's self-portrait is evident. It should also be noted that Rib-Hadda is familiar with the argument and the language of reward we saw used by Suppiluliumas. "He (the king) knows my *kittu*. The king (also) knows how long he has been showing me favor because I have no divided allegiance (lit. second heart), my only intention being to serve the king, my lord."[38] Suppiluliumas: to see the *kittu*, and, literally, to favor a favor (*dumqa dummuqu*); Rib-Hadda: to know the *kittu*, and, literally, to do a favor (*dumqa epēšu*).

All of these various themes—loyal service, the enticements and hostility of the disloyal, a unique loyalty, the reward of loyalty—shape and pattern Rib-Hadda's thought of himself and the world about him. With them and through them he sees his life and tells his tale. And so the tale begins to make no sense, to trouble and perplex, to become, as it were,

[35] Ibid., 40–41:1–19.

[36] *JAOS* 90 (1970) 184–203.

[37] *CBQ* 38 (1976) 512. See earlier his *Theology of the Program of Restoration of Ezekiel 40–48*, HSM 10 (Missoula: Scholars Press, 1976), esp. 146–47.

[38] See n. 32.

an anti-tale. For though uniquely loyal, Rib-Hadda remains unrewarded. How can this be? "Why has the king done nothing for me?" Rib-Hadda's last words concern an ideal and an ethos. He writes them, not as a Job, but as a puzzled and unrewarded Caleb.

THE NEW JEWISH VERSION:
GENESIS OF THE FOURTH GREAT AGE OF BIBLE TRANSLATION

Harry M. Orlinsky

Hebrew Union College–Jewish Institute of Religion, New York

A LL translations of the Bible that came to be regarded as official had their origin, or acquired authorization, in communities whose needs they served; it should therefore come as no surprise to learn that the social forces that brought these needs into being also influenced the translations that fulfilled these needs.[1]

The Jewish community of Alexandria, Egypt, following its counterpart in the motherland, Judah, operated with the concept that the Hebrew text of the five books that constituted the Torah of Moses[2]

---

[1] See § A, "The Four Great Ages of Bible Translation," 4ff. of the Introduction in H. M. Orlinsky, ed. *Notes on the New [Jewish] Translation of The Torah* (Jewish Publication Society, 5730/1969); parts of this were drawn from "The New Jewish Version of the Torah: Toward a New Philosophy of Bible Translation," *JBL* 82 (1963) 249–64 (= chap. 22 in Orlinsky, *Essays in Biblical Culture and Bible Translation* [New York: KTAV, 1974], 396–417).

[2] The Torah may have been God's, but the Bible uses the phrase "the Torah of Moses" (*tōrat Mōšeh*) more frequently than is realized; thus in the account of how Ezra had the Torah canonized, Nehemiah 8 (see n. 3 below), the phrase *sēper tōrat Mōšeh* is employed in v 1 (to which *hattôrāh* in vv 2, 3, and 7 refers), *tōrat hā-ʾĕlōhîm* in vv 8 and 18, and *tôrāh ʾăšer ṣiwwāh YHWH bĕyad Mōšeh* in v 14. Of course it is only as God's spokesman to Israel that Moses acquired this distinctive status (cf., e.g., out of many other [Exodus 24; Deut 1:1–3; 4:44f.; 33:4; Jos 1:1, 7], v 14 just cited). Yet a close study of the phrases used for Torah-*cum*-God/Moses in the various parts of the Bible—thus the pre-exilic prophets are not credited with associating the Torah with Moses and Sinai, any more than the non-Deuteronom(ist)ic parts of the Pentateuch are—would reveal interesting data in the matter of authorship and date (i.e., the social-political forces and the identity of the establishment at any given time, e.g., the domains of the Davidic-Judean and Israelite interests, or the priestly group).

Among the numerous studies of torah and "the Torah" see, e.g., W. D. Davies, *Torah in the Messianic Age and/or the Age to Come* (JBL Monograph

preserved the original words of God; so that when the Hebrew language had ceased to be readily understood by the majority of the considerable Jewish population of Alexandria, in the third–second century b.c.e., the Hebrew Torah had to be turned into their new vernacular, Greek. And since every work in the Hebrew was for them God's to begin with, the Greek translation of the Torah had to reproduce these words faithfully. Accordingly, the Old Greek (Septuagint) translation of the Torah that came into being and that became the official Bible of Alexandrian Jewry— indeed, the Letter of Aristeas has it that the Jewish comminity actually canonized this translation[3]—constituted overwhelmingly a literal (often what we tend to call colloquially a crib or pony) translation of the Hebrew.[4] As I put it elsewhere:[5]

> One would hardly claim divine inspiration [and canonical authority] for a translation of the Hebrew Torah that tended to be free or paraphrastic, that was inclined to render two words by one or to combine two sentences into one, that was disposed to leave out from the Hebrew—or add to it—a word or a phrase, that perverted the plain meaning of the Hebrew, and the like. One did not deal lightly with the text of the Holy Law. . . .[6]

Series 7 [1952]); J. G. Gager, *Moses in Greco-Roman Paganism* (SBL Monograph Series, 16, 1972), especially chap. 1 on "Moses the Wise Lawgiver of the Jews" (25–79) and chap. 2 on "Moses as a Deficient Lawgiver" (80–112); F. Gottschalk, "Aḥad Ha-Am's Midraš on Moses," 113ff. of his "Aḥad Ha-Am as Biblical Critic," *Hebrew Annual Review* 7 (1983). For the Jewish community of Alexandria in the last few centuries b.c.e. it was enough, as evident from the *Letter of Aristeas*, simply to refer to "the Law," sometimes described as "holy, divine" (cf. §§ 3, 5, 38, 45, 46, 122, 129, 133, 171, 176, 309, 313); Moses is referred to once as "our lawgiver" (*ho nomothétēs hēmōn*, 131), and in §§ 177 and 313 mention is made respectively of "God whose holy words these are" and "the Law is holy and has come into being through God. . . ."

[3] The burden of the introductory data (89–94) and § A ("For Whom was the Letter of Aristeas Composed? The Septuagint as Holy Writ," 94–102) of Orlinsky, "The Septuagint as Holy Writ and the Philosophy of the Translators" (*HUCA* 46 [1975] 89–114) was to determine the technical term for the procedure of canonization of the LXX version as the Bible of the Alexandrian Jewish community, making the LXX *nomos* the equivalent of the Hebrew *torah*." See also my forthcoming chapter on "The Septuagint and its Hebrew Text" in *The Cambridge History of Judaism*, ed. W. D. Davies.

[4] Cf. § B of the aforementioned article, "The Septuagint as Holy Writ," etc., 103–14.

[5] Ibid., 102. The biblical passages dealt with there specifically are Gen 15:2 and 1:1–3.

[6] The expressions "tended (to be . . .)" and "inclined (to render . . .)" are important, for here and there a LXX translator will—for any of several possible reasons—be less than literal. It is easy to generalize about the nature of the LXX as a translation—cf., e.g., II. B. Swete, *An Introduction to the Old Testament in*

The philosophy of translation employed in the LXX has held unparalleled sway over the Christian world down to our very day; indeed, when the Protestant schism developed within European Christian society, this essentially word-for-word philosophy became even more entrenched. As the religious aspect of the new social order (the increasing primacy of commercial capitalism) in its struggle against the old (feudalism), Protestantism vigorously opposed the authority of the Roman Catholic Church's official version of the Bible, the Vulgate, and the Church's authority to interpret the Bible; it even rejected a whole section of the Church's Bible, specifically, the additional books in the OT (sometimes constituting an Appendix), which have come to be called the Apocrypha or the Deuterocanonical Books.[7]

In pursuing this course, the new Church argued that it was God's own words to Moses, and to his other select spokesmen, that were authoritative, and that it was impermissible for anyone to add anything to these words or to subtract anything from them. So that if God uttered wĕḥōšek ʿal-pĕnê tĕhôm in Gen 1:2, it was not right to add "was" in the phrase "(and darkness) was upon (the face of the deep)," any more than it was correct to include "land" in the phrase "(and let) the dry land (appear)" for (wĕteraʾeh) hayyabbāšāh in 1:9.[8] And so the eighth or so revision of William Tyndale's English translation of the Pentateuch (1531), the Appointed/Authorized Version of 1611 (popularly known as the King— and not infrequently in certain circles nowadays as the "Saint"!—James Version), made sure that the reader (if not the listener) recognized the words not actually uttered by God by printing them in italics: was and land—as though yabbāšāh (as distinct from the adjectives ya-beš/yĕbešāh) meant simply "dry."

Greek, rev. ed. R. R. Ottley (1914; KTAV reprint, 1968), chap. V, 315ff., and the more recent and critical survey offered by S. Jellicoe, The Septuagint and Modern Study (Oxford, 1968; Reprint, Winona Lake: Eisenbrauns, 1978), chap. X, "Language and Style," 314ff.; S. Brock, "Aspects of Translation Technique in Antiquity," Greek, Roman, and Byzantine Studies 20 (1979) 69–87 (to be used with reserve)—but each biblical book, even "part of a book, or more than one book" (Jellicoe, 315), must be studied per se. I hope to pursue this aspect of the LXX elsewhere.

[7] A convenient and lucid summary of the matter may be found on viiiff. ("The Revised Standard Version, the Apocrypha/Deuteronomical Books") of the Preface in the Common Bible: The Holy Bible, Revised Standard Version . . . an Ecumenical Edition (1975), or in C. C. Torrey, The Apocryphal Literature (1945) 3–40; a detailed treatment is offered in The Cambridge History of the Bible, vol. 3 (1963), The West from the Reformation to the Present Day—though the treatment (see the review by Orlinsky, JQR 54 [1965] 342–44), unfortunately, is hardly satisfactory from the point of view of the historian.

[8] Note that the LXX added no word in v 2 (kaì skótos epánō tês abússou) and reproduced yabbašāh in v 9 by its correct equivalent, (kaì ophthḗtō) hē chērá.

Hardly a verse in Biblical Hebrew prose lacks at least one occurrence of conjunctive *waw*, and hardly ever was the *waw* reproduced by anything but "and" (rarely by "but," let alone by such other appropriate conjunctions as "although," "when," "then," "after," "however") or simply left untranslated—to the point where it is not unfair to label the King James Version, along with its predecessors all the way back to the LXX and to its successors down to this day, as "And Bibles." So that even this meaningless and dreary reproduction of simple *waw* helps justify the assertion that in "liberating" the Bible from the control of the Roman Catholic Church, the Protestant Church actually assisted in increasing the slavish acceptance of the literal approach to the Bible, the sort of thing that is currently being equated in the United States—where the political-social climate at the moment is favorable for it—with the viewpoint of the so-called Moral Majority, and is used to support even such tenets as the "Scientific Creationism" of the fundamentalist wings of some organized religious bodies.[9]

It is of more than passing interest at this point to note that the Judean community during the late Persian–early Hellenistic period adopted the view that, along with the Written Law (*torah še-biktab*), God had given Moses on Mount Sinai also the Oral Law (*torah še-bě-ʿal-peh*), so that to comprehend God's Law fully and correctly it was essential to make use of both versions. As a matter of fact, from the time that this view came to prevail, it was the Oral Law—as decided by those in power, e.g., the Sadducees and then the Pharisees—that determined what the Written Law, i.e., the Hebrew text proper, really indicated. As a result, the Jewish community of Judah did not lay undue emphasis on the literalness of the Hebrew text, unless it suited their viewpoint and interests, and instead gave relatively free reign to interpretation.[10]

---

[9] In an unsigned notice of F. F. Bruce, *History of the Bible in English*[3] (1978), in the May 1980 issue of *The Bible Today* (196), the plea is made: "Wouldn't it be better to let the cinders of religious bias, Catholic and Protestant, cool off and be stored in a museum?" On some aspects of "(Scientific) Creationism," see the discussion in *Academe* 68 (March–April, 1982) 6–36; Orlinsky, "The Plain Meaning of Genesis 1:1–3," *BA* (Dec. 1983) 207–9.

[10] In Deut 4:1–8, a notable "Exhortation to Israel to observe diligently the law now about to be set before it" (S. R. Driver, *Deuteronomy*[2] [ICC; Edinburgh: T. & T. Clark, 1896] 62), the adjuration in v 2, "You shall not add anything to what I command you or take anything away from it, but keep the commandments of the Lord," (cf. Deut 13:1) was meant by its author, clearly, to apply to the legal enactments. In time, however, when the priestly establishment acquired control of restored Judah, this adjuration was applied to the very words of the Hebrew text, with the interpretation of the words (and the laws that they expressed) now the domain of the other half of the twofold Law, the Oral. So that when Deut 4:2 is applied in §§ 303–311 of the *Letter of Aristeas* to the newly

Not only that. In Jewish circles, both in Judah/Judea and in the Babylonian diaspora, it was the Hebrew text itself, rather than a translation of it, that counted. It was not the essentially literal LXX translation of the Alexandrian Jewish community but the at times interpretive Aramaic Targums that appealed to the Judean and Babylonian communities; and even there—again unlike the Alexandrian, and subsequently also the Christian community—it was the Hebrew text, to which the Jewish population at large had direct access, that continued to hold primacy over the Aramaic Targums.[11]

In this light, it becomes clear that when a translation of the Hebrew Bible into the Arabic vernacular was deemed necessary for the considerable Jewish community in Moslem regions, the noted tenth-century philologian and philosopher, and community leader, Saadia, proceeded to produce a version that was far less literal than any Christian translation before that time and up to 1970, when the New English and the New American Bibles appeared. M. L. Margolis put it well in his *multum in parvo* book, *The Story of Bible Translations* (1917) 53–54:

> Though not a paraphrase, the version [of Saadya] is by no means literal. Where necessary a word is added to bring out the sense clearly; several verses are frequently joined together in a syntactical nexus, and thus, though the original coloring is lost, the translation gains in lucidity. . . . What is principally aimed at is clarity and elegant diction. . . . Though not free from faults, Saadya's version served as a mine in the hands of successive generations of Bible students; but it was intended in the first instance for the people, the Jews in the vast domain of Arabic culture. . . ."

(For some specific cases in point in the Pentateuch, see pp. 12–13, 21–22, 23 in Orlinsky, *Notes on . . . The Torah* (and cf. *sub* "Saadia" in the Index, 278).

---

canonized LXX translation of the Torah, it is the text proper that is involved, not the comprehension of the laws contained in the text; see 99f. and n. 14 in Orlinsky, § A of article cited in n. 3 above. A useful survey of this important and complex development may be found in E. Rivkin, "Pharisees," in *IDBSup.* (1976), 657b–663b (with reference especially to S. Zeitlin's basic studies).

[11] It is idle to speculate how the Alexandrian Jewish community would have developed vis-à-vis the twofold Law and the Hebrew text itself and its Greek version had not the catastrophic events of 70 and 135 transpired; for a case in point see Orlinsky, "The Septuagint: a Little Known Fact about the First Translation of the Torah," *Essays*, chap. 20, 383–86. For a survey of recent studies on the origins of the Targumim, see the "Introduction" in L. Smolar-M. Aberbach, *Studies in Targum Jonathan*—in conjunction with the re-issue of P. Churgin, *Targum Jonathan to the Prophets* (1927)—forthcoming in KTAV's *Library of Biblical Studies* (1982) [appeared in 1983].

Haven't there been then, one may ask, any literal Jewish translations of the Bible? What about, for example, the version made by Rabbi Isaac Leeser in Philadelphia (1845–53), or the version sponsored by the Jewish Publication Society in 1916–17 with Margolis as its editor-in-chief (and the only Bible scholar on the translation committee), or Moses Mendelssohn's version and the translation-cum-commentary by the Biurists, or the Yiddish *Tsĕʾénah Urĕʾénah*, (cf. Cant. 3:11), or Yehoash's Yiddish translation?[12]

The answer is simple and forthright: True! Of course there have been literal Jewish translations. But when did they appear, and under what circumstances? For the fact is that all the aforementioned Jewish translations of the Bible—and of course the Jewish revisions of Christian Bibles—were produced in recent times, in the midst of Christian society and under the influence of the Christian (Roman Catholic, Greek Orthodox, and Protestant) Bibles.

The social forces that began to prevail in the United States and Europe in the period following World War I—inflation, the Wall Street Crash, the world-wide Depression, the rise of various forms of totalitarianism, in short, the loss of confidence in the ability of man to comprehend the world order and to solve its problems by reason and science alone— brought about a return to Holy Scripture and to religious thought.

And so, in the 1930s and 1940s, the period dominated by the threat and then the actuality of World War II, the Revised Standard Version, sponsored by the International Council of Churches of Christ, was planned and achieved; its purpose, in the light of the English of twentieth century America and of the results of archaeology since World War I, was to "embody the best results of modern scholarship as to the meaning of the Scriptures, and express this meaning in English diction which is designed for use in public and private worship and preserves those qualities which have given to the King James Version a supreme place in English literature." This was essentially true also of the Roman Catholic Bible that was planned at the same time by the American Episcopal Committee of the Confraternity of Christian Doctrine: "The supreme goal to be sought in rendering the word of God into the vernacular is rigorous fidelity to the meaning of the original, expressed in simple and

---

[12] See the detailed and informative article by R. Gottheil on "Bible Translations" in *Jewish Encyclopedia*, III (1902), 185a–197b; Orlinsky, "Yehoash's Yiddish Translation of the Bible," *JBL* 60 (1941) 173–77 (= *Essays*, chap. 23, 418–22); B. J. Bamberger, "American Jewish Translations of the Bible," *Jewish Book Annual* 15 (5718/1957-58), 33–40; E. R. Levenson, "An Addition [chiefly Moses Mendelssohn and the Biurists] for the J. P. S.' *Notes on the New Translation of The Torah*," *Gratz College Annual of Jewish Studies* 6 (1977/5738) 51–61. On Isaac Leeser, see 292f. (and nn. 12–14) and 353f. in Orlinsky, *Essays*.

intelligible language." So that by and large the Protestant Revised Standard Version was a modest revision of the King James (1611), British Revised (1881–85), and American Standard (1901) Versions, and the Catholic *Confraternity Holy Bible* a similarly modest revision of the Rheims-Douay (1582 and 1609–10) and Challoner (1750) Versions. They mark the end of the Third Great Age of Bible translation, begun by William Tyndale and Martin Luther in the sixteenth century, and they constitute the transition to the Fourth Great Age.[13]

It is no mere coincidence that the break with the age-old word-for-word philosophy of Bible translation and the introduction of the current Fourth Great Age was achieved by the American Jewish community. World War II had come and gone; but the consequences of that phenomenon, considerable and ongoing as they have been for Europe and the world generally, were nothing short of epochal for world Jewry in particular. The three main consequences, all interrelated, were: the annihilation of six million European Jews by the Nazis and their cohorts, the creation of the State of Israel, and the coming of age of the North American Jewish community. A new epoch, at one and the same time frightening, promising, and challenging, confronted the meager twelve million Jews who survived, now concentrated in two main centers, America (close to half of the total) and Israel.

The Jewish Publication Society of America, having published in 1916–17 a Jewish revision of the King James and British Revised Versions,[14] began in the latter part of the 1940s to consider a revision of it for the English-speaking Jewish communities of North America and

[13] In this connection, H. J. Cadbury's article on "Revision after Revision" (*The American Scholar* 15 [1945–Summer 1946] 298–305) merits careful reading; and the chapter (8) on "Translations of the Text—Modern English" in S. Rypens, *The Book of Thirty Centuries* (1951) 209–49—while of uneven merit and to be read with reserve—offers numerous interesting facts. H. G. May, *Our English Bible in the Making* (1952), 74, has noted that ". . . as one scholar has phrased it, both the *English Revised Version* and the *American Standard Version* were undertaken prematurely. The discoveries of the first half of the twentieth century have been so revolutionary that they have demanded a new translation that incorporates the fruits of our newer knowledge. . . ." By the same token, one may wonder what the Revised Standard Version would have been like had it been undertaken even a decade or so later than it was; look at how the Catholic *New American Bible* (1970) differs from the *Confraternity Holy Bible* (1941ff.) which it replaced.

[14] See M. L. Margolis, *The Story of Bible Translations* (1917), chaps. 6 and 8, and his (unsigned) article on "The New English Translation of the Bible," *American Jewish Year Book* (*AJYB*), 19 (5678/1917–18) 161–93 (reprinted by J.P.S., 1917, 33 pp.); C. Adler, "The Bible Translation," *AJYB* 15 (5674/1913–14) 101–21.

Europe and elsewhere, a revision in the manner of the Revised Standard and Confraternity Versions. But American Jewry was already no longer what it had been in the 1930s and early 1940s, when the Protestant and Catholic communities had planned their revisions. The American Jewish community had grown by 1950 to some five million souls, secure, mature, and optimistic in the continued opportunity to develop freely in every important aspect of its economic, political, cultural, and religious life. In keeping with its status and verve, unprecedented in the two-and-a-half millennia of the Jewish Diaspora, New World Jewry was not attracted—as it would have been a decade or two earlier—by the prospect of a modest revision in the early 1940s of a modest revision (the JPS Bible of 1916–17) of the modest British Revised Version (1881–85).

The latter part of the 1940s had passed in desultory talks about the need of a revision and its scope, and there then followed some four years of more intensive discussion and ad hoc meetings; as an ongoing participant in all this, the writer argued against a revision of the existing JPS (1916) version and for a fresh translation of the Hebrew Bible with a new philosophy of translation. Finally, at the annual public meeting of 1953 (May 10), on invitation of the Society—most of whose officers had by then been won over to his view—the writer delivered the main address on the subject, "Wanted: A New Bible Translation in English for the Jewish People"; emphasis for the new translation was laid upon "intelligibility and correctness, the accord with the new English style, and the latest scholarly truth," at the same time that stress was laid upon the use of the traditional (so-called masoretic) Hebrew text and on the avoidance of emendation of it in the translation of the text.[15]

A number of additional official and informal discussions followed, and the Society formally agreed to the conditions set forth by the writer. It appointed a committee of six scholars to assume responsibility for the new translation, with the writer as editor-in-chief. The Committee held its first session in June, 1955, with a draft of Gen 1:1–5, accompanied by

---

[15] The text of the address constitutes chap. 18 in Orlinsky, *Essays*, 349–62. It may be noted here that emendations of the preserved Hebrew text, frequently based on at least one ancient version (mostly the LXX), were offered only in the footnotes, in the *Torah* (1962), *Prophets* (1978), and *Five Megilloth and Jonah* (1969); this was in contrast to the procedure of, e.g., the Revised Standard Version, where emendations of the consonantal Hebrew text appeared in the body of the translation and usually indicated by "Cn" in a footnote (cf. Orlinsky, "The Hebrew Text and the Ancient Versions of the Old Testament," Chap. IV, in *An Introduction to the Revised Standard Version of the Old Testament* [by Members of the Revision Committee, Luther A. Weigle, Chairman; 1952] 24–32 [=chap. 21 in *Essays*, 387–95]). The Committee responsible for the rest of the *Writings-Kethubim* (1982) of the New Jewish Version decided arbitrarily not to offer any emendations even in the footnotes.

voluminous data, prepared by the writer for its consideration and collective decision.[16]

Thus the New Jewish Version was born; and the Fourth Great Age of Bible Translation had begun.

It is generally agreed that the Alexandrian Jewish philosopher Philo, about 1,950 years ago, helped lay—even if unwittingly—much of the philosophical foundation of Christianity; and it has been argued that it was another Jewish philosopher, Baruch Spinoza (1632–77), sixteen hundred years later, who was largely responsible for destroying Philonism and for helping give Christianity new direction. In Bible translation, it was the Jewish LXX version, some 2,200 years ago, that set the norm for word-for-word reproduction of the Hebrew, and it is precisely this philosophy of literal, essentially mechanical translation that the New Jewish Version set out to discard. There was, further, good reason to believe that with the appearance of the *Torah* in 1962, with its internal and external break with the past, a new pattern would be set which the new authorized Protestant and Catholic translations would tend to follow.

This has come to pass. The Confraternity Bible has been abandoned, to be replaced by the much more modern New American Bible, much more modern not only in its philosophy of translation but also in the fact that whereas the Confraternity Bible had been based directly on the Latin text of the Vulgate version, the NAB derived directly from the Hebrew (-Aramaic) and Greek texts. The British Revised Version has been succeeded by the altogether different New English Bible. And the Revised Standard Version—let alone the American Standard Version that it had replaced—is in the process of being superseded by the ongoing revision of the RSV.[17]

It may well be that the Fourth Great Age of Bible Translation, which began shortly after the middle of the century and consisted chiefly of the New Jewish Version, the New American Bible, and the New English Bible—to which the Good News Bible (Today's English Version), among

---

[16] The other five members of the Committee at the time consisted of E. A. Speiser, M. Arzt, B. J. Bamberger, H. Freedman, and S. Grayzel, the last-mentioned serving also as Secretary. H. L. Ginsberg joined the Committee later (early in 1956). On how the Committee functioned, see § B2 of the Introduction in Orlinsky, *Notes on the New [Jewish] Translation*, etc., 14–19.

[17] See the special issue of the *Duke Divinity School Review* 44/2 (Spring 1979) 67–195, ed. L. R. Bailey, "Recent English Versions of the Bible" (republished with some additions as *The Word of God* by John Knox Press); and J. P. Lewis, *The English Bible/From KJV to NIV: A History and Evaluation* (1981). As for the "New" Bibles that have been appearing on the market increasingly, e.g., the New King James and the New American Standard Versions, the less said about them the better.

the unauthorized, more freely rendered versions, may be added—will come to a close with the appearance of the new edition of the Revised Standard Version at the turn of the decade; in the meantime, and probably well into the twenty-first century, the dominant practice will continue to consist of "revision after revision."

ISAIAH AND HIS CHILDREN*

J. J. M. Roberts
Princeton Theological Seminary

I SA 8:18 says that Isaiah and the children whom Yahweh gave him were for signs and portents in or against Israel. This statement raises several questions. How many children did Isaiah have? How were they signs and portents? What did they signify? And whom or what is meant by the term Israel? In this paper I will attempt to demonstrate that Isaiah had at least three children, each of whom received a symbolic name—Shear-jashub, Immanuel, and Maher-shalal-hash-baz. All three were born during, or in the case of Shear-jashub, perhaps shortly before, the Syro-Ephraimite conflict, when the northern kingdom, Israel, together with Syria tried to force Judah into a defensive alliance against Assyria. Isaiah's children with their symbolic names functioned as living embodiments of Isaiah's message during this time.

But the oracles of Isaiah given during this period were reworked, probably first by Isaiah himself later in his ministry, and then perhaps by disciples after Isaiah's death, in order to make the oracles speak to new situations in the life of God's people. As a result it is often very difficult to recover the original intention of an oracle. The interpreter who wants truly to penetrate the meaning of the text is faced with a two-fold or even three-fold task. One must reconstruct the original context and the meaning of the oracle in that context, one must trace the transformation of the oracle's meaning in its later context or contexts, and one must ask about the meaning of the oracle for the contemporary community of faith.

The key to the historical situation in which Isaiah's children embodied their father's message is provided by Isa 7:1-9:

> In the days of Ahaz the son of Jotham, son of Uzziah, king of Judah, Rezin the king of Syria and Pekah the son of Remaliah the king of Israel marched on Jerusalem to fight against it, but they could not mount an attack against it. When it was reported to the house of David, "Syria has entered into league with Ephraim," their heart and the heart of their people shook as the trees of the forest shake before a wind.

* It is a pleasure to contribute this study in honor of Prof. Iwry, a former colleague, teacher, and cherished friend.

193

But Yahweh said to Isaiah, "Go to meet Ahaz, you and Shear-jashub your son, at the end of the aqueduct of the upper pool, by the road to the fuller's field. You shall say to him, 'Take care and remain calm! Do not fear, and let your heart not be troubled by these two stumps of smoldering firebrands, at the anger of Rezin and Syria and the son of Remaliah. Because Syria—with Ephraim and the son of Remaliah—has plotted evil against you, saying, "Let us go up against Judah and cut her off[1] and conquer her[1] for ourselves, and appoint the son of Tabiel as king within her," thus says the lord Yahweh:

"It will not stand, and it will not come to pass;
For the head of Syria is Damascus, and the head of Damascus is Rezin.[2]
The head of Ephraim is Samaria, and the head of Samaria is the son of Remaliah.
If you do not believe, you will not stand firm."

Isaiah's mission to Ahaz was one of reassurance. His message to him was a message of salvation. The evil plan of Syria and Israel against Judah, Jerusalem, and the Davidic house would not come to fruition. Ahaz need not fear. He need only trust Yahweh, and he would remain secure on the throne. The promise was dependent on Ahaz's faith, but this condition should not be overly stressed to turn this oracle into an oracle of judgment. In the original historical context, it could only have functioned as an oracle of salvation with an attendant demand for faith in the divine promise.

[1] The derivation and meaning of *unĕqîṣennāh* is disputed. The RSV derives it from *qûṣ*, "to feel a sickening dread," hence in the hiphil, "to terrify." One could see the Syrian and Israelite campaign as an attempt to intimidate Jerusalem into capitulating. The fact that the allied kingdoms could not mount a successful attack on Jerusalem may suggest that the allies were not really prepared for a prolonged siege, and the use of this verb would give added weight to Isaiah's admonition not to fear. The plans of these kings were at absolute cross purposes with Yahweh's plans.

On the other hand, the use of the verb *bāqa*[c] suggests that the allies planned to "breach" the city by siege (see 2 Chr 32:1 for a similar construction). The verb *bāqa*[c] can be used for an attack on a territory (2 Chr 21:17), but it is more normally used for breaching a city's fortifications (cf. 2 Kgs 25:4; Jer 39:2; 52:7; Ezek 26:10). That, however, raises the question of what antecedent is intended by the third feminine suffix on the two verbs. The immediate antecedent is Judah, but since the attack was aimed specifically at Jerusalem and had the allies' plans materialized, the new king would have been installed in this city, one wonders if the intended antecedent is not Jerusalem. If so, one might consider analyzing the first verb as an otherwise unattested hiphil of *qāṣaṣ*, reading *unĕqēṣṣennāh*, "Let us cut her (Jerusalem) off and conquer (breach) her for ourselves."

[2] The line, "Within sixty-five years Ephraim will be broken to pieces so that it will no longer be a people," has been deleted following the common judgment that it is a later gloss. It is a very peculiar gloss, however, since the sixty-five years refer to nothing of which we have any knowledge, while Ephraim actually fell within three years, which any later glossator should have known. One should

God's explicit instruction that Isaiah's son Shear-jashub accompany Isaiah to this meeting suggests that the child's symbolic name somehow embodied Isaiah's message for this occasion, but the text here gives no explanation of the name. In the sequel, in verses 10–17, a child with the symbolic name, Immanuel, is also mentioned, but since the interpretation of this passage is very complicated, perhaps it is best to begin with the third child, Maher-shalal-hash-baz. Of the three children bearing symbolic names the symbolic significance of his name is the least problematic and the least debated. That is not to say there is complete unanimity on the symbolic significance of the name Maher-shalal-hash-baz, but compared to the other texts Isa 8:1–4 is relatively clear and may serve as a starting point for interpreting the other names.

> Yahweh said to me, "Take a large tablet[3] and write on it with an ordinary[4] stylus,[5] 'To Maher-shalal-hash-baz.' Then have it witnessed for me[6] by reliable witnesses, Uriah the priest and Zechariah the son of Jeberechiah."
>
> Then I had intercourse with the prophetess, and she conceived and bore a son. Yahweh said to me, "Name him Maher-shalal-hash-baz, for before the lad knows how to cry, 'Daddy!' or 'Mommy!' one will carry away the wealth of Damascus and the plunder of Samaria to the king of Assyria."

It is clear from the new introduction in v 5, that these following verses were given to the prophet on a separate occasion, so they should not be used to interpret the original intention of vv 1–4. There are a number of uncertainties in the passage to which we must return later, but several things are clear: 1) The name given to the child means something like "The-Spoil-Hastens-the-Booty-Speeds."[7] 2) The name was

---

also note that the notice comes before the line about Ephraim, and therefore seems out of place. One wonders if this is not a misplaced, garbled, conflate reading from a fuller original oracle in which the judgment against the two kingdoms was explicitly expressed, perhaps originally following v 9a:

whnh b^{c}wd šš šnh	And, behold, within six years
dmśq mwsr m^{c}yr	Damascus will cease to be a city;
wb^{c}wd ḥmš šnh	And within five years
yḥt $^{\circ}$prym m^{c}m	Ephraim will cease to be a people

Cf. Isa 17:1.

[3] The precise meaning of *gillāyôn* is uncertain; it might also refer to a sheet of papyrus.

[4] The meaning of $^{\circ}$*ěnôš* in this context is uncertain; "ordinary" is only a guess.

[5] The word *ḥereṭ* might also designate the ductus rather than the writing tool itself. In this case one could translate the phrase as "in an ordinary script."

[6] Reading the imperative with IQIsa^a and the LXX.

[7] The precise grammatical analysis of *mahēr* and *ḥāš* is irrelevant for the purposes of this article.

given before what it signified had come to pass—the function of the witnesses was presumably to protect the prophet from the charge of composing a prophesy after the event. 3) The prophet expected the fulfillment of what the name signified before the child spoke his first words, that is, within a year of the child's birth. 4) This concern for the time of fulfillment reflected also in the symbolic name's emphasis on speed, indicates that the symbolic function of the child was primarily to provide a time limit for Isaiah's prophecy. 5) The prophecy itself was that both Damascus, the capital of Syria, and Samaria, the capital of Israel, would be destroyed and plundered by Assyria within the year. 6) Since these two states were threatening Jerusalem at the time, the prophecy could only be heard by the Judean royal court as an oracle of salvation. If Syria and Israel were going to fall within the year, one need not be overly concerned about their plans. In other words the original intention of the oracle was similar to that in 7:4-9. It was to reassure Ahaz in the hope that he would trust in God's promise and refrain from entering into negotiations with Assyria.

The interpretation of the symbolic significance of Maher-shalal-hash-baz in 8:4 has a very similar structure to the explanation of the symbolic significance of Immanuel in 7:16, so we turn now to this earlier passage. Isa 7:16 must be discussed in the context of 7:1-17. Some scholars see v 10 as beginning a new unit and would place this incident somewhat later than Isaiah's meeting with Ahaz at the aqueduct, but this is problematic. Vv 10 and 11 begin with the prophet offering a sign to Ahaz as an inducement to faith. God had done the same with Moses (Exod 3:11-12; 4:1-9), Gideon (Judg 6:15-18, 26-40), Saul (1 Sam 10:1-7), and he later did the same with Hezekiah (2 Kgs 19:29; 20:8-11). But such signs always presupposed a prior message that the sign is given to confirm. If one severs vv 1-9 from v 10, however, there is no prior message. V 10 could never have opened an independent literary unit. It is dependent on vv 1-9, or a similar opening unit, for the prior message which alone gives it meaning. Thus, unless one assumes a lost introduction, it seems likely that vv 10-17 represent a continuation of Isaiah's conversation with Ahaz at the aqueduct.

The promise made to Ahaz in the preceding oracle was contingent on Ahaz's faith, and Isaiah continues the confrontation by offering Ahaz a sign from God as an inducement to such faith. Perhaps Ahaz's response to the initial oracle was less than encouraging, for while even the offer of a choice of signs is not unparalleled (2 Kgs 20:8-11), the scope of the choice offered Ahaz is unusual, and it underscores the importance Isaiah attached to the king's decision at this critical juncture. Yahweh was willing to pull out all the stops to secure Ahaz's faith.

Ahaz, however, refused to play by the rules. Hiding behind a false piety, he declined the invitation to ask for a sign. From Isaiah's response it is clear that the prophet regarded Ahaz's refusal to ask for a sign as a pious smokescreen. The king's real concern was not over "testing God" but with preserving his own freedom of choice in the situation. If he accepted the prophet's offer of a sign, and it was forthcoming, Ahaz would be locked in to a quietistic policy of waiting out the expected siege. Without the confirmatory sign the king would have more freedom to go against the prophet's advice in considering other political choices such as an appeal to Assyria. Ahaz did not believe, and he did not want to be forced into a belief that would limit his freedom.

Apparently Ahaz's response reflected the views of the royal court, because Isaiah's retort is addressed to the whole Davidic house, not just to the king. The royal court had gone too far with this refusal. It was bad enough to exhaust the prophet's patience by their refusal to believe, but when one refused the offer of a sign from God himself, that was to exhaust the patience of Isaiah's God. The expression "my God" suggests the close relationship between the prophet and Yahweh, but it also contains a note of judgment. By the choice of this expression rather than "our God" or "your God," Isaiah pointedly excludes the Davidic house from that relationship of intimacy with God. It was a relationship sustained only by faith, and by their lack of faith the Davidic house had forfeited it. Nevertheless, even the court's faithfulness does not prevent God from trying again. Though Ahaz had refused to ask for a sign, God gives him one anyway, albeit now God chooses it, not Ahaz.

There is a lively debate about the nature of that sign, but two things should be kept in mind. The sign must have some meaning for Ahaz and the royal court, and the remarkable parallel between 7:16 and 8:4 must be given its due. I translate 7:14-17 as follows:

> Therefore the Lord himself will give you a sign. Look, the young woman is pregnant and will soon bear a son, and she will name him Immanuel. He will eat curds and honey when he learns to reject the bad and choose the good, for before the lad learns to reject the bad and choose the good, the land before whose two kings you cringe shall be deserted. Yahweh will bring upon you and upon your people and upon the house of your father days that have not come since the day that Ephraim turned aside from Judah.[8]

Isa 7:14 has the form of a traditional announcement formula by which the birth of a child is promised to particular individuals (Gen 16:11; Judg 13:3; the same basic construction is even found in an earlier Ugaritic text, *CTA* 24:7), and that together with the definite article indicates that Isaiah is speaking of a particular woman. He does not call her a virgin; ᵓalmâh does not have that meaning in Hebrew.[9] Moreover, the parallel with the announcement to Hagar in Gen 16:11 suggests that

---

[8] Deleting "—the king of Assyria" as a gloss, see below.

[9] The literature on this subject is too vast to cite; see the commentaries.

the woman was already pregnant at the time Isaiah called attention to
her. Nothing in the Hebrew text suggests that the conception lay in the
future. In fact, the use of the participle *wĕyōledet* implies that the birth
itself was imminent. The woman was "about" or "soon" to give birth.
Unfortunately, one cannot translate this so-called *futurum instans* use of
the participle into a specific time frame. It might be as easily said of a
woman one month into her term as of a woman nearing the end of her
term.

Precisely who this woman was is a subject of debate, but two suggestions seem most probable. Either Isaiah was referring to a wife of
Ahaz or to his own wife. The close parallel with the prophetic oracle in
8:1–4, where Isaiah's wife is clearly the mother of the child, suggests that
Isaiah is also referring to his own wife here. We do not know exactly
how old Shear-jashub was at the time of this encounter, but he could not
have been very old. The fact that Isaiah gave him a symbolic name pre-
supposes that he was born after Isaiah's call to be a prophet, hence after
the death of Uzziah. Thus he could hardly have been older than seven,
and he may have been several years younger. If he were just old enough
to accompany Isaiah, say three or four, Isaiah could still refer to his wife
as a "young woman." Apparently Shear-jashub was Isaiah's firstborn,
and since Israelite women married quite early and had children as soon
as possible, his wife could still have been in her teens. The presence of
the young child at the meeting might also explain Isaiah's reference to
the young woman. It is unlikely that any pregnant woman from the
royal court would have been present at this meeting by the aqueduct,
and had Isaiah's wife been present, it is strange that she is not mentioned
along with her son. But with Shear-jashub present, Isaiah might have
referred to the boy's young mother, who was presumably well-known to
Ahaz, as the young woman who was again pregnant. Isaiah does not say
"my wife," but neither does he use that unequivocal expression in 8:3,
where it is clearly his wife who is meant.

If one is correct in identifying the young woman as Isaiah's wife
who was pregnant with her second child, in what does the sign actually
consist? It does not consist in a miraculous birth. Does it consist in the
symbolic name alone, or is there more to it? Here one must compare 7:16
and 8:4. Both verses begin with a time limit introduced by *ky bṭrm yd^c
hn^cr*, "For before the lad learns," followed by an infinitive construction
that states the content of that learning or knowing. While 8:4 with its
reference to the child's first words suggests a time limit of only a year
after the birth of Maher-shalal-hash-baz, 7:16 with its reference to
Immanuel's choice of foods, suggests a terminus after the weaning of
this earlier child, thus a somewhat longer time limit of two to three
years. Since the Immanuel prophecy antedates the conception of Maher-
shalal-hash-baz, it is likely that the different time limits attached to the
two children actually have in mind the same terminus for the fulfillment

of Isaiah's prophecy, and the sign of Immanuel like the sign of Mahal-shalal-hash-baz was a positive sign to Ahaz. By the time Immanuel is weaned, he will be able to choose the richest foods appropriate for his age. Whatever shortages that have resulted or will result from Syria and Israel's attempts to besiege Jerusalem will have been made good within three years of the birth of Immanuel. Accordingly, v 17 should be taken in a positive sense. Yahweh will bring upon Judah days of abundance such as she had not known since the northern tribes split off under Solomon's successor. The final words of v 17, "the king of Assyria," give the verse a negative slant, but these words are generally considered a late gloss, even by those scholars who understand the oracle as a threat, not as an oracle of salvation.

The word Immanuel also occurs in two other places in Isaiah (8:8b and 8:10), both of which appear to be reworked fragments, and for both of which an original positive connotation may be reconstructed. V 8b makes little sense in its present context as the continuation of 8:8a. Isa 8:7–8a describes the Assyrian invader under the metaphorical image of a rampaging river in flood:

> Therefore the Lord is about to bring upon you the mighty flood waters of the River, the king of Assyria and all his glory; and it will rise above all its channels and overflow all its banks; and it will sweep on into Judah as a flood, and pouring over, it will reach up to the neck.

V 8b continues with the statement, "And the outspreading of his wings will fill the breadth of your land, Immanuel." The imagery is strangely mixed. One does not normally speak of a river having wings.[10] In the OT the normal content of the imagery of outspread wings is the idea of protection. One takes refuge under the wings of Yahweh.[11] Though it is impossible to reconstruct a complete original setting for 8:8b, it is probable that it once functioned as a positive word. Yahweh's wings stretched out over the whole land to protect it.[12] Such a positive interpretation of the name in 8:10 is certain. It occurs as part of an oracle addressed to the nations in which their plans against Judah are doomed to failure:

> Be shattered,[13] O peoples, be broken.
> Listen all distant parts of the earth.

[10] This is the only passage where *kānāp* is so used.

[11] See Pss 17:8; 36:8; 57:2; 61:5; 63:8; 91:4; Ruth 2:12. The image is probably connected to the temple iconography of the cherubim of the ark with their outspread wings. The cherubim served as Yahweh's throne and together with the ark, Yahweh's footstool, clearly symbolized Yahweh's presence.

[12] See the translation and notes on this passage in the new Jewish Publication Society translation.

[13] Or possibly, "Band together," deriving *rʿw* from *rʿh*, "to associate with," following the Targum and the Vulgate.

> Gird yourself and be broken,
> Gird yourself and be broken.
> Make a plan, but it will be frustrated.
> Speak a word, but it will not come to pass,
> For God is with us (Immanuel).

The language of the shattered plans has numerous points of contact with 7:7–9, and one may suspect that this fragment was originally aimed at Syria and Israel, and that it was originally given in the same context of Isaiah's meeting with Ahaz, when the name Immanuel was undoubtedly explicated. In any case, 8:10 interprets the name positively.

Although, as I have already noted, no interpretation of his symbolic name is offered when Shear-Jashub accompanies Isaiah to meet Ahaz in chap. 7, one is probably correct in assuming that there was once an oracle explicating the name for the people. The closest thing to such an explication in the Isaianic corpus is the material preserved in 10:20–24a:

> In that day the remnant of Israel and the survivors of the house of Jacob shall no longer lean on the one who smites him, but he will lean on Yahweh the Holy One of Israel in truth. A remnant will return (*Shear jashub*), a remnant of Jacob to El Gibbor. For even if your people, O Israel, are like the sand of the sea, only a remnant of it will return. Destruction is decreed overflowing with righteousness. For the lord Yahweh of hosts will make the decreed destruction in the midst of the whole land. Therefore, thus says the lord Yahweh of hosts, "Do not fear, my people, who live in Zion. . . ."[14]

One should note that the element *shear* occurs in this passage four times, and the full form *Shear-jashub* occurs twice. In the present context of chap. 10, this material functions to reassure Judah in the face of the Assyrian threat, hence must be dated to the time of Sargon, or more probably Sennacherib, and therefore is far too late to serve as an interpretation of the symbolic name Shear-jashub. There are indications, however, that these verses as well as parts of vv 16–19 and 27d–34 originated in the context of the Syro-Ephraimitic war and were originally directed against Damascus and Ephraim, not Assyria.

Thus the remnant (*shear*) discussed in vv 20–24a is defined as the remnant of Israel, the survivors of the house of Jacob, and the remnant of Jacob. They are set in contrast over against the inhabitants of Zion. Note the contrasting vocatives with contrasting personal pronouns: "Though *your* people, O Israel . . ." (10:22) versus, "Therefore . . . do not fear, *my* people, who live in Zion. . . ." Isaiah clearly uses the term

---

[14] The text continues with the mention of Assyria as the object of that fear, but I will argue that this is part of Isaiah's reworking of the original oracle. See below.

Jacob in several passages to refer to the northern kingdom in distinction to Judah (9:7; 17:4), and that usage would explain the contrast here very nicely, including the contrast between the threat to Israel and the promise to the inhabitants of Zion.

Shear also occurs in 10:19, and the judgment pronounced on the enemy army in 10:16–19 has its closest parallels in the oracle against Damascus and Samaria in 17:1–6, which speaks of the remnant (*shear*) of Syria (17:3) and describes Israel as left only a remnant (*nishʾar*), like a thoroughly picked vineyard (17:6). Both passages speak of the "fatness" (*mishman*) of the enemy and of the emaciation (the verb *rāzâh* or the noun *rāzôn*) that will strike him (10:16; 17:4), both use the term "glory" (*kābōd*) of the enemy (10:16; 17:4), and both use agricultural imagery involving trees to indicate the utter decimation of the enemy (10:18–19; 17:4–6).

Finally, the description of the enemy march on Jerusalem in vv 27d–32 has long raised questions, since it does not conform to the line of march portrayed in Sennacherib's account of his Judean campaign, or of any other Assyrian campaign against Jerusalem of which there is any record. For that reason a number of scholars have seen in these verses an account of the approach toward Jerusalem of the Syro-Ephraimite army.[15] That would fit both the line of march, and the reaction of the threatened territories corresponds exactly to the reaction of Judah portrayed in Isa 7:2. Moreover, the goal of this march is Jerusalem as in the Syro-Ephraimite war (7:1, 6). Nothing in the account in 10:27d–32 suggests the systematic reduction of Judah's outlying fortresses, which characterized Sennacherib's campaign.

If this reconstruction of the original historical setting for 10:20–24a is correct, then the original interpretation of the name Shear-jashub falls completely into line with the interpretation of Maher-shalal-hash-baz and conveys the same message as Immanuel. All three names were to reassure Judah and the Davidic house in the face of the threat from Syria and Israel. Only a remnant of the attacking enemy would survive God's judgment. Zion was secure because God is with us, but both Damascus and Israel would soon be plundered.

This analysis brings us back to 8:16–18:

> Bind up the testimony, seal the instruction with those I had instructed. But I will trust in Yahweh, who is hiding his face from the house of Jacob. Yes, I will wait for him. I and the children, whom Yahweh has given to me, are signs and portents against Israel from Yahweh of hosts, who lives on Mount Zion.

---

[15] See especially H. Donner's monograph, "Israel unter den Völkern," *VTSup* 11 (1964) 30–38, and his later article, "Der Feind aus dem Norden," *ZDPV* 84 (1968) 46–54.

As Clements has recognized, these verses must mark the original conclusion to the narrative in 8:1–4; the sealed testimony or instruction
originally referred to the scroll inscribed with the name Maher-shalal-
hash-baz and witnessed by Uriah the Priest and Zechariah the son of
Jeberechiah.[16] These two men are presumably the ones referred to as
Isaiah's *limmūdîm*, in which case the term does not mean "disciple" in
the normal sense of that word, but "those instructed by" someone.
Apparently they were to keep the scroll in order to attest the truthfulness
of Isaiah's message when the prophecy was fulfilled. Since the children's
names all foretold a judgment on the northern kingdom, both Israel and
the house of Jacob in this passage should be taken as originally referring
to the northern kingdom. At the time of the Syro-Ephraimite war Yahweh
was hiding his face from the northern kingdom. Despite the ancient
promise to make them numerous, they would be left a pitiful remnant
(10:22), because they did not lean upon Yahweh (10:20). In contrast,
Isaiah would wait upon Yahweh (8:17). Moreover, as in 10:22–24; 8:16–18
shows the same contrast between Israel, from whom Yahweh is hiding
his face, and Jerusalem/Zion, where Yahweh dwells.

But if Isaiah and his children with their symbolic names originally
served to embody God's message of judgment against the northern kingdom, these oracles were soon reedited to include Judah in Yahweh's net
of judgment. This is clear from the way in which the insertions in
8:5–15 have split apart 8:1–4 and 8:16–18, giving the whole passage a
more ambivalent note. The insertions, however, have taken place in
stages. Apparently when Ahaz, despite the reassurances given him by
Isaiah's repeated oracles against Israel and Syria, decided to appeal to
Assyria for help, Isaiah saw this as a final refusal to trust in Yahweh,
and drew the conclusions implicit in the conditional promise of 7:9. If
the Davidic house and its people refused to delight in the gentle waters
of Shiloah, that is, to trust in Yahweh's promises to Zion and its Davidic
king, they would not stand firm; the raging flood of Assyria would
sweep them away with the feeble enemies they so feared. The oracle in
8:5–8a would appear, therefore, to stem from relatively soon after Ahaz
had definitively turned his back on Isaiah's advice and had implored
Assyria for help. Vv 11–15 would also appear to stem from the same
period because of its announcement of judgment on both houses of
Israel. It is probable that Isaiah himself is responsible for the insertion of
this material into his memoirs, which has the effect of extending his
announcement of judgment against Israel to also include Judah.

The same effect is achieved in chap. 7 by the addition of vv 18–25, at
least once it was connected to the preceding by the concluding gloss on
v 17, "the king of Assyria." How much of this material may be attributed to Isaiah, however, and whether it was added at one point, or in
stages, is very difficult to decide.

16 R. E. Clements, *Isaiah 1–39* (NCB; Grand Rapids: Eerdmans, 1980) 100.

The insertion of 8:8b-10, however, must stem from later in Isaiah's ministry. Isaiah threatened that Yahweh would use Assyria to punish God's people, but once it was clear that Assyria had overstepped her assigned role, Isaiah began to announce God's impending judgment on Assyria (10:5ff.). In doing so he appears to have reused old oracles that were once directed against other enemies of Judah. Thus in 10:16-24a and 27d-34 Isaiah, or less probably a disciple, works old oracles against Syria and Ephraim, stemming from the period of the Syro-Ephraimitic war, into the judgment oracle against Assyria. The same appears to be true in 8:8b-10. These verses were probably inserted as the last element in 8:1-18, at a time when Isaiah felt it was important to stress that Assyria's haughty plans against Jerusalem would no more be realized than the earlier plans of Syria and Israel. The reuse of 8:8b-10 in this way was appropriate, because both in its original setting and in this secondary reapplication the oracle was directed against political powers who in their human arrogance plotted against Yahweh and his city, Jerusalem.

The reuse of the Shear-jashub oracle in 10:20-24a, however, gave a new dimension to this material. Whereas the original oracle functioned as a reassurance to Judah by threatening that *only* a remnant of Israel would return, that is, by giving the idea of the remnant a negative connotation, when the oracle was placed in this new setting, it functioned as a reassurance to Judah by promising that at least a remnant of Israel would return, that is, by giving the idea of the remnant a positive connotation. Though Assyria was used by God to punish his people, at least a remnant of Israel would return to God, the punishment would not last forever, and therefore the inhabitants of Jerusalem need not fear Assyria. The reworking of the oracle was not carried through thoroughly enough to strip the remnant concept totally of its earlier negative connotations, however, with the result that the concept remains curiously ambivalent in the present text, a fact that has produced the lively scholarly debate over Isaiah's understanding of the remnant.

If this reconstruction of the original meaning of the names of Isaiah's children is correct, it has far-reaching implications for the redactional study of the book of Isaiah. In contrast to most contemporary students of the book who attempt to explain the inconcinnities in the material as the result of late glossing and post-Isaianic redactional work, my work suggests a far larger component of very early Isaianic oracles reworked and redacted by the prophet himself in later stages of his own ministry. This interpretation also has implications for a contemporary Christian appropriation of the Immanuel prophecy, but that is a topic for another paper.

ISAIAH 66:1-4:
JUDEAN SECTS IN THE PERSIAN PERIOD AS VIEWED BY TRITO-ISAIAH

Alexander Rofé

Dept. of Bible
The Hebrew University, Jerusalem

O NE of the conspicuous differences between the prophecies of Deutero-Isaiah (Isaiah 40-53) and Trito-Isaiah (Isaiah 54-66)[1] lies in their respective descriptions of redemption. Deutero-Isaiah portrays the redemption of Israel at the hands of Cyrus, the anointed of the Lord, who will vanquish the Chaldeans (48:14), establish a new imperial kingdom (45:1), restore the Judean exiles to their land and rebuild Jerusalem (45:13; 44:28).[2] This redemption is brought about by a foreign king, who unwittingly serves as a tool in the hands of the Lord (45:4-5), the God who hides himself (45:15). Trito-Isaiah, in contrast, describes the redemption as a direct intervention of the Lord (59:16-20), unaided by anyone from the nations (63:3), executing an apocalyptic judgment upon the wicked (66:15-16) and establishing the imperial rule of Israel over the nations (55:3-5; 60; 61:5-6). Deutero-Isaiah presents the redemption as unconditional, in accordance with his view that the word of the Lord always comes to pass (40:8; 45:23; 46:8-11); consequently, the fulfillment of the announcement of redemption is in his view a criterion for the truthfulness of the Lord as opposed to the falsity of idols (41:21-29;

---

[1] The first to recognize, in the 1880s, that Isaiah 54-66 (and in his view also 50-51) are not part of Deutero-Isaiah was Kuenen. He attributed these chapters to the prophet's disciples. The German translation of this part of his book was published only after his death; see: A. Kuenen, *Historisch-kritische Einleitung in die Bücher des Alten Testaments*, IIer Teil: Die Prophetischen Bücher (Leipzig, 1892) 128-44. Elliger came to a similar conclusion and attributed in addition some portions of chaps. 40-53 to Trito-Isaiah's editing. See K. Elliger, *Deuterojesaja in seinem Verhältnis zu Tritojesaja*, (Stuttgart, 1933). Different criteria, of content and outlook justify, in my opinion, the basic conclusions of Kuenen and Elliger. A detailed discussion of these conclusions and other outlooks concerning Trito-Isaiah requires a separate study.

[2] In these points it is possible that Deutero-Isaiah was influenced by the political and religious propaganda of the Persians. See M. Smith, "II Isaiah and the Persians," *JAOS* 83 (1963) 413-21.

43:9–10, 11–13; 44:24–26; 45:20–22). Contrariwise, according to Trito-Isaiah redemption depends on obedience to the Lord (55:3; 58:6–9a; 9b–12, 13–14), in accordance with his view that the word of the Lord does not come to pass automatically, since its nature is like that of rain and snow: as they are designed to water the earth, making it fruitful, the Word is designed to fertilize the hearts of men, restoring them to the Lord (55:6–11) and giving them salvation.[3] Otherwise, sin and disobedience delay redemption (59:1–2). Henceforth an additional difference: Deutero-Isaiah promises redemption to all Israel, indiscriminately; Trito-Isaiah, in contrast, designates redemption to a certain group only, referred to by different names: "the servants of the Lord" and his "chosen ones" (54:17; 65:8–9, 13–15, 22; 66:14), "those who take refuge in him" (57:13), "those who fear the word of the Lord" (66:2, 5), "his people who seek him" (65:10), "those of Jacob who have repented of rebellion" (59:20), "the poor" (66:2), "the broken," "the humble," "the humble in spirit" (57:15), "the broken of spirit" (66:2), "the afflicted," "the broken-hearted" (61:1), "the mourners," "the mourners of Zion" (57:18; 61:2–3). The others, variously called wicked (57:20–21), those who have forsaken the Lord and have forgotten his holy mountain (65:11), the enemies of the Lord (66:14), rebels against the Lord (66:24)[4]—since these are responsible for the plight of the nation (65:1–7), they will thus be punished by fire and sword (65:12; 66:24).

The words of Trito-Isaiah clearly refer to two well-established and well-defined opposing groups (65:8–15; 66:5). There are two aspects to this opposition: a sociological aspect, as witnessed by such terms as "poor," "oppressed," "humble"; and a religious aspect, since in opposition to "rebels against the Lord" stand "those of Jacob who have repented from rebellion." There is also a political angle to the conflict, since one party is called "mourners," "mourners of Zion," whereas the other party is called "those who have forsaken the Lord and forgotten his holy mountain." Nevertheless, it is difficult to determine from the words of the prophet who is actually being referred to. Both the accusations and acclamations are broadly addressed. Part of the prophet's words are formulated in fixed literary patterns which belong to the heritage of psalmic literature (such as the praise of the poor and humble) or of prophetic literature (such as the political rebuke—57:9). Alongside these literary patterns are found some more concrete terms, but these remain obscure both because of the indetermination of the texts and because of our meager knowledge of the beginning of the Second Commonwealth. Who

---

[3] Cf. A. Rofé, "The Question of the Fulfillment of Prophecies, Isaiah 55:6–11 and the Problem of Trito-Isaiah," *Proceedings of the Sixth World Congress of Jewish Studies*, Vol. I (Jerusalem, 1977) 213–21 (Hebrew).

[4] In Deutero-Isaiah, by contrast, there is no confrontation between "rebels" and "repenters from rebellion." All Israel is called "a born rebel" (48:8), but the Lord forbears with them (v 9) and blots out their sins like a cloud (44:22).

are then, the two antagonistic groups which take up such a considerable space in the invectives and consolations of Trito-Isaiah?

It seems to me that the solution to this question is found in Isa 66:1-4, since the prophet here identifies his opponents unequivocally. From this identification it is possible subsequently to proceed to a fuller reconstruction of the prophet's time and the historical circumstances of his prophecy.

In Isaiah 66:3 we read:

שוחט השור מכה איש
זובח השה ערף כלב
מעלה מנחה דם חזיר
מזכיר לבנה מברך און
גם המה בחרו בדרכיהם
ובשקוציהם נפשם חפצה

There are four pairs of deeds here, described by participles, and in each pair the first member describes a legitimate cultic act, whereas the second member an abominable and sinful action. How should these pairs be interpreted?

One way, largely accepted, is to add *Kap comparationis* and to interpret: one who slaughters oxen is like one who strikes a man," etc. However, this results in an absolute denial of the cult,[5] which is not found in any prophet's words, and particularly not in Trito-Isaiah (cf. Isa 60:7, 13; 66:20-23). Accordingly, efforts have been made to qualify the issue and to propose in various ways that those meant are some of the Lord's worshippers who lack inner sincerity,[6] or a certain group of Jerusalemite evil-doers,[7] or the Jews of Elephantine in Southern Egypt,[8] or the Samaritans.[9] Yet the problem remains: in the lack of any clear

---

[5] H. Gressmann, *Ueber die in Jes. c. 56-66 vorausgesetzten zeitgeschichtlichen Verhältnisse*, (Göttingen, 1898) 25; K. Budde, "Das Buch Jesaja, Kap. 40-66,": E. Kautzsch and A. Bertholet, *HSAT*[4] (Tübingen, 1922); J. L. McKenzie, *Second Isaiah* (AB 20; Garden City, NY, 1968).

[6] F. Delitzsch, *Biblischer Kommentar über den Prophet Jesaia* (Leipzig, 1866); K. Pauritsch, *Die neue Gemeinde: Gott sammelt Ausgestossene und Arme* (Rome, 1956) 195-201.

[7] This interpretation, already recognizable in LXX, is offered by Ibn-Ezra and Kimhi; later on, cf. W. Gesenius, *Kommentar über den Jesaia* (Leipzig, 1821); C. C. Torrey, *The Second Isaiah* (New York, 1928); P. Volz, *Jesaia II* (KAT; Leipzig, 1932).

[8] M. Haller, *Das Judentum* (SATA; Göttingen, 1915, 1925[2]).

[9] B. Duhm, *Das Buch Jesaia* (GHAT; Göttingen, 1922[4]); A. Dillmann and R. Kittel, *Der Prophet Jesaja* (KEHAT[6]), (Leipzig, 1898); K. Marti, *Das Buch Jesaja* (KHAT; Tübingen etc., 1900); J. Skinner, *Isaiah, Chs. XL-LXVI* (CB; Cambridge, 1917[2]).

reference to such a group,[10] commentators have had to supply one out of their own mind, with no warrant in the text. And should one claim that the clue is to be found in the second member of the pair—עורף כלב, מכה איש, etc.,[11]—the difficulty remains because it is then implied that all participants in the cult are sinners, whereas "the poor and brokenhearted, and who is anxious about my word" have quit the cult and take no part in it.[12] To be sure, such an interpretation would not entail a fundamental denial of the cult, but rather a reproof of the cult in Jerusalem at the time.[13] However, such a reproof cannot be inferred from the words of Trito-Isaiah, who accuses his opposers of "forgetting my holy mountain" (65:11), and recalls how the children of Israel used to bring offerings in a pure vessel to the house of the Lord (66:20).[14]

The meaning of the verse is, in my opinion, quite simple: the four first members of the pairs which describe legitimate cultic acts contain the addressees of the words of rebuke which follow, and their identity is clear—the priests who serve in the temple.[15] The first member of each pair of participles comprises, then, the subject,[16] which describes the priestly profession; the second member comprises the predicate and

[10] As noted by Ehrlich, who tried to complete the indication by making it antithetical to the preceding verse; see A. B. Ehrlich, *Miqra Kifshuto*, vol. 3 (Berlin, 5661 [= 1901]).

[11] Thus Rashi; S. D. Luzzatto, *The Book of Isaiah* (Padua, 1867 [Hebrew]); A. Dillmann, *Der Prophet Jesaia* (KEHAT⁵; Leipzig, 1890); C. Westermann, *Isaiah 40–66* (Engl. Transl.: OTL; London, 1969).

[12] This situation came about, to be sure, hundreds of years later, in the days of the Qumran sect. Members of the sect testify concerning themselves: וכל אשר הובאו בברית לבלתי בוא אל המקדש להאיר מזבחו ויהיו מסגירי הדלת, אשר אמר אל "מי בכם יסגיר דלתו, ולא תאירו מזבחי חנם" (Damascus Covenant 6:11–13, which interprets Malachi 1 as referring to the sect). And perhaps it is no coincidence that the reading in 1QIsᵃ is: שוחט השור כמכה איש.

[13] A new attempt to explain this difficult verse was made by J. M. Sasson, "Isaiah lxvi 3–4a," *VT* 26 (1976) 199–207. He distinguishes different tenses for each member of the pairs and interprets: the one who used to slaughter oxen now smites men. However, it is difficult to confirm such a distinction of tenses.

[14] Some modern interpreters, such as Westermann (above, n 11), remove this verse from its context, pronouncing it an addition. In my opinion their view derives from Protestant theology which would not admit the possibility that a great prophet such as Trito-Isaiah would support the cult. See below, n 48.

[15] This interpretation was suggested by my students, Rina Mizrahi and Michal Frumovici, in a Hebrew University seminar on Isaiah 55–66 offered in 1974.

[16] The subject comes in the construct state. The vocalization of מַעֲלֵה with ṣereh is thus correct. Possibly a haplography occurred here and we should read: מעלה המנחה with the article, as in the first two pairs. The omission of the article in the third pair may have caused its omission also in the last pair: מזכיר (ה)לבונה.

object,[17] relating the priests' abominable deeds. This explanation will be substantiated by examining the content of these expressions.

‏שוחט השור . . . זובח השה‏   "slaughterer of oxen . . . sacrificer of sheep." The root ‏שח״ט‏ appears at times synonymous to ‏זב״ח‏,[18] whereas "oxen and sheep" comprise a fixed word pair indicating sacrificial animals.[19] Both expressions thus express a single concept: those who slaughter sacrifices. To be sure, according to the Priestly Code slaughtering was permitted to all Israelites, whereas the function of the priest began only upon receiving the blood and continued with the service at the altar (Lev 1:2–9, 10–13; 3:1–5, 6–11, etc.), since approaching the altar was prohibited any outsider (cf. Num 17:1–5). But in the course of time, apparently after the Restoration, there was a rising tendency to limit permission to slaughter sacrifices. At first the slaughtering was limited to the Levites, as evidenced by the prescriptions of Ezekiel[20] and from the accounts of the Passover in the books of Ezra[21] and Chronicles.[22] Later, the priests claimed slaughter for themselves. It is related already in Chronicles that the priests slaughtered a sin-offering which came to atone for all Israel,[23] and this is not at all required by the Priestly Code.[24] Still later, Philo describes slaughtering as being done by a priest.[25]

---

[17] Accordingly, the word ‏מכה‏ should be vocalized ‏מַכֵּה‏, with *segol*.

[18] Compare Exod 23:18 with 34:25: ‏לא תזבח/תשחט על חמץ דם זבחי‏.

[19] Exod 21:37; 34:19; Lev 22:23, 28; 27:26; Deut 14:4; 17:1; 18:3; 1 Sam 14:34; 15:3.

[20] Ezek 44:10–11: "But the Levites . . . they shall slaughter the burnt offerings and the sacrifices for the people. . . ."

[21] Ezra 6:20; the verse should be translated, in my opinion: "For the priests purified themselves; and the Levites were altogether pure, they slaughtered the passover for all the children of the captivity and for their brethren the priests and for themselves." From the end of the verse it is clear that the subject of "slaughtered" is the Levites.

[22] 2 Chr 30:16–17: ". . . the priests splashed the blood which was handed them by the Levites. For, as a large number in the assembly had not purified themselves, the Levites had the duty of slaughtering the passover lamb for anyone who was unpurified. . . ." 35:3–6: "And he addressed the Levites . . . stand in the sacred place according to the divisions of the fathers' houses . . . and slaughter the passover." See also 35:10–11; 1 Esdr 1:6: "slaughter the passover and make ready the sacrifices for your brethren."

[23] 2 Chr 29:23–24: ". . . then the he-goats for the sin-offering were brought before the king and the assembly, who laid their hands on them; and the priests slaughtered them. . . ."

[24] Lev 4:15 (concerning the communal sin-offering): "The elders of the community shall lay their hands upon the head of the bull before the Lord, and the bull shall be slaughtered [unspecified subject] before the Lord."

[25] Philo, *De specialibus legibus*, 1.199: καὶ μετὰ ταῦτα, λαβών τις τῶν ἱερέων καταθύετο.

Perhaps such a view is alluded to already in the LXX.[26] The Talmud makes various comments on this issue. On the one hand it is related (*b. Ketub.* 106a) that "The learned men who taught the priests the laws of ritual slaughter received their wages from the Temple funds." Thus the status of slaughter was equated to that of the "handful," which was fundamentally a priestly duty. On the other hand, some sayings forcefully deny that slaughtering is a priestly prerogative. Thus *b. Pesaḥ* 64b: "An Israelite slaughtered and the priest caught (the blood),' etc. Is then an Israelite dispensable? He (the Tanna) informs us of that very fact, viz., that the *shechitah* is valid (when done) by a lay Israelite." And the Rabbinic legend in *b. Ber.* 31b describes a dispute between the young Samuel, who represents the type of a precocious student of the Beth-HaMidrash, and Eli the priest of Shiloh, seen as the typical representative of the priestly aristocracy. Eli seeks a priest to come and slaughter and Samuel asks: "Why are you looking for a priest to slaughter? Slaughter by a layman is permitted!" This he proves from scripture. It appears that alongside the practice of the Temple-priests to monopolize slaughtering, the Pharisaic law emphasized that any person of Israel was entitled to slaughter.[27]

מעלה מנחה   "offerer of meal-offerings." As shown by the verb על״ה what is meant is an offering entirely consumed on the altar, as described in the older sources (Judg 13:19–20) or such as the "oblations offering" (מנחת נסכים; *m. Menaḥ* 6. 2) which is offered alongside a holocaust or a peace-offering (Num 15:2–16).[28] Since this offering is made on the altar, it must be performed by a priest.

מזכיר לבונה   "offerer of incense." According to the instructions of Leviticus (2:2, 9, 16; 5:12; 6:8; 24:7), the phrase means the one who burns the "remembrance-offering" (אזכרה) that is, the "handful" from the meal-offering mixed with frankincense.[29] The act of taking the handful and burning on the altar is reserved exclusively for priests.[30]

Thus, out of three legitimate cultic acts mentioned by Trito-Isaiah in our verse, two are original priestly prerogatives whereas the third was appropriated by the priesthood in the course of time. As for the deeds described in the predicate, they cover several different spheres: מכה איש

---

[26] LXX to Lev 1:5, 11; 4:15, 24, 29 reads καὶ σφάξουσι ("and they slaughtered"). In most of these places the LXX implies that the bringer of the sacrifice does not slaughter it, but rather the servants of the temple.

[27] A similar situation came about in relation to the scapegoat. See *m. Yoma* 6, 3: "They delivered it (the scapegoat) to him that should lead it away. All were eligible to lead it away, but the priests had established the custom not to suffer an Israelite to lead it away. R. Jose said: It once happened that Arsela of Sepphoris led it away and he was an Israelite."

[28] Cf. M. Haran, "Minḥah," *Enṣiklopedia Miqra'it*, vol. 5, cols. 23–30.

[29] Cf. D. Hoffmann, *Das Buch Leviticus*, I–II (Berlin, 1905–6).

[30] See J. Milgrom, "Qᵉtoret", *Enṣiklopedia Miqra'it*, vol. 7, cols. 112–18.

("strikes a man") refers to acts of physical violence;[31] מברך און ("blesses iniquity") means blessing of idols;[32] and ערף כלב ("immolates a dog"), דם חזיר (read probably הֹדֵם חזיר, "cuts a swine")[33] upbraid the participation in magic or mystery cults which are censured also in Isa 65:4–5; 66:17.[34]

But why does the prophet use oblique language without referring to the priests by name? Two complementary reasons explain his diction. First, the proclivity of biblical language for synonymity, which apparently derives from poetic parallelism, brought about the creation of synonyms for the names of professions by use of the participle, especially a participle in construct state. For example, חרש ("smith")—נפח באש משליכי ביאור חכה (Isa 54:16); הדגים ("fishermen")—פחם ומוציא כלי למעשהו כל תפשי משוט . . . (Isa 19:8); המלחים ("sailors")—ופרשי מכמרת על פני מים כל חבלי הים (Ezek 27:29). Occasionally, biblical rhetoric foregoes the use of the actual name and makes use of oblique language only. Thus instead of the name מלך ("king")—ישב על כסא . . . מושל ב- (Jer 22:30), or also יושב . . . תומך שבט (Amos 1:5, 8). Second, since in the course of generations several priestly families were ousted from the cult, such as the family of Abiathar in Anathoth (1 Kgs 2:26–27; Jer 1:1), a further advantage in the verse's diction is that it does not indicate priests in general, but only those who actively serve in the temple.

This manner of expression is found in additional passages in biblical and post-biblical literature. In Jer 48:35 we read: והשבתי למואב, נאם ה', מעלה במה ומקטיר לאלהיו. Here also those who function in the cult are meant. So also in Jer 33:18: ולכהנים הלוים לא יכרת איש מלפני, מעלה עולה ומקטיר מנחה ועשה זבח כל הימים; that is, there will always be levitical priests serving in the temple. It should be remembered that the entire pericope in Jer 33:14–26 is not represented in the LXX. Apparently this section is not an original prophecy of Jeremiah but rather was composed later, at a time when doubt was cast on the election of Israel and the continuation of the Davidic dynasty. At that time, the beginning of the Second Commonwealth, the quarrels over who were the legitimate priests were renewed. The passage in Jer 33:18 is thus close in time to the days

---

[31] As expressed in Isa 58:4: "Because you fast in strife and contention, and you strike with a wicked fist." There is no support for interpreting מכה איש as a murderer or one who offers human sacrifice.

[32] Cf. Isa 65:11 which censures the worship of "Gad" and "Měni." for און in the meaning of "idol" cf. 1 Sam 15:23; Hos 4:15; 5:8; 10:5; 12:12.

[33] See D. Leibel, "Variant Readings," Beth Miqra 8 (1964) 187 (Hebrew).

[34] R. de Vaux, "Les sacrifices de porcs en Palestine et dans l'Ancien Orient," BZAW 77 (Fs. O. Eissfeldt; Berlin, 1958) 250–65. On the basis of the evidence from Israel's neighboring nations, he concludes that the eating of pork was rare and limited to certain cults or magical practices which were low forms of religious practice. In his opinion, these customs spread to Israel in the sixth century B.C.E.

of Trito-Isaiah.[35] About the same time the prophet Malachi declares (3:3): "מעלה מנחה. וטהר את בני לוי... והיו לה׳ מגישי מנחה בצדקה" "Who offers up the meal-offering," מקטיר מנחה "who burns the meal-offering," מגיש מנחה "who presents the meal-offering"—all these expressions mean the same: priests who officiate in the temple.[36] Later, in the language of the Tannaim the expression מזה בן מזה "a sprinkler (of blood) son of a sprinkler (b. Ber. 28a; y. Ber. 5:1): indicates a priest of legitimate lineage. Here again the participle, which describes a function, serves as an indirect way of referring to the priestly profession!

The rebuke of Trito-Isaiah is thus directed against the priests of his time, and lacking any indication to the contrary, it should be understood that the priests of Jerusalem are referred to. His eschatological speech on the future ingathering of the exiles (66:20–22) is also in line with this view: "they shall bring [the subject is the nations and the distant coasts mentioned in v 19] all your brothers out of all the nations as an offering to the Lord . . . and from them likewise [that is, from your brothers who will be brought by the nations back to Jerusalem] I will take some to be levitical priests, said the Lord. For as the new heaven and the new earth which I will make shall endure by my will—declares the Lord—so shall your seed and your name endure." In other words: the diaspora, even those across the seas and furthest away, will be returned to Jerusalem by those nations in whose midst they live. The Lord will take levitical priests from among those returning from the diaspora in order to serve him.[37] The monopoly of the Jerusalemite priests will thus be broken.[38] And should one ask: How could those of the diaspora avoid assimilation, and the priests among them prove their lineage?—"So shall your seed and your name endure." They shall certainly survive and their genealogical lists will be preserved and give witness to their ancestry.[39] In these words also, which announce the establishment of a new priesthood, the antipathy of Trito-Isaiah towards the Jerusalemite priesthood of his time is apparent.

From these words, as illuminated by the explanation of Isa 66:3, the character of the antagonism between Trito-Isaiah and the Jerusalemite priests becomes clearer. We have seen that he accuses them of acts of idolatry, apostasy, and participation in idolatrous mysteries. It should be emphasized that he does not in principle reject the cult. He does not censure the cult as being a web of rituals, sacrifices, stringency in matters of purity and impurity, or the confinement of the sacred and its custody

---

[35] P. Volz, Der Prophet Jeremia (KAT; Leipzig, 1922).

[36] Accordingly, ומגיש מנחה in Mal 2:12 should be explained in the same way.

[37] In my view, we should read in v 21: וגם מהם אקח לכהנים לוים, אמר ה׳. Later scribes were interested in distinguishing between priests and Levites. For the interpretation of the verse see Kittel (above, n 9).

[38] See in Marti's commentary (above, n 9).

[39] Thus Duhm (above, n 9).

in the hands of the Zadokite priests. Trito-Isaiah does not represent a religious movement fundamentally at odds with the priestly faith. He is no spokesman for some prophetic movement which rejects the restoration of the cult in Judah and centers upon an eschatological-apocalyptic anticipation of an impending revelation of the Lord.[40] On the contrary, the establishment of a renewed cult is for Trito-Isaiah an essential factor in the restoration of Israel.[41] His prophecies deal with entirely different issues. In order to recognize these issues it is first necessary to compare his words to the testimony of the historical books which give account of the period and shed light on the historical background of his prophecies.

The historical background is apparently the first half of the fifth century B.C.E., before the time of Ezra and Nehemiah.[42] In the book of Ezra-Nehemiah, a sharp reproof—both explicit and implicit—is sounded against the Jerusalemite establishment, including priests and notables. The high priest Eliashib was a friend of Tobiah (Neh 13:4–8), and his son Joiada was related by marriage to Sanballat the Horonite (13:28). Similar relations to Tobiah obtained between the other Judean noblemen and Jerusalemite notables (Neh 6:17–19).[43] This friendship with the noblemen of the neighboring nations which vigorously opposed the

[40] *Pace* P. D. Hanson, *The Dawn of Apocalyptic* (Philadelphia, 1975) 32–208: "Chapter II—Isaiah 56–66 and the Visionary Disciples of Second Isaiah." Hanson's book is written out of a transparent theological bias: the legacy of the confederation of the Israelite tribes passed on to prophecy, from prophecy to apocalyptic, and from here to Christianity. The essence of this legacy was the revelation of the Lord, "the divine Warrior," in order to execute judgment and salvation. Opposite this legacy stood the pragmatic community which inherited the hierocracy of the beginning of the Second Commonwealth which in turn continued the line of the Zadokite priests of Jerusalem in monarchic times. Hanson sees in Isaiah 56–66 the words of the first apocalyptists who inherited the message of Deutero-Isaiah and now organize themselves into an opposition party: they oppose the cultic restoration in the name of the impending Kingdom of God. Their religion is the one to answer the existential problems of modern man (402–13). In my opinion, this conclusion of Hanson looks like a resuscitation of the old controversy over who is the true Israel.

[41] 56:5–7; 60:6–7, 13; 62:9; 64:10; 66:20, 23; and see above, n 14 and below, n 48.

[42] The hypothesis that the time of Trito-Isaiah is in this period was expressed already by Duhm (above, n 9) and Littmann; see E. Littmann, *Über die Abfassungszeit des Tritojesaia* (Freiburg i.B., 1899). For a description of the events in Judea in the Persian period see Morton Smith, *Palestinian Parties and Politics that Shaped the Old Testament* (New York and London, 1971) 99–147; J. M. Grintz, "From Zerubabel to Nehemiah," *Zion* 37 (1972) 175–82, esp. 164–74 (Hebrew); E. Stern, *The Material Culture of the Land of the Bible in the Persian Period* (Jerusalem, 1973 [Hebrew]); N. Avigad, *Bullae and Seals from a Postexilic Judean Archive* (= *Qedem* 4), (Jerusalem, 1976).

[43] Cf. Neh 3:4, 30, in which verses appears Meshullam son of Berechiah, father-in-law of Tobiah's son (Neh 6:18) among those rebuilding the walls.

building of the walls of Jerusalem surely aggravated the zealots of Zion, who called themselves "mourners," "mourners of Zion" (Isa 57:18; 61:2–3), and defined their opponents as "those who have forsaken the Lord and forgotten his holy mountain" (65:11). Marriages with foreign women were commonplace and the Jerusalemite aristocracy, again including the priests, condoned such (Neh 6:18; 13:28; Ezra 9:1–2; 10:18–22). To these marriages were opposed "all those anxious (concerned) for the words of the God of Israel" (Ezra 10:3).[44] A similar epithet appears in our verses indicating the group opposed to the slaughterers of oxen and offerers of meal-offerings (Isa 66:2, 5). They saw in mixed marriages an invitation to idolatry (Neh 13:26). And to be sure, it is only natural that such marriages brought about closer social ties which provided an inlet for the invasion of idolatry and syncretistic practices.[45] The poignant, probably exaggerated, accusations of Trito-Isaiah concerning such are thus understandable (Isa 57:4–8; 59:12–13; 65:3–5; 66:17). From the passage discussed above it is understood that these charges were addressed also to the priests (66:3).

On the other hand, this prophet's silence on the matter of mixed marriages is conspicuous and requires explanation. It may be that the prophet was silent on this issue because his view did not coincide with that of Ezra and Nehemiah. In one of his speeches (Isa 56:1–8), he supports the right of "those who attach themselves to the Lord" to be absorbed into the Jewish community. To be sure, this is a different sort of foreigner; they do not intermingle with the return-community in the land of Israel by marriage but rather are joined to it in the diaspora by their faith in the Lord. Nevertheless, one who supported the right of these first proselytes to be accepted into the Jewish community, and did this against an opposition which is well-echoed in his words (56:3), was not prone to solve the question of foreign wives in the simple way of divorce, but was open to another solution—of making them "attached" to the Lord. In another speech (54:11–17) Trito-Isaiah actually claims that the "sojourners"—and this time those dwelling in Judah are meant—dwell there only by the will of the Lord,[46] and their destiny is to "fall-in with Israel," that is, to receive its rule and become attached to it (54:15): הן גור יגור אפס מאותי מי גר אתך עליך יפול. It may be surmised that also

---

[44] The ideology of these circles against mixed marriages and against emigration to Mesopotamia was paradigmatically expressed in the story of Genesis 24. See A. Rofé, "The Betrothal of Rebekah (Genesis 24)," *Eshel Beer-Sheva—Studies in Jewish Thought*, vol. I (Beer-Sheva, 1976) 42–67 (Hebrew).

[45] And even for mystery cults; see above, n 34.

[46] אפס = "but" (Num 22:35; cf. 22:20). מאותי = "according to my will" (1 Kgs 12:24). [Both the ass episode (Num 22:22–35) and the prophecy of Shemaiah (1 Kgs 12:22–24) are late, post-exilic additions; one should expect them to be linguistically affinitive to Trito-Isaiah.] The thrust of the verse is thus: if a sojourner should dwell in the land, it is only by my will.

among Trito-Isaiah's party, "those anxious over the word of the Lord," there were differences of opinion regarding various actual issues of the day.

An additional topic of Trito-Isaiah's prophecy which is clarified by the historical account of the book of Ezra-Nehemiah is the Sabbath. Neh 13:15–22 amply describes the situation in Judea and Jerusalem before Nehemiah's intervention. Work in the fields did cease on the Sabbath, but commercial life went on without restraint. Even Phoenician merchants from the coastal cities would come to Jerusalem's gates on this day. The Sabbath came to serve as a sort of weekly market day in Jerusalem.[47] It was only natural that the day on which people were free of work in the fields and other labors would become a day for bargaining and business. Alongside Nehemiah's protests we also read the rebuke and urging of Trito-Isaiah (Isa 56:2, 4, 6; 58:13–14), which include general warnings against "pursuing your affairs," that is, taking care of one's daily needs on the Sabbath.[48]

The book of Nehemiah also describes a deep class schism in Judea.[49] The rich notables exploited the impoverished masses, took control of their property and sold their women and children into slavery (Neh 5:1–8). Further on we read of the Temple being emptied of its lower-ranking personnel because of the rulers' neglect (13:10–13). This class schism echoes in the words of Trito-Isaiah who takes the side of the poor (66:2), the oppressed and humiliated (57:16) against the priests and other aristocrats. In his sermon on a day of fast the prophet expressed poignant indignation over the prevailing social injustice (Isa 58:1–12).

Some of these issues reappear in the words of another anonymous prophet, "Malachi," who apparently flourished in this period as well. In Malachi there also is a harsh rebuke against the priests who make the people stumble in iniquities (2:1–9). In Malachi there also is the expectation of an impending judgment against the wicked (3:1–5, 19, 21). And most significantly, also in Malachi there is a sharp schism between "the arrogant and doers of evil" on the one hand, and "those who revere the Lord" on the other hand. This schism in Malachi is institutionalized, since the prophet announces in the name of the Lord that the names of those who revere the Lord have been written before him in a scroll of

---

[47] This situation continued in Europe up to the present: in some places the weekly market day took place on Sunday, in spite of the rulings of the Catholic church.

[48] Without any ground whatsoever, scholars (e.g., Hanson, above, n 40) detach the "Sabbath prophecy" and pronounce it to be an editorial addition to Trito-Isaiah. The only explanation which can be found for such a pseudo-critical operation is a Protestant theological axiom that no prophet of stature would give expression to the normative requirements of Judaism. See above, n 14.

[49] The economic factors of this schism were discussed in detail by Smith (above, n 42).

remembrance (3:16). However, differences do exist. Malachi does not mention the Sabbath or the sin of idolatry, and his social reproach is routine (3:5). He strongly affirms the value of the cult and accuses the priests of neglecting it (2:10, 13–16).[50] Malachi employs the term 'ה יראי, which frequently occurs in the Psalms but is not found at all in Trito-Isaiah. These differences between the two prophets testify to a certain distance between them, either in the time of their activity or in their party affiliation.

The agreement between Trito-Isaiah and the views of Ezra and Nehemiah against the Jerusalem establishment explains the origin of his prophecy. In the more than one hundred years since the exile of Jehoiachin, Judaism took shape in the Babylonian exile.[51] This denomination clearly delineates itself from its environment by prohibiting mixed marriages on the one hand, and by the formation of an institutionalized body of נלוים—"Gentiles who join themselves to the Lord"—on the other. It maintains a firm communal solidarity expressed, for example, in the obligation to redeem brethren slaves (cf. Neh 5:8). It strictly enforces cessation of commerce on Sabbath as an extension of the ancient prohibitions against land cultivation. It also nurtures impassionate dreams of rebuilding the city of Jerusalem which conflict with the more realistic policies of the Jerusalemite notables. Trito-Isaiah represents these ideals. In a Jerusalem controlled by Joiakim (Neh 12:10), Eliashib and their cohorts, Trito-Isaiah represents a vocal opposition, an opposition of mourners and afflicted (61:1–2).[52] Some time (a generation?) afterward Nehemiah's time was ripe. However, Nehemiah did not act as an oppositionist but as a ruler. Thanks to his standing in the Persian court he was appointed governor of Judea by Artaxerxes I (465–424 B.C.E.). The dreams of rebuilding Zion became with him a realistic plan for building the walls of Jerusalem.[53] This plan was the basis of a consensus between Nehemiah, the official who came from Susa, and the Jerusalem

[50] In contrast to this it seems that the issue of foreign women (Mal 2:11–12), which does not fit organically in its context, may be an addition to the words of Malachi. Cf. E. Sellin, *Das Zwölfprophetenbuch* (KAT; Leipzig and Erlangen, 1922).

[51] For a fitting characterization of the opposition between the "children of the exile" and the Jews of the land of Israel see S. Talmon, "Return to Zion—Consequences for Our Future," *Cathedra* 4 (1977) 29 (Hebrew).

[52] In literary works which can be dated to the beginning of the Second Commonwealth, the word ענוים refers to a specific group, a sort of sect, as scholars have already assumed. For a survey of views and bibliography see R. Martin-Achard, "ענה ʿnh II—elend sein," *Theologisches Handwörterbuch zum Alten Testament*, vol. II (München, 1976) 341–50.

[53] On the questions concerning the location of the wall and the extent of the building see now Y. Tsafrir, "The Walls of Jerusalem in the Period of Nehemiah," *Cathedra* 4 (1977) 31–42 (Hebrew) and the bibliography there.

elite. Afterward, in the wake of this first success, Nehemiah was able to impose other planks of his platform: the shaping of Judaism in the land of Israel in the image of the Eastern Jewish diaspora.[54]

---

[54] The main points of this paper were given in a lecture at the Seventh World Congress of Jewish Studies (Jerusalem, 1977). I am grateful to Mr. Menahem Ben-Yashar and to Dr. Devorah Dimant for their important comments and to Mr. Galen Marquis for the English version. Translations of the Talmud mainly follow the Soncino Talmud.

MATERIALS TOWARD A BIBLICAL GRAMMAR IN THE BIBLE EXEGESIS OF THE TOSEFTA

Samuel Rosenblatt†
Dept. of Near Eastern Studies
The John Hopkins University

S INCE the authorities quoted in the *Tosefta* correspond by and large to those mentioned in the *Mishnah*, it is not surprising that the grammatical views of the former should coincide on the whole with those held by the latter.

The קַל or simple form of the verb is taken to denote spontaneous and deliberate action. Thus for example the clause כי יגח (Ex 21:28) is interpreted as meaning עד שיתכוין ליגח "until he gores intentionally" (B Kam 4:6). The intensive nature of the פִּעֵל is recognized in the comment on וקדשתו "and thou shalt sanctify him" (Lev 21:8) of על כרחו "perforce" (Snh 4:1). It is not only the הִפְעִיל that has a causative meaning as in לא יַחֵל דברו "he shall not profane his word" (Num 30:3), which is rendered לא יעשה דבריו חולין "he shall not make his words profane." The פִּעֵל, too, often has such force as in מְשַׂנְאֶיךָ (Ps 139:21), which is construed מַשְׂנִיאֶיךָ "those that cause hatred of Thee." In fact the הִפְעִיל of hollow verbs in the biblical texts is usually rendered by the פִּעֵל rabbinic Hebrew equivalents. Thus, for instance, תכין לבם "Thou wilt direct their heart" (Ps 10:17) becomes צריך שיכון לבו "he must direct his heart" (Ber 3:6); and יקימנו "he may let it stand" (Num 30:14) becomes מקיים לאיזו שירצה "he may carry out whichsoever he wishes" (Ned 7:4).

The denominative use of the פִּעֵל is illustrated by the interpretation of תְּשַׁקְּצֶנּוּ "thou shalt utterly detest it (i.e., the idol)" (Deut 7:26) as implying that idols were "to be considered unclean like a reptile שקץ." Another example is לְבַכֵּר "to declare as being the firstborn" (Deut 21:16) by investing the "son of the beloved wife with the rights of primogeniture in the matter of inheritance" (Bek 6:1).

The transitiveness of the פִּעֵל, which is implied rather than spelled out in the *Mishnah*'s comment on מעות לא יוכל לתקון "what has been perverted cannot be straightened" (Eccles 1:15), is clearly indicated by

Reprinted by the kind permission of Dropsie College for Hebrew and Cognate Learning, Philadelphia, Pa © 1983 from Dropsie University *Monograph Series IV*

the inference in the *Tosefta* from the פָּעַל participle מְאָדָּמִים (Ex 25:5) that coloring ram skins died red on the Sabbath is a direct violation of the prohibition of work on the Sabbath (Sabb 8 [9]:21).

As for the tenses, it is noted that at times the perfect has a pluperfect meaning. Thus for instance the statement in the decalogue of ועשית כל מלאכתך (Ex 20:9) is supposed to indicate that all manual labor has to be completed before the Sabbath sets in, while ושמואל מת (1 Sam 28:3) is construed "and Samuel had already died." With the waw conversive the perfect might indicate purpose as in (Lev 18:5) וחי בהם "that he might live by them" or the simple future as in ושבתי את שבות עמי ישראל (Amos 9:4) "then will I return the captivity of My people Israel."

The imperfect is capable of denoting option, as, according to one opinion, in the case of ולו תהיה לאשה (Deut 22:19, 29), which is construed "she may become his wife," and in the case of אישה יקימנו (Num 30:14), which is taken to mean "her husband may sustain it" (Ned 7:4). There are, however, numerous occasions in which it has a jussive force. Thus, for instance, ששת ימים תעשה מלאכה (Ex 35:2) is understood as meaning "in six days shall work be done" (Sabb 1:21). Also so far as the husband is concerned, who has brought false charges against his wife, or the rapist, ולו תהיה לאשה (Deut 22:19, 29) is an order to the effect that, whether he consents to it or not, "she shall become a wife unto him." With a negative the imperfect may serve the function of a warning, as in ולא ימותו (Ex 30:20), which is construed "lest they incur the death penalty." The waw conversive turns the imperfect into an ordinary past. Thus וימת שמואל (1 Sam 25:1) is rendered "Now Samuel just died."

The cohortative is recognized as having an optative connotation. Illustrative hereof are אשימה עלי מלך (Deut 17:14), which is interpreted to mean "I would like to appoint a king over me" and אוכלה בשר (Deut 12:20), which is rendered "I would fain eat meat."

The employment of the infinitive absolute prior to the finite verb to express the compulsive character of a command has already been noted in the Bible exegesis of the *Mishnah*. Examples bearing out this point of view in the *Tosefta* are המול ימול (Gen 17:13), which is taken to indicate that "the circumcision must be undertaken repeatedly" until it is carried out properly, and שום תשים (Deut 17:15), which is regarded as implying the absolute power wielded by the king over his subjects. There is, furthermore, on record one instance in which the infinitive is believed to have been employed in the place of a finite verb. Thus, for example, עד בש (II Kings 2:17) is rendered "until he became ashamed."

That the active participle of a stative verb may point to completed rather than still continuing action is borne out by the construction of נופל (Deut 21:1) as "fallen" rather than falling. As for the passive participle of a transitive verb like בלל it may indicate potentiality rather than actuality. Thus בלולה בשמן (Lev 2:5) is taken to mean "mixable with oil" rather than "mixed."

Ordinarily the singular of nouns is used to refer to a single item of a given species or category. Thus for example it is inferred from the term הפרוכת (Ex 26:34) employed by the bibilical text that only one curtain separated the holy from the holy of holies in the tabernacle. The expression דבר הרוצח (Deut 19:4) is intended to underscore the fact that the murderer must not repeat the declaration that he has committed the crime with which he has been charged. The use of the singular תורת החטאת (Lev 6:18) indicates that there was to be a uniform procedure for all sin-offerings. From בהמה בהמה (Lev 27:10) it is deduced that substitutions were to be made solely on a one for one basis.

On the other hand the context may indicate that the singular employed in the case on hand is collective. Thus, for example, when it is said that in the city of Nineveh were to be found בהמה רבה (Jonah 4:14), it is obvious that the reference was to a large number of cattle. Likewise when בהמתך "thy cattle" (Ex 21:35) is listed as one of a series of possessions, the entire species is meant, not just an individual beast (B Kam 6:18). By the same token, however, when in the prohibition of the acquisition by the king of Israel of unnecessary equipage the singular is employed, as in למען הרבות סוס (Deut 17:16), the implication is that even a single superfluous horse was forbidden.

The plural, as in הזכרים לה' (Ex 13:12) could be construed as either generic or numerical. When it is the latter, any number of the article referred to may be indicated. This applies to שלחנות "tables," which occurs in 2 Chron 4:19 and to עדים "witnesses" mentioned in Deut 19:15. All that the use of the numerical plural without the mention of a figure warrants is that more than one is meant. Thus the statement (Ex 12:7) על הבתים אשר יאכלו אתו בהם reveals that the paschal lamb was to be eaten in a multiple number of houses. Usually, however, the minimum of two only is all that can be deduced from a plural not modified by a numeral. Thus, for instance, two is the smallest number of children a man is required to beget in order to comply with the commandment of פרו ורבו "be fruitful and multiply" (Gen 1:28). This is borne out by the passage in 1 Chron 23:15, where the expression בני משה "the sons of Moses" is amplified by the listing of only גרשום and אליעזר (Yab 8:4). The indefinite plural ערבי נחל "willows of the brook" (Lev 23:40) authorizes the use of no more than two willow twigs in the ritual of the feast of booths. Implicit in the term עצים (Lev 6:5) is that the cuttings of wood to be burnt on the altar were to be limited to two. The minimum number of harvests permitted to be consecrated prior to the jubilee was two (Arakh 4:8) because the biblical text uses the expression על פי השנים (Lev 27:18). Similarly at least two years had to elapse after the jubilee before land sold during the jubilee cycle could be redeemed (Arakh 5:1) on account of the statement במספר שני תבואות ימכר לך (Lev 25:15).

The plural may also denote continuity over a stipulated period of time. Thus the intervals at which Absalom, the son of David, was accustomed to shave his hair (2 Sam 14:26) are described as מקץ ימים. It may furthermore point to perpetuity as in לבקרים (Job 7:18) which is taken to mean "every morning."

Of the genitive relationship between substantives following each other there is noted above all the descriptive genitive. Examples hereof are ווי העמודים (Ex 27:10), which is rendered "columnlike hooks," and פסילי אלהיהם (Deut 7:25), which is construed as "their sculptured deities." To be included in this group are מי אפסים (Ezek 47:3) "water up to the ankles" (Suk 3:3), מי מתנים (Ezek 47:4) "water up to the loins" (Suk 3:5), and לקט קצירך (Lev 19:9) "the gleaning at the time of thy harvest." In the interpretation of קללת אלהים תלוי (Deut 21:23) as "a hanged man is a belittlement of God" (Snh 9:7) אלהים is obviously regarded as an objective genitive.

A special kind of descriptive genitive is the word דבר in the phrase ערות דבר (Deut 21:1), where it is construed as "some unseemliness." It has the same function as the Arabic enclitic ـما following an indefinite noun.

The locative ending ה = appended to substantives is clearly recognized as indicating direction to a locality. Thus ארצה כנען (Num 35:10) is construed "toward the land of Canaan." Also from the statement על ירך המזבח צפונה (Lev 1:11) it is deduced that the altar was located entirely on the north side of the tabernacle.

Like that of the infinitive absolute preceding the finite verb the function of the cognate accusative is generalization. Thus when it is said חטאתו אשר חטא (Lev 4:23), "any type of sin" is implied. When an accusative follows both a verb and an active participle, it is susceptible of being construed as the object of either. This applies, to cite one instance, to שלם ישלם המבעיר את הבערה (Ex 22:5). When a substantive precedes a verb, as in the case of בוצע ברך נאץ ה' (Ps 10:3), it may serve as either subject or object.

An adjective following a noun as well as another adjective could modify either. Illustrative hereof is כלי נחושת מוצהב טובה שנים (Ezra 8:27), the meaning of which could be either that there were two golden vessels or vessels having the value of two golden ones (Arakh 2:5).

Proper names in apposition to those preceding them often serve to define further those that they follow. Thus when the Israelites were told that they were crossing the Jordan on their way to Canaan (Num 35:10), the implication was that the Jordan River was part of the territory of Canaan (B Kam 8:19). Also when a curse was pronounced on any one who would rebuild "this city, namely Jericho" את העיר הזאת את יריחו (Josh 6:26), what was implied was not only that the city was not to be rebuilt even under another name but also that no city bearing the name of Jericho was to be built elsewhere (Snh 14:6).

It has already been pointed out by me in my study of the Bible exegesis of the *Mishnah* (p. 13) that the definite article was recognized as having at times a particularizing function and at others a generic force. An illustration in the *Tosefta* of the first is שבעת הימים (Gen 7:10), i.e., *the seven days* of mourning over the death of Methuselah (Sot 10:3). Examples of the second are חטמא (Num 19:19) "the unclean" (in general) (Demai 1:14) and בדרך (Deut 6:7) "on the highway." Per contra the absence of the article indicates that the reference does not extend to the entire class or category. Hence בין דין לדין (Deut 17:8) means "between one lawsuit and another" but not every lawsuit (Hor 1:7).

The demonstrative adjective with the definite article, which follows a noun determined by an article, points to the context immediately preceding. Thus, for example, the phrase כַּמשפט הזה (Ex 21:31) can mean only "in the manner just described" (B Kam 3:2).

The use of a disjunctive pronoun in the biblical text, where a conjunctive one could just as well have been employed, is interpreted as denoting restriction. Thus when it was said ונתתם אותה אל אלעזר (Num 19:3), what was intended was that the particular portion was to be given exclusively to Elazar (Parah 4:6).

The personal pronoun הוא, even when used as a copula, too, usually has a restrictive sense. Thus זבח פסח הוא (Ex 12:27) implies that the victim must be slaughtered specifically as a Passover offering. Similarly חטאת הוא (Lev 5:9) betokens that the sacrifice is valid only when it is intended as a sin-offering. Likewise אשם הוא (Lev 5:19) indicates insistence on intending the sacrifice in question as a guilt-offering (Zeb 1:1).

The conjunctive personal pronoun in the genitive may point to the essence of the individual referred to. Thus it is inferred from the clause יֵעָשֶׂה לו (Ex 21:31) mentioned in connection with the ox, who gored a human being, that restitution is to be made with the body of the goring animal (B Kam 3:2). Such a pronoun may also serve as a reflexive. Thus it is deduced from the statement לא יחל דברו (Num 30:3) that even a scholar, who is authorized to absolve others of their vows does not have the power to nullify his own.

Of the particles the adverb אך "howbeit, yet" is considered as being restrictive. It is thus interpreted in connection with the Sabbath laws. אך את שבתתי תשמרו (Ex 31:13) indicates that there were exceptions to the prohibition of all labor on the weekly day of rest. Similarly the employment of this term in conjunction with the Day of Atonement in the declaration אך בעשור לחודש הזה יום הכפורים (Lev 23:27) indicates that the atoning effect of this solemn festival is not absolute but conditioned upon the individual's conduct.

Of the prepositions the following meanings are implicit or explicitly given in the *Tosefta*: אל indicates direction with the meaning of "toward." The purport of ותקהל העדה אל פתח אהל מועד (Lev 8:4) is that the congregation faced the sanctuary (Meg 4 [3]:21). When it was said אל הבית הזה (1 Kings 8:42) it was clear that prayer was to be directed to the temple built by Solomon. Similarly in the statement והתפללו אל ה'

(1 Kings 8:44), though direction could not have been meant literally, it was to be thus understood figuratively (Ber 3:16). The noun דרך could also be used as a preposition with the same meaning (Ber 3:16).

The basic significance of the preposition ב is "in" or "within." Thus, for example, the implication of מחית בשר חי בשאת (Lev 13:10) is that the raw flesh is within the rising, and of הנגע בעור הבשר (Lev 13:3) that the symptom of the plague is surrounded by the skin. This preposition is also used in the sense of "by means of" in such remarks as כי ביום הזה יכפר (Lev 16:30), from which it is deduced that the Day of Atonement itself serves as a means of atonement. ב is furthermore employed to indicate the agent of a passive verb, as in ונקרא שמו בישראל (Deut 25:10), which is to be rendered "and his name shall be called Israel." Finally it might serve the function of a genitive. Thus הדם הוא בנפש (Lev 17:11) is equated with דם הנפש "the life-blood" (Zeb 8:17).

The composite preposition מלבד "besides" (Num 28:23; 29:11) is understood as implying simultaneity.

The ground meaning of the preposition בין "between" is difference. An example hereof is שבועת ה' תהיה בין שניהם (Ex 22:10), which implies that there exists a difference between the two litigants so far as their credibility is concerned.

The preposition ל most commonly indicates the purpose for which, or the individual in whose interest or for the sake of whom something is done. Thus it is inferred from the phrase למשמרת (Num 19:9), which figures in connection with the ashes of the "red heifer," that these ashes had to be deposited in a special place for safe-keeping (Parah 3:4, 14), as well as for guarding them against being used for any purpose other than that of purification (Mikw 7 [8]:11). The remark about the unemancipated Hebrew female slave חפשה לא נתן לה (Lev 19:20) implied that a writ of emancipation had to be drawn up specially for the individual who was to be emancipated (Gitt 2:7). The prescription ועשה לה הכהן (Num 5:30) concerning the scroll to be used in the ordeal of the wife suspected of infidelity indicated that it had to be inscribed for her individually (Gitt 2:7). The same applied to the bill of divorcement to be handed to the divorcee. The implication of the words וכתב לו (Deut 24:1) is that every such document had to be prepared specially for the woman to be divorced (Gitt 2:7). The expression וכתב לו (Deut 17:8) used in connection with the scroll of the Torah that the king of Israel was expected to have in his possession and read from constantly indicates that a copy had to be prepared afresh for each successive ruler (Snh 4:7). Furthermore when it was said with reference to the slaughtering of a beast as a sin-offering ושחט אותה לחטאת (Lev 4:33), it was clear therefrom that the intention to offer it for the purpose had to be present at the time of the slaughtering (Zeb 1:1). This meaning is clearly inherent in the remark כל פעל ה' למענהו (Prov 16:4), where instead of the simple ל the composite preposition למען is employed.

Sometimes the preposition ל is used in the sense of "by." Thus, for example, תמימים יהיו לכם (Num 28:31) is interpreted to mean: "if they are found by you to be unblemished" (Pes 5:5). It also occurs with the meaning of "in exchange for" (B Kam 9:16) in the directive לא תקחו כופר לנפש רוצח (Num 35:31).

The preposition מן usually has a partitive meaning in the sense of "of" or "from." Thus מאלה (Lev 5:13) is interpreted as signifying "some of these." מאדם (Lev 27:28) signifies "some persons" (Arakh 4:24). משדה אחוזתו (Lev 27:28) points to "a portion of the field that is his property" (Arakh 4:24). מבקרך ומצאנך (Deut 12:21) connotes "some of thy cattle and thy sheep." It may also serve as the "by" of agency, as in והכהן הגדול מאחיו (Lev 21:10), which is rendered "the priest who is magnified by his brothers." It may be used furthermore to introduce the infinitive of a verb of completion, as in the case of וכלה מכפר (Lev 16:20), which is to be translated "and he shall finish atoning."

The preposition עד in the phrase עד רדתה (Deut 20:20) has the meaning of "up to and including."

The preposition על is most commonly construed as signifying "on" or "upon." The expression על לחם הבכרים (Lev 23:20), for instance, indicates that the sacrificial animals were to be placed on top of the bread of the first-fruits. Also when it was said with reference to the silver and gold decorations of the idols that were to be destroyed כסף וזהב עליהם (Deut 7:25), it was what was placed on them that was included in the prohibition. Occasionally, however, as in the placing of the incense על המערכה (Lev 24:7), it may have the meaning of "alongside" or "adjacent to."

עם often denotes proximity in time. It does so in the case of בעליו עמו (Ex 22:14) and בעליו אין עמו (Ex 22:13). Most commonly, however, it points to special contiguity (B Mez 8:21, 22). The implication of כסף וזהב אשר עמהם (Deut 29:16) was that it was the silver and gold garments actually worn by the idols that were considered an abomination. The meaning of ויקח משה את עצמות יוסף עמו (Ex 13:19) was that the remains of Joseph were in the same camp with Moses, namely that of the Levites (Kelim 1:8). As for the scroll of the Torah that the king of Israel was to have with him always, as it is said והיתה עמו כל ימי חייו (Deut 17:19), it was in his palace that it was supposed to have been deposited (Snh 4:8). Of course when employed in connection with God the sense of contiguity implied in this preposition perforce had to be purely figurative. The meaning of ועמכם בדבר המשפט (2 Chron 19:6) could be only "God supports your judicial verdict" (Snh 1:9).

In the injunction of עזב תעזב עמו (Ex 23:5) the preposition עם lends itself to two different interpretations. One is that the enemy is to be assisted in the reloading of his beast that succumbed under the weight of its burden, עמו being construed in this instance as meaning "on its back." The other is that the help is to be a joint effort of the owner as well as of him who comes to his rescue and that the benefits, too, are to be shared (B Mez 2:28).

The particle of relationship אשר in such clauses as אשר נתן לך (Deut 8:10) may be construed as either an indefinite relative pronoun with the meaning of "whatever" or as the indefinite time conjunction "whenever."

The most common function of the conjunction ו in linking nouns or verbs is to indicate equality between the items linked. Thus it was deduced from the statement והנותרת מן המנחה לאהרן ולבניו (Lev 2:10) that Aaron's share of the remnants from the meal offering was to be equivalent to that of his children. The injunction אישה יקימנו ואישה יפירנו (Num 30:14) was understood to imply that only vows capable of being fulfilled could be annulled. The apposition with הבשר והדם or עלתך (Deut 12:27) indicated that both the blood and flesh had to be on hand to carry out the requirements of the burnt-offering. The duty of procreation was, according to one view, fulfilled only when at least one male and one female child had been begotten on account of the phraseology of the text of Scripture, which states זכר ונקבה בראם (Gen 5:2) "male and female did He create them" (Yab 8:4). Also because it is said with reference to the owner of a vicious beast that has made a practice of goring human beings והועד בבעליו ולא ישמרנו (Ex 22:29), that there was no case if the owner, who had been warned, was no longer alive when the goring, against which he had been cautioned, took place (B Kam 4:6).

The conjunction ו might also indicate the chronological order in the execution of operations incapable of being carried out simultaneously. Thus, for instance, when it was said וכפר בעדו ובעד ביתו ובעד כל קהל עדת ישראל (Lev 16:17) what was meant was that the high-priest was to atone first for himself, then for his household and lastly for the entire congregation of Israel (Zeb 10:2).

However it is also possible, without doing violence to the actual intent of the biblical text, to construe the conjunction ו as an alternative with the meaning of "or." זכר ונקבה בראם (Gen 5:2) signified to one of the authorities quoted by both the *Mishnah* and the *Tosefta* nothing more than that the human species, like other members of animal kingdom, was created in two different sexes, whence it was inferred that by begetting two of either a person had complied with the duty of procreation. Similarly the meaning of אישה יקימנו ואישה יפירנו (Num 30:14) is that the husband possesses the option of either sustaining or nullifying the vows taken by his wife.

One more use of the conjunction ו recognized in the *Tosefta* is that of introducing the apodosis of a conditional sentence כי תחטא ושמע (Lev 5:1) is taken to indicate that there exists no obligation to listen in order to testify unless a sin has first been committed.

A STUDY OF THE RELATION-SHIP OF THE SYRIAC VERSION
TO THE MASSORETIC HEBREW, TARGUM JONATHAN, AND SEPTUAGINT TEXTS IN JEREMIAH 18

Leona Glidden Running
Andrews University

T HE question has often been raised concerning the Syriac Peshiṭta (SP), whether it is a faithful translation of the Masoretic Hebrew text (MT), or whether it shows greater or lesser dependence on the Aramaic Targum (*Tg-14.*),[1] with much or little influence from the Septuagint (LXX). This brief study tests the situation in a limited section of Jeremiah 18.[2]

[1] For discussion and references to scholars who have dealt with this question, see Arthur Vööbus, *Peschitta und Targumim des Pentateuchs* (Stockholm: Estonian Theological Society in Exile, 1958) 9–17.

[2] The MT is from the *Biblia Hebraica Stuttgartensia* (Stuttgart: Deutsche Bibelstiftung, 1966/77), transliterated. The *Tg.* transliteration has been compared with the consonantal text of Paul de Lagarde (*Prophetae Chaldaice*, Leipzig: B. G. Teubneri, 1872), with the voweled text printed in Walton's Polyglot, 3 (Brian Walton, *Biblia Polyglotta*, London: 1656), and with the supralinear voweled text in Alexander Sperber, *The Bible in Aramic*, 3, *The Latter Prophets According to Targum Jonathan* (Leiden: E. J. Brill, 1962) 178–80. The SP is transliterated from the Nestorian vocalized Urmia text published by the Trinitarian Bible Society, London, 1852, compared with the Jacobite vocalized text in Walton's Polyglot, 3. By these comparisons scribal errors have been corrected as far as possible in *Tg.* and SP. Though no Syriac script indicates doubled consonants or vocal *shewa*, these have been included in the transliteration where required by the formations (as Pael or Ethpaal verbs) or as indicated by the dot with a *bĕgadkĕpat* letter, above it if hard (therefore often doubled) or below if it is spirantized (therefore often with a vocal shewa preceding). The transliterated Greek text is from *Septuaginta*, ed. Alfred Rahlfs (Stuttgart: Privileg. Württ. Bibelanstalt, 2, 6th ed., n.d.). The NIV quotations are from the *The Holy Bible: New International Version*, Copyright © 1978 by The New York International Bible Society. Used by permission of Zondervan Bible Publishers.

1: MT haddābār ʾăšer hāyâ ʾel-yirmĕyāhû mēʾēt YHWH lēʾmōr:

Tg. pitgam nĕbûʾâ dahăwâ ʿim yirmĕyâ min qŏdām YĔYĀ lĕmêmār:

SP petgāmāʾ dahĕwāʾ ʿal ʾĕramyāʾ men qĕdām māryāʾ: lĕmēʾmar:

LXX Ho logos ho genomenos para kyriou pros Ieremian legōn

NIV This is the word that came to Jeremiah from the Lord:

All three versions are very close to MT. Tg. adds "prophecy" which SP does not follow, but otherwise SP is almost identical to Tg.

2: MT qûm wĕyāradtā bêt hayyôṣēr wĕšāmmâ ʾašmîʿăkā ʾet-dĕbārāy:

Tg. qûm wĕtêḥôt lĕbêt paḥărāʾ wĕtammān ʾašmĕ ʿînāk yat pitgāmāy:

SP qûm ḥôt lĕbêt paḥḥārāʾ: wĕtamman ʾašmĕʿāk petgāmay.

LXX Anastēthi kai katabēthi eis oikon tou kerameōs, kai ekei akousę̄ tous logous mou.

NIV "Go down to the potter's house, and there I will give you my message."

The only difference is in LXX, "you will hear," instead of "I will cause you to hear," like the other three.

3. MT wāʾērēd bêt hayyôṣēr wĕhinnēhû ʿōśeh mĕlāʾkâ ʿal-hāʾobnāyim:

Tg. ûnĕḥātêt lĕbêt paḥărāʾ wĕhāʾ hûʾ ʿābēd ʿĕbîdtāʾ ʿal sĕdānāʾ:

SP wĕneḥtēt lĕbêt paḥḥārāʾ ʾayk petgāmēh dĕmāryāʾ: wĕhāʾ hû ʿābēd ʿăbādāʾ ʿal saddānāʾ.

LXX kai katebēn eis ton oikon tou kerameōs, kai idou autos epoiei ergon epi tōn lithōn.

NIV So I went down to the potter's house, and I saw him working at the wheel.

SP inserts "according to the word of the Lord"; otherwise they are all alike.

4: MT wĕnišḥat hakkĕlî ʾăšer hûʾ ʿōśeh baḥōmer bĕyad hayyôṣēr wĕšāb wayyaʿăśēhû kĕlî ʾaḥēr kaʾăšer yāšar bĕʿênê hayyôṣēr laʿăśôt:

Tg. wĕʾitḥabbel mānāʾ dahăwâ ʿābid dĕṭînāʾ bĕyad paḥărāʾ wĕtab wĕʿābdêh min ʾôḥărān kĕmāʾ dĕkāšar bĕʿênê paḥărāʾ lĕmeʿbad:

SP wĕʾetḥabbal (h)wāʾ māʾnāʾ dĕṭînāʾ dĕʿābēd (h)wāʾ bʾîdēh dĕpaḥḥārāʾ: waḥĕpak wĕʿabdēh māʾnāʾ (ʾ)ḥĕrēnāʾ ʾayk daṣĕbāʾ.

LXX kai diepesen to aggeion, ho autos epoiei, en tais chersin autou, kai palin autos epoiēsen auto aggeion heteron, kathōs ēresen enōpion autou tou poiēsai.

NIV But the pot he was shaping from the clay was marred in his hands; so the potter formed it into another pot, shaping it as seemed best to him.

Tg. is with MT; SP is close, but transposes "of clay" before "which he was making" and omits the last phrase of both MT and *Tg.*, condensing the thought—though the Syrohexapla[3] adds "in his eyes" with LXX and Aquila, omitting "potter."

5: MT   *wayhî děbar-YHWH ʾēlay lēʾmôr:*

    Tg.   *wahăwâ pitgam něbûʾâ min qŏdām YĚYĀ ʿimî lěmēmār:*

    SP   *wahěwāʾ ʿălay petgāmēh děmāryāʾ: lěmēʾmar:*

    LXX *kai egeneto logos kyriou pros me legōn*

    NIV Then the word of the Lord came to me:

SP transposes "to me" in comparison with the other three. *Tg.* again inserts "prophecy."

6: MT   *hăkayyôṣēr hazzeh lōʾ-ʾûkal la ʿăśôt lākem bêt yiśrāʾēl něʾum-YHWH hinnēh kaḥōmer běyad hayyôṣēr kēn-ʾattem běyādî bêt yiśrāʾēl:*

    Tg.   *hakěpahărāʾ hādên hălāʾ yûkělāʾ qŏdāmay lěmeʿbad lěkôn bêt yiśrāʾēl ʾāmar YĚYĀ hāʾ kěmāʾ děṭînā běyad pahărāʾ kēn ʾattûn hašîbîn qŏdāmay bêt yiśrāʾēl:*

    SP   *ʾayk pahhārāʾ hānāʾ lāʾ meškah (ʾ)nāʾ dʾeʿbed lěkôn bêt yisrāêl: ʾāmar māryāʾ: hāʾ ʾayk ṭînāʾ bʾîday pahhārāʾ hākanāʾ: ʾattôn bʾîday bêt yisrāêl.*

    LXX *Ei kathōs ho kerameus houtos ou dynēsomai tou poiēsai hymas, oikos Israēl; idou hōs ho pēlos tou kerameōs hymeis este en tais chersin mou.*

    NIV "O house of Israel, can I not do with you as this potter does?" declares the Lord. "Like clay in the hand of the potter, so are you in my hand, O house of Israel."

Tg. typically expands with "before me" and "are reckoned before me." SP does not follow but is close to MT, though with plural "in my hands," with LXX. LXX omits "declares the Lord." This is, however, included by Aquila, Symmachus and Theodotion, followed by the Syrohexala. SP has it.

7: MT   *regaʿ ʾădabbēr ʿal-gôy wěʿal-mamlākâ lintôš wělintôṣ ûlěhaʾăbîd:*

    Tg.   *zěman ʾămalêl ʿal ʿamāʾ wěʿal malkûtāʾ lěmeʿqar ûlětāră-ʿā ûlěʾabbādāʾ:*

    SP   *ʾen men šelyāʾ ʾěmar ʿal ʿammāʾ wěʿal malkûtāʾ: lěmeʿqar walěmestar: wělaměsahhăpû walěmawbādû.*

    LXX *peras lalēsō epi ethnos ē epi basileian tou exarai autous kai tou apollyein,*

    NIV If at any time I announce that a nation or kingdom is to be uprooted, torn down and destroyed,

---

[3] Frederick Field, ed., *Origenes Hexaplorum . . . Fragmenta*, 2 (Hildesheim: Georg Olms, 1964) 619–21.

All are closely alike, but MT and *Tg.* (and NIV) have three verbs of destruction at the end, while SP has four and LXX has two!

8: MT   *wĕšāb haggôy hahû^ɔ mērā^cātô ^ɔăšer dibbartî ^cālāyw wĕni-hamtî ^cal-hārā^câ ^ɔăšer hāšabtî la^căśôt lô:*

Tg.   *wîtûb ^camā^ɔ hahû^ɔ mibbîštêh digzārît ^călôhî wĕ^ɔêtûb min bîštā^ɔ dĕhašbêt lĕme^cbad lêh.*

SP   *wanĕtûb ^cammā^ɔ hāw men bîštēh: ^ɔahpek menēh bîštā^ɔ d^ɔethaš-bēt lĕme^cbad lēh.*

LXX   *kai epistraphḗ to ethnos ekeino apo pantōn tōn kakōn autōn, kai metanoēsō peri tōn kakōn, hōn elogisamēn tou poiēsai autois·*

NIV   and if that nation I warned repents of its evil, then I will relent and not inflict on it the disaster [lit. evil] I had planned.

LXX inserts "all" and makes "evil" plural both times. SP simplifies (like LXX), omitting in mid-verse what is otherwise a repetition at the end.

9: MT   *wĕrega^c ^ɔădabbēr ^cal-gôy wĕ^cal-mamlākâ libnôt wĕlințôa^c:*

Tg.   *ûzĕman ^ɔămalēl ^cal ^camā^ɔ wĕ^cal malkûtā^ɔ lĕmibnî ûlĕqa-yāmā^ɔ:*

SP   *w^ɔen ^ɔĕmar ^cal ^cammā^ɔ wĕ^cal malkûtā^ɔ lĕmebnā^ɔ walĕmeşab:*

LXX   *kai peras lalēsō epi ethnos kai epi basileian tou anoikodo-meisthai kai tou kataphyteuesthai,*

NIV   And if at another time I announce that a nation or kingdom is to be built up and planted,

All are very close to MT with small differences (SP begins with "if" but the Syrohexapla follows Aquila with "suddenly" or "at a certain time," closer to MT, *Tg.* and SP end with the infinitive meaning "to establish" rather than "to plant."

10: MT   *wĕ^cāśâ hāra^ch [sic; Massoretic note] bĕ^cênay lĕbiltî šĕmōa^c bĕqôlî wĕnihamtî ^cal-hațțôbâ ^ɔăšer ^ɔāmartî lĕhêțîb ^ɔôtô:*

Tg.   *wĕya^cbêd dĕbîš qôdāmay bĕdîl dĕlā^ɔ lĕqabbālā^ɔ lĕmêmrî wĕ^ɔêtûb min țabtā^ɔ da^ɔămārêt lĕ^ɔêțābā^ɔ lêh:*

SP   *wĕne^cbed dĕbîš qĕdāmay: wĕlā^ɔ nešma^c bĕqāl(y): ^ɔahpek menēh țābtā^ɔ d^ɔemrēt lĕmaț^ɔābû lēh.*

LXX   *kai poiēsōsin ta ponēra enantion mou tou mē akouein tēs phōnēs mou, kai metanoēsō peri tōn agathōn, hōn elalēsa tou poiēsai autois.*

NIV   and if it does evil in my sight and does not obey me, then I will reconsider the good I had intended to do for it.

SP begins like *Tg.*, then is close to MT in the second clause and slightly different from both in the third clause, ending like the others. LXX alone has plural for "evil" and "good," otherwise being closer to MT.

11: MT   *wĕ^cattâ ^ɔĕmor-nā^ɔ ^ɔel-^ɔîš-yĕhûdâ wĕ^cal-yôšĕbê yĕrûšālaim lē^ɔmōr kōh ^ɔāmar YHWH hinnēh ^ɔānôkî yôşēr ^călêkem rā^câ*

        wĕhōšēb ᶜălêkem mahăšābâ šūbû nāʾ ʾîš middarkô hārāᶜâ
        wĕhêṭîbû darkêkem ûma ᶜallêkem:

Tg.   *ûkĕᶜan ʾămar kĕʾan le ʾĕnaš yĕhûdâ ûlĕyatbê yĕrûšlēm lĕmê-*
      mar kidnan ʾămar YĔYĀ hāʾ ʾănāʾ bārê ᶜălêkôn bîšāʾ ûmḥaš-
      šēb ᶜălêkôn mahṣābāʾ tûbû kĕᶜan gĕbar mĕʾo(w)rḥêh bîštāʾ
      wĕʾatqînû ʾo(w)rḥatkôn wĕᶜôbādêkôn:

SP   *wĕhāšā ʾĕmar lĕgabrēʾ dîhûdāʾ: walĕᶜāmōrêh d ʾorešlem:*
      hākanāʾ ʾāmar māryāʾ: hāʾ bārēʾ (ʾ)nāʾ. ᶜălaykôn bîštāʾ:
      wĕmethaššab (ʾ)nāʾ ᶜălaykôn mahšabtāʾ: tûb(w) w ʾetpĕnāw
      gĕbar men ʾu(w)rḥēh bîštāʾ: w ʾaṭʾeb(w) ʾu(w)rḥatkôn wa ᶜă-
      bādaykôn:

LXX *kai nun eipon pros andras Iouda kai pros tous katoikountas*
      Ierousalēm Idou egō plassō eph' hymas kaka kai logizomai
      eph' hymas logismon· apostraphētō dē hakastos apo hodou
      autou tēs ponēras, kai kalliona poiēsete ta epitēdeumata
      hymōn.

NIV   "Now therefore say to the people of Judah and those living in
      Jerusalem, 'This is what the Lord says: Look! I am preparing
      a disaster for you and devising a plan against you. So turn
      from your evil ways, each one of you, and reform your ways
      and your actions.' "

While the first two use a collective singular before "Judah," SP and
LXX have plural there as well as before "Jerusalem." LXX has plural
for "evil" (NIV "disaster") and omits "saying, 'thus says the Lord.' "

12: MT *wĕʾămĕrû nôʾāš kî-ʾahărê mahšĕbôtênû nēlēk wĕʾîš šĕrīrût*
      libbô-hārāᶜ na ᶜăšeh:

   Tg. *wa ʾămārû tabnāʾ mibbātar pu(w)lḥānāk ʾărê bātar ᶜaštônā-*
      nāʾ nĕhāk ûgĕbar hirhu(w)r libbēh bîšāʾ na ᶜbêd:

   SP   *w'ĕmar(w) henôn nethayyal: wĕbātar mahšĕbātan nēʾzal:*
      wĕ(ʾ)nāš ṣebyānay lebbēh bîšāʾ ne ᶜbed.

   LXX *kai eipan Andrioumetha, hoti opisō tōn apostrophōn hēmōn*
      poreusometha kai hekastos ta aresta tēs kardias autou tēs
      ponēras poiēsomen.

   NIV But they will reply, 'It's no use. We will continue with our
      own plans; each of us will follow the stubborness of his evil
      heart.' "

All say the same thing in slightly different words, SP not following *Tg.*
exactly. *Tg.* alone expands a bit from MT in the second clause. SP with
LXX has plural "desires of his evil heart."

13: MT *lākēn kōh ʾāmar YHWH šaʾălû-nāʾ baggôyim mî šāma ᶜ kāʾēl-*
      leh ša ᶜărûrît ᶜāśĕtâ mĕʾōd bĕtûlat yiśrāʾēl:

   Tg. *bĕkēn kidnan ʾămar YĔYĀ šĕʾîlû kĕʾan bĕᶜammayāʾ man*
      šĕmaᶜ kĕʾilên (šĕnûy) ᶜābādat lahădāʾ kĕništāʾ dĕyiśrāʾēl:

   SP   *meṭul hānāʾ hākanāʾ ʾămar māryāʾ: šaʾel(w) bêt ᶜammēʾ*

manū ʿăbad ᵓayk hālên: šatyûtā ᵓ rabbětā ᵓ ʿebdat bětu(w)ltā ᵓ dîsrāēl.

LXX   *dia touto tade legei kyrios Erōtēsate dē en ethnesin Tis ēkousen toiauta phrikta, ha epoiēsan sphodra parthenos Israēl;*

NIV   Therefore this is what the Lord says: "Inquire among the nations: Who has ever heard anything like this? A most horrible thing has been done by Virgin Israel.

All are essentially alike. SP has "who has done" instead of "who has heard."

14: MT   *hăya ʿăzōb miṣṣûr śāday šeleg lěbānôn ᵓim-yinnātěšû mayim zārîm qārîm nôzělîm:*

Tg.   *hā ᵓ kěmā ᵓ dělêt ᵓepšar děyipsôq mê tělag děnāḥêt ʿal haqlê libnān kēn lā ᵓ yipsěqûn mimṭar naḥătîn ûmê mabbûa ʿ nāb ʿîn:*

SP   *ᵓen ʿānēd men ṭûr tědayyā ᵓ talgā ᵓ wěmen lebnān: w ᵓen metkělên mayyā ᵓ qarîrē ᵓ nu(w)krāyē ᵓ děrādên.*

LXX   *mē ekleipsousin apo petras mastoi ē chiōn apo tou Libanou; mē ekklinei hydōr biaiōs anemǭ pheromenon;*

NIV   Does the snow of Lebanon ever vanish from its rocky slopes? Do its cool waters from distant sources ever cease to flow?

The Hebrew of this verse is difficult. NIV has done excellently in making sense of it. *Tg.* takes the first letter of the third word, with MT, as *sin*, giving it the sense of "fields," while SP and LXX take it as *šin*, resulting in the sense of "breasts." In the second half all are slightly different, *Tg.* inserting "rain" and "spring" and LXX the idea of water violently windforced. SP is close to MT. The question of MT (implying negation) is made explicitly negative in *Tg.* and made into two conditional clauses in SP, also implying negation. The LXX had the interrogative *mē* twice, implying a negative reply, as do the clauses in NIV.

In Dr. Iwry's class in Hebrew Rapid Reading in the fall of 1959 we were reading Jeremiah. When we came to this verse, he referred to Prof. Albright's small emendations that made better sense. These were mentioned as an aside in Albright's article "A Catalogue of Early Hebrew Lyric Poems (Psalm 68)," in *HUCA* 23, part 1, 1950–51, 1–39. Albright stated,

> This convincing emendation I owe to Dr. S. Iwry, who is publishing it in *JBL*; only simple haplography and vertical dittography are involved, and there is an excellent parallel in Jer 18:14, where I should render (with one small emendation of the consonantal text and simple haplography):
>
> Will flints (*ṣōr*) forsake   Or snow Lebanon?
>   the fields
> Will flowing (*zābîm*) water   Or running springs (*měqôrîm*)?
>   dry up
>
> Since most fields in the Palestine hill-country are strewn with pieces of flint, the pertinence of Jeremiah's words is obvious. The verb for melting

or disappearance of snow and drying up or disappearance of water is the same: *ntš* is a transposed doublet of *nšt*, 'to dry up, disappear' " (23, 24).

Dr. Iwry's article was published in *JBL* 71 (1952) 161–65. In it he gave primacy to Prof. Albright, stating in a footnote, "This suggestion was developed by Prof. Albright in a seminar on Psalm 68 held at Johns Hopkins in 1949; cf. now W. F. Albright," and he cited the *HUCA* article. Both scholars were being real gentlemen! It would appear that Albright, the generous mentor, was as usual boosting a former student, by then a colleague teaching part-time in his department.

The changes involve merely removing the *mêm* from *miṣṣûr* to the end of the preceding word as an enclitic *mêm*, leaving *ṣōr*, "rock"—or "flint" ("which is strewn abundantly over the plains of northern Palestine." Footnote: "So I am informed by Professor Albright.") Also *zārîm* is read as *zābîm*, changing one letter to a similar one—as Iwry said, "a case of confusion of similar letters"; and putting a (lost) *mēm* on *qārîm*, making *mĕqōrîm*, "lost by a simple haplography." Dr. Iwry summarized in class,

"Will the flint ever leave the field? Can snow ever leave Lebanon? Can foreign water be dried up?—running water, fountains; *nôzĕlîm*, running fountains; foreign water (Isa [45:8; 48:21]) from a foreign country (source of rivers). [With appreciation to my esteemed teacher, Dr. Iwry.]

15: MT   *kî-šĕkēḥūnî ʿammî laššāwᵓ yĕqaṭṭĕrû wayyakšīlûm bĕdarkê-*
          hem šĕbîlê ʿôlām lāleket nĕtîbôt derek lōᵓ sĕlûlâ:

   Tg.   *ᵓărê šĕbāqû pu(w)lḥānî ʿamî lāᵓ lahănāᵓâ ᵓasîqû bu(w)smîn*
          wĕᵓaṭ ʿîᵓûnûn bĕᵓo(w)rḥathôn bîštāᵓ mišbîlîn taqnān dĕmin
          ʿalmāᵓ lĕmêzāl bĕᵓo(w)rḥan dĕlāᵓ taqnān bišbîlîn dĕlaᵓ mĕkab-
          bĕšîn:

   SP   *meṭul daṭĕʿāᵓûn(y) ʿam(y): wĕlasĕrîqûtāᵓ sam(w) besmēᵓ:*
          w'ettĕqel(w) b'u(w)rḥāthôn bašĕbîlê dĕʿālam: lĕmēᵓzal bašĕ-
          bîlēᵓ b'u(w)rḥāᵓ dĕlāᵓ dĕrîšā̃.

   LXX   *hoti epelathonto mou ho laos mou, eis kenon ethymiasan· kai*
          asthenēsousin en tais hodois autōn schoinous aiōnious tou
          epibēnai tribous ouk echontas hodon eis poreian

   NIV   Yet my people have forgotten me; they burn incense to worth-
          less idols, which made them stumble in their ways and in the
          ancient paths. They made them walk in bypaths and on roads
          not built up.

SP is closest to MT, though with the first verb "wandered, strayed" instead of "forgot."

16: MT   *lāśûm ᵓarṣām lĕšammâ šĕrîqōt ʿôlām kōl ʿôbēr ʿālêhā yiššōm*
          wĕyānîd bĕrōᵓšô:

Tg.   *lĕšawā ᵓâ ᵓarᶜăhôn lĕṣādû ᵓištĕmāmût ᶜălām kol dĕyeᶜbar*
        ᶜălāh yiklê wĕyānîd bĕrêšêh:

SP   *lĕmeᶜbad ᵓarᶜăhôn lĕtemhā ᵓ walĕmašrôqîtā ᵓ lĕᶜālam: wĕkul*
        dĕneᶜbar ᶜălēh: netmah wanĕnîd bĕrēšēh.

LXX   *tou taxai tēn gēn autōn eis aphanismon kai syrigma aiōnion·*
        pantes hoi diaporeuomenoi di' autēs ekstēsontai kai kinēsousin
        tēn kephalēn autōn.

NIV   Their land will be laid waste, an object of lasting scorn; all
        who pass by will be appalled and will shake their heads.

All versions are close to MT (with active voice rather than passive, as in
the first clause of NIV). But SP does not use the same vocabulary as *Tg.*

17: MT *kĕrûaḥ-qādîm ᵓăpîṣēm lipnê ᵓôyēb ᶜōrep wĕlō ᵓ-pānîm ᵓer ᵓem*
        bĕyôm ᵓêdām:

Tg.   *kĕbîdûr rûaḥ qiddûmā ᵓ kēn ᵓĕbadrînûn qŏdām baᶜălê dĕbābê-*
        hôn qĕdal wĕlā ᵓ ᵓappîn ᵓaḥzînûn bĕyôm tĕbārêhôn:

SP   *ᵓayk rûḥā ᵓ dĕšawbā ᵓ ᵓĕbaddar ᵓennôn qĕdām bĕᶜeldĕbābē ᵓ:*
        qĕdāla ᵓ wĕlā ᵓ ᵓappē ᵓ ᵓĕḥawwē ᵓ ᵓennôn bĕyāwmā ᵓ dĕᶜāqa-
        thôn.

LXX   *hōs anemon kausōna diasperō autous kata prosōpon echthrōn*
        autōn, deixō autois hēmeran apōleias autōn.

NIV   Like a wind from the east, I will scatter them before their
        enemies; I will show them my back and not my face in the
        day of their disaster."

Again *Tg.* and SP are close to MT but with different words; LXX is less
literal in translation than NIV and the others, omitting "back" and
"face."

18: MT *wayyō ᵓmĕrû lĕkû wĕnaḥšĕbâ ᶜal-yirmĕyāhû maḥăšābôt kî lō ᵓ-*
        tō ᵓbad tôrâ mikkōhēn wĕ ᶜēṣâ mēḥākā wĕdābār minnābî ᵓ lĕkû
        wĕnakkēhû ballāšôn wĕ ᵓal-naqšîbâ ᵓel-kol dĕbārāyw:

Tg.   *wa ᵓ ămarû ᵓĕtô wĕneḥšab ᶜal yirmĕyâ maḥšĕbān ᵓărê lā ᵓ*
        tipsôq ᵓôraytā ᵓ mikkāhên ûmĕlak mēḥakkîm wĕ ᵓu(w)lpan
        mēsāpar ᵓĕtô ûnĕsāhădîneh sāhidwān dišqar wĕlā ᵓ nĕṣît lĕkol
        pitgāmôhî:

SP   *w ᵓĕmar(w) tāw netḥaššab maḥšabtā ᵓ ᶜal ᵓĕramyā ᵓ: dĕlā ᵓ*
        nē ᵓbad nāmôsā ᵓ men kāhnē ᵓ: wĕtarᶜîtā ᵓ men ḥakkîmē ᵓ:
        wĕmeltā ᵓ men nĕbîē ᵓ: tāw nemḥêw(hy) bĕlešānēh: wĕlā ᵓ nĕṣût
        kulhôn petgāmāw(hy).

LXX   *Kai eipan Deute logisōmetha epi Ieremian logismon, hoti ouk*
        apoleitai nomos apo hiereōs kai boulē apo synetou kai logos
        apo prophētou· deute kai pataxōmen auton en glōssȩ̄ kai
        akousometha pantas tous logous autou.

NIV   They said, "Come, let's make plans against Jeremiah; for the
        teaching of the law by the priest will not be lost, nor will
        counsel from the wise, nor the word from the prophets. So

come, let's attack him with our tongues and pay no attention to anything he says."

All are very close to MT except that *Tg*. has "scribe" instead of "prophet" (plural in NIV), and *Tg*. also interprets "let us smite him with (our) tongue" as "let us give false testimony against him." LXX alone omits the negative in the last clause. Syrohexapla has the negative, with asterisk, following Origen's Greek text. Various commentators justify this omission, to mean paying close attention to all he says in order to entrap him. John Bright joins these in his note, saying, "both readings are possible, and attractive."[4] But in comparison with MT, *Tg*., and SP, which here all have the negative, LXX appears to be in error (or, the negative particle may have been lost from the *Vorlage* of LXX).

In vv 19–23, SP is with MT and the others do not stray far from it. SP is not, however, always using exactly the vocabulary of *Tg*. *Tg*. and LXX expand and interpret here and there.

To summarize: The SP seems to be translated quite closely from the MT in every verse. There are small differences, such as an addition in v 3, omissions in vv 4 and 8, small transpositions in vv 5 and 20, "it" in v 9, a different verb in vv 13 and 15, different wording in part, as in vv 10 and 14, and three plural instead of singular nouns in v 18.

The vocabulary of SP is almost identical to that of *Tg*. in vv 1 through 11. Otherwise the same thoughts are expressed in mostly different words.

The influence of LXX on SP in this chapter seems slight: plural noun(s) in vv 6, 11 and 12; an omission in v 8; "breasts" instead of "fields" in v 14; perhaps *nāmôsā*ʾ (= *nomos*) in v 18 (though that is the usual Syriac word for *tôrâ*—it is used for 207 of the 216 occurrences of *tôrâ* in the Hebrew OT according to Young's Analytical Concordance; in v 8 the SP uses another word for "law," and for one, in that part of the verse SP is lacking). The influence of LXX consists of five or six small points, possibly, at most.

From this small, one-chapter sample it would seem that the Syriac translator worked directly from the Hebrew text, in the first half paying attention also to the Targum, and only occasionally casting his eye on the LXX!

---

[4] *Jeremiah* (AB 21 Garden City, N.Y.: Doubleday, 1965) 124.

ERNEST RENAN'S INTERPRE- TATION OF BIBLICAL HISTORY

Leivy Smolar
President, Baltimore Hebrew College

I N his presidential address to the Society of Biblical Literature in 1970, Harry M. Orlinsky called for studies of "the interpretation of the Bible in the light of changing historical circumstances." Describing the historian's approach, he wrote, "is only preliminary to the systematic attempt to account for their kind of Biblical exegesis."[1] This study of Ernest Renan's interpretation of the kings and prophets of ancient Israel is part of a larger assessment of Renan as a historian of ancient Israel. It is a privilege to present it in honor of Dr. Samuel Iwry, my senior colleague and mentor in the Department of Near Eastern Studies at the Johns Hopkins University, and Distinguished Professor of Literature and Dean of the Baltimore Hebrew College.

Ernest Renan was one of the most famous and notorious literary figures in nineteenth century France. Dozens of his books and hundreds of articles, remarks, and notes on past and present alike fill the pages of the *Journal des Débats, Revue des Deux Mondes, Journal Asiatique* and other more popular and scholarly forums. Renan's notoriety began with the publication of his *Life of Jesus*, one of the best-selling works of the century in France. In Renan's inaugural lecture as the newly-elected holder of the Chair of Hebrew at the Collège de France in 1862, he had described Jesus as "an incomparable man."[2] The *Life of Jesus* was Renan's full account of Jesus. Once a candidate for the priesthood, Renan became known as the enemy of the Catholic religion.[3]

For over thirty years, Renan dominated biblical and Semitic studies in France.[4] In 1860, Renan directed an expedition to Phoenicia, under-

[1] Harry M. Orlinsky, "Whither Biblical Research?" *JBL* 90 (1971) 1 n. 1.

[2] E. Renan, "De la part des peuples sémitiques dans l'histoire de la civilisation," (vol. II of *Ouevres complètes d'Ernest Renan*, edited by Henriette Psichari [10 vols., Paris: Calmann-Levy, 1947–1961]; hereafter cited as *OCP*) 329.

[3] Philip Spencer, *The Politics of Belief in Nineteenth Century France: Lacordaire, Michon, Veuillot* (London, 1954) 179–80.

[4] Jean Pommier, *Renan d'après des documents inédits*[2] (Paris: Perrin et Cie., 1923) 10; Rene Dussaud, *L'ouevre scientifique d'Ernest Renan* (Paris:

written by the Emperor and protected by his troops in Lebanon who had been sent there to defend the Maronite Christians from the attacks of Moslem Druzes.[5] Renan's *Mission to Phoenicia* (1864) was a model of scholarly analysis and reporting, overshadowed only by his founding of the *Corpus Inscriptionum Semiticarum (1871-)*.[6] Renan served as secretary of Société Asiatique from 1863 to 1882 and was elected its president in 1884. In the latter decades of his life, Renan was the administrator of the Collège de France.

Renan's biblical studies were capped by the history of ancient Israel (1887-94) which ranged from the patriarchal period to the eve of the Revolt of the Jews against Rome in 66.[7] In this brief essay, we will analyze Renan's interpretation of government and prophecy during the First Commonwealth of Biblical Israel in the light of his opinions of the politics and events of his age.

While his view of the Prophets was influenced by the social and political revolutions of mid-century France, Renan had no love for the regime of Napoleon III, although he initially benefited from the Emperor's largesse. Renan had been disappointed by the Revolution of 1848. His basically conservative political nature had no place for crowds and revolutionaries.[8] Following the Revolution, Renan had written to his sister Henriette:

> I am not a socialist. I am convinced that none of the theories of the hour is destined to triumph in its actual form. A system—a narrow, partial, thing by its very essence—can never realize itself. The system is a burgeon which must burst its sheath in order to become a truth, universally recognized, universally applied.... I am a progressive, that is all.... I persist in believing that from petty passion to petty passion, from personal ambition to personal ambition, through misfortune, through crime and bloodshed, we are none the less in the act of a great transformation for the greater good of humanity.[9]

Renan was opposed to socialism, which he believed was geared to attaining materialist ends. His sense of social idealism did not include

---

P. Geuthner, 1951) 51-69; A. Dupont-Sommer, "En marge d'un centennaire, Ernest Renan et les débats des études phéniciennes," *Archeologia* 20 (1968) 6-11.

[5] James B. Pritchard, *Archaeology and the Old Testament* (Princeton, N.J.: Princeton University, 1958) 91-101.

[6] Renan was secretary to the commission that was charged by the Société Asiatique with investigating the project. See Renan's report to the Society, *Journal Asiatique* VIe siècle, 9 (1867) 398-409.

[7] *Histoire du peuple d'Israël OCP* VI.

[8] Joseph Onno, "Renan et Tocqueville," *Information Historique* 36 no. 3 (May-June 1974) 107-11.

[9] E. Renan, "Lettre à Henrietta Renan," (1 July 1848) in *Lettres de Famille, OCP* IX, 1085-87; "Lettre à Henriette Renan," (24 February 1849) 1172.

economic benefits. Nor did Renan believe that a socialism based on economic gain could be realized. "It is clear," he wrote,

> that an association in which the dividends are according to the needs of each, and are not according to the capital contributed, can repose only on exalted abnegation and on ardent faith in a religious ideal.[10]

The ascent of Louis Napoleon to the presidency of the Second Republic after the Revolution had pleased Renan. Renan's concept of a government and society ruled by a provincial noble élite did not brook a powerful monarchy centered in Paris and, as a result, the *coup d'état* in 1851, in which Louis Napoleon transformed himself into the Emperor Napoleon III and his government into an Empire, repelled Renan.[11] Renan was no friend of religious orthodoxy. He was detested by the Empress who was a champion of Catholic orthodoxy.[12] On the other hand, Renan was often found in the entourage of Prince Napoleon and with the Princess Mathilde to whom Renan had been introduced by Sainte-Beuve in 1862.[13] In fact, Renan was sailing off the coast of Scandinavia with Prince Napoleon when the Franco-Prussian War broke out eight years later and the prince had to sail home.[14]

Renan's earlier career in scholarship had evidently not been hindered by the coolness of the imperial atitude towards him. In 1847, Renan had won the competition leading to the Volney Prize for his essay on the development of the Semitic languages, which was published in 1855 to great scholarly acclaim as the *Histoire Générale des Langues Sémitiques*.[15] Napoleon III sponsored Renan's archaeological expedition to Lebanon in 1860.[16] When Renan returned to France in November, 1861, he was in a very strong position to press his case for the appointment to the chair in Semitics at the Collège de France that had been vacant since the death in 1857 of the famed Orientalist, Quatremère.[17] The appointment depended on the recommendation of the Faculty of

[10] E. Renan, *Les Apôtres*, OCP IV, 543.

[11] Albert L. Guerard, *French Prophets of Yesterday: A Study of Religious Thought Under the Second Empire (London, 1913)* 235.

[12] Joseph N. Moody, ed. *Church and Society: Catholic Social and Political Thought and Movements, 1789–1950* (New York: Arts, 1953), pp. 135–57; idem, *The Church as Enemy: Anticlericalism in Nineteenth Century French Literature* (Washington: Corpus Books, 1968) 122ff.

[13] Robert Chabanne, "L'Affaire Renan et le politique de Second Empire." *Annales de Faculté de Droit, Science et Economie d'Université de Lyons* (1973) 36.

[14] Chabanne, "L'Affaire Renan," 40–41.

[15] *OCP* VIII, 125–589.

[16] A. Dupont-Sommer, "Ernest Renan et ses voyages," *Comptes rendus de l'Académie des Inscriptions*, November–December, 1973, 601–18.

[17] Chabanne, "L'Affaire Renan," 40–41.

the Collège de France and the leadership of the Académie des Inscriptions et Belles-Lettres to the Minister of Education. But it was the minister's recommendation to the Emperor that was critical and the Emperor's approval that was decisive.

Following Renan's remarks on Jesus, his courses were suspended three days later by order of the Emperor on February 26, 1862.[18] Even the more liberal Minister of Education, Victor Duruy, who had been appointed by Napoleon III after the Renan affair had taken place, could do no more than terminate Renan's professorship and offer him a post at the Imperial Library as a consolation—which Renan refused. The *Life of Jesus* had gone through ten editions in five months, been translated into eleven languages, and placed on the Index of Prohibited Books within two months of its appearance. Duruy, however personally sympathetic, had been appointed to maintain public order in education, which did not include Renan's lecturing on religion.[19] The disaffection of the Emperor in no way diminished Renan's enthusiasm for scholarship or the growing admiration of his colleagues. In January, 1870, Renan was elected president of the Académie des Inscriptions et Belles-Lettres. The following November, after the overthrow of the defeated Napoleon III, the new Republican regime, in the midst of the turmoil of reorganizing the government of France, marked its new spirit of liberalism with the reappointment of Renan to his Chair.

Renan's disaffection for the Bonapartist regime and the Emperor on political as well as personal grounds was reflected, as we shall see, in Renan's overall view of centralized government and his criticism of the centralized governments of ancient Israel. However, even more telling as sources of influence which played upon Renan's treatment of the politics of ancient Israel are his views on Germany and France before and after the Franco-Prussian War of 1870.

Renan believed that Germany had become a great nation while France had declined in power and spirit.[20] In "L'instruction supérieure en France," (1863) Renan argued that Germany envisaged its history as a "parallel to geology, history seeking the past of humanity, the same as geology sought the transformation of the planet."[21] Renan argued that weakness of Germany in the eighteenth century had perhaps accounted

---

[18] Chabanne, "L'Affaire Renan," 43.

[19] Roger L. Williams, *The World of Napoleon III, 1851–1870* (Glencoe, Ill,: Free Press, 1957) 173–208; Chabanne, "L'Affaire Renan," 50–52.

[20] Claude Digeon, *La Crise Allemande de la pensée Française (1870–1914)* (Paris: Presses Universitaires de France; 1959), 181–88, 536–41; Allan Mitchell, *The German Influence in France After 1870: The Foundation of the French Republic* (Chapel Hill, N.C.: University of North Carolina, 1979) 43.

[21] E. Renan, "L'instruction supérieure en France," in *Questions contemporaines* (Paris: Michel Levy, 1863) 82; E. Renan, "La monarchie constitutionelle en France," in *La Réforme Intellectuelle et morale* (1871), edited with an introduction by P. E. Charvet (Cambridge, 1950) 145.

for her intellectual superiority. He also warned that the entry of Germany into the field of political and military activity would spell the beginning of her intellectual decline.[22] Renan viewed the centralization of the German state with deep concern and stressed his admiration for Germany's diverse tribal origins which in his view embodied the triumph of the individual against the state.[23]

In "La Monarchie constitutionelle en France," which appeared in 1869, Renan criticized the centralized monarchy of France, the destruction of provincial liberties during the fourteenth century by Philip IV of France, and the absolutism personified by Louis XIV in the seventeenth century. He decried the French Revolution for having introduced materialism into society. Once again, Renan demanded that a new form of government, if not a new society, be created, characterized by a restrained monarchy, less central government, and a localized administration. The commune, the canton, and the department would gain new strength. Renan attributed France's low estate as a cultural force to the Revolution. A society had to be led by men of "merit and virtue" who could best be found in a society where the ranks are regulated by birth rather than by wealth alone. Otherwise, France would be dominated by the mediocre.[24] Besides, he wrote,

> France excels only in the exquisite, it loves only the distinguished, it knows only how to create the aristocratic. We are a race of gentlemen. Our ideal has been created by gentlemen, not, like that of America, by honest bourgeois, by serious men of affairs.[25]

As a candidate for the Chamber of Deputies in 1869, Renan ran on a platform devoted to the preservation of peace and the expansion of personal and corporate liberties.[26] His platform included: reduction of the army and of the term of armed service, termination of the state of armed peace, opposition to imperialist expeditions, immediate French evacuation of Rome, a budget controlled by Parliament, popular education, liberty of the press and association, and the eventual separation of Church and State.[27]

Renan's opinions about French politics also represented his direct reactions to the German siege of Paris and defeat of France and to the

---

[22] "L'instruction supérieure en France," 85, n. 1.

[23] E. Renan, "Philosophie de l'histoire contemporaine," in *Questions contemporaines*, 10.

[24] "La monarchie constitutionelle," 145, 151, 153, 179–82.

[25] "La monarchie constitutionelle," 171.

[26] Chabanne, "L'Affaire Renan," 35–54; Richard M. Chadbourne, *Ernest Renan as an Essayist* (Ithaca, N.Y.: Cornell University, 1957) 127ff.

[27] Francis Espinasse, *The Life of Ernest Renan* (London, 1895) 141.

civil war triggered by the rise of the Paris Commune in 1871. On July 19, 1870, Napoleon III declared war on Prussia. His armies were soundly defeated and the Emperor captured on September 2 along with his army of 80,000 men. On September 4, the Empire was replaced by an emergency government of National Defense that was led by the Republican deputies of the former Imperial Corps Legislatif dedicated to continuing the war.[28] On September 6, the new foreign minister exhorted his diplomatic corps: "We will not yield one inch of our territory, nor one stone of our fortresses. . . ."[29] On October 27, the French army surrendered at Metz and Bismarck offered an armistice. When Paris surrendered, the National Assembly left Paris and resumed its deliberation at Bordeaux on February 13, 1871.

The Germans entered Paris on March 1, 1871.[30] Negotiations were already underway for a peace settlement between Prussia and France and it was clear that Germany would annex Alsace and Lorraine. On March 11, 1871, the national government moved from Bordeaux to Versailles and executive offices were opened in Paris. But the Parisian deputies opposed the national government. On March 18, revolution broke out in Paris and the national government fled to Versailles. On March 26, 1871, a Parisian revolutionary council was elected and on May 1, following the idealized model of the French Revolution, the radical members of the Paris government seized power and elected a Committee of Public Safety. The political leaders in Paris readied themselves during the next weeks while the French national army regrouped for an attack on the Paris Commune. Regular officers were returning from Germany and taking charge of the upper ranks of the French army.[31] In the first week of civil war in Paris from May 21–28, 20,000 defenders of Paris were killed.[32]

The War and the Commune deeply troubled Renan. After the French defeat, in a public letter (September 13, 1870) to the NT theologian David Friedrich Strauss, Renan contended that France should be allowed to keep Alsace and Lorraine. Renan appealed to Germany's unparalleled historic sense of idealism. He cautioned against chauvinism and argued that nationalism be placed in a secondary role. "My philosophy," he wrote, "is idealism. When I see the good, the beautiful, the true, that is my *patrie*."[33]

Political or military defeat, he believed,

[28] Williams, *The World of Napoleon III*, 2–3.

[29] Robert Baldich, *The Siege of Paris* (New York: Macmillan, 1964) 26.

[30] Baldich, 229–32.

[31] Robert Tombs, *The War Against Paris* (Cambridge, 1981) 98.

[32] Mitchell, *The German Influence*, 7.

[33] E. Renan, "Lettre à M. Strauss (18 August 1870)," in *La Réforme Intellectuelle*, 112–13; cf. 103, 111.

is the expiation of a past glory and often the guarantee of a victory for the future. Greece, Judea paid with their national existence for their exceptional destiny and the incomparable honor of having established their teachings for all of humanity.[34]

In a second letter to Strauss a year later, after the French cession of Alsace and Lorraine to Germany, Renan attacked Germany for its racial politics. "You have raised in the world the banner of ethnographical and archaeological politics in place of liberal politics," he wrote, "this *politique* will be fatal to you."[35]

Above all, Renan denounced Germany for rejecting its own mission and spirit:

> Your Germanic race seems always to believe in Valhalla; but Valhalla will never be the Kingdom of God. With this military *eclat*, Germany risks losing its true vocation . . . to find a rational and as just as possible an organization for humanity.[36]

At the same time, however, Renan praised Germany and condemned France. In the *Goncourt Journal*, a few days after the French defeat (September 6, 1870), Renan is described as bursting out, "Yes, gentlemen, the Germans are a superior race!" Ignoring the immediate objections, Renan severely criticized French education, the Jesuits and the Catholic Church in France, and praised German education and Protestantism. The narrator then picks up the description of Renan:

> Renan has gotten up and is walking around the table with uneven steps, his little arms beating the air, reciting fragments of Scripture in a loud voice, saying that all is set down there.[37]

In a second episode recounted in the *Journal* (Tuesday, April 18, 1871), Renan deplored the lack of resistance by the French liberals against the Paris Commune. The narrator continues:

> He [Renan] says that if he had been honored by his fellow citizens' mandate, he would not have failed in what he calls a duty: "I would have wanted," he adds, "to make myself seen carrying on my back something that spoke to the eyes which would be a sign, a symbol, something like the yoke the prophet Isaiah bore on his shoulder!"[38]

---

[34] Renan, *La Réforme Intellectuelle*, Preface, 6.

[35] E. Renan, "Nouvelle Lettre à M. Strauss," in *La Réforme Intellectuelle*, 123–24.

[36] "Nouvelle Lettre à M. Strauss," 127.

[37] George J. Becker, ed. *Paris Under Siege, 1870–1871: From the Goncourt Journal* (Ithaca and London: Cornell University, 1969) 58.

[38] Ibid., 61.

Renan fled from his home in Paris during the Commune. A few days before he took refuge in Versailles, Renan wrote to his good friend, Bertholet (April 29, 1871):

> We are particularly necessary objects of the patrie; we have benefited from its institutions, from its past, from its ancient glory; we are its pupils, its alumni; leaving, we dissipate in advance the capital that it invested in us, even though we could have formulated a personal and legitimate gripe against her. We cannot leave France except if she chases us, or restrains us from freely deploying our intellectual activity, or if she permits us to die of famine.[39]

Frustrated, loyal, and sharply critical in his *La Réforme Intellectuelle et Morale de France*, published in October 1871, Renan complained that France had lost her military spirit and nobility, and now stood without privilege or the sword to defend French honor because she had expelled her German characteristics.[40]

To return France to its needed position of strength, it was necessary to revive the institutions of the French historic past and resuscitate its spirit of individual liberty. A revived nation, however, would have to express itself in more than political terms. A nation had to create religion, art, science, which is to say, matters of universal significance, or remain the embodiment of an arrested development and unwanted ideas.[41] A limited and controlled constitutional monarchy which accorded conspicuous autonomy to the provinces and was itself liberal in spirit, devoted to peace, and conservative in its social outlook, would sustain a stable and creative nation.[42]

Renan condemned democratic republicanism and universal suffrage and pleaded for power to be given to an elite whose origins, education, and inborn superiority would bring strength to France. Renan was convinced that France had to assume the aristocratic form of German government. France needed to reorganize itself, to reestablish the monarchy, reconstitute a landed nobility, reject ecclesiastical instruction, reconstruct public instruction on a secular basis, and inspire individuality in the arts. There would be an end to political aggrandizement and war. The right people would govern the country.[43]

---

[39] E. Renan, *Correspondence Renan-Bertholet* (Paris: Calmann-Levy, 1898) 404.

[40] Renan, "La réforme intellectuelle," in *La Réforme Intellectuelle*, 21. In general, see Edouard-Felix Guyon, "Gobineau et Renan: temoins de 1870," *Revue d'histoire diplomatique* 87, no. 3–4 (1973) 211–31.

[41] E. Renan, "La Guerre entre la France et l'Allemagne," in *La Réforme Intellectuelle*, 145–50.

[42] Renan, "La monarchie constitutionelle," 178, 180.

[43] Renan, "La réforme intellectuelle," in *La Réforme Intellectuelle*, 36, 39, 42, 44.

Renan urged Frenchmen to emulate Germany's military ability after the war and restore the ancient Germanic tribal institutions of the earliest periods of French history when wars were won. Renan recalled that the backbone of medieval France was a Germanic military aristocracy. In later French history, the provincial estates existed to rubberstamp royal decisions while the forces of the princes of the blood had been converted into "complacent servants of the absolute power." Nevertheless, the monarchy had provided France with enduring stability over the centuries and, consequently, Renan wrote, "the day that France decapitated its king, it committed suicide." The French Revolution had replaced its singular valued older institutions with an egalitarianism that rejected the aristocratic and military spirit and injured France itself. "A society," he wrote, "is only as strong as its ability to recognize the fact of natural superiority . . . that of birth."[44]

Renan believed the national rejuvenation would occur once the aristocratic leadership of France was invited to take its natural position at the helm of state. Indeed, Renan argued that the victory of Germany over France was a defeat for French revolutionary principles and a victory for the Old Regime in France where monarchy and aristocracy had prevailed. The "old dynasties and aristocracies" had to be restored to power. Renan had no use for republican government. A republic, he wrote, "cannot exist, except in a country that is defeated or absolutely pacified. In all countries exposed to war, the cry of the people will always be the cry of the Hebrews to Samuel, 'A king to march at our head and make war with us.'" A "young and serious king, austere in his way had to be restored to the throne." But there could be no monarchy without aristocracy. The critical role of the provincial élites in the management of the state had to be recognized. This meant a restructuring of government and the decentralization of political and administrative power in France.[45]

In *La Réforme*, Renan repeatedly condemned the materialism of France. He criticized France for trying to ape the democracy of America, condemned the French for expelling the Germanic element in their heritage, and denounced Bonapartism and the materialism of the society of Napoleon III. Renan was aghast at the Paris Commune: the "horrible episode" of May 18, 1871 marked the lowest point in French history.[46]

Renan believed in the primacy of noble rule and the centrality of rural and provincial responsibility in the governance of the French. He was torn between his conviction that Paris was necessary to provide France with culture and style and his unqualified rejection of Paris as the sole and unrivaled center of French political power. Again, he

[44] Renan, "Lettre à M. Strauss," 112–13.
[45] "La réforme intellectuelle," 39, 46, 47, 53, 61.
[46] "La réforme intellecutelle," 22–24, 27, 30, 40.

returned to the attack on the rampant industrial and commercial materialism that he felt was holding western Europe and especially France in its grip. He held the growing power of the republican bourgeoisie of France and England in contempt. Again, he argued that France had lost its military capacity and aristocratic elan, the values of the spirit, thought, nobility, and moral distinction which he attributed to France's Germanic origins. England, too, had discarded the pride of her leadership, the "obstinate" nobility who were also scions of Britain's Germanic heritage. Again, Renan attacked the Commune, the pernicious influence of international Jacobinism, and the wild dreams of rampant population of Paris.[47]

Renan was not alone in his repudiation of the centralized state and in his belief that the destiny of France lay in the hands of France's provincial leadership. As Louis M. Greenberg pointed out in his definitive study of the reactions of Marseilles, Lyons, and Paris to the idea of a centralized France in the years prior to and after the War and the Commune:

> The decentralist reaction to the Second empire was an essential aspect of the movement of 18 March [1871, which proclaimed the Commune]. The same reaction that found conservative expression in the departmental council of law of 1871 and in the effort to gain more freedom for the provinces, to move the capital from Paris, and to restore monarchy to France had its leftist expression in the communalist movement. Its goal was a republic of republics based on extended freedom for the department, the commune, and the individual.[48]

One by one, Greenberg documents the protests against Napoleon III's regime. Renan concurred with the decentralists, and proclaimed in *La Réforme*: "This desire for a political state involving the least possible central government, is the unanimous work of the provinces. . . . This is the spirit of what might be called provincial democracy."[49]

A decade later, it was spirit of the nomadic tribes of the patriarchal age, the pastorale of the age of the Judges, and the return of authority to the tribes under Jeroboam that Renan lauded. It was anything but the spirit of David or Solomon or Bonaparte or the materialist revolution. Ideally, it was an ongoing spirit of political reform, the prophetic spirit of Renan himself. But that excluded the radicals and religionists of the present and the prophets and kings of the past.

[47] "La réforme intellecutelle," 22–25, 36, 42; cf. Guyon, "Gobineau et Renan," 223.

[48] Louis M. Greenberg, *Sisters of Liberty: Marseilles, Lyons, Paris and the Reaction to a Centralized State, 1868–1871* (Cambridge, Mass: Harvard University, 1971) 4.

[49] "La réforme intellecutelle," 25.

Later critics of Renan accused him of cynicism, dillentantism, and inconsistency, all of which they summed up in the derogatory term, *rénanisme*. But, as we shall see, if the attitude of Renan to Paris and France in the 1870s and to Jerusalem and Israel is any testimony, then Renan was, in this case, remarkably consistent.

In writing on ancient Israel, Renan maintained his basic principle that nationhood was a stumbling block to the achievement of universal greatness. Thus, in his third Hibbert lecture (1881):

> Almost all the nations designed to play the part of civilizers on the great scale—as, for instance, Judea, Greece, the Italy of the renaissance—exercise their full influence on a world only after they have fallen victims to their own greatness. They must first die, then the world lives by them, assimilating what they have created at the cost of their own fever and suffering. Nations, indeed, have to choose between the slow, quiet, obscure destiny of one who lives for himself, and the stormy and troubled career of one who lives for humanity.[50]

Renan abhorred Israelite nationalism, which he identified with barbarity, fanaticism, and war. He viewed the centralization of the state under David and Solomon as the decline of Israel's importance to the world, a disorder at birth. He regarded with praise those efforts which disrupted the centralized state, such as the rebellion of the tribal aristocracy of the north under Jeroboam, and considered Israelite nationalism to be inimical to the true mission of Israel, which was to be the agent of universal monotheism. Universalism and nationhood had been expressed in the two concepts of God which the ancient Israelites espoused: the universalist Elohim of the desert nomad Semites and the Israelite national god, Iahveh.

In Renan's analysis, the god Iahveh had been introduced to the Israelites following the period of their enslavement in Egypt. In Renan's interpretation, the acceptance of Iahveh by the Israelites as their national god represented not the beginning of their freedom but the climax of their enslavement. Israel had learned all about the *trappings* of religion and nationhood during their period of slavery in Egypt. The Egyptian cult, priesthood, superstitions, symbols, rites, and hierarchical form of government were all assimilated by the Israelites. And thus, when the Israelites came out of Egypt, they had been prepared for nationhood.[51]

The introduction of the religion of Iahveh into the life of ancient Israel sometime during its wandering in Sinai was the capstone of an experience which marred the very essence of Israel's mission. Once the Israelites formed themselves into a nation, Renan believed, they inevitably

---

[50] E. Renan, *Conférence d'Anglerre*, *OCP* III, 616, 640.

[51] E. Renan, *Histoire de peuple d'Israël*, *OCP* VI, 114–49, 194–206; hereafter cited only as *Histoire*.

went to war, captured the land of Canaan from its rightful inhabitants, forced the native population to leave its soil, and engaged in all of the other bloodletting activities that were part of national warfare and existence. The savagery of nationhood was a far cry from the peaceful and ethical desert life of the patriarchal ancestors of Israel. But it was to be the Israelite way of life until the monarchy in Jerusalem was destroyed.

Renan attacked Israelite nationalism by sarcastically dismissing their primitive idea of the god called Iahveh. The very nature of a god partial to one people was unappetizing to Renan.

> This capricious god is the very embodiment of partiality. . . . He gets angry with people for no apparent cause. Then he is made to sniff the smoke of the sacrifice and his wrath is appeased. . . . The wars of Iahveh all end in terrible massacres in honor of this cruel god.[52]

Renan approved of David for not having been a complete monotheist totally committed to the worship of the national god Iahveh. Renan saw David's henotheism as responsible for his religious tolerance. While Renan accused Iahveh of ordering massacres and acts of savagery, he considered the wars of David to be political and not religious wars. There were as yet no holy wars because religious nationalism or exclusivism had not firmly set it.[53]

As a result of his openness to other peoples and cultures, David did not become an isolated fanatic religious nationalist. In David's time, no great national transformation in society had taken place. Tribal custom still guided society and family life as it had in the days of the patriarchs. Aside from David's palace guard and Cretan mercenaries, there was no standing army except for the continuation of the tribal levy.

Renan was more critical of Solomon. While David had provided the institutional basis for the centralized monarchy and for the primacy of Jerusalem, Solomon laid the groundwork for the religious ceremonialism which was displayed during the First and Second Temples.[54] Solomon acted to centralize power but in reality set the stage for revolution, for it was clear to Renan—and in his opinion to the Israelites—that the king had been laboring on behalf of his dynasty with no appreciable popular support.[55] Individual worship at local shrines evidently had continued to be favored by most Israelites. Renan also criticized Solomon for bringing material prosperity to his kingdom, which, in Renan's view, was contrary to Israel's destiny.[56]

[52] *Histoire*, 344.
[53] *Histoire*, 345.
[54] *Histoire*, 413.
[55] *Histoire*, 504.
[56] *Histoire*, 418.

Most of all, Renan considered the construction of the Temple to have been completely against the grain of the true destiny of ancient Israel. In Renan's opinion, the Temple immediately created resentment and was not accepted as a religious symbol.[57] Renan believed the first Torah, which he identified as Exodus 20:24 f., or the Book of the Covenant, to have been a protest against the Temple, and "Mosaisme," the study and life of the Torah, to have been a repudiation of Solomon. In the future, Renan maintained, Jesus, "the great living summary of Israel," would prophesy the destruction of the Temple in Jerusalem and the rebuilding of the Temple in spirit.[58]

Renan's conception of the destiny of the Jewish people was unambiguous: "The fate of the Jewish people was not to form a separate nationality: it is a race which always cherishes a dream of something that transcends nations: its ideal is not the city but the synagogue, the free congregation."[59] Renan consequently believed Israelite political nationalism to be a major threat to Israel's authentic destiny among the nations. Ultimately, politics and royal dynasties would have to surrender and disappear.

> The causes of this crisis were of old standing and the crisis itself inevitable. The Mosaic law, the work of lofty idealists, possessed by a powerful socialistic thought, but the least politic of men, was like Islam, exclusive of a civil society existing side by side with the religious. The law which appears to have taken the form in which we now read it in the eighth century B.C., would, even if the Assyrian conquest had never taken place, have broken into fragments of a little kingdom of the descendents of David. From the time that the prophetic element took the upper hand, the Kingdom of Judah, on unfriendly terms with all its neighbors, full of enduring hatred for Tyre, at enmity with Edom, Moab and Ammon, no longer had any possibility of a life in it. I repeat, a nation which devotes itself to social and religious problems, loses itself in politics. The day when Israel became 'a peculiar treasure' unto God, 'a kingdom of priests, a holy nation,' it was decreed that it should never be a people like any other. It is impossible to unite contradictory destinies: excellence is always atoned for by abasement.[60]

Renan's anti-monarchism and his view of the prime role of the aristocracy was strongly reflected in his interpretation of three ages in the history of biblical Israel: the rebellion of the northern tribes against Rehoboam, the period of the Judges, and the age of the Patriarchs.

After Solomon, according to Renan, ancient Israel was "a pompous Sultanate," with its functionaries, finances, and central shrine. Against

---

[57] *Histoire*, 405-406.

[58] *Histoire*, 419.

[59] Renan, *Conferences*, 642.

[60] E. Renan, *Nouvelles études d'histoire réligieuse*, OCP VII, 731-32.

this repressive centralism stood the northern tribes ready to return to a premonarchic state of affairs. The northern tribes had never accepted the concept of unlimited centralized monarchy in Renan's outlook, and were furious at being subjected to severe taxation, including a corvée, all of which served only to enhance the glory of the Judean monarch. The Judeans had been weakened by their dependence upon an absolute government. In the North, a former appointee of the king, Jeroboam, had been contacted by a prophet, the natural enemy of wealth and material possession, and an alliance between them had been forged.[61]

The rebellion of the northern tribes against Jerusalem and Judah was not only important as a reaction against national centralization, but as a return to their ancient tribal values. In fact, in Renan's scheme of Israelite history, the rebellion of the tribes was not the first time that the Israelites had acted in search of their destiny.

The return of the Israelites to a tribal society during the period of the Judges symbolized a return to a semblance of religious purity, in Renan's view. The time of the Judges was no era of peace. There were revolts against oppressors, battles among the tribes themselves, internal struggles for supremacy, and attempts at setting up a monarchy. There were severe acts of barbarity committed in the name of the national god of Israel. Moreover, the national god Iahveh, which Renan regarded as the evil impulse in ancient Israel, had begun to overcome the ethical and universal concepts which were the attributes of the Elohim of the patriarchs.

Renan also believed that the period of the Judges was an age of gold, an ideal age that was never forgotten. The society of the Judges was based on tribal organization and an agrarian economy. But even more so, he wrote, "Those days

> were represented as an epoch of gaiety, of intermittent good fortune, fre-
> quently of pure morality, always of liberty, when the individual master of
> his land, unexposed to the abuse of the monarchy, lived in the state nearest
> to a perfect state, which is the primitive nomad state.[62]

The rebellion of the northern tribes against Rehoboam took place because

> the tribal spirit, the habits of the nomad and patriarchal life, were still
> keen among the Josephites (the northern tribes). This spirit did not lend
> itself to any great organization, whether civil, religious or military. Thus
> the first fifty years of the independent kingdom of Israel are quite identical
> with the centuries of the Judges.[63]

[61] *Histoire*, 417–18.
[62] *Histoire*, 252.
[63] *Histoire*, 433–34.

The ideal age of the history of Israel was, however, the age of the patriarchs. In patriarchal society, the tribe was the most significant unit. Society functioned on the basis of patriarchal authority within the tribe, without military organization, or priests or prophets, and yet with life and property secure. Renan followed the Book of Genesis closely in describing marriage and kinship, legal rights of children, primogeniture, slavery, and the mode of daily living among the Semites down to the details of the furnishings of their tents and food they ate. The Semites valued honesty, truth, and the family tradition, all of which demonstrated the presence of a rudimentary moral code with some notion of reward and punishment. The code of the tribe, maintained Renan, worked as effectively as the more complicated jurisprudence of the nineteenth century in limiting violence. It was such an age of religious perfection that the author of the Book of Job used it as the background for his work.[64]

The patriarchal way of life, in Renan's view, had projected the Semites into the foremost place in the history of humanity. Although there were no external signs of power in patriarchal society, these illiterate men—thus Renan—were able to maintain a society based simply on the principle of respect, without recourse to violence, the popular vote, the hereditary principle, or an established constitution.

The society of the Semites was also elaborately described by Renan in the *Histoire Générale* and later in the *History*. There were no political or judicial institutions in patriarchal times and no authority outside of the family. Semitic society was that of the tent and the tribe. The Semites were not warlike; they were militarily inferior. The late history of the Israelites shows that they were in constant need of mercenaries. But the society of the Semites was the society which highlighted the free individual. A feeling for hierarchy was antipathetic to the Semites. Finally, while the Semites believed that the bond linking them to divinity had given them a special place in the eyes of God, they only evidenced what Renan considered to be an egoistic spirit, loving God but considering him their special protector, calling upon him to avenge the wrongs done to them and to lead them successfully against their enemies.[65]

Renan's antimonarchism and desire for social change were very influential in shaping his interpretation of the role of the prophets of Israel. Renan praised the prophets. To Renan, the prophets sought to restore the ideal patriarchal age from which Israelite society had departed. However, discontent was provoked by the materialist Israelite society, the unequal condition of the rich and the poor, and the conviction that wealth was produced by injustice. Renan also viewed the prophets as the

[64] *Histoire*, 41–45.

[65] *Histoire*, 41–47; E. Renan, *Histoire générale et systemè comparée des langues semitiques* (Paris: Calmann-Levy, 1874) 13–15.

spokesmen for ethical monotheism and social justice and the monarchy as representing the antithetical principle of nationalism. His understanding of the chapter on the constitution of kingship, 1 Samuel 8, quite strikingly reflected this outlook.[66]

In this episode, the Israelite tribal leaders, oppressed by the Philistines, confront the prophet Samuel with a request to place a king over them who will rule them like all the surrounding nations. Samuel at first refuses the claim that the rule of a king would be a repudiation of his own leadership. Samuel then puts the request before Iahveh. He is told that the Israelites are rejecting God and not Samuel. Nevertheless, divine permission is granted. Samuel returns to the people and agrees to search for a king, but not without first describing the burdens that the royal might will inevitably inflict upon the people.

Renan considered this narrative to be a superbly "theatrical" exposition of the dilemma of Israel over the nature of its destiny. Here, he wrote,

> The duality was already established. Israel aspired after two contradictory things: It wanted to be like everyone else and to be apart. It wished to enjoy at the same time a real and practical existence and an ideal and impossible dream. Prophetism and royalty were placed in absolute opposition to each other from their very beginnings. A lay state obeying all of the necessities of lay states, and a theocratic democracy perpetually undermining the bases of civil order, this was the struggle which in its development filled up a stamp of originality.[67]

During the course of events which spelled out the destruction of the United Kingdom of David and Solomon and as a result of the absence of finished or fixed institutions of government and worship, the prophets arose. They were final interpreters of the ancient dream of a universalist ethical religion without form or nation or place. "These men of God were a source of great embarrassment to the secular authority, but the true tradition of the spirit was really preserved in them."[68]

Renan also viewed the prophets as forerunners of the archetypes of the medieval, monastic, and mendicant orders—proto-communalists. He conceived of the organization of the prophets as consisting of masters and novices called "sons of the prophets" who took their meals together, assembled in common rooms, and were subjected to periodic visits by the master of the order.[69] In a fashion similar to that of the medieval friars who in Renan's view were driven by the desire to return to the primitive ideal of Christianity, the Israelite prophets were attempting to retrieve

[66] *Histoire*, 268–69.
[67] *Histoire*, 269–70.
[68] *Histoire*, 437.
[69] *Histoire*, 486.

the purity of the patriarchal age. The prophets were enormous in number, very poor, and generally idle. Jerusalem in the prophetic age reminded Renan of medieval Paris with its hordes of beggars congregating under the shadows of Notre Dame.[70]

Renan valued the prophets for their opposition to the materialist social order which had overcome ancient Israel in the days of the monarchy. Worldliness, luxury, and intellectual brilliance—Renan was evidently referring to Solomon's court—combined with disregard of the poor, was not the destiny of Israel.[71] Thus, Renan pointed out, the failed attempt by King Jehoshaphat of Judah to continue Solomon's work in building a navy to sail to India only inspired the prophet Eliezer ben Dovadah to rejoice.[72]

Renan praised the prophets' vigorous criticism of the central monarchy and their overall antipolitical message which fitted in well with Renan's anticentralist conception of the political structure and his view of the purposeful fate of ancient Israel in history. Thus, Renan considered the fall of the northern kingdom in 722/21 B.C.E. to have removed an obstruction from the path of ancient Israel's true destiny.[73]

The prophets of Israel had secured its place in world history and human progress. The prophets had crystallized the idea of one, universal god, and asserted the primacy of righteousness over ritual.[74]

The prophetic spirit remained in sharp contrast to Israel's worldly politics. Renan believed that Israel's departure from a role as a power-gathering nation would return it to a pursuit of its true destiny. The Israelite prophets down to Ezekiel in the sixth century were less concerned with political success or national destiny than they were in quest of an eternal ideal, which to Renan was inimical to the continuation of nationality.

Renan's favorable response to the ideals of the prophets also resulted from his view that they were about to destroy the religious nationalism, which according to Renan, was personified by the ancient Israelite god Iahveh. The prophets would then lead the people of Israel back to the "primitive elohim, the patriarchal god, the El of the large tent, to the true god."[75] In terms of Renan's conception of human destiny, he viewed the prophets as having reformulated the idea of Iahveh to express the ideal of a universal divine creator who was also a god of righteousness and law.[76]

---

[70] *Histoire*, 680–85.
[71] *Histoire*, 572–75.
[72] *Histoire*, 504–5, 562.
[73] *Histoire*, 643.
[74] *Histoire*, 624, 647, 985.
[75] *Histoire*, 191.
[76] *Histoire*, 516.

Renan, the candidate of peace in his first abortive foray into politics, voiced deepest appreciation for the role of the Israelite prophets in systematizing future history by laying out the plan that history should follow, a way of universal peace and social justice. The prophets had raised ancient Israel to its greatest heights in human history by proclaiming the need for "a democratic puritanism of morals, hatred of luxury, of profane civilizations, and of obligation resulting from a complicated civil organization . . . (and for) the worship of Iahveh consisting above all else in purity of feeling" and not in ritual.[77]

The impact of the prophets of Israel upon Christianity represented their most significant contribution, since Christianity would carry the prophetic ideal of universal peace and justice to the world. Thus, Renan lauded the age of the prophets as

> the most fruitful one in all religious history. Even the initial movement of Christianity, in the first century of our era, takes second place, by comparison, with this extraordinary movement of Jewish prophetism in the eighth century B.C. Jesus is all contained in Isaiah. The humanitarian destiny of Israel is as clearly written about 720 as that of Greece will be two centuries later.[78]

Beginning with the premise that one God was "the unique cause of the phenomena of the universe," that the divine justice "should be realized on earth" and "for each individual within the limits of his existence," the prophets went on to proclaim a revolution in society, "that all the Old Testament will some day become the figure that which is realized by the New. . . ."[79]

Renan's praise of the Israelite prophets was nevertheless thoroughly mixed with severe criticism. Social reformers though they were in his view, the prophets were also considered by Renan to have been fanatics who were in the main responsible for the growth of theocratic nationalism in ancient Israel. While attacking the monarchy and the Temple, the prophets had also been inspired by the new religious nationalism which confined the free spirit of ancient Israel and, in Renan's view, had given birth to the narrow clericalism that would characterize Israel's future.[80]

Renan contemptuously condemned the fanaticism of the prophets. Equating them with French journalists who "carried every political question to a sort of paroxysm," he had no use for the utopianism and suicidal pacifism of the prophets.[81] Renan considered the prophets to be religious fanatics as well, forerunners of later Christian inquisitors who

---

[77] *Histoire*, 624, 647.
[78] *Histoire*, 647.
[79] *Histoire*, 958, n. 2.
[80] *Histoire*, 494, 688, 690, 729, 775, 782, 795–96.
[81] *Histoire*, 597, 624.

were exacting in their cruelty while shedding tears over their God. His most laudatory comments on the role of the prophets as revivers of the ancient patriarchal values were practically nullified by his angry denunciation of their fanaticism.

Renan believed that the prophets had been dangerous men capable of destroying society, revolutionaries, "visionaries, utopists, and inspired democrats commanding revolutions and making or unmaking dynasties," who could very well bring society to a chaotic end. The attack of the prophets on the centralized monarchies of ancient Israel was welcome from Renan's vantage, but not the extent and ferocity of their attack on society.[82]

Renan's condemnation of religious and nationalist fanaticism and of social revolution controlled his selective praise of the prophets. He favored the social reformers Amos, Micah, and Zephaniah, and Isaiah, the visionary Joel, and the unknown prophet of the last chapter of the Book of Zachariah, whose work, in Renan's opinion, heralded Christianity.[83] On the other hand, Renan criticized Hosea and Habakkuk as overly nationalistic and Obadiah and Nahum as violent chauvinists. Renan denounced Jeremiah as the blindest, most suicidally fanatic prophet of all, and saved his tenderest praise for the unknown prophet called Second Isaiah whose description of the "Suffering Servant" of Israel foreshadowed the advent of Jesus.

Renan maintained that the religious fanaticism of the prophets was responsible for the evolution of Judaism as an exclusive faith. The strict directives of Judaism and the fanaticism of the prophets who directed its growth created the barrier which eventually separated Israel from the nations of the world. To Renan, the national and religious institutions of the Judean state in the seventh and sixth centuries were departures from the true vocation of the Hebrew people, superseding the brief glimpse of Israel's universal mission which some of the eighth century prophets had envisioned. For the centralizing forces introduced by Solomon were perpetuated, after the defection of the northern tribes, in the southern kingdom of Judah and in Jerusalem. Under Kings Hezekiah and Josiah, religious nationalism and royal centralization reached new heights. Josiah brought Solomon's work to an effective climax. He eliminated all paganism, suppressed all sanctuaries outside of the Temple in Jerusalem, brought the unemployed Levites to the Temple where they became a wholly dependent sacerdotal caste, fixed the festival calendar, and made pilgrimage to Jerusalem obligatory. "A pious Jew in the time of Josiah," Renan wrote, "was almost as happy in his religion as a Christian in the time of Saint Louis."[84] Religious orthodoxy had reached its crest during

[82] *Histoire*, 514, 600, 623.
[83] *Histoire*, 588.
[84] *Histoire*, 784.

the rule of Josiah as the god of the nation was transformed into the universal divinity.

Finally, all of this centralization based on religious and national orthodoxy was codified in the Deuteronomic Code. Renan could not abide the existence of this code. "These mischief-making texts were destined to bear fruit and they sent to the stake, more specifically, a host of unhappy Israelites. . . . In this respect, the Deuteronomic code has not been exceeded even by that of the Dominican Inquisition. . . ."[85] "The savage egotism of an exclusive nationality which confiscated the Divinity for its own advantage is certainly far from the ideal of religious truth," he wrote.[86]

The existence of religious nationalism, whether in his own day or in ancient Israel, was a source of great anguish to Renan. In his writings, where past and present were often fused, he condemned religious chauvinism:

> Germany, by the philosophy to which it has given birth, by the voice of its men of genius, had more successfully proclaimed than any other race the absolute, impersonal and supreme nature of the Divinity. But when she became a nation, she was led, according to the way of all flesh, to particularize God. The Emperor William on several occasions spoke of *Unser Gott* and the god of the Germans. . ." "*Iahveh, elohenu,* our god," said the Israelite. *Unser Gott* says the German. . . Strange contradiction, fearful blasphemy! As well say, *my absolute, my infinite, my Supreme Being.*[87]

There was one justification for Israelite nationalism in Renan's view: it was a necessary step in keeping the message of monotheism alive. Renan even admitted that the later prophets, the Torah, and the priestly postexilic state were necessary in the historical scheme of things to preserve the universal message of the prophets which was ultimately destined to go forth to humanity at large by means of Christianity.[88] As the immediate precursors of Christianity, the prophets alone had kept alive the authentic universal message of ancient Israel, the Elohism of the patriarchs. For the sake of preserving monotheism and social justice until the advent of Christianity, Renan accepted the nation, religion, and prophets of Israel as an unwelcome means to a desirable end.

In his *Debates with Historians,* the Dutch historian Pieter Geyl wrote:

> History is often thought of as a study contentedly remote from the present, or as a hobby of scholars who have elected to fly from the world around

---

[85] *Histoire,* 796.
[86] *Histoire,* 493.
[87] *Histoire,* 190–91.
[88] *Histoire,* 729.

them into the dead and gone past. The truth is rather that history is an active force in the struggles of every generation and that the historian by his interpretation of the past, consciously or half-consciously or even unconsciously, takes his part in them, for good or for evil.[89]

Renan participated in the struggles of his generation, all too often as a frustrated observer. As a result, his interpretation of ancient Israel, was hardly ever "contentedly remote" from the tumultuous events of his own time.

[89] P. Geyl, *Debates with Historians* (New York: Meridian Books, 1958) 264.

NEW GLEANINGS ON RESHEPH FROM UGARIT

Yigael Yadin†
The Hebrew University, Jerusalem

R ESHEPH is one of the most enigmatic deities of the Canaanite pantheon.[1]

Sam Iwry in his by now classic article on belomancy in ancient Palestine and Phoenicia[2] deals, *inter alia*, also with some aspects of Resheph, about whom he aptly says: "The extreme fluidity of the personality and function of this god is indicated in many ways."[3] He was

---

[1] Of the vast literature dealing with Resheph, the following are the more recent and contain references to earlier bibliography. (Additional studies will be mentioned in the course of the article.) The most recent comprehensive study of Resheph is William J. Fulco, S.J., *The Canaanite God Rešep* (New Haven, 1976). Although the book was severely criticized, it is still the most handy, and frequent references will be made to it; of review-articles of Fulco's study, I would like to single out R. Giveon, "Review Article: Resheph in Egypt," *JEA* 66 (1980) 144–50. Another very important study (with many thought-provoking suggestions and good references to earlier literature) is D. Conrad, "Der Gott Reschef," *ZAW* 83 (1971) 157–83; A. R. Schulman, "Reshep Times Two," in W. K. Simpson, and W. M. Davies (eds.), *Studies in Ancient Egypt, The Aegean and the Sudan: Essays in Honor of Dows Dunham on the Occasion of his 90th Birthday, June 1, 1980,* (Boston, 1981) 157–66. This paper may also be considered as a review of Fulco's book; on this study, see further my remarks in n 64 below. On Resheph consult also D. Collon, "The Smiting God . . . ," *Levant* 4 (1979) 111ff. See there, also, on the connection of Resheph with the lion, 128ff. Of the earlier studies I would like to mention the following: J. Leibovitch, "Quelques nouvelles représentations du dieu Rechef," *ASAE* 39 (1939) 145–60; pls. XV–XXII; *idem*, "Amon-Raᶜ, Rechef et Houroun sur une stèle," *ASAE* 44 (1945) 163–72; F. Vattioni, "Il dio Resheph," *Annali del Istituto Orientale di Napoli* NS 15 (1965) 39–74; R. Stadelmann, *Syrisch-Palästinensische Gottheiten in Ägypten* (Leiden, 1967) 47–76; H. O. Thompson, *Mekal, The God of Beth-Shan* (Leiden, 1970) 144–163; and lastly, but not the least, the concise article of S. Löwenstamm in *Encyclopaedia Biblica* (Hebrew), 7, (Jerusalem, 1976) 437–41, particularly for the treatment of Resheph in the Bible. On this, see also the article by M. Weinfeld, below, n 36.

[2] S. Iwry, "New Evidence for Belomancy in Ancient Palestine and Phoenicia," *JAOS* 81 (1961) 27–34.

[3] Ibid., 31.

right, too, in emphasizing one of Resheph's functions "as gate-keeper of the sun," as may be inferred from one of the Ugaritic texts.[4]

S. Iwry's discussion of Resheph was prompted by the fact that Resheph is sometimes referred to as Resheph ḥṣ—and ḥṣ (ḥz) was the main subject of his article.

Apropos of Resheph, Iwry mentioned, albeit briefly, another of his epithets: gn. It is therefore appropriate, I believe, to dedicate this article which deals with one of the objects on which the name of Resheph and this epithet was written to my good friend and esteemed colleague, Sam Iwry.

* * *

THE LION-FACE RHYTON

The late C. F. A. Schaeffer-Forrer has published one of the most interesting inscribed objects discovered at Ugarit.[5] The object is a terracotta lion-faced rhyton bearing an inscription in the Ugaritic cuneiform alphabet (fig. 1).[6]

It is surprising that Schaeffer did not mention two similar—although not inscribed—rhyta from Ugarit[7] (a drawing of one is published here; fig. 2). The common elements of all three rhyta are readily apparent, although their artistic quality is different, and one may assume that they were made by different potters.

The inscription, which was incised prior to the baking of the vessel, is not only a clear indication that the pot—and thus the other two as well—was made at Ugarit (or its vicinity), but—and this is even more important—that the lion rhyton was deliberately chosen by the offerer who ordered the vessel.

It is only natural that the unusual inscription was the focus of the studies of Schaeffer, Dietrich, and Loretz[8]—so much so that the archaeological aspects of the vessel itself were not treated at all. Yet, it is important to note at the outset of the discussion that the discovery of 14th-13th centuries B.C. Canaanite lion-face rhyta is of the utmost importance for

----

[4] Ch. Virolleaud, PRU II 189, No. 162; Conrad, "Der Gott Reschef," 169; and now, J. Gray, "Canaanite Religion and Old Testament Study in the Light of New Alphabetic Texts from Ras Shamra," in Ugaritica VII (1978) 91, and see further below.

[5] Ugaritica VII (1978) 149.

[6] After Ugaritica VII (1978) 152, fig. 4.

[7] The first: C. F. A. Schaeffer, Syria 19 (1938) 194, pl. XIX; the same rhyton, ILN (Jan. 1940) 26. The second: Land des Baal (Catalogue of an Exhibition; Mainz am Rhein, 1982) Nos. 128, 138.

[8] M. Dietrich and O. Loretz, "Die Keilalphabetische Krugaufschrift RS 25.318," Ugaritica VII (1978) 147-48.

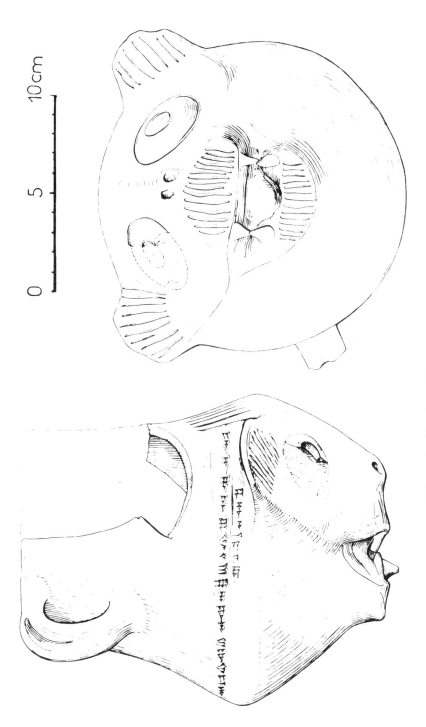

Figure 1. After Ugaritica VII, figure 4 (p. 152).

Figure 2. Rhyton from Ras Shamra.

the study of the lion rhyta discovered in Philistia (including the other territories occupied by the Sea-Peoples in Palestine), belonging to the 12th–11th centuries B.C. It is instructive to mention some of the observations on this subject in two of the most recent and penetrating studies on the Philistine rhyta.

Trude Dothan stresses mainly the fact that the Philistine rhyta "seem to be the last echo of a long Mycenaean-Minoan tradition of animal-headed rhyta."[9] Prof. Dothan, furthermore, accepts the view that Philistine rhyta "were part of the widely distributed *koine* of Myc.III.B."[10] However, she rightly admits the astonishing fact that "among all these animal-headed rhyta [Mycenaean style rhyta found in Cyprus and Ugarit] there is not a single example of a lion's head in Mycenaean ware and decoration, although plain examples are known from Thera and Ugarit."[11] Obviously, the three Ugaritic rhyta provide not only the missing link between the Mycenaean metal prototypes and the pottery Philistine uses, but are, in a way *sui generis*, created by the Canaanites (probably originally in Ugarit) to suit their ritual needs.

A. Mazar follows in the main the trend of thought of Dothan in his thorough discussion of the beautiful lion-face rhyton found in the *favissa* of the Philistine temple at Tell Qasile.[12] However, he felt that there existed "a long chronological gap between the appearance of the object in the Aegean world and its appearance in the Philistine culture."[13] One of the explanations put forward by Mazar is worth quoting: "One could also claim that the Aegean rhyton type was accepted in the East already in an early phase of the Late Bronze Age, and that rhytons in this tradition continued to be produced in the Levant throughout the Late Bronze Age."[14] Indeed this hypothesis is corroborated now by the three lion-face rhyta from Ugarit. As we shall see, the Canaanite products may have had much more importance than just being examples of the artistic bridge between the cultures.

THE INSCRIPTION

There can be no doubt that a very important aspect of the find is the two-line, pre-firing inscription on the carination line of the vessel, immediately under the lion's face, placed to be read facing the beast's face. The inscription reads as follows:

[9] Trude Dothan, *The Philistines and their Material Culture* (New Haven and London/Jerusalem, 1982) 231.

[10] Ibid.

[11] Ibid., 232. The reference is to the one published in *Syria* 19 (1938). Cf. also *ILN*, where the rhyton is described as "a large feline statue in terra-cotta."

[12] A. Mazar, "Excavations at Tell Qasileh, Part One," *Qedem* 12 (1980) 101–3.

[13] Ibid., 102.

[14] Ibid.

bn agptr
pn arw d šᶜly nrn l ršp gn

The first to mention this inscription—and it is now clear that the data at his disposal at the time were not complete—was C. Gordon:[15] "Virolleaud informs me of a terra cotta lion's head (sic!) with the following inscribed on its neck: *pn arw d šᶜly ršp gn* the lion's face that N has offered to R. of the Garden."[16]

Before discussing the epithet *gn*, it is imperative to understand the relation of the first line—*bn agptr*, son of Agaptar—(not known to Gordon) to the second line.

The name *Agptr* occurs several times in the Ugaritic alphabetic texts (also: *Agbtr*), as well as in the Akkadian form: *A-gab Lugal*.[17] An *Agptr*, who is *aldy*, i.e., Alašian (Cypriote) is also known.[18]

Dietrich and Loretz seem to be right in assuming that the scribe forgot to write the words *bn agptr* and added them later; thus they must be inserted somewhere in the second line.[19] Of the two possibilities either that *bn agptr* is the maker of the vessel and the offerer or that he is the priest in *bt ršp gn* ("The temple of Resheph GN"), they[20] prefer the first and understand and translate the inscription as follows:

Pn arw bn agptr d šᶜly nrn l ršp gn: "Löwengesicht des Agaptarri,[21] das Nrn dem 'schützenden Reschef' dargebracht hat."[22]

The two possibilities are difficult to accept. The mentioning of two personalities in such a dedicatory inscription, inscribed before firing, is very unusual. As a matter of fact they do not make sense: Why should *Nrn* act on behalf of *bn agptr*? I therefore suggest inserting the words *bn agptr* after *nrn*, to be read thus: *Pn arw d šᶜly nrn bn agptr l ršp gn*, i.e., "The lion's face that Nrn son of Agptr has offered to Resheph GN."

---

[15] *Ugaritic Textbook* (Rome, 1965) (= UT) 486, No. 2356.

[16] Cf. also Virolleaud in *PRU* II 135: "*R. du jardin.*"

[17] See Dietrich and Loretz, *Ugaritica* VII (1978) 147.

[18] Ibid. The fact that *Agptr* is a Cypriote, where the cult of Resheph is known to have been very popular (at least in later periods) may be of some significance.

[19] In a way, the same technique is attested in the much later Dead Sea Scrolls (cf. Y. Yadin, *The Temple Scroll*, vol. I, [Jerusalem, 1983] 21). On the long traditions of scribal techniques, see R. D. Barnett, "A Legacy of the Captivity: a Note on the Paleo-Hebrew and Neo-Hebrew Scripts," *Eretz-Israel* 16 (1982) 1*ff.

[20] *Ugaritica* VII (1978) 177–78.

[21] Should have been "Sohn des Agaptarri."

[22] The second alternative implies that *bn Agptr* was deliberately written separately. In this case, Loretz and Dietrich understand the text as follows: "Nrn (hat) stellvertretend für *bn agptr* den Löwenkopf in den Tempel gebracht"; obviously, an even less probable meaning.

Another expression in this inscription deserves discussion: *pn arw*. The word *pn*, "face," is used here not in an abstract way but clearly as a description of the face on the vessel. The scribe did not resort to a word like *head* (which seems to the modern eye to be more natural).[23]

The final problem connected with the inscription is the meaning of the epithet *gn*. Gordon, followed for a time by Dahood,[24] translated it as: "Resheph of the Garden." So, too, Virolleaud: "*R. du jardin*." Samuel Iwry[25] and D. Conrad[26] understood it as "Resheph of the Shield," while Aistleitner suggested: "*Resheph von Gn (GN),*"[27] i.e., *gn* designates here a place name. Dietrich and Loretz rejected all of these interpretations: "shield" is out of question since this object is called *mgn* in Ugaritic; "garden"—since why should Resheph be associated with a garden, particularly since there was a temple of Resheph *gn* (*bt ršp gn*) in Ugarit? Also, *gn* as a place name is not acceptable since "Warum der Reschef eines unbekannten und wohl auch unbedeutender Orten in Ugarit ein

---

[23] Cf. "Rhyton léoncéphale" in Schaeffer's description of the vessel (above, n. 5), or "lion-headed rhyta," in Trude Dothan's definition (*Ugaritica* VII [1978] 149). Note the following phrase in A. Mazar's study (*Excavations at Tell Qasile, Part One*, 102): "the lower part of the vessel was moulded in the shape of an animal's head." Mazar's hesitancy to define the animal as a lion—"The identification of the animal on the rhytons from Tell Qasile and Tell Jerisheh as a lion is not definite"—(although, he finally does so), and not a pig was influenced by A. Kempinsky's insistence that these animals are pigs (p. 113, n 3). These ideas are now to be definitely eliminated; the Ugaritian scribe, as if anticipating modern speculations, wrote plainly: "lion's face"! The word "face" is obviously a reference to the mask-like form of the vessel. Apropos of this usage I would like to mention the fact that Tanit—the consort of Baᶜal Ḥammon the chief god of the Phoenician-Punic pantheon—is frequently called *pn baᶜal*, "the face of Baᶜal" (cf. my article "Symbols of Deities at Zinjirli, Carthage and Hazor," in J. A. Sanders, ed., *Near Eastern Archaeology in the Twentieth Century: Essays in Honor of Nelson Glueck* (Garden City, 1970) 216ff. This epithet was still used in the (later) coins of Ashdod: φανηβαλος. In the above-mentioned paper I suggested that the term "face" should be understood in this context not in an abstract way, but as an actual mask (i.e., *tanit* was depicted in a mask form as the face of Baᶜal) and to identify it with the many clay masks found in the Punic sphere: "It may be asked whether these very masks were not the 'face of Baᶜal'" (p. 220). The usage of the word *pn* in the Ugaritic rhyton, not only strengthens this possibility, but provides us with a semitic technical term for an "image of a face" object depicted in clay or other materials. The word is used in a similar—although not identical—way in Ezekiel in several places (cf., e.g., 1:6, 10; 10:14; 41:19, as well as 25:20, etc. In contrast see *pn š*; *pn ʾalp*, in the Kilamuwa inscription, line 11. See Y. Abishur, *Phoenician Inscriptions and the Bible* (Jerusalem, 1979) 209 (Hebrew). See also below, n 43.

[24] M. Dahood, *Psalms III 101–150* (AB 17A; (Garden City, 1970) xxv.

[25] Iwry, "New Evidence."

[26] Conrad, "Der Gott Reschef," 173.

[27] Dietrich and Loretz, *Ugaritica* VII, 147.

Heiligtum haben solte."[28] The suggestion of Dietrich and Loretz is "In gn sehen wir einem Namen, das von gnn, 'beschützen' abzuleiten ist: ršp gn, "Reschef des Schutzes, der schützende Reschef."

However, in *Orientalia* in 1977, Dahood and Pettinato published new data from Ebla[29] which seem to support Aistleitner's interpretation (without being aware of his suggestion). According to this article, Resheph (^{d}ra-sa-ap) in the Ebla tablets "is associated with various cities."[30] But the epithet which has a direct bearing on our subject and appears in Ebla several times is "Resheph of Gunnu(m)." The name of the city, according to Dahood and Pettinato, is written in the following ways: gú-nu; gú-nu^{ki}; gu-núm and gú-núm^{ki}.[31] Bearing in mind that in the Ugarit texts a [b]l.ršp.gn is mentioned, it is most interesting to note the following information provided by Dahood and Pettinato: "Moreover, a temple of Resheph of Gunu is expressly mentioned in TM (= Ebla) 75 G. 1560 rev. X 15–17: é-^{d}ra-sa-ap gú-nu^{ki}. Again, remembering that our rhyton was used most probably for libations or anointing ceremonies it is interesting to learn that in the tablets there is mentioned also "a priest for anointings of the same divinity (íl-ba-Ma-lik pa$_4$: šeš ^{d}ra-sa-ap gú-núm)."[32] Dahood and Pettinato opine that both the Ebla texts and the one a thousand years later from Ugarit refer "to the same temple."[33] One must wait for the full publication of these texts.

Was there any reason why a lion rhyton was offered? Or, in other words: is there any connection between Resheph and the lion? This important problem, not raised by the first publishers, must be treated within the discussion of the nature of Resheph in the light of the documents and monuments.

RESHEPH AND THE LION

As noted at the beginning of our discussion the nature of Resheph is still quite enigmatic and has caused heated discussion and produced a vast literature.[34]

[28] Ibid, 148.

[29] M. Dahood and G. Pettinato, "Ugaritic ršpgn and Eblaite rasap gunu(m)^{ki}" Or 46 (1977) 230ff.

[30] Dahood and Pettinato even suggest seeing in ^{d}ra-sa-ap sí-é-am^{ki}, "Resheph of Shechem," Or 46 (1977) 231.

[31] Could gn be identified with the mound and bay of Junya, between Byblos and Beyrouth?

[32] Dahood and Pettinato, "Ugaritic ršpgn," Or 46 (1977) 231.

[33] On the other hand, they adhere to the interpretation of ršphs as Resheph of the arrow, rejecting the other suggestions (hs as place name, "street," and by implication they reject also "Resheph of luck"). On the possible connection between Resheph and the arch and arrows, see below.

[34] See the literature quoted above, n 1.

Since Resheph was venerated, albeit in a syncretistic manner, for thousands of years and in countries far apart, such as Anatolia, Egypt, Syria, Phoenicia (including the Punic orbit), Mesopotamia, Palestine, and Cyprus,[35] it is not surprising to find that Resheph had different epithets, traits, and identifications in the various countries. Our main purpose is to find out whether there was any connection between Resheph and the lion.

For a long time a nexus between Resheph and Nergal was perceived.[36] Now that we know for certain, thanks to the fairly-recently published tablets from Ugarit,[37] that the Ugaritic Canaanites identified Resheph with Nergal, we can affirm this connection.

The clearest association of Nergal with the lion is manifested on some of the kudurrus.[38] Nergal's symbol is clearly the lion-headed mace or staff. This by itself is deciding proof that the lion is Nergal's/ Resheph's symbolic animal. In other words, the fact that the rhyton offered to Resheph at Ugarit bore a lion's face must have been the result of a deliberate act of choice by the offerer.

From one of the Ugaritic mythical texts it was inferred that Resheph was the gate-keeper of the Sun goddess: ʿrbt špš ṯgrh ršp, i.e.: "the Sun setting and Resheph being her porter."[39] If this interpretation is a correct one—and from the bibliography mentioned it is clear that it is widely accepted—we have here corroborative data to an idea, suggested a long time ago, that the lion orthostats in Anatolian temples may represent the lion of Nergal in his role of porter[40] or guardian.[41] I may also

[35] See conveniently Fulco's and Conrad's studies.

[36] See Thompson, *Mekal*, 144ff. See also his article in *BA* 30 (1968) 20, with references to Mekal, Resheph, Nergal and the lion (including the connection between Resheph and *MKL* in Cyprus). Conrad ("Der Gott Reschef," 159ff. For the most recent treatment of the subject, see M. Weinfeld, " 'They fought from heaven'—Divine Intervention in War in Ancient Israel and in the Ancient Near East," *Eretz-Israel* 14 (1978) (H. L. Ginsburg volume) 26 (Hebrew).

[37] On the most recently published tablet, see A. Herdner, "Nouveaux texts alphabétiques de Ras Shamra—XXIVᵉ Campagne 1961," *Ugaritica* VII (1978) 3; cf. also M. Nougayrol, *Ugaritica* V, 42ff. See also end of n 38.

[38] L. W. King, *Babylonian Boundary Stones* (London, 1912), e.g., pl. XCII; on the whole subject see now E. von Weiher, *Der babylonische Gott Nergal* (Neukirchen-Vluyn, 1971) 45; on the equation Nergal = Resheph, see there, 90ff.

[39] Ch. Virolleaud, *PRU* II (1981) No. 162; see the most recent treatment by Gray in *Ugaritica* VII (1978) 91. For earlier discussion, see Fulco, *Rešep*, 38; Conrad, "Der Gott Reschef," 169, n 85.

[40] See the detailed discussion of the subject by Thompson, *Mekal*, 93.

[41] Thompson's discussion is apropos of the suggestion of A. Rowe to see in the lion relief of Beth-Shean "the Mesopotamian god Nergal in the form of a lion" (ibid., 93).

mention the two temples from Hazor—particularly the big one in Area H dedicated to the weather god—which were guarded by lion orthostats.[42]

In the light of the above, an inscription from Kition discovered in 1860[43] deserves mention:

3. וארום אשנם || אש עתן בדא כהן רשפחץ בן וכנש

4. לם בן אשמנאדן לאדנן לרשפחץ וברך.

The ארום אשנם was understood a long time ago as two lions, i.e., "two (statues of) lions."[44] In those days the form *arwê* in Ethiopian was quoted as a parallel to the singular *arw*.[45] However, this correct interpretation was later rejected for an unproved alternative: "altar hearth."[46] Now that the Canaanite singular *arw* appears clearly in Ugarit, and the association between the lion and Resheph is established, it seems that there can be no doubt that the meaning of the Kition inscription is *two lions*, and thus: "The two lions (orthostats?) given by Bdᵓ, *priest of ReshephḤṢ* to his Lord ReshpehḤṢ", i.e., to his temple.

[42] See my *Hazor* (The Schweich Lectures 1970), (London, 1972) 67. It is noteworthy that in the *favissa* of the lion-temple in Area H we found two pieces of clay liver models. In fragment B it is written (according to Landsberger and Tadmor): *Ištar(?) will eat the land//Nergal will . . . (Hazor,* 83). Prof. M. Weinfeld kindly drew my attention (in a letter of 2/24/82) to the following: "In these days I came across some information which may be helpful in your study on the 'lion face' and Resheph. Here it is (based on a Hittite text published by M. Otten in *Istanbul Mitteilungen* 17 (1967) 60): 'The elders of the city of Urah vow to offer a rhyton to the god Ya-ri, the god of plague and war.' This deity is related to *Era*, Nergal (H. Kümmel, *Erstatzrituale etc.,* 101). I found him standing on a lion (M. Güterbock, *Or,* 15 494). Even more important, it is stated in a Hittite text (a king's dream) that the king must offer to the god Ya-ri a lion-shaped ivory object (*KUB*, XV 5 II 39; see also L. Oppenheim, *Dreams,* 193). The god Ya-ri is called the "Lord of the arch" like Nergal. I believe that in the above theme there is supporting evidence for your suggestion." On the arch and Resheph see further below. Weinfeld's letter followed a private seminar of some of my colleagues, in which I first presented the gist of the present article.

[43] *CIS* I, no. 10; G. A. Cooke, *Textbook of North-Semitic Inscriptions* (Oxford, 1903) nos. 12, 55; N. Slouschz, *Thesaurus of Phoenician Inscriptions* (Tel Aviv, 1942) nos. 59, 68 (Hebrew); A. Donner and W. Röllig, *Kanaanäische und aramäische Inschriften* (Wiesbaden, 1964) no. 32.

[44] See Cooke, *Textbook,* 56. He cites also a Greek inscription from Near Sidon: τοὺς δύο λευητας.

[45] See Slouschz *Thesaurus,*.

[46] Cooke, Donner-Röllig, and others.

THE PHILISTINES' LIONS RHYTA AND THEIR MEANING

We began our article by pointing out the importance of the lion rhyta of Ugarit[47] in closing a gap between the Aegean prototypes and the very similar Philistine rhyta; in fact, I submit that they are more than just a gap-closing: they may be the very missing link between the two. It is appropriate, therefore, to conclude this paper with a brief discussion of the Philistine lion rhyta and their cultic significance. Until now five such rhyta have been found,[48] one in each of the following sites: Tell Zeror and Megiddo (within the northern limits of the Sea Peoples' dominions), Tell e-Ṣafi (probably Gath) in Philistia in the south, and in Tell Jerisha and Tell Qasile, on the Yarkon river, in the center and heart of the Sea Peoples' territories. In other words, they cover all the great centers of the Sea Peoples' territories.[49]

Having established the cultic association of the lion element in the Ugaritic rhyton with Resheph, we may pose the question whether the Philistine lion rhyton also is connected with the worship of Resheph. The original deities worshiped by the various Sea Peoples are not known, but by the time they settled in Canaan, and definitely as reflected in the Bible, all the known gods are in fact Canaanite in nature and name:[50] Dagon (with temples at Gaza and Ashdod—two of the principal cities of the Pentapolis), Baal—Zebub, or Zebul (the local god of Ekron), the goddess Ashtoreth, or Ashtaroth (whose temple was most probably located at Beth-Shean). It has been noted by many scholars that the Philistines' religion after their contact with the Canaanites was eclectic and

[47] A most intriguing object is held by an offerer to Resheph (garbed in typical Sea-Peoples dress) on a newly published stela from Memphis (first published by Fulco, *Rešep*, pl. II) and re-discussed in detail by Schulman ("Reshep," 160, and fig. 2 there). On this object writes Schulman: "With his upraised right hand he pours out a libation from a scarcely visible jar" (p. 162). In n 27 he adds: "Probably a hemisperical spouted libation can rather than a spouted *ḥṣ*-jar." However, to my (biased?) eyes it looks clearly like a lion-faced rhyton! This observation can be ascertained only by examining the stela, which is in the University Museum, University of Pennsylvania (E.13620). I would like to mention another recent find of importance to our discussion. In the 1982 season of excavation at Acco, a seal impression (ca. 600 B.C.) was found with the name of Resheph and a depiction of a lion. I wish to thank Prof. M. Dothan for this information and for his permission to mention it here.

[48] See the thorough discussions in T. Dothan and B. Mazar, *The Philistines*, "Excavations at Tell Qasile, Part One."

[49] On the division of Palestine between the various Sea Peoples see my paper: "And Dan, Why Did He Remain in Ships?", in *Western Galilee and the Coast of Galilee* (The Nineteenth Archaeological Convention, October, 1963) (Jerusalem, 1965) (Hebrew) 42; the same in English in *AJBA* 1 (1968).

[50] See T. Dothan, *Philistines*, 20.

the names of their previous deities were identified with the Canaanite pantheon.

T. Dothan, dealing with the 11th century B.C. Philistines, defines the nature of their religion aptly: ". . . the Philistines had begun to assimilate the main elements of Semitic Canaanite beliefs into their own religion. Even the names of their deities are Canaanite. In this context it is important to remember that the worship of these deities was widespread in Canaan before the coming of the Philistines."[51] One may go even one step further—as Prof. A. Malamat and others have—and suggest that it was at Ugarit (or in my opinion, partly already in Cyprus) that the Sea Peoples had their first glimpse of the Canaanite Pantheon: "Both these deities [Dagon and Baal-Zebul] it should be noted had been venerated earlier especially at the port of Ugarit, where, interestingly, many Ashdodite merchants seem to have settled."[52] Therefore it would not be wrong to assume that Resheph, too, was one of those Canaanite deities absorbed by the Philistines, either already in Cyprus (which was always an important center of Resheph veneration)[53] or at Ugarit. The fact that the lion rhyton from Tell Qasile was found in the *favissa* of the Philistine temple strengthens this assumption.[54]

Do we possess any additional clues to corroborate the suggestion that Resheph the lion-god was worshiped in Philistia? I think we do. First, in the very vicinity of Tell Qasile there existed an important cult center of Resheph—at least in the Persian-Hellenistic periods. I refer, of course, to the well-known place called Arsuf (= Resheph)—Apollonia.[55] Although until now no relics were found from the early Iron period, it is reasonable to assume that the establishment of a Resheph-Apollo[56] cult-

---

[51] Ibid.

[52] See A. Malamat, "Origins and the Formative Periods," in H. N. Ben-Sasson (ed.), *A History of the Jewish People* (Cambridge, 1976) 84. On the Ashdodites at Ugarit see also M. Dothan, "Ashdod I," *ʿAtiqot* 7 (1967) 8.

[53] Particularly during the Persian period; see Fulco, *Rešep*, 47.

[54] It is interesting to note that lions or lionesses also feature very conspicuously on a cult stand found in the temple of Tell Qasile; see A. Mazar, "Excavations at Tell Qasile, Part One," pl. 32, and the discussion on pp. 89–90. Another find from Tell Qasile is perhaps related. I refer to the famous ostracon which mentions "Gold of Ophir" for "Beth Ḥoron." Could it refer to a temple of Ḥoron at Qasile, which is associated with Resheph? On Resheph/Ḥoron, see in particular J. Leibovitch, "Quelques nouvelles représentations." On a fragment of a lioness from a karnos found at Ashdod, see, M. Dothan, "Ashdod I," pl. XVIII, 1.

[55] I. Roll and E. Ayalon, "A Coastal Town in the Southern Sharon Plain," *Qadmoniot* 15 (1982) 16.

[56] On the equation Resheph-apollo in Cypriote inscriptions, see Conrad, "Der Gott Reschef," 165; Fulco, *Rešep*, 50. Fulco rightly emphasizes that both Resheph and Apollo are archers. On this see further below.

place would have been at a site which was associated with an older tradition, as was the case in many cult centers in the Ancient Near East.[57]

A very striking and unique find was made by H. and J. Kaplan, several years ago, in a small, 12th-century chapel discovered at Jaffa. There was found[58] an actual skull of a lion—an obvious indication of the connection between the deity and the lion. In my paper on Dan,[59] I suggested that the solar character of Samson, his association with the lion, the striking similarity between his feats and those of Hercules (whose hallmark was the skin of the Nemean lion), who was also identified with Resheph[60]—all indicate that a solar deity associated with the lion was a very important deity among the Philistines. I believe that now I can be more specific and suggest that the deity was none other than Resheph.

Of some interest may be the fact, mentioned briefly above, that on many Egyptian monuments the consort of Resheph (called Qudšu, i.e. "holy," which could be an epithet of Anath or Ashtoreth) is standing on a lion (or perhaps a lioness, in some cases?).[61] It is easy to follow the "logical" development in the Canaanites' thinking: If Resheph is symbolized by a lion, then his consort is a lioness. In fact the Canaanite goddess called "lioness" (lb ʿt-lbia) in all probability can be identified with the consort of Resheph. She is definitely associated (like ʿAnat[62]) with the bow and arrows (symbolically equated with lightning and fire arrows of Resheph in the Bible—see below). This association is perhaps manifested also in the unique find of the inscribed arrow-heads from el-Khadr.[63] On three arrows of a larger group there is an inscription

[57] In my article "And Dan," I enumerated the sites on the Philistine coast which were intimately connected with Greek mythology (see in particular the connection between Perseus, Andromeda, and Jaffa—S. Tolkowsky, *The Gateway of Palestine: History of Jaffa* [London 1924] 27; and those of Mopsus the "son of Apollo" with Ashkelon which he conquered—Athanasius, VII, 37; cf. T. Müller, *Fragmenta Historicorum* I, 38).

[58] Cf. Haya and J. Kaplan, "Jaffa," in M. Avi-Yonah, ed., *Encyclopedia of Archaeological Excavations in the Holy Land* II (Jerusalem, 1976) 540 and photo on 538.

[59] See above, n 49.

[60] Fulco, *Rešep*, 48.

[61] See *ANEP*, nos. 470–74; cf. also T. G. H. James, *An Introduction to Ancient Egypt* (London, 1979) 134.

[62] See my article [Y. Sukenik], "The Composite Bow of the Canaanite Goddess Anath," *BASOR* 107 (1947) 11ff.

[63] F. M. Cross and J. T. Milik, "Inscribed Javelin-heads from the Period of the Judges: A Recent Discovery in Palestine," *BASOR* 134 (1954) 5; idem, "A Typological Study of the El-Khadr Javelin- and Arrow-heads," *ADAJ* 3 (1956) 15. Cf. also S. Iwry's article, "New Evidence." For the most recent and enlarged treatment on these inscriptions as well as others discussed since, see F. M. Cross,

which reads: *ḥṣ ᶜabd lb ʾt* = "the arrow of servant of the lioness," or in a less literal translation but more correct in its meaning: "servant of the Lion-lady." [64] Interestingly, Cross identifies—I believe rightly—"the Lion-lady" without hesitation with ᶜ*Anat*. [65]

It is noteworthy that among the lists of bowmen and slingmen from Ugarit we find not only ᶜ*bdlbit.qšt*—i.e., "servant of the lioness (goddess), bowman," [66] but also a bowman-slingman whose name is *ršpab.qst w qlᶜ* (i.e., "my father is Resheph" [67]). It has been suggested by Milik, discussing the el-Khadr missiles and the Ugarit lists, that there may have

---

"The Origin and Early Evolution of the Alphabet," *Eretz-Israel* 8 (1967) (The E. L. Sukenik Volume) 13*ff.; on the possible association of these arrow-heads with professional archers in David's army (in his pre-monarchical period), see B. Mazar, "David's Heroes" in *Canaan and Israel* (Republication and updating of Historical Essays), (Jerusalem, 1974) 186 (Hebrew).

[64] F. M. Cross, *Eretz-Israel* 8 (1967) 13*. Although Cross refers to the inscribed weapons as "darts," he considers the whole lot as a "hoard of arrowheads" which is "more easily explained as the contents of the quiver of an archer," "Origin," 13*, n 33. The total length of the three inscribed blades (including their tangs) is between 10.5–9.2 cms. (cf. also *ANEP* I, *Supplementary Texts and Pictures*, 1968, no. 805). Thus there is no reason to consider them as "darts" and not arrowheads. Whatever the case, Schulman's suggestion (164), that the quivers of Resheph, as depicted on some Egyptian monuments, are "filled with feathered missiles" (i.e., not arrows), is not convincing. Not only were ancient darts, as depicted on monuments, not equipped with feathers, but Schulman's arguments from the Bible and the Semitic inscriptions in support of his suggestion are partially wrong and partially not accurate. It is surprising to note that he had to acknowledge some of his colleagues for bringing to his notice that "a number of inscribed objects have *ḥṣ* PN [sic!]." This reference is to the El-Khadr weapons. There are no further references to the studies dedicated to this crucial find. He also mentions the epithets "Rsp ḥṣ or Rsp bʾl ḥẓ" [sic!] and suggests understanding them as "Reshep, (lord) of the feathered missile." As further support for the assumption that *ḥṣ* may denote a dart, he acknowledges his thanks to another colleague for the information "that Hebrew *ḥṣ* is used to describe the javelin head of Goliath of Gath (I Samuel 16 [should be 17]:7." Again, no further treatment of this important subject is given. In fact, in this verse the word *ḥṣ* does not refer to the javelin head but should be read (with the Masoretes' emendation, the LXX and the Vulgate as *ʾeʾṣ*, i.e., wood, or the javelin shaft. This is quite clear from the verse itself: (Q רעץ =) רחץ חניתר כמנור ארגים ולהבת חניתר שש מאות שקלים ברזל, "And the shaft of his spear was like a weaver's beam, and his spear's head weighed six hundred shekels iron" (*RSV*). It is clear that the javelin head is called להבת. On the whole subject, see my article: "Goliath's Javelin and the *Menor Orgim*," *PEQ* (1955) 58–69.

[65] Cross, "Origin," 13*.

[66] *UT*, 321:III:38; Cross, "Origin," 13*; B. Mazar, "David's Heroes," 186.

[67] *ršp ʾb.qšt.w.qlᶜ*, *UT*, 321:III:45. Cf. also ibid., 321:I:35: ᶜ*ba rsp.qst*. On the dual functions (bowman and slingman) see also 1 Chr 12:2, נשקי קשת מימינים ומשמאלים באבנים ובחצים בקשת.

existed "a mercenary body of soldiers, and especially of bowmen [and slingmen—Y. Y.], surviving the migrations and the changing of ruling class, the profession being hereditary among certain families." [68]

B. Mazar, as we mentioned, went one step further and suggested a connection between the el-Khadr arrowheads and the mercenaries who joined David, which included bowmen and slingmen. These included, *inter alia*, the professional Gadite soldiers from Trans-Jordan, "whose faces were like the faces of lions and who were swift as gazelles upon the mountains." [69] It is also important to mention that B. Mazar, in dealing with the mercenary soldiers who joined David (and the el-Khadr arrowheads) drew attention to Ps 57:5 as another proof of mercenaries, nicknamed "Lebaites," i.e., "a military unit whose emblem was the lioness goddess." [70] I would like to add that these "Lebaites" are further defined there as "men aflame, their teeth are spears and arrows, their tongues sharp swords." Again, I would go one step further and suggest that we have here an exact definition of "Reshephites" (even according to the biblical traits of Resheph):[71] flame-like arrows, etc. In other words, perhaps we have here, both in the el-Khadr arrows and the biblical verses, a clue to the existence of Sea Peoples, professional bowmen, whose patron deities were Resheph and his consort the "lady lioness."

*   *   *

In conclusion we may sum up the main points raised in this paper.

The discovery of a lion-face rhyton dedicated to Resheph at Ugarit not only fills in an important gap in the history of these peculiar vessels but indicates—supported by other data—that the lion was Resheph's symbolic animal. The lioness, most probably, was the animal of his consort (probably ᶜAnat), who was called "lady lioness." She was the patron goddess of the archers.

The discovery of several lion-face rhyta in greater Philistia (including one actually found in a Philistine temple) probably indicates that the Canaanite god Resheph, like Dagon and Ashtoreth, was among the Canaanite deities adopted by the Sea Peoples in an early stage of their history, during their sojourn in Cyprus and Ugarit.

---

[68] Cf. Cross, "Origin," 13*, n 33.

[69] 1 Chr 12:9: ופני אריה פניהם. It may perhaps be assumed that these warriors actually wore "lion-face" masks. Of interest, too, is the combination of the lion and the gazelle, in defining the prowess of these warriors. Resheph is frequently depicted on Egyptian monuments with gazelle horns on his crown.

[70] Mazar, "David's Heroes," 186.

[71] On the biblical epithets of Resheph, see in particular S. Löwenstamm, *Encyclopedia Biblica* VII, 437–41; M. Weinfeld, "'They Fought from Heaven,'" see also Fulco, *Rešep*, 56.

The mention of Resheph in the Bible, with his typical epithets and traits, points clearly to him as having penetrated at an early period into Israelite culture, only to be later emasculated and lose most of his divine epithets, although enough remains to indicate his original Canaanite traits.

ADDENDUM

After the manuscript was at the printers, I read a paper on this subject to the Biblical Archaeology and History group of the Institute for Advanced Studies of the Hebrew University. Two members drew my attention to articles which are relevant to the subject:

1. Prof. H. Cazelles to the article of P. Xella, "Le dieu Rashap à Ugarit," in *Les annales archéologiques arabes syriennes*, 1979–1980, 145ff. This article hardly touches upon the main points discussed in my article, but is important, mainly, for the *Appendice* (159ff.), which lists all the references to Resheph in the Ugaritic texts, including those recently discovered at Ras Ibn Hani. Xella, who basically maintains the view that Resheph is an underworld deity and argues against Conrad's views, discusses, albeit briefly, the problems of *gn*.

2. Prof. A. Millard, to the article of W. F. Hallo, "Haplographic Marginalia," in *Ancient Near Eastern Studies in Memory of J. J. Finkel-stein*, Memoirs of the Connecticut Academy of Arts and Sciences, 1977, 101ff.